THE EDUCATION
OF A COLLEGE PRESIDENT

THE EDUCATION
OF A COLLEGE PRESIDENT
A Memoir

James R. Killian, Jr.

The MIT Press
Cambridge, Massachusetts
London, England

© 1985 by The Massachusetts Institute of Technology

This book was set in Palatino by Achorn Graphic Services and printed and bound by The Murray Printing Company in the United States of America.

Library of Congress Cataloging in Publication Data

Killian, James Rhyne, 1904–
   The education of a college president.

   Bibliography: p.
   Includes index.
   1. Killian, James Rhyne, 1904–   . 2. Massachusetts
Institute of Technology—Presidents—Biography.
3. College presidents—Massachusetts—Biography.
I. Title.
T171.M495K543   1985   607'.1174'6 [B]   85-122
ISBN 0-262-11096-2

Opening page: Letter K from *Neues, ABC Buchlein,* 1627, by the German engraver Lucas Killian. The Museum of Fine Arts, Boston

To the Corporation, Faculty, and Students of the
Massachusetts Institute of Technology whose warm fellowship
has generously provided me with continuing education for
three-score years

where the ships of youth are running
   close-hauled on the edge of the wind,
with all adventure before them,
   and only the old behind. . . .
—Humbert Wolfe, *Humoresque*

CONTENTS

ACKNOWLEDGMENTS

This memoir would not have been written had MIT bid me farewell in customary fashion on my retirement. But MIT cherishes its idiosyncrasies, and one is its custom of inviting its retired presidents and chairmen discreetly to remain on campus in ample but out-of-the-way quarters. The theory is that the presence of these retirees symbolically and sometimes actually provides a valuable continuum of experience. Although totally free of any administrative responsibilities, they serve as a peripatetic archive of past events, policies, and experience and are even occasionally asked by the powers that be to undertake unusual and sometimes covert missions. In no sense is the arrangement an entitlement; it is a benefice that the Institute is not obligated to offer nor the recipient to accept.

I have been the beneficiary in the most gracious way imaginable of this unusual and forbearing MIT custom, and I give it first place in this list of acknowledgments.

This anomalous custom has been made more valuable for me by assuring the continued service of Elizabeth Pigott, who first teamed up with me in 1952 when I was president and has served with me continuously during my presidency, my chairmanship, and my retirement. As secretary and administrative assistant she has been the discreet custodian and rapid selector of my files, dictator of my schedule, curator of my whimsical memory, and decipherer of my increasingly shaky script. Her valiant services on my books and speeches have included all of the above plus professional editorial and research skills of the first order. Not the least has been her sibyllic use of her patented divining rod in the subterranean recesses of libraries and archives to locate buried documents and other hidden treasures sought by me and other members of the MIT community. As she worked on my manuscript, she became acutely aware of the truth of the old observation that there is no good writing, only good rewriting.

Friends and colleagues in and out of the ivory tower have generously contributed in greater or lesser degree to my manuscript. Some recalled a fact or name I missed, others read and corrected paragraphs or chapters or most of the document, still others debated my prejudices. Their name is Legion, for they are many. Below is but a partial list of the people to whom I am indebted:

David Beckler, Edward Pennell Brooks, Gordon Brown, John Buchanan, Perry Crawford, Richard Douglas, Harold Edgerton, Robert Everett, James Fisk, Royce Flippin, Walter Gale, Bernard Gould, Paul Gray, Harold Hanham, Ada Louise Huxtable, Carl Kaysen, Gyorgy Kepes, Edwin Land, Henry Loomis, Margaret MacVicar, Boris Magasanik, William McCune, Walter Milne, Elting Morison, Charles Myers, I. M. Pei, William Porter, Frank Press, Francis Reintjes, Walter Rosenblith, Paul Samuelson, Francis Schmitt, Robert Schrock, Abraham Siegel, Irwin Sizer, Philip Smith, Ross Smith, Louis Smullin, Robert Solow, Guyford Stever, Jerome Wiesner, Karl Wildes, and Robert Wood.

Warren Seamans of the MIT Museum and Historical Collections read an early version of the whole manuscript and made available from his unmatched collection many of the photographs, and Vincent Fulmer, secretary of the Institute and of the MIT Corporation, read a near-final version and made generously available from his encyclopedic files and comprehensive memory information otherwise unavailable. I have of course relied greatly on the Institute Archives and feel deeply grateful for the skilled professional services of Helen Samuels and her associates. David Ferriero and his reference colleagues in the Hayden Library have repeatedly located hard-to-find material. I also welcomed the assistance of members of the staffs of the Eisenhower and Kennedy Libraries.

I then turned to John Mattill, the editor of *Technology Review*, and asked him if he would give me the benefit of his sharp editorial eye by reading my text. He responded generously; in fact he went well beyond what I had any right to expect of him by his searching emendations and his wise comments. One of my happy accomplishments was to find John and to bring him to MIT in 1948.

In 1977 I published a memoir, *Sputnik, Scientists, and Eisenhower* (The MIT Press), reporting my unique and memorable experiences in mobilizing science advice for President

Eisenhower in 1954 to 1959. The memoir I now publish brackets that retrospective essay, and I am grateful for the permission of the MIT Press to draw occasionally on it to complete my record.

In 1979 Professor Harold E. Edgerton and I published *Moments of Vision: The Stroboscopic Revolution in Photography* (The MIT Press), with Edgerton providing the remarkable photographs and I the supporting text. I wrote for that book a tribute to Edgerton. Since that book is currently available, I have avoided repeating myself by omitting from this book an otherwise essential chapter on "Papa Flash" and Strobe Alley. His career at the Institute and mine have run almost concurrently, and my moments of vision over many years have been multiplied and brightened by his "let's get going" spirit.

As I embarked on this memoir, the Alfred P. Sloan Foundation made a modest but generous grant to MIT which covered necessary expenses. For this aid I express my deep appreciation.

INTRODUCTION

A man doesn't learn to understand anything unless he loves it.

—Goethe[1]

Mencken described the publication of memoirs as flapping one's wings in public, which is a fair observation of my memoir. It is brazenly egotistic in charting my own career, and, in addition, it is exuberantly chauvinistic in its description of MIT. With this note of atonement, I proceed.

I describe episodes and personalities that have imprinted themselves on my memory from my first years at MIT as a student. In gathering together these memories, I first recall my experiences in educational administration that unpredictably led to my appointment to the MIT presidency and chairmanship. I then move on to my assignments in the public service, several to undertake tasks and science advisory responsibilities for Presidents Truman, Eisenhower, and Kennedy. In these pages, I write at times as an administrator and at times as a witness.

In signing his celebrated painting, *The Arnolfini Wedding*, the Flemish artist Jan van Eyck wanted it known that he was both painter of the wedding couple and witness to their wedding, and so he painted his signature in flourishing script: *Johannes de Eyck fuit hic* or, in translation, "Jan van Eyck was here." In recollecting many of the episodes in this memoir, it would be appropriate to declare "James Killian was here," to avoid leaving any impression that in every episode I was the impresario.

The first part of this memoir spans my MIT career: the apprenticeship years (1926–1939); executive assistant to President Compton (1939–1943); vice president (1943–1948); president (1948–1959); chairman or honorary chairman of the Corporation (1959–1979); and on into my years of grace as a pensioner, entirely free of any executive responsibilities but with a ringside seat.

During these six stages a pride of six presidents, starting with Karl Taylor Compton, has presided over the Institute, each contributing to its transformation into a research university. President Jerome B. Wiesner and Chancellor Paul E. Gray once described MIT as a "university *sui generis*." "It is unique," they said, "because of its international character, which does justice to the fact that the natural sciences are invariant under different skies. And it is unique in its concern not only with the sciences and engineering but with their human and societal consequences."

In explaining this achievement, I give special attention to two pivotal events. One was the appointment of Karl Taylor Compton to the presidency of the Institute. As Charles Eliot did at Harvard, Compton transformed a college into a university. When he came in 1930, Compton found a leading school of engineering, mainly undergraduate. He left it a research university, strong in both science and engineering and with a flourishing graduate school. Observing how he accomplished this was a profound contribution to my educaton as a science administrator.

The second pivotal event, and one I witnessed close up, was MIT's acceptance and conduct of large research projects during World War II. The location of the Radiation Laboratory at MIT in 1940 was a dramatic turning point in the Institute's history. This project ultimately became "the largest research organization in the world," as President Compton described it. It was a remarkable demonstration of the creative power of large, integrated research programs conducted in the benign environment of an educational institution.

Throughout the part of this memoir devoted to MIT, I have sought to identify the operative causes of its achievement of a place among the institutions in the forefront of the world's research universities. As it moved into this position, the Institute also became a seed bed of fresh initiatives in education. Among these initiatives, as Jerome Wiesner once remarked, was the shaping of an educational program for the twenty-first century. My participation in these transformations was a further contribution to my education for a highly unconventional career as educator and professional science administrator.

The path of a research university president in the decade of the fifties led through the Delectable Mountains, and I seek to explain why in my text. The government was a helpful partner to higher education, federal funds were generously granted, regulations were few, U.S. presidents sponsored measures to strengthen education, and research universities were the beneficiaries of the great adventure in scientific productivity and technological achievement that occurred mainly in Europe in the 1920s. Once in a relaxed moment, historian Elting Morison ventured the freewheeling observation that the MIT presidency is "one of the twenty most interesting jobs in the world." When I was climbing through the Delectable Mountains in the fifties, I would have agreed.

Throughout these pages are echoes of a statement that I made in my inaugural address, when I described MIT as a "university polarized around science, engineering, and the arts." "We might call it," I also said, "a university limited in its objectives but unlimited in the breadth and thoroughness with which it pursues these objectives." These two sentences of mine in 1949 have become, to my surprise, the most quoted and long-lived of any metaphors I have ever used about MIT.

Later, in my first President's Report, I advocated "better linkages between science and the humanities, with the object of fusing the two into a broad humanism that rests upon both science and the liberal arts and that does not weaken either. We need a bifocal vision to thread our way among the problems of our technological society."

As illustrations of how universities adapt their programs to the advancement of knowledge, to changing societal needs, and to the visions of new academic leaders, I have explored in some detail two examples at MIT, one the development of the Sloan School of Management and the Department of Economics, and the other, the growth of biology and other human sciences at the Institute. In addition I illustrate how the social sciences and the life sciences flourish in association with technology and how technology in turn finds new dimensions by living and working in close harmony with the humane sciences.

The second part of my memoir describes experiences outside academe, including a series of major assignments in the service of President Eisenhower. At his request I chaired a task force in the midfifties to study ways to prevent a surprise attack against the United States. Then came my two-year stint as Special Assistant for Science and Technology, the first full-time presidential science adviser. Other assignments under Eisenhower were to serve as chairman of the President's Science Advisory Committee and chairman of the President's Board of Consultants on Foreign Intelligence Activities, an appointment for which Kennedy also tagged me. I seek to convey the heady experience of being at the fulcrum of great events in the post-Sputnik period when President Eisenhower moved to quiet the national jitters, when NASA and our national space program were created, when efforts to initiate restrictions on nuclear tests were undertaken, and perhaps most important of all, when educational reform and federal aid to education were placed near the top of the national agenda.

My work in government service, particularly in the new and precarious post as presidential science adviser, proved to be profoundly important to my maturation. I had spent nearly three decades in the closure of an ivory tower, and although the experience was marked by opportunity, challenge, and growth, I still needed to be tested in the electrifying and exposed environment of the White House.

Another assignment in the public sector to which I give special importance was the chairmanship of the Carnegie Commission on Educational Television. A superb committee and staff formulated the concept of public television, invented the name, and prepared an eloquent report, whose major recommendations were accepted by Congress within a year—something of a record for congressional action. I look back on the launching of this system of public broadcasting, including public radio, with the greatest pride and satisfaction.

To tell my story, I rely greatly on tributes to the many colleagues in and out of MIT on whose shoulders I have stood and who have enriched my life. "History is not events, but people," said Jacob Bronowski in *The Ascent of Man*. The same can be said of the ascent of institutions.

At the opening of this preview I recalled Jan van Eyck's unusual signature. As this memoir is finished, it delights me to discover that in lectures at the University of Virginia in 1958, William Faulkner, when asked what he wanted to achieve as a writer, confessed that he could describe it best by saying that in passing through the "wall of oblivion," he wanted to "leave a scratch," like the immortal Kilroy of World War II. This is my scratch.

THE EDUCATION
OF A COLLEGE PRESIDENT

James R. Killian, Jr., 1949. Photo by Fabian Bachrach

1
THE WINDING STAIR TO THE MIT PRESIDENCY

All rising to great place is by a winding stair.

—Francis Bacon, *Essays*, "Of Great Place"

TIMES REMEMBERED: MY START UP THE STAIR

In 1926 I never dreamed in even my most uninhibited fantasies that I was destined to be president of MIT. If I had entertained the idea, I would have considered it preposterous. After spending two years in liberal arts studies at Trinity College, now Duke University, I had transferred to MIT to prepare for a job in the textile industry, my father's field. In fact on graduation I was on the verge of accepting one of two offers, one from the textile division of the Goodrich Tire and Rubber Company and the other from Goodyear, but the fates had already planned to direct me down a less traveled road.

It came about this way. In my senior year at MIT I served as editor of the undergraduate newspaper, *The Tech*. In those callow days when slide rules adorned all students and raccoon coats a few, I was an ardent addict of H. L. Mencken (I still read him for his slashing prose and his lusty tributes to the great composers he loved), and in my best imitation of Mencken's style I occasionally lambasted the Institute's administration. This did not go unnoticed in the office of the dean of students, and I received from time to time invitations to call on Harold Lobdell, who was on the dean's staff. "Lobby" had mastered an amiably stern adroitness in handling student discipline, and without resorting to discipline, he usually left me fully aware that my diatribes were jejune, revealing an obvious ignorance of academic administration and the amenities of a company of scholars. Surprisingly several of these episodes led to an unexpected camaraderie between Edwardian Lobdell and culprit me, and when he started to moonlight as publisher of the alumni magazine, the *Technology Review*, he asked me to contribute an occasional column on undergraduate affairs. In this role as an embryonic journalist and Mencken-inspired critic, I wrote a number of occasional pieces for the *Review*, including one in November 1925, that spotlighted a decline in the Institute's enrollment. "For the fourth successive year," I pointed out, "the undergraduate registration of the Institute has declined. . . .

"The immediate problem for the Institute," I pontificated, "is thus twofold: first, how may the number of applicants be increased . . .; second, how may the increased numbers be selected with more intelligence?" With remarkable devotion to the First Amendment, Lobdell did not censor these contributions, and later he boldly invited me to serve as a full-time assistant to editor Eric Hodgins, a graduate of MIT's Department of Chemical Engineering who had been recruited by Lobdell to join him in transforming the *Review* into a distinguished institutional journal. Hodgins later claimed that he was awarded his degree in chemical engineering on condition that he never practice that profession. Anyway he never did, becoming instead a nationally prominent journalist and writer, publisher of *Fortune,* and author of the novel *Mr. Blandings Builds His Dream House* and other successful books. And ultimately I surprised everybody, including myself, by being elected president of the Institute. It is not fantasy to conclude that my election to the editorship of the triweekly undergraduate newspaper, *The Tech*, proved to be a long drop kick into the territory of the Institute's presidency.

MEMORABLE TEACHERS
My relationship with Dean Lobdell grew into a warm friendship—a friendship so cherished by us both that he officiated as best man at my wedding to Elizabeth Parks in 1929. Later, as I watched his skill in chairing a faculty committee in the thirties and forties on the stabilization of enrollment and the fixing of quotas for overcrowded or undercrowded courses, I learned about the subtleties of academic politics from him. I learned much about the art of writing and editing from Hodgins. I shared his literary interests and his enthusiasm for MIT's Department of English and History, which he described as a "miracle" in his posthumously published autobiography, *Trolley to the Moon.* "I don't understand," he wrote, "how, in those days, it was possible to attract and hold, on the faculty of an engineering school, so many men of scholarship or intellectual brilliance or

both"[1] and how it kept them contented without teaching graduate studies.

The architect and leader of this brilliant liberal arts college within an engineering school was Associate Professor Frank Aydelotte, later to become president of Swarthmore and, later still, president of the Association of Rhodes Scholars and director of the Institute for Advanced Study. During his years at MIT he became a strong advocate of honors courses in engineering, doubtless as a result of his experience with honors courses while a student at Oxford. His belief in the importance of such courses led him to introduce an honors program at Swarthmore, which in its prime was considered to be a major educational innovation. While in the Department of English and History at MIT he assembled a volume of essays for English classes in schools of engineering, and in the second edition he stated its purpose:

1. To teach the student to write not by telling him how, not by doing his thinking for him, but by stimulating him to think for himself about his own problems, about his work and its place in the world.

2. To lead the engineering student to think of the occupation for which he is preparing himself not as a trade but as one of the liberal professions.

3. To lead him to see how his work of designing material conveniences for men is bound up with the spiritual advancement of the race—with the world of science, of literature, and of moral ideals.[2]

Recently, in reading the autobiography of Richard Soderberg, I found testimony to the high quality of teaching in this Department of English and History. As a graduate student fresh from Sweden in 1919, Soderberg was inspired by a special course in English given by Professor Matthew Copithorne. "It presented," he wrote, "a mature and fascinating introduction to the American scene, made doubly interesting by informal discussions of American politics."

Aydelotte's able successor as head of the Department of English and History, Henry Greenleaf "Molly" Pearson, was able to maintain and even to strengthen Aydelotte's strong teaching corps, and during my period as an MIT student I came under his benign influence and the stimulating teaching of Professors W. A. Crosby, Winward Prescott, Henry Latimer Seaver, William Chace ("Profanity Greene") Greene, and above all, Robert Emmons Rogers, better and affectionately known as Tubby. Although not a brilliant scholar, Rogers was a beguiling lecturer on English literature and sundry other matters as he "poured forth gleeful inspiration" and his "merry bitterness." He inadvertently achieved international fame by advising Institute graduates, in an extemporaneous speech, "Be a snob. Marry the boss's daughter." This bit of practical advice was delivered at a senior banquet where the seniors and their invited faculty and friends drank beer chug-a-lug. A student newspaper reporter, representing the late and unlamented *Boston Post*, rushed to file a story on Tubby's ironic advice. That this episode occurred during the Great Depression, when tycoons sold apples on street corners, surely enhanced the story's reach, and in the months that followed, Tubby was engulfed by newspaper clippings from all over the world.

Tubby was an extraordinarily gifted teacher. He was possessed, to use a Shavian phrase, of a "cherubically adipose" manner and sometimes lectured with his eyes apparently closed, but these physiological eccentricities did not inhibit the vigor of his teaching. Hodgins was to eulogize him as the greatest teacher of his educational career. I too found Rogers an exceptional teacher, and I listened in on or took several of his courses. He turned my attention to the impact of science on English literature, and I was inspired to widen my reading by his course on the English novel. He introduced me to Wells, the Brontës, Hardy, Gissing, Chesterton, Thomas Love Peacock, and above all to George Meredith, who was to become, despite his "elegant opacity," one of my literary hobbies. It was Tubby Rogers who led me to Meredith's *An Essay on Comedy and the Uses of the Comic Spirit* and the application of this philosophy in several of his novels. Meredith's explication of the comic spirit as a means for maintaining balance, proportion, persuasion, and self-revelation in one's conduct and living has helped me throughout my career to rely on the corrective and healing power of laughter during times when the going was rough or the outlook grim.[3]

I have kept alive my interest in Meredith, even though he has long since faded into obscurity. I continue to collect books about and by him and have a small assortment of Meredithiana, including first editions, biographies, critical evaluations, and some manuscript fragments. I have also found in his robust philosphy a guiding light in fair weather and foul. "Life is but a little holding lent to do a mighty labor," he wrote in *Vittoria,* and when he described the "rapture of the forward view," he struck a responsive note. If Meredith was thus influential during my green days, W. B. Yeats has become increasingly the poet of my old age.

Thus I was stimulated by my teachers in the Department of English and History to develop personal affirmations and to become more reflective and more discerning of human values. This experience also led me, when I became president of the Institute, to give strong support to the humanities, as did my predecessor, Karl Compton. I welcomed the favorable action of the faculty in approving the recommendation of the Lewis Committee that MIT give the social sciences and humanities full professional status by establishing a School of Humanities and Social Studies. Today, thirty years later, offerings in the humanities and related fields, though occupying an uneasy place in this intense scientific environment, go far beyond the ably taught but limited courses that I found so stimulating in the 1920s. The enthusiasm I now hold for the educational value of study in the humanities is as great as it was then, and I find no sound reason for the belief that the humanities at MIT must always be cringing from a crisis of identity.

The course of study in which I was registered was designated as Course XV, Business and Engineering Administration, with Mechanical Engineering option. It too had gifted undergraduate teachers, including its head, Erwin Schell, author of *The Technique of Executive Control* (sales: over 100,000 copies); Davis R. Dewey, well-known economist and brother of the philosopher

John Dewey; and Floyd Armstrong, specialist on corporation organization and envied for his personal success in the stock market. As this memoir advances, I will have more to say about Dewey, Schell, and Course XV. Another teacher I remember with gratitude was Jay Balsbaugh, who taught a course in electrical engineering for those like me who were not aiming to become electrical engineers. He was young, but he had mastered the art of being a communicator—not in the political but in the academic sense.

Beginning in its green years the Institute also offered a group of electives, known as General Studies, gathered together in what was once called Course IX. I elected several of these, and one was notable for giving me new insights into the canons of evolutionary science and lasting contempt for "creationism." It was "Organic Evolution," taught by an outstanding teacher and scholar, long dead, Henry Woodburn Shimer, professor of paleontology in the Department of Mining, Metallurgy, and Geology. What James Russell Lowell said of Louis Agassiz might also be said of Shimer:

He was a Teacher: why be grieved for him
Whose living word still stimulates the air?[4]

These teachers and courses served to reduce my intellectual parochialism and to foster new values in which technology and the liberal arts comfortably coexisted. But there were other inputs to my education.

In the late twenties and during the thirties I was reading avidly and widely but unsystematically. How widely was recently confirmed for me when my classmate and lifelong friend, Robert C. Dean, presented me with a 1973 memoir of his (unfinished and unpublished) entitled "All That He Could Remember Without Actually Looking It Up." He recalls that he had received an AIA silver medal for the best four years' work leading to a bachelor's degree in architecture. Along with this medal came a copy of Henry Adams' *Mont-Saint-Michel and Chartres*. He already had read "under Killian's tutelage" *The Education*. He further noted that "Killian led him to many significant books," including *A History of Science and its Relations with Philosophy and Religion* (1930) by the Cambridge University historian with the formidable name of William Cecil Dampier Dampier-Whetham and Oswald Spengler's *The Decline of the West.* Apparently Spengler's fantasies in pessimism were both startling and fascinating, and Dean recalled that it "certainly dampened the enthusiasm of a young architect out to do great things."

Some other unforgotten books on my reading list were the abridged edition of *The Golden Bough* by Sir James George Frazer, *The Expanding Universe* and other books by Sir Arthur Stanley Eddington, *The Rise of American Civilization* by Charles A. Beard and Mary R. Beard, *The Time Machine* and *Outline of History* by H. G. Wells, anything by H. L. Mencken and his friend James Huneker, and *Studies in Literature* by Sir Arthur Quiller-Couch. I found in R. Vallery-Radot's *Life of Pasteur* an inspiring portrait of a man who opened a new era in the life sciences and who also possessed, as Hans Zinsser once said, "infinite goodness and tenderness of heart." Thomas Henry Huxley stood at the head of this list, and I found inspiration in his convictions and his prose. Of course I broke away much of the time from this heavy fare to read F. Scott Fitzgerald and other fiction writers.

During the closing years of the 1920s I discovered the delights of the theater, from balcony seats of course. Together with Elizabeth Parks, a widely read Southern girl majoring in English literature at Wellesley College and whom I courted for her four student years there and married in 1929, we saw as many plays and musicals as our limited funds permitted. We had the good fortune to be around at the time when the American Winthrop Ames staged his elegant productions of Gilbert and Sullivan, which we found to be several imaginative cuts above the very best versions the D'Oyly Carte company could achieve. Of the musicals, Jerome Kern's *Show Boat* still rings sentimental bells, for it has provided a theme song for us through the years.

To cite an example of how a great play can indelibly stir the emotions and steer acquaintances toward a lasting friendship, my wife and I recall vividly seeing in the Boston of the late 1940s

Paul Vincent Carroll's prize-winning play, *Shadow and Substance.* Liz and I had gone to the theater with our neighbors, the Donald Durrells, whom today, a half-century later, we number among our cherished friends. While driving back to our homes in Wellesley, we found ourselves unforgettably moved—and united in a lasting friendship—by the spiritual qualities of this powerful play.

In the early, impecunious years of our marriage, when we lived in a tiny apartment in Cambridge, I remember how Liz and I read to each other substantial parts of Meredith's *The Ordeal of Richard Feverel.* She too was one of my most sensitive teachers. Later, in reading Roy Harrod's biography of the economist, Lord Keynes, I was delighted to find that Keynes was a fan of Meredith's. He wrote in a letter: "I have enjoyed Richard Feverel immensely. . . . When I am reading it, I get absorbed in a way that is not very usual with me." So it was with Liz and me.

By pure coincidence, our daughter and her husband, when searching for an apartment after their marriage, without consulting us and without having any knowledge that we had lived there when she was born, rented the very same Holden Green apartment. This led my wife to remark that it appeared that this was like the salmon instinct to return upstream to the place where they were spawned.

At the time we lived at Holden Green in Cambridge, it had the interesting feature that each apartment had its own furnace in the basement. This forest of furnaces could be confusing to new families moving into the building, and numerous instances were reported of apartment occupants firing up a furnace that heated someone else's apartment. The theory of this self-service heating arrangement was that it would bring young occupants of the apartment building together in rewarding community life in the basements.

While a student at Trinity College, I was initiated into the Sigma Chi Fraternity, and when I transferred to MIT, I was invited to continue my association with its Alpha Theta Chapter, the first fraternity at the Institute (1882), and to live in its chapter house. The members managed the house. They were cosmopolitan in their backgrounds and in their fields of study. The chapter house was once a private home and among its amenities was an organ, which some members were competent to play and occasionally did all through the night when mice had not deflated the bellows. In the dining room was a stained glass (Tiffany?) window containing lines from Shakespeare's *The Taming of the Shrew:*

Do as adversaries do in law
Strive mightily but eat and drink as friends.

And so we did, and at meal times the singing of lusty songs was frequently on the menu and gave a lift to our spirits and warmth to our fellowship. As Lewis Thomas would say, there was no entropy.

While living at the chapter house, I became a close friend of James Bamford of Reading, Pennsylvania, where he was elected reform mayor in later life. Aside from our committed preoccupation with physics, chemistry, and engineering, Jim shared my interest in the theater and in Mencken's and Nathan's new magazine *The American Mercury,* both of us sharing a single copy which we read avidly.

I also came under the benign influence of Mrs. Ellen King, who served as librarian of the Walker Memorial Gymnasium Library, a collection of books for browsing—another example of MIT's unexpected resources in the humanities. Earlier, when Tech was on Boylston Street in Boston, she ran a lunch counter for students in the Rogers Building. She was a jewel of a lady who in her widowhood devoted herself to MIT students and in my day kept a rapt group of us up to date on current books.

Another aspect of the humanities to which I was exposed came through my association with students studying architecture at the Institute, including the Bob Dean who advanced his education by reading the books I called to his attention. From him and others I had the benefit of fallout from Professor John O. Sumner's celebrated two-year subject, "European Civilization and Art." This sweeping treatment of the history of architecture and art was an approximation of a liberal arts education and, along with the teaching in the Department of English and History, provided an excellent opportunity for bridging the two cultures.

In these green days I lost some of my conventionality through my association with architectural students. By their more uninhibited personal styles and their emulation of what they had heard about glamorous student life at the great École des Beaux Arts in Paris, they introduced liberating touches of gaiety into MIT student life. Much later and of greater importance was the influence of architects and our Department of Architecture on my perception of the arts, especially the visual arts.

STUDENT SOCIETY *SUI GENERIS*

In 1925 I was elected a student member of a senior society that bore the name of Osiris and thus came to know its long and unusual history and its importance. It was founded in 1904 (the year I was born) by Arthur J. Sweet, a transfer student who wanted to promote more contact between members of the student body and the administration and faculty.

Each year the active student members, numbering fifteen, selected their successors and in addition a member of the administration or faculty or alumni body to be an honorary member. Over the years every president of the Institute during the society's existence accepted honorary membership, beginning with Henry Pritchett in 1904.

In the period when Osiris was founded, it was fashionable in the collegiate world to use Greek letters and mythology for the names and rituals of fraternities and other student organizations, but Sweet wanted his society to be different and based its name and ritual on Egyptian mythology.

Initiation into the society involved the customary ordeal frequently associated with the admission of new members of fraternities, but all of this ritualistic jargon was quite unimportant compared to the function of the society. In the early days it met at a club, no longer in existence, located at 270 Beacon Street, which led to the society's being referred to for the rest of its life as "270."

The important aspect of the society was its bringing together students, alumni, and a group of honorary members consisting mainly of administrative officers, faculty members, and others the students felt to be important to their interests.

To promote free discussion and equality among the members, everyone was called by his first name, including the presidents of the Institute. Following the dinner that was usually a part of the monthly meetings, the group addressed a wide range of topics of interest to students and from time to time formulated proposals later to be introduced to the Institute community without reference to the society. I know that the presidents of the Institute, the deans, and other dignitaries brought into the society as honorary members attached great importance to the opportunity it provided to develop useful relations between students and their seniors. I know, for example, that President Compton and earlier presidents, as did I, valued the opportunity to have this informal contact with students and to participate in a free-for-all discussion of Institute affairs. It was an opportunity for the undergraduate members freely to air their complaints and to introduce their ideas for improving the quality of life at the Institute, both living and academic. Thus, despite its pseudomythology, ritualistic procedures, and the fun that marked its meetings, the society proved itself of great value, and the members, both student and honorary, in their later careers, looked back on their experience as members with pleasure and pride.

I have before me what I believe to be the last published directory of the student members and the honoraries. It is a stellar group. Each June, on Alumni Day, Marshall Dalton used to arrange for a breakfast gathering of present and past members at the Braeburn Country Club, and these reunions attested to an enduring fellowship.

In the late 1960s, I regret to report, the society disappeared. In that tumultuous period the student temper found the secrecy and the elitism highly objectionable, and the society that had so long existed to the benefit of the Institute perished in the turmoil.

THE *TECHNOLOGY REVIEW* YEARS

While an undergraduate, the required subjects—management, accounting, economics, the humanities—of Course XV commanded my best attention, but they did not divert me from pursuing a way through the required core studies in engineering. I became adequately familiar with thermodynamics and mechanics, the subtleties of entropy, and the elementary basics of machine design and electrical engineering. I machined an elegant but useless specimen in the now-discontinued machine shop, and in the drafting rooms I mastered one visual art by producing some elegant mechanical drawings which my mother wanted framed. In mathematics, however, I was an even poorer student than I was in the engineering subjects and as a result did not complete the requirements for a degree on schedule. My job on the *Review*, however, gave me the freedom to complete all the mathematics subjects needed to qualify for a bachelor's degree. This *Review* assignment also made it practical to turn down the jobs in industry which had been offered me and, by remaining at MIT, to fill gaps in my education by intensive study and reading on my own. "Education is . . . hanging around until you've caught on," Robert Frost shrewdly observed in 1963.

After a contretemps with Lobdell, Hodgins resigned from the *Review* in 1930 and I succeeded him as editor, determined to carry on the Hodgins editorial elan and style. This style had been aided and abetted by a young electrical engineering graduate, John D. Crawford, who had joined the *Review* staff in 1927 and lighted up the office with his pink cheeks and bright humor. Another stalwart who had joined this *Review* team was Ralph Jope, who had been highly successful as the energetic president of the undergraduate student body in 1927–28. He had entrepreneurial gifts of a high order and did much to extend the circulation and build the advertising revenues of the *Review*. Later, and until his premature death, he dedicated himself to the advancement of the Institute's fund-raising and athletics programs. With freewheeling and joyful editing inherited from Hodgins and salted and promoted by this team, the *Review* gained additional prestige within and without the community and reached many non-MIT readers.

The *Review* headquarters was on "Wienerweg," the office-to-office trail taken almost daily by MIT's genius mathematician, Norbert Wiener, and these visits permitted me to recruit him as an occasional author. In his visits to the stations on "Wienerweg," he usually asked, "How are things?"—meaning not "How are things with you?" but rather "How are things with me?" Of the many anecdotes about Wiener that are still recalled in the MIT community, I think of the one about his driving to Providence with his wife to give a lecture at Brown. He finished the lecture in so euphoric a mood that he took the train back to Boston leaving his automobile and his wife waiting in Providence.

The staff of the *Review* was always awed by Wiener's ability to dictate rapidly and accurately articles containing intricately erudite ideas and many dates and names. He needed no references or notes, and the resulting manuscripts usually required almost no editing to be ready for publication. As he read his manuscript coming from the secretary's machine, he would thank her magisterially for *her* skill!

The *Review* was not the medium to publish Wiener's profound mathematics work. That found ample outlet in his several books such as the classic *Cybernetics, or Communication and Control in the Animal and the Machine,* and his many papers, but Wiener turned to the *Review* for publishing pieces in a lighter vein. He became delightedly interested in the murder stories of S. S. Van Dine, who wrote with some sophistication about murders involving mathematics and mathematicians, and on one occasion Wiener wrote for the *Review* with obvious enjoyment a review of Van Dine's *The Bishop Murder Case.* Without having read the last installment, he tried with elaborate exegesis to identify the murderer—and was wrong. His effort to dope out the plot, as well as his acknowledgment of failure, provided entertaining and learned reading. He corresponded a number of times with Van Dine, and "having passed all the tests prescribed by the Constitution and By-Laws of the Society" was later declared a full and participating member of the Speckled Band of Boston, Scion Society of the Baker Street Irregulars.

Thus did this ex-prodigy and prodigious scholar, with encouragement by the *Review*, occasionally forget some of his profound woes and worries about the coming apocalypse and have fun. In many places in this memoir I recall how his genius engendered new programs and enriched the intellectual life of our company of scholars.

Another contributor to the *Review* was Wiener's acerbic colleague in mathematics, Leonard "Prince" Passano, who wore spats, carried a cane, and proudly showed his first editions, including one from his favorite author, Herman Melville *(Moby Dick)*. Chemist-humanist Tenney Davis; John E. Burchard, then of the Bemis Foundation, architectural critic; and Vannevar Bush, vice president and dean of engineering—all contributed memorable articles, while Harold Edgerton brought to me his earliest strobe photographs, which gave the magazine pioneering photographic distinction before Gjon Mili used the Edgerton flash photography with spectacular results in the then-new *Life* magazine.

The authors and the articles which I drew to the *Technology Review* contributed importantly to my preparation for science administration. I recall a witty piece, a riotous romp, written by Bush in which he stationed himself at some date long in the future and from that vantage point looked back at the primitive state of affairs in the 1930s. He titled it "The Inscrutable Thirties," but I fear he would have found the eighties far more inscrutable.

The associations I had with the architects made me a better editor of the *Review*. I turned to Sam Chamberlain, etcher, photographer, and gourmet, to do sketches for the *Review* covers and in other ways to embellish its pages. My interest in the graphic arts led me to seek out the gifted typographers W. A. Dwiggins and Daniel Berkeley Updike. In the late thirties Henry Seaver of the Department of English and History took over Sumner's course, and for one brief shining term he and I gave a "General Study" in typography. As a moonlighting assignment

I also taught a course for three years at Simmons College, which grew into a course in magazine editing. I have never lost my fascination with the graphic arts, and in my slight graphic arts collection are typographic specimens and prints, including etchings by all four of the distinguished etchers who were graduates of the Institute's Department of Architecture.

A number of the younger members of the Institute's staff, including me, were occasionally asked to double in brass by doing odd jobs for the administration. President Samuel Stratton, for example, was urged by John R. Freeman, a distinguished engineer, to strengthen education and research in hydraulics and fluid mechanics at MIT. Already Freeman had financed several fellowships for American graduate students to go to Germany to study these subjects under some of the leading German scholars in these fields. At his request I traveled with Dr. Stratton by day coach to see the famous engineer at his office in Providence. At that meeting Freeman secured Stratton's agreement to have MIT sponsor the translation and then publication of several important texts. When we returned, Stratton asked me to arrange for their translation and publication in English. I of course accepted. Out of this came the start of what was first called The Technology Press and now stands as a major university press under the rubric The MIT Press. I look back with much satisfaction on the founding of this successful university press. Today the catalog of the Press reveals a wide range of scholarly books and journals. I note particularly that it is one of the principal sources of books on architecture and that it has an outstanding series of publications devoted to the history of computing and computer technology.

When Karl Compton became president in 1930, he undertook a well-conceived and tasteful public relations program for the Institute including attractively written, illustrated, and printed brochures, which he asked me to edit. These widely distributed brochures were designed for seniors in high schools and students preparing for graduate study. Dr. Compton felt that MIT's light had been hidden under a bushel.

In preparing the brochures, I had to inform myself in some

detail about departments, programs, and faculty at the Institute, and I thus increased, at least superficially, my knowledge of science and engineering. In addition President Compton arranged for MIT to have an exhibit at the Chicago World's Fair, and in this exhibit there was a demonstration of the spectacular new Van de Graaff electrostatic generator and a generous supply of publications about MIT.

In this period Dr. Compton sparked the initiation of the Institute's first Alumni Fund, and since I was also serving as treasurer of the Alumni Association, I was called upon to help launch the fund. This was my introduction to fund-raising, an activity that has intimately engaged me in massive campaigns to build much-needed new resources for the Institute.

In such assignments I was drawn closer to the president's office and came to know numerous leading faculty members. I found myself achieving a special relationship with Bush, for whom I ran minor errands. Soon we developed a personal friendship, and Bush found me a rapt listener when he wanted reactions to his theories of education or to some of his incipient inventions. "I cannot avoid inventing," he said to me over and over as I once drove with him to Cape Cod. (As Bush was later to conclude, the making of inventions provides an "elation of creation" similar to that experienced by poets.) After planting a dozen or so fruit trees at his summer home in Dennis, we quickly got back to inventing radical new courses of study and whole experimental colleges.

It was during this decade of the 1930s that I became increasingly aware of the beneficial exchanges taking place between American and European scientists. The effects of these exchanges began to have an impact in the decade of the twenties and grew more influential in the thirties. We sometimes forget that in these decades there was a steady development of American graduate institutions, a process that Robert Oppenheimer described as a "rather sturdy and indigenous effort" in American research. The versatile forces that were at work in this period to bring a greater sophistication to science in our universities came about in part as a result of American students going to Europe for graduate study. In a Compton Lecture he gave at MIT in 1962, I. I. Rabi pointed out that these American graduate students probably knew as much or more basic physics as the Europeans they visited but the Americans lacked the taste, style, and sense of what was important in science. When they returned to their American institutions, they brought back these sophisticated attributes which added greatly to the quality of American scientific research. This injection of the European style of research was increased by physicists coming from Europe in the wake of Hitler's ascendancy. The Europeans migrating to this country not only brought their style but they in turn were inspired by the brashness and boldness of spirit they found in Americans. Indeed, it was these two qualities that quickly led American research institutions to achieve such stature as to provide continued attraction to scientists overseas, bringing them in increasing numbers to this country. Einstein, for example, came in 1933, and his presence both symbolically and actually made the United States an even more powerful mecca.

During the thirties and forties I perceived this symbiotic effect at work at MIT and later came to understand its role in transforming a leading school of engineering into the research university it was becoming.

THE PRESIDENT'S EXECUTIVE ASSISTANT

My career as an academic administrator started in 1939 when Bush left MIT to become president of the Carnegie Institution of Washington. In discussing with President Compton the rearrangements that would have to be made as a result of his departure, Bush suggested, to my surprise, that I be asked to join the staff of the president's office to take over some of the more routine responsibilities that he had been carrying. Dr. Compton accepted Bush's suggestion, and I remember the day in October 1938 when with characteristic courtesy he looked in on me at my office and asked if I would be willing to join his staff as his "executive assistant." I was thirty-four years old. Compton had already asked Edward L. Moreland to take over Bush's responsibilities as dean of engineering. In a burlesque song gaily sung at a retirement dinner much later, my move from the *Review* to the office of the president was limned:

I flourished that pen with such manifest joy
That K.T. appointed me his office boy.

"In his new position, which becomes effective January 1," said the formal news release, "Mr. Killian will participate in the Institute's administration and will take over some of the responsibilities which have been carried by Vice President Vannevar Bush, who on the first of the year becomes president of the Carnegie Institution of Washington. . . ."

No one knew in January 1939 that war was to start in Europe in September 1939, or that the United States would later become an active participant. But a group of leading scientists, including Bush, Compton, and James B. Conant, were already worrying about the combat readiness of the country if it should be drawn into the war. Under the leadership of Bush they organized the National Defense Research Committee months before we were drawn into the conflict and started planning a war research program. Out of this foresighted planning and organizing came the decision to request universities to undertake war research, and in October 1940 MIT was asked to accept responsibility for the radar research project mentioned in my introduction that, with many other projects, was to transform it into a great research arsenal.

As an initial member of this National Defense Research Committee, President Compton was to become heavily involved in the war research program planned and administered by the Office of Scientific Research and Development. This meant that much of his time was pre-empted by the war and that my responsibilities as his aide would become far greater than any contemplated by him or me. It meant that I found myself deeply involved in the nonscience aspects of the Institute's administration of what was to become a massive wartime responsibility. It meant in fact that I became a Cambridge surrogate for President Compton in the day-to-day executive direction of the Institute.

Compared to the scientists who were principals in the great

war research projects, I was an inconspicuous, behind-the-scenes administrator. But I had breathtaking opportunities to be tested and educated for any future responsibilities that might come my way.

Dr. Compton's choice of me to join his staff was a startling one to many of my associates and above all to me. I was "magnificently unprepared." I was not a scientist. I had not sought the job. And my previous career could best be described as idiosyncratic preparation for university administration.

In the formal Executive Committee action appointing me as executive assistant, it was specified that my term of appointment was for six months. Clearly I was on trial, and there was even debate about my title. My office was to be in the presidential suite, the same room that Bush had occupied, and in my amateur status I naturally found this arrangement a daunting experience. On occupying this office, I found this pleasant note on my desk:

Dear Jim:

May your occupation of this desk bring you a full share of satisfaction and enjoyment; the sense of true accomplishment which renders tolerable the many irritations of an executive officer.

Don't forget to put your feet on the desk once in a while, drive everyone out, and take time to think.

Cordially yours,
V. Bush

While still a puppy and not yet housebroken, I was soon involved in the preparation of the Institute's annual budget. Under Bush the budget was mostly a product of authoritarian decisions made by him, a procedure I dared not follow. Instead, I formed a budget and review committee (which was later formalized as the Academic Council), a group including the deans of all the schools. This was an innovation that was to prove itself later on by removing fears that the departments and schools were not being treated equitably and by cultivating confidence in the administration.

My future was uncertain, and I experienced moments of insecurity and considerable doubt that I was cut out for the job, in Robert Frost's phrase, "vaguely realizing" the road ahead. Since I do not find in the files any formal action extending my appointment, I suppose the six months' term was forgotten. I just continued, largely, I suppose, because Compton increasingly was caught up in his wartime duties away from the Institute. I am sure, however, that from time to time Compton hardly knew what to make of his anomalous assistant, and that there must have been occasions when it seemed to him that the arrangement would not fly.

In the opening months of 1939 our national affairs were marked by a deceptive tranquility soon ruptured by Hitler's invasion of Poland on September 1. In effect World War II had started, and perceptive Americans, including our leading scientists "with the future in their bones," could not escape forebodings about the impact of these events on the United States and on a college with resources that would obviously be drafted if the United States went to war. Among the stanzas W. H. Auden was to write at white heat and publish in his poem "September 1, 1939" was a moral protest:

Waves of anger and fear
Circulate over the bright
And darkened lands of the earth
Obsessing our private lives;
The unmentionable odour of death
Offends the September night.[5]

I shared this moral anger but accepted without reservation the conclusion that Hitler was to make war inescapable for the United States. No doubts remained in my mind that I must serve the war effort in uniform or in some other assignment requiring my total commitment. I reproduce in appendix B a letter written by Dr. Compton to my draft board, which argued that I could best fulfill my duty by civilian service on his staff, and apparently the draft board agreed.

This period led to a steady increase in my responsibilities as an administrative officer at the Institute. Despite these mounting concerns I did not in my wildest Walter Mitty dreams anticipate what was ahead.

As a nonscientist I was challenged to keep au courant with science and technology, even though I might be unprepared to achieve the rank of a working scholar in any field of science. In the most modest sense my relationship with scientists was similar to what Winston Churchill described as his in World War II. "I knew nothing about science," he wrote, "but I knew something of scientists . . . and I had much practice in handling things I did not understand."[6]

I was greatly aided in handling things I did not understand by the presence across the corridor from my new office of Virginia-bred Edward L. Moreland, who had assumed Bush's portfolio as Dean of Engineering. Moreland had been head of the Department of Electrical Engineering since 1935 and prior to that had been a partner in the distinguished firm of consulting engineers, Jackson & Moreland. I had come to know him as a car-pool neighbor in Wellesley and during the period in which he was president of the Alumni Association. At his firm Moreland had been involved with the design of steam and hydroelectric plants, power transmission systems, the electrification of railroads, and many other major engineering studies and projects.

In 1942 Bush and Conant recruited him to serve as executive officer of the National Defense Research Committee. This was to lead to his appointment as adviser to General MacArthur's High Command and, after V-J Day, as head of the Scientific Intelligence Survey in Japan.

I was to miss him greatly following my learning period as executive assistant to the president. Our work together permitted me to observe his skills in resolving diverse points of view, aided by the way his face could light up with an utterly engaging smile when making tough administrative decisions. I greatly admired his power to radiate a gentle warmth and his considerate courtesy in dealing with his colleagues at the Institute. In these ways he was a nonpareil teacher for me as a tyro administrator.

2
THE WAR YEARS AND THEIR EDUCATIONAL LEGACY

MIT's evolution into a major research university was dramatically accelerated by its research in support of World War II. In this chapter I present selected examples of spectacular research projects undertaken in an academic environment but wholly dedicated to the wartime needs of the nation. Several of these laboratories grew out of research already under way, but the major wartime laboratory was a project entirely new to the Institute and staffed by personnel from many institutions. As I describe these great undertakings, however, I seek to show that while devoted totally to the winning of the war, they also extended the boundaries of technology and generated educational sequels that vitalized the Institute's postwar education.

THE RADIATION LABORATORY
One of the earliest major projects the National Defense Research Committee decided on was a program for the development of microwave radar. Already the British had developed long-range radar, and the combination represented one of the major wartime scientific achievements of what Churchill called the Wizard War. The NDRC division responsible for this microwave project was headed by Compton. After several failures to find a suitable location, he was persuaded on October 16, 1940, to permit the establishment of the new laboratory at MIT. I have documentation for this in a memorandum Dr. Compton wrote to Drs. Bush and Conant dated February 26, 1942. I quote the pertinent paragraphs:

The events which led to the selection of MIT as the sponsoring institution for the Radiation Laboratory should be a matter of record. The Microwave Committee first considered the new Cyclotron Laboratory of the Department of Terrestrial Magnetism of the Carnegie Institution of Washington as a suitable location, but soon abandoned this idea because another NDRC activity had already become established in these quarters and it was even evident that the Radiation Laboratory would require more than the remaining space there available.

It was next arranged with the Army Air Corps to establish the laboratory in a temporary building on Bolling Field in Washington. This would have been a central location with airplanes available for practice but without the advantage of lookout over the sea. However, immediately prior to submission of this recommendation by Section D to NDRC word was received from the Army Air Corps that a change of plans made the Bolling Field location impossible. Drs. Bush and Loomis [Alfred Loomis, investment banker and physicist, and also a member of the MIT Corporation and active on the NDRC Microwave Committee] asked whether MIT could make space available and could get any facilities at the East Boston Airport. I telephoned the situation up to Mr. Killian at MIT, who phoned back in a few hours that MIT could make available 11,000 square feet of good laboratory space, and the National Guard hangar at the East Boston airport would soon be available. On the basis of this information, NDRC proceeded to make the contract with MIT for the establishment of the Radiation Laboratory. Since that time MIT has handled the business arrangements, but the selection of personnel and the technical direction of the program have been in the hands of officers chosen by Section D-1.

When I called Compton back to say that Professor Edward Bowles's laboratory in the Department of Electrical Engineering could be vacated and made available but not much more, he then told me that a secret project would be located in this space and that there would soon be some new boys in town to occupy it. The selection of Bowles's space was especially appropriate because as early as 1922, along with Carleton Tucker, he had pioneered a program in communications and had undertaken work on microwave theory, both of which were to prove useful to the new project, and this pioneering work was also a factor that led Drs. Bush and Loomis to persuade Dr. Compton to consider MIT.

Several of those present, including Bowles, at the Washington meeting where the decision was made to ask MIT to undertake the Radiation Laboratory wrote for the record or expressed slightly different versions of the discussion that took place. Apparently it was difficult for NDRC member Frank Jewett to believe that a group of young scientists located in an academic institution could provide the resources that would be required. (Jewett, who had risen to the presidency of the Bell Laboratories, in fact had graduated from MIT in 1903.) Vannevar Bush, in his Oral History Collection, recollected the strained relationships between Compton and Jewett:

Frank Jewett and Karl Compton did not get along very well, and the reason was fundamentally this. Under Compton, there was assembled at the Radiation Laboratory probably the hottest crowd of physicists on electronic gadgetry and the like that was ever put together. A lot of them were prima donnas; there were a couple of thousand people in the Laboratory and it was quite a show. Frank Jewett had been the fellow who had really put the Bell Laboratories together, and he'd directed it. It was the pride of his whole career. It was just too much for him to think that a crowd of youngsters could do something better than the Bell Labs could.[1]

It is also of interest to recall that Robert A. Millikan of CalTech expressed concern about the hazards of concentrating at one place "fifty" physicists. As it turned out, before it completed its job, the Radiation Laboratory had brought together an estimated 20 percent of the nation's top-ranking physicists, without disastrous results.

Promptly after the decision was made to sponsor the Radiation Laboratory at MIT, new boys were "walking around in room 4-133, deciding where their benches would go and what they ought to buy" and indicating how inadequate this space was and how much more would certainly be needed. This was the modest start of an enterprise that ultimately employed nearly 4,000 men and women and at its peak occupied two-thirds of a million square feet of floor space.

With Ernest Lawrence of the University of California undertaking the first recruiting, MIT volunteered to aid the new laboratory to build its initial staff. This included making the arrangements with the individuals so selected and negotiating with their home institutions for their leaves of absence. Because the United States was not yet at war, these first leaves of absence were negotiated for only one year, and because of the highly classified nature of the laboratory, it proved to be at times very difficult to convince other institutions to grant the necessary leaves.

There were rumors that came to my ears in 1941 or 1942 that a discussion had taken place in Washington as to whether the Radiation Laboratory might grow too large and that the concentration of so many scientists working on war research in a single academic institution might become the subject of criticism or attack.

In an effort to clear up this rumor for the record, I wrote, toward the end of the war, to the historian of the laboratory, Professor Henry E. Guerlac, and on August 17, 1945, I received a letter from him which included the following conclusions:

As far as I can ascertain, the discussions that took place during these first months were the result of several events in combination: (1) America's entrance into the war on December 7 and the necessity of deciding how much the Laboratory should expand under the pressures of war; (2) criticism from other institutions, just then faced with the threat of losing their tuition fees and not yet rescued in part by Army and Navy programs, that the NDRC contracts had not been spread widely enough; (3) an attack led by Dr. Jewett of NDRC who opposed the growth of the Laboratory. It is not my impression that there was an actual proposal that it be divided into several pieces.

The memorandum of Dr. Compton referred to above was designed to meet all these criticisms. It summarizes the decisions reached by the Microwave Committee and by the NDRC, the latter meeting in special session without the attendance of the Army and Navy members. It calls attention to the plans already underway for letting new NDRC radar contracts under Radiation Laboratory supervision to other institutions. A document in my possession written by Dr. Linford on January 16, 1942, and addressed to the Committee on Farming Out Projects, shows that such a committee had been constituted and that institutions were already answering a circular that had been sent around.[2]

It is not within the purview of this memoir to describe in any detail the magnificent accomplishments of the Radiation Laboratory. Extensive accounts of its work may be found in *Scientists Against Time* that brought, in 1947, the Pulitzer Prize in history to its author, James Phinney Baxter III, and further information is in *Q.E.D., M.I.T. in World War II* by John Burchard.[3]

The Radiation Laboratory devoted itself to three major missions: (1) to develop a 10-centimeter airborne set for use by night fighters, (2) to achieve an accurate precision gun-laying radar, (3) to design a long-range navigational system (which came to be called LORAN and that today is in worldwide use). In the course of its work it carried on fundamental research on the behavior of microwaves, including the development of new tubes, new circuits, and new components.

In one of his reports its director, Dr. Lee A. DuBridge, described the laboratory as primarily one of engineering and production: "By June 1943 nearly 6000 radar sets of Radiation Laboratory design had been delivered to the Army and Navy, 22,000 were on order, and production was climbing past the rate of 2000 sets per month of all types. The total dollar value of Service orders had by that time grown to three quarters of a billion dollars. Production mounted rapidly during the latter half of the year, and equipments with trained personnel were reaching the theaters in large quantities."

As Baxter was to write in this history,

The 150 radar systems which the Radiation Laboratory had produced or helped to produce had speeded the day of victory. The high resolution of 10-cm radar as compared to that of longer-wave sets had come to seem dull and unsatisfactory compared with the wonderful clarity of the 3-cm radar and that of still shorter wave length. With these glowing outline maps before their eyes navigators had guided our bombers over Italy, Germany, and Japan. Thanks to the blind-bombing techniques they made possible, the pressure of strategic bombing had been kept so steadily on the Axis powers that they could not rebuild their towns, cities, and railroads, when they were bombed and blasted into ruins.

By applying science to the technology of the war, the laboratory was to play a decisive role in the defeat of Germany. It was DuBridge, I think, who summed up matters by remarking that radar won the war; the atom bomb ended it. Rabi said it stronger: had it not been for radar, the Allies would have lost the war.

By its early provision of a home for the Radiation Laboratory—and by its ability to make quick decisions—and by its forehanded acceptance of other war research projects mostly initiated by its faculty, MIT demonstrated leadership in mobilizing university resources for the prosecution of the war and later for the prosecution of peace.

In an introductory note to the Index volume of the *Radiation Laboratory Series*, Lee DuBridge wrote that it was fortunate that the laboratory was organized as a part of MIT: "The flexibility of its administrative organization and the kind and wise leadership of President Compton and Vice President Killian were vital factors in the Laboratory's operation and success."

By its success the Radiation Laboratory provided a demonstration of the power of integrated research, which was later to be influential in the organization of research by universities and industry. It also encouraged universities, especially MIT, to devise postwar interdepartmental organizations for integrating new fields of learning and research requiring a partnership of disciplines. Of this I will have more to say.

More than most of the other large-scale wartime university research projects, this laboratory contributed directly to the conduct of fighting in the theaters of war and brought its civilian research personnel in operational contact with the personnel of the fighting military forces. This brought to the laboratory a sense of urgency and of direct sharing in battle operations and bequeathed to those Radiation Laboratory members who continued at MIT a realistic sense of the importance of further contributions to our national security after the war. And these scientists and engineers continued to undertake creative programs such as the summer study projects which MIT later sponsored. (Professor Zacharias has made the interesting comment to me that this sense of realistic involvement which marked the work of the Radiation Laboratory group led to the initiation of such programs as the Physical Science Study Committee organized in the 1950s to reform and improve the teaching of science in precollege schools.) It created a closer working relationship between scientists, government, and the educational apparatus of the country. It "was the first appearance, in the national fabric, of science as an autonomous force, and of the scientific method as a way of work. Here for the first time significant energy was set free." It was especially notable that attitudes of young scientists in the Radiation Laboratory had been changed by their experience there. In a taped interview recalling in 1982 his experience in the Radiation Laboratory, Professor Louis D. Smullin, Dugald C. Jackson Professor of Electrical Engineering, observed:

Because of that free interchange, not having to say "Yes, sir," things got solved in a more rational way. . . . That was a very unique time that carried all the way through to postwar MIT. We still weren't old, but we were used to speaking up and knowing that we . . . had done an important job without having to defer to our elders other than politeness. They weren't smarter because they were older. That made a big ferment at MIT in subsequent years . . .[4]

In writing as historian of the Navy in World War II, Rear Admiral Samuel Eliot Morison bluntly noted that the U.S. Navy was woefully unprepared for the German U-boat blitz on the Atlantic Coast. How this problem was solved involved a number of characters including Secretary Stimson, Bush, the president, Admiral King, and others. But for the purposes of this memoir I recall the important role played by Edward Bowles and the Radiation Laboratory. Bowles, who had been closely associated with the early arrangements in the NDRC for the Radiation Laboratory, was invited at Bush's suggestion by Secretary Stimson to be an expert consultant to his office. In this capacity Bowles was informed about the latest radar developments in the Radiation Laboratory, and it was he who recommended that planes be equipped with the laboratory's new centimeter radar for spotting U-boats on the surface. Other devices were brought to bear and rapidly turned the tide against the German U-boats. This defeat of the German U-boats off the Atlantic Coast was one of the great victories of the war.

Later, still in his capacity as consultant, Bowles recommended that a large number of the Radiation Laboratory's newly developed SCR-584 radars be shipped to England to defend against the German buzz bombs; they proved to be decisively effective.

Julius Stratton was also asked to serve as expert consultant to the Secretary of War and contributed importantly in solving communications problems for the ferrying of fighters and bombers to Britain by northern routes. Later he participated in the application of ground radar in air defense.

SERVOS, FIRE CONTROL, AND COMPUTERS

Although its huge size tended to overshadow the others, the Radiation Laboratory was by no means the only war research project at the Institute. Indeed, during World War II MIT undertook four hundred contracts for work in furtherance of the national war effort. A number of these other wartime projects were wholly indigenous to MIT, had been started prior to the war, and were continued after the war by its staff. Like the Radiation Laboratory and its successor, the Research Laboratory of Electronics, they were to be of profound importance to postwar education at the Institute.

Let me now proceed invidiously to select for description several of these research programs not only to celebrate their war achievements but to show how they too came to make lasting contributions to education and to pay deserved tribute to the brilliant teachers who directed them. In a very real sense these case histories show the genesis of major postwar technological advances that strengthened both graduate and undergraduate education, notably in engineering. I present as examples Gordon Brown's Servomechanisms Laboratory, Stark Draper's Instrumentation Laboratory, and Jay Forrester's Whirlwind Computer Project. In the next chapter I describe the highly productive summer study projects that served the nation in the cold war period and describe the genesis of the Lincoln Laboratory, the large peacetime laboratory MIT was drafted to undertake.

THE SERVOMECHANISMS LABORATORY[5]

During the course of his research in the Department of Electrical Engineering, Professor Harold Hazen made pioneering contributions to computer technology, notably to Bush's differential analyzer, and to automatic control. Among these were fundamental contributions to the theory of servomechanisms, and in 1935 he was awarded the Levy Gold Medal of the Franklin Institute for his publications on this new technology. (Simply defined, a servomechanism is a device that enables a small force to control a large force; power steering in a car is an elementary servomechanism.) His student and later colleague, Professor Gordon Brown, had worked closely with him, and this antecedent experience came to maturity in Brown's wartime Servomechanisms Laboratory, where invaluable new servo technology was developed for the accurate direction of gunfire and, ultimately, for revolutionary use in industry.

In a tribute to Hazen (*Annals of the History of Computing*, January 1981), Brown gives an impressive account of Hazen's research, much of it in association with Vannevar Bush and Brown himself during the exciting decades of the 1920s and 30s. There was a remarkably creative, freewheeling group in the Department of Electrical Engineering at that time making the department world famous as a center of advanced research, notable inventions, and advances in education. As Brown has recently said to me, those were the days when the bets were on people and not on programs and people were shaping the future by developing their own ideas through the technique of brilliantly uninhibited theses. Among graduate students and faculty, companionship was memorably close despite the insistence of each researcher to do things in his own way. Here was a spirit of free-enterprise scholarship, which was another one of the qualities that made MIT a very special research university.

Out of this laboratory research also came refinements in engineering education. When Professor Brown later became head of the Department of Electrical Engineering and then dean of engineering, his experience had prepared him well to initiate major reforms in teaching and curriculum design.

In his history of electrical engineering at MIT, Professor Karl Wildes has written that the Servomechanisms Laboratory and its successor, the Electronic Systems Laboratory, under the leadership of Frank Reintjes, seem "in retrospect to exhibit close to the ideal interaction of research and education. Real problems, whether of war or of peace, have attracted innately bright students and staff to work together in an atmosphere of professional engineering attainment. While engaged in these pursuits, the participants have prepared themselves to take on increasingly responsible positions in industry and in society generally. During the eight years 1963 to 1971 the annual reports show that thesis research in the Electronic Systems Laboratory contributed to 377 degrees . . . an average of 47 a year."

The Servomechanisms Laboratory provided important educational opportunities to gifted engineer, Jay W. Forrester, whose development of a pioneer computer in the postwar period I celebrate in a following section. Stark Draper, who worked in close association with the Servo Lab, was to become recognized as one of the great engineers of our time as he evolved the renowned laboratory that was ultimately to bear his name.

While he was with the Servomechanisms Laboratory during the war, Forrester agreed to go to Pearl Harbor to investigate the cause of a breakdown in a radar on board the aircraft carrier USS *Lexington (II)*. While at work repairing this radar equipment, which had been designed by the Radiation Laboratory, Forrester was asked if he would be willing to continue his work aboard the carrier when she went to sea. He agreed and unepectedly found himself "in the midst of an assault on the Gilbert and Marshall Islands." As Professor Wildes records the incident, "an enemy plane launched a torpedo into *Lexington's* stern, destroying her steering equipment and setting her rudder to port. . . . Other attacks were repulsed by antiaircraft fire while the disabled rudder was centered and the carrier steamed toward Pearl Harbor, steered by her screws." And, as Gordon Brown noted, "Jay became quite a hero at Servo Lab."

In 1949 the Servomechanisms Laboratory embarked on a research program that was to lead to the wide industrial adoption of a new system by which machine tools were controlled automatically by means of programmed instructions stored in punched cards, magnetic tape, or computer memory. Work in this field began in the Servomechanisms Laboratory under a contract with the Parsons Corporation of Michigan and continued through a contract negotiated with the Air Force in 1951. By 1952 the pilot design of a machine that was the basis of the invention of programmable, general-purpose numerically controlled machine tools was in operation. The achievement of this invention grew out of much earlier work in servomechanisms and machine computation in the 1920s and 1930s by Professor Hazen and Vannevar Bush. With this background and through Forrester's experiences with the Whirlwind computer and the research of William K. Linvill, a graduate student in the 1940s who developed the theory of operating servomechanisms with Whirlwind-type signals, the laboratory was able to make a landmark contribution to numerical control.

In an address presented in 1968, Willard F. Rockwell, Jr., of the North American Rockwell Corporation, spoke of the achievement that emerged from this MIT work as an "astonishing new system." Said Mr. Rockwell, "The marriage of numerical control, the digital computer, and machine tools is one of the stunning technological innovations of our time—an achievement to rank with nuclear power . . . and with space flight . . . as a third great development of our generation."

While Mr. Rockwell's statement may be hyperbolic, there has come to be clear recognition that basic work on numerical control proved to be of fundamental importance to the U.S. manufacturing industry, despite the initially conservative position the machine-tool industry took toward this technological breakthrough. It is an eloquent example of how the universities, working with the support of government and industry, can underwrite American leadership in advanced manufacturing technology. The pioneering computer technology introduced by Hazen, Bush, and others in the 1930s was fertile intellectual soil for Hazen and Brown to advance the conceptualization and design of servomechanisms, especially digital-servo design. The ground was rich for the develoment of computer-controlled machine tools and for the digital control of processes. This brilliant, pioneering technology was inevitably to lead to the current era of robotics.

While Japanese industry grabbed the lead, the Americans

fiddled. The automobile industry was at first cool to the advances in numerical control and let the Japanese take the lead in applications. I count it one of my failures as a corporate director not to have adequately aroused General Motors to the robotics in its future.

The National Defense Research Committee sponsored a program in the Servomechanisms Laboratory that led to some very early studies of missile flight. The contribution of these studies led the Navy after the war to induce MIT to undertake a guided missile program. Despite suggestions that this research be undertaken in a formal laboratory arrangement, the decision was made that the program would be carried out as an Institute-wide project with various programs conducted in half a dozen or more departments. This was a uniquely organized program. Its technical coordination was the responsibility of a technical steering committee, and its policy direction was by an MIT guided missile committee under the chairmanship of Dr. Stratton. The executive officer selected for the program was then an assistant professor in aeronautical engineering, H. G. Stever. In participating recently in an oral history program, Stever described how this unusual arrangement made fundamental contributions later useful in the design and development of guided missiles and stimulated work of broad importance in several MIT departments. Stever later became head of the Departments of Mechanical Engineering and Naval Architecture and Marine Engineering; from there he moved on to the presidency of the Carnegie Institute of Technology, thence to the directorship of the National Science Foundation, and, in the closing days of the Nixon administration, science adviser to the president.

In the postwar period the Mechanical Engineering Department, under the leadership of Jerome Hunsaker, Richard Soderberg, and their successors, achieved recognition as the nation's top-ranking department in its field. The recruiting of able department heads was another of the accomplishments of Compton and Bush as they moved to strengthen not only science but engineering as well.

In much the same way that the Research Laboratory of Electronics was the wellspring of new electrical science and disciplines, the Servomechanisms Laboratory was the seedbed of new technologies, and especially the critical decisions required to achieve numerical control.

By 1949 these various engineering breakthroughs, together with Draper's Instrumentation Laboratory, had become a collection of enterprises that was to have revolutionary impact on bold military and industrial technology. They contributed to my realization that the decade of the fifties was a dramatic time to be an administrator.

The enormous productivity of these assemblies of engineering professors and graduate students working in the freedom and cognation of American universities was to shape the future of American society. I am emboldened to say that only in our research universities and in the Bell Telephone Laboratories did there exist in those bright days the freedom, the interconnected web of technology and science, and the existential scholarship required to achieve the technological achievements I have summarized.

Let me now turn to the spectacular achievements of Stark Draper's Instrumentation Laboratory and then Jay Forrester's Project Whirlwind. Forrester had been brought up to innovative speed in the Servomechanisms Laboratory.

THE INSTRUMENTATION LABORATORY

Professor Stark Draper's Instrumentation Laboratory developed a family of computing gunsights to enable our naval vessels to defend themselves against the Japanese Kamikaze planes that attacked our ships in the Pacific war. As President Julius Stratton was to write in an appreciation of Dr. Draper, "In 1941, the United States was shocked by the sinking of the *Repulse* and the *Prince of Wales*, with all the implications for the future of naval power. Out of a discussion with the late Nathaniel McL. Sage, whom he deeply admired and respected, Draper was led to the development of the Mark 14 [gyroscopic] gunsight. Two years later, at the battle of Santa Cruz, *Battleship X* (USS *South Dakota*) gave a spectacular demonstration of its effectiveness.

"From the Mark 14 gunsight, in turn, there came a whole new concept of fire control."[6]

Draper next applied the same technology to the invention of gunsights for the Air Force.

Even more spectacular developments in guidance, navigation, and control technology came from his hand after the war as the Instrumentation Laboratory developed and produced an impressive series of inertial navigation systems for aircraft, ship, missile, and submarine use, and the highly precise gyroscopes required by these systems. Perhaps the most famous achievements of the Laboratory were the systems that guided Apollo to the moon, permitted surface exploration, and safely guided the spacecraft to earth.

Professor Draper was also a stellar performer as a teacher and as head of the Department of Aeronautical Engineering. In the classroom he applied to engineering education his philosophy of cradle-to-grave research and development, which characterized the Instrumentation Laboratory's work. Instruments developed in the laboratory, Draper insisted, should remain under its responsibility from creation to completion by subcontracting industrial companies.

In his appreciation Jay Stratton recalls a course in advanced mechanics in which he was the teacher and Stark Draper was a student. "Clearly," said Stratton, "I can claim Stark as one of my former students. However, to make much of that point would be a travesty of the facts; it would be difficult to say whether it was teacher or student . . . who learned most from the other." Stratton also graphically described how Draper beguiled him to take a flight in Draper's plane, Draper piloting, in order to demonstrate some of the matters that had been under discussion in the classroom:

I sat behind Stark as he lectured with shouts and gestures on the idiosyncrasies of instruments. Then, at a point directly over the harbor, it happened. The nose went sharply up. For a moment we hung on the propeller, as if suspended in the stillness of space. Suddenly the plane pitched forward; I gazed down on the water far below. We began to pick up speed. I became aware of a strange phenomenon: slowly, then more rapidly, the Boston skyline began to rotate about the plane. The Customs House tower moved in a majestic circle. It occurred to me that I had left a good many things undone and that the Department would be hard put to find someone to teach mechanics. The plane leveled out, rolled over, and settled down on a quiet course. I said nothing. No student but Draper has ever done such a thing to me before or since.[7]

Courtland Perkins, former president of the National Academy of Engineering, recently recalled for me the reactions of graduate students to Stark Draper's teaching in the late 1930s and early 40s. Perkins had come to MIT to study aeronautical engineering after graduating from Swarthmore, and found Draper's teaching, by contrast with that at Swarthmore, unconventional and exciting. Draper would come to class wearing a green eyeshade and accompanied by assistants to help him in handling his props. "Today," he might announce to his class, "we are going to discuss the genesis of an invention we made overnight." Using his own system of units and symbols, which would take his students some time to master, he then proceeded to illustrate the brand of creative engineering he was using in his embryo Instrumentation Laboratory. Draper thus taught engineering by *doing* engineering; learning and research were intermingled, and the students' learning experience became memorably provocative and exhilarating. The art he brought to teaching was another of the advances in MIT education in the 1950s.

PROJECT WHIRLWIND

Although not a wartime laboratory, Project Whirlwind benefited from the experience of its director, Jay W. Forrester, who was associated with Professor Gordon Brown in the Servomechanisms Laboratory. It is appropriate to describe Whirlwind as one of the legacies of wartime research.

During the war, as a result of his experience in the use of flight trainers to train pilots for Navy planes, an imaginative and charismatic Naval officer, Captain Luis de Florez, in the Navy's Special Devices Division, began thinking about more sophisticated simulation devices for pilot training and for yielding information about the reaction of pilots to wind tunnel tests of model planes that might be useful in the design of new planes. He discussed his ideas about trainer-analyzers with friends at MIT and found strong support on the part of Nathaniel Sage, Professor Hunsaker, and professors in the Department of Aeronautical Engineering. Consequently Professor John R. Markham was appointed project engineer for research on an "airplane stability and control analyzer," and he, together with Professors Joseph Bicknell and Otto C. Koppen, prepared a report on "a proposed method of ensuring satisfactory handling characteristics of new airplanes." In this report they included a statement that "a specialized calculating machine could be built that could be set up for a particular airplane according to data obtained by experimental means, and the pilot's control motions could be fed into the system by actually having the pilot fly the resulting airplane." In this statement appeared the first suggestion that a new kind of computer would be required for such a system. This speculation was to lead ultimately to the concept of the Whirlwind computer.

Research to achieve Captain de Florez's objectives eventually moved from aeronautical engineering over to electrical engineering, and specifically into the domain of Professor Gordon Brown's Servomechanisms Laboratory. In 1944 Professor Brown brought the Navy project to the attention of one of his assistant directors, Jay Forrester, who was challenged by the concept and agreed to direct a project. He enlisted another Servomechanisms Laboratory staff member, Robert R. Everett.

Among the "hot" graduate students and research assistants of those days was Perry Crawford, who studied under Bush and Samuel Caldwell and did a master's thesis under the title "Automatic Control by Arithmetical Operations," which considered the control of antiaircraft gunfire. Perry was a wellspring of current ideas about digital as well as analog devices. He was a vital source of information to both de Florez and Forrester about work at other places. Later both Forrester and Everett "were to attribute to Perry Crawford the suggestion, which they came to take seriously, that digital numerical techniques merited serious study."[8] In after years Forrester recalled standing on the steps in front of one of the Institute buildings talking with Crawford, whose remarks turned on a light in his mind. His recollection is that from that time on he began to consider the digital mode seriously. After concentrating too long on analog computing, MIT was belatedly to recognize that digital technology was the road to the future.

The fascinating history of the electronic digital computer is reviewed by Brian Randell in the October 1982 *Annals of the History of Computing*, and appropriately he gives credit to the pioneer work of Vannevar Bush and his associates. It can be argued, he said, that Bush had a direct influence on the course of the development of the modern computer, even though his development of the differential analyzer has identified him principally with the analog technology. Randell concluded, however, that Bush was the first to conceptualize, but not to construct, an electronic digital computer. He did this as he addressed himself to the research leading to the highly classified Rapid Selector—an almost forgotten project at MIT in which John H. Howard played a major role—for the Navy's cryptographic agency.†

Perry Crawford has convinced me that Bush drew up comprehensive proposals for an electronic digital computer in a series of memoranda in 1937 and that he had succeeded in launching in late 1937 or early 1938, working with William Radford, the first electronic digital computer machine. Bush also, with the assistance of a grant from the Carnegie Corporation, succeeded in founding a Center of Analysis which would house and coordinate the computational devices developed at MIT, including the Rockefeller analyzer, which was already virtually obsolete.†

At the Moore School of the University of Pennsylvania, J. Presper Eckert and John W. Mauchly were proceeding successfully with the digital development of ENIAC (Electronic Numerical Integrator and Calculator) which has been justly described as the first all-purpose, all-electronic digital computer.

In 1944 Professor John von Neumann of the Princeton Institute for Advanced Study visited ENIAC with results profoundly important to the future of computers. It led him, as logician and mathematician, to think profoundly about computers and their design and to undertake the building of EDVAC (Electronic Discreet Variable Automatic Computer). Historians of the computer view the years 1944, 1945, and 1946 as perhaps the most eventful years in the intellectual history of computers.

Von Neumann went on to gain the support of the Institute for Advanced Study to undertake the construction of EDVAC. He was supported in his desire actually to construct a computer embodying his advanced ideas by Frank Aydelotte, onetime head of the Department of English and History at MIT but then head of the Institute for Advanced Study.

As Forrester and Everett plunged ahead at MIT, they also saw the possibility of a computer that possessed real-time control, and this capability with "men in the loop" placed very different demands on the machine from those dictated solely by pure computation. Out of their determined efforts ultimately emerged the "first high-speed electronic digital computer to operate in real time," a computer with synchronous parallel logic that was the first computer "to use a random access magnetic core memory," an element invented by Professor Forrester.

In 1946 the Navy transferred the sponsorship of the Forrester project from the Special Devices Division to the Office of Naval Research, and thus Whirlwind came under the sponsorship of ONR. But when the project came to concentrate on a new kind of digital computer, rather than on the machine application originally proposed, ONR continued its sponsorship with increasing discomfort. A major problem with Project Whirlwind was that it had been assigned to ONR's mathematics branch but did not seem significantly oriented toward mathematical uses; moreover it was costly.

As I have said, von Neumann approached his concept of a computer as a brilliant logician and mathematician, Forrester, as a brilliant engineer. As to be expected, the sponsorship of the two computers by ONR tilted in its sympathies toward the von

Neumann computer. The elegant engineering and the emphasis on reliability which Forrester and Everett insisted on resulted in costs that contrasted with von Neumann's less-expensive profoundly conceived EDVAC. Whirlwind also at this stage had largely lost any defined, specific objectives for its use, although there were of course visions in the minds of its leaders. The two projects provided a dramatic demonstration of how an engineering philosophy of design as exploited by Forrester and Everett focused on reliability, capability, and reproducibility, whereas the von Neumann group proceeded as logicians and mathematicians.

When I invited his comment on my story of the Whirlwind computer, Professor Brown expressed the view that in retrospect, Forrester and Everett appear to have been among the earliest workers in the field who clearly visualized the capability of these digital machines to process vast amounts of information in new and novel ways, rather than to view them as merely manipulators of numbers and compilers of tables with lightning speed.[9]

When the personnel of ONR questioned the rising cost of Whirlwind, as did MIT, Forrester and Everett insisted that they could not proceed with the project unless they could do it in terms of their concepts of the quality of the engineering, adaptability, and multiple use that should be built into the computer. In computer jargon they were determined not to wind up with a computer susceptible to "kluges."

A point was reached where the Navy probably would have canceled its contract because of the mounting cost of Project Whirlwind and its seeming lack of a clear objective, although the MIT administration, after two reviews, decided to back it without reservation. A dramatic reversal of this situation then occurred when there appeared a proposal from the Air Force to use Whirlwind as the heart of an air defense system. This concept had come out of a committee of the Scientific Advisory Board of the Air Force that was chaired by Professor George Valley of the MIT Physics Department. The engineering characteristics, the reliability, and the other qualities of Whirlwind seemed to provide the best available computer for an air defense system, the SAGE system as it came to be called. (SAGE is an acronym for *Semi-Automatic Ground Environment*.) And so the Air Force began to pick up the tab of the still growing costs of completing Project Whirlwind and of adapting it to the air defense development program. Whirlwind was thus saved, justified, and put to important national use. Here was another example of how funds from the Department of Defense, flowing through the Office of Naval Research and from the Air Force, contributed enormously to the development of the new university about which I have been writing.

To my abbreviated account of the origin and uses of the Whirlwind computer, let me add some historical notes about a differential analyzer which Bush planned in the early thirties and to which the Rockefeller Foundation was to make large grants. As I have indicated, Bush's brilliant achievement, his successful "differential analyzer," was in the analog mode, and the new Rockefeller machine was to be a major improvement and upscaling of the original. Bush "envisioned a computer larger, faster, more flexible and convenient but still a version in principle of the 1931 machine."[10] Bush had written to Warren Weaver of the Rockefeller Foundation that the new computer "will become a center of analysis of a certain important type to which research workers everywhere will turn for their solutions and their equations."[11]

This bold vision was not to be realized. Bush's departure for Washington to head the Carnegie Institution, the coming of World War II, and technical difficulties were to plague the analyzer as work on it continued into the upper forties. In the intervening period the digital type of computer clearly became the computer of the future, and projects such as ENIAC at the University of Pennsylvania and Whirlwind itself provided a demonstration that the analog type of computer, except for special purposes, was rendered obsolete by the new digital technology. Until the Whirlwind project was undertaken, MIT electrical engineers had been largely diverted over the years from the development of digital computers.

In May 1947, I received a memorandum from Dean George R. Harrison reporting that he and Professor Hazen had concluded that Whirlwind "completely overshadows the Rockefeller project." "It might prove desirable," said Harrison, "to stop work on this and offer to return to the Foundation all funds expended on it" out of grants recently made to the Institute. "We could then throw all of our effort into the Forrester project, which is much more amply financed, and of such scale that it would be likely to absorb any results of the Rockefeller project. . . ."

These evaluations of the Rockefeller differential analyzer came to Karl Compton's attention and led him to write to Warren Weaver in June 1947 as follows:

At the end of our first year certain conclusions have become evident that alter our original program in a major way and which I wish to report to you at this time. The major conclusion is that the Navy Whirlwind project here under the direction of Mr. Jay Forrester has so evolved in objectives, scope, and security aspects that it is doing what we had expected to do under the Rockefeller Grant. It is doing this on a substantially larger scale than we had planned under your grant and with such vigor that the purpose of your grant to us is being met as fully as we know how to meet it. This being the case, we think the expenditure of Foundation funds for competitive work in the same institution is not justified and is in fact foolish. Our conclusion therefore is to terminate the work under your grant and to return to the Foundation the monies that have been sent to us by the Foundation.

In July Compton received this understanding letter from Weaver:

I think that the conclusion you have reached is entirely characteristic of the intelligence and, if I may use so Victorian a phrase, the scrupulous honor which we all confidently expect from MIT. It does not seem to me that there is any aspect of the situation which need cause anyone any regret. After all, our common object was to forward this very important field of work. It is being forwarded at MIT, and in a very distinguished way.

While director of the Research Laboratory of Electronics and later as provost, Dr. Stratton played a key role of appraiser and policymaker with respect to MIT's computer activities. He too had concluded that the Rockefeller differential analyzer should be terminated. And it was he who conceived an ongoing program at the Institute that led to the selection of Professor Philip Morse to direct a computation center, a post from which he skillfully shaped future information-processing policies and services at the Institute.

The availability of Whirlwind made it possible for MIT mathematicians and geologists to make a breakthrough in revealing information, long hidden, in seismic records used in the search for oil. It was also used for the preparation of computer programs for the digitally controlled machine-tool project described earlier. Perhaps more important, its great achievement in computer technology made it one of the great pioneer computers. It has provided a training ground for a group of experts who were to have a lasting influence on computer technology. It has led to enormous developments in the computer industry and to a solid demonstration that engineers no less than scientists can carry through successfully a great high-technology undertaking.

There had arisen during World War II a canard that it required physicists to do the advanced engineering required by the development of radar and other military weapons systems. The achievements of the programs that I have singled out for description—the Servomechanisms Laboratory, the Instrumentation Laboratory, and Project Whirlwind—all established beyond any cavil the capacity of first-rate engineers, no less than of physicists, to carry through remarkable breakthrough technological developments.

The story of Whirlwind's development has been admirably told in a book by Kent C. Redmond and Thomas M. Smith entitled *Project Whirlwind: The History of a Pioneer Computer*. The Whirlwind project stands as another testimony of the educational impact of wartime projects that trained new breeds of engineers for the furtherance of ever more complex technology.

Professor Forrester, after this highly successful development of the Whirlwind computer and his basic invention of its magnetic storage system, decided to move on into the application of computers in the broad field of management and economics and social movements.

MIT was responsible both to Forrester and to the government for the management of the patent arising out of Professor Forrester's invention of the magnetic storage system. This proved to be a long, difficult, and vexing engagement for an academic institution. It was resolved ultimately in the Stratton administration following intensive negotiation with IBM, which agreed to pay a lump-sum royalty subject to certain reductions for its use of the patent. Settlements proportional to that with IBM were negotiated over a period of years with other companies using the Forrester invention in their digital computers. The negotiation with IBM had come to a head during President Stratton's absence from the country, and it fell to my lot and that of Vice President Carl Floe to respond to the proposal from Thomas Watson, Jr., of IBM that we undertake to settle the matter. At a dramatic meeting at the Armonk headquarters of IBM with Watson and Albert Williams, Floe and I presented a proposed settlement figure; after some deliberation IBM countered with a modified total (far higher than any royalty they had earlier been willing to consider), which we of MIT had agreed in advance to accept.

Had MIT not earlier formulated a patent policy, there could have been no such settlement. It is worthy of note that the University of Pennsylvania had no patent policy and consequently Eckert and Mauchly were unable to receive any royalties for their invention of ENIAC.

In 1979 Forrester was elected to the Inventors Hall of Fame for his invention of the magnetic-core memory device. Once, in talking with me, Professor Gordon Brown had commented that among his associates he placed Forrester in the category of genius.

THE RADAR SCHOOL
Progress in the Radiation Laboratory brought realization that special radar training programs would be required as microwave radar came into use. Through initiatives taken by Professor Bowles, Dean Moreland, and President Compton, a Radar School, independent of the Radiation Laboratory, was estab-

lished by MIT in June 1941, with Wilmer L. Barrow serving as director.

The Harbor Building in Boston ultimately housed this School, which trained nearly 8,900 officers, enlisted men, and civilians in radar techniques. It was MIT's largest wartime educational program and again demonstrated the interaction of research and education. As Professor Reintjes has stressed, its legacies were substantial. Many of its alumni found their way into the academic community and pointed their engineering courses in entirely new directions through courses in pulse circuits, microwaves, and servomechanisms—topics that were unheard of in the prewar era. In these endeavors they were materially aided by the Radar School's textbook *Principles of Radar*, first published in 1947, as well as by the 28-volume "bookshelf" prepared by the Radiation Laboratory as documentation of its wartime efforts.

The Institute of course had both V-12 and ASTP. It also trained many officers, including WAVES, in meteorology. I remember Captain Charles Joyce, senior naval officer on campus and a bachelor, being nonplussed by the arrival of the WAVES. When their senior officer reported in to him, he gruffly asked why she didn't remove her hat as all the male officers did when in his office. As they settled in, however, he went to great pains to see that they were made to feel welcome, properly housed, and provided with appropriate amenities.

THE RESEARCH LABORATORY OF ELECTRONICS: SEQUEL TO THE RADIATION LABORATORY

Prime among the examples of educational legacies of the Radiation Laboratory was a seminal postwar innovation that came to be called the Research Laboratory of Electronics.

The Radiation Laboratory, in its contributions to the winning of World War II, had provided an unprecedentedly impressive demonstration of how interdisciplinary research with a clearly defined mission could provide scientific support and new technology for meeting an urgent national need.

It was not surprising then that as early as 1943 the MIT faculty and administration, observing the success of this laboratory, began to conceive an academic successor smaller in size but with a similar interdisciplinary structure for basic research. Professor John Slater, head of the Department of Physics, who had been on leave working on wartime research at the Bell Telephone Laboratories, came forward with a proposal that the Institute undertake a laboratory to succeed the Radiation Laboratory and to continue its basic research. As a result of his initiatives, which he discussed with Dr. Compton, Professor Stratton, and me, a conference was held in August 1944 to discuss the formation of what Slater called a research laboratory of electronics. Present at this conference, in addition to Dr. Compton and Professor Slater, were Dean Harrison and Professors Hazen and Stratton. As a result of the enthusiastic endorsement of this group, the Executive Committee of the Corporation in September formally approved the establishment of an "Interdepartmental Electronic Laboratory to conduct research in the field of electronics in association with the Departments of Physics and Electrical Engineering and to approve the appointment of Professor Julius A. Stratton as Director of the Laboratory." The Committee also authorized an appropriation of $250,000 for the purpose of ensuring $50,000 a year for five years to support the laboratory— another example of the Executive Committee's willingness to earmark funds for new ventures. This was in addition to $50,000 it had already appropriated for the cost of materials and equipment necessary to establish a research program in the field of electronics. I was active in running interference for the founders of this new academic venture and, along with Horace Ford, in proposing to the Executive Committee actions to provide the necessary seed money.

In later years Slater, in looking back, further expressed his belief that interdepartmental laboratories such as RLE helped scientists to get things done that they could hardly have accomplished otherwise. Slater proposed other interdepartmental laboratories or centers and thus contributed in a very fundamental way to the structural arrangements at the Institute which have furthered research in a variety of fields. It was Slater of course who also promoted the Research Laboratory for Nuclear Science, and his desire for a laboratory for chemical and solid-state physics contributed to the ultimate organization of MIT's Materials Science and Engineering Center.

The creation of the RLE was also facilitated by a decision on the part of the Office of Scientific Research and Development to finance for a brief term a Basic Research Division of the Radiation Laboratory, and for the first six months of 1945 OSRD provided a special grant of $50,000 for the support of this division, which was later to be folded into MIT's academic RLE program.

Under the strong and imaginative leadership of Dr. Stratton and successive directors, which included Professors Albert Hill, Jerome Wiesner, Henry Zimmerman, Peter Wolff, and Jonathan Allen, this new academic venture has flourished. It has grown into an entity impressive in its beneficial relationships with government, impressive in the fruitful interplay it provides between science and engineering, and impressive in its exciting successes in opening up new intellectual territory and in providing new interconnections between many fertile minds working in diverse fields. Although sponsored by the Departments of Electrical Engineering and Physics, the laboratory provides an attractive environment for students and staff from many departments without diminishing the role of these departments in the academic structure of the Institute. In fact the "center" concept RLE embodied and the successful exploitation of this concept by other centers modeled on it were major factors in MIT's postwar evolution into a new kind of research university.

Let it also be noted that it nurtured two MIT presidents, J. A. Stratton and J. B. Wiesner, who were thus well prepared to further the development of this university.

In the 1979 report of the President and Chancellor of the Institute, which reviews the evolving intellectual map of MIT over the past fifty years, an account is given of how a book written by MIT's famed mathematician, Norbert Wiener, and published under the title *Cybernetics, or Control and Communication in the Animal and the Machine*,[12] became an intellectual endowment for the early years of RLE. Wiener's seminal book provided a synthesis of statistical communication theory, servomechanisms, and feedback along with advanced views on the potential—and dangers—of computers. Out of the resonance prompted by Wiener's book and out of the research it promoted in RLE grew "most of MIT's contemporary work in human communication, including the neurosciences, psychology, and linguistics, as well as much of the computation activities." The Center for the Brain Sciences now in gestation, the Center for Cognitive Science, and Whitaker College devoted to the health sciences, technology, and management, had their roots in the Research Laboratory of Electronics. The RLE gave sustained attention to the applications of information theory, and it was George Miller, the psychologist at Princeton, who said that it was a symposium on information theory at MIT in 1956 that led to the birth of the cognitive sciences.[13] Profound conclusions can be drawn from the startling fact that the dramatic growth at MIT of the human sciences owe so much to a laboratory engaged in the sciences dealing directly with the inanimate.

With an assist from William Locke of modern languges, the laboratory attracted such figures as Morris Halle and Noam Chomsky, who were to pioneer a new approach to linguistics. The great linguist and literary scholar, Roman Jakobson, at Harvard was attracted by the linguistics activity at MIT and came to spend much of his time at the Institute, thus providing another distinguished example of the versatility of the program in the Research Laboratory of Electronics.

RLE also became a center for research by graduate students, and it provided men and ideas for a new industrial technology that undergirded an industrial renaissance, particularly on Route 128 in Massachusetts. It further enabled the Institute to move rapidly to respond to the urgent plea of the Air Force to create the Lincoln Laboratory devoted initially to air defense. It also provided a demonstration of how university research can be effectively supported by government. Under an ingenious "tripartite" contract with three services, this pioneering form of government support was wholly benign and appropriate for a university because in those days there were in the military services administrators who understood the collegial, self-governing character of universities.[14] Those of us in educational institutions who experienced this benign, nonintrusive relationship with government wish desperately that the same spirit will be renewed in the 1980s.

At dinner during the festivities marking the dedication, in March 1982, of Whitaker College, President Donald Kennedy of Stanford emphasized with antic wit the challenges of interdisciplinary work. It "is a little like making love: it requires patience, finesse, and a deep devotion to getting the job done."

RLE successfully met this challenge.

The late Leo Szilard was once asked to identify the qualities that make a good laboratory great. An atmosphere of wholeness that transmutes it into a kind of magic was his perceptive answer. The MIT wartime and postwar laboratories seemed endowed with Szilard's "a kind of magic."

In this period many other achievements were occurring in other parts of the Institute. The recent death (1984) of Professor Samuel C. Collins recalls to mind his work in the Department of Chemistry that led to the invention of the Collins Helium Liquefier, which dramatically advanced the science of extremely low temperatures. Professor Collins is a vivid figure in my memory not only because he was a delightful man but because it fell to my lot, in the early days of my service in the president's office, to arrange in 1943 his transfer from the Department of Chemistry, where he was not entirely happy, to the Department of Mechanical Engineering, where he prospered.

WARTIME ADMINISTRATORS

With support from an outstandingly able staff, three men carried the major administrative oversight of the legion of nontechnical war tasks assigned to MIT—Nathaniel McL. Sage, director of the Institute's Division of Industrial Cooperation, Horace Sayford Ford, treasurer of the Institute, and myself as executive assistant to the president.

Basically the responsibility resting on the three of us was to make sure that no impediments were placed in the way of the

Institute's conduct of its many war-research projects and military training programs. Along with Dr. Compton and the Corporation's Executive Committee we were acutely aware of the challenge to manage the fiscal aspects of this huge commitment so that the Institute would not be wrecked financially and in reputation; in discharging our responsibilities for the Radiation Laboratory, we had constantly in mind the responsibility to ensure that the introduction of this huge foreign body did not become thrombogenic for the Institute.

Sage was a creative negotiator and contract officer and contributed immensely to the sound contractual relationships I have mentioned between universities and the federal government in the conduct of sponsored research. Fiscal officers found him a relentlessly tough negotiator. But regardless of the outcome of a negotiation they reacted to him with warm admiration for his mettle, his color, and his barracks-room humor. In a brusque and crusty manner he dealt with them as man to man and in speech that was colorful, uninhibited, and unambiguous. Along with "Doc" Foster and Professor R. H. Robnett, he originated policies and procedures that enabled MIT to maintain an excellent record in responsibly accounting for its use of public funds, and it was he who prompted a witty government contract officer to observe wryly that it was treaties and not mere contracts that he had negotiated with MIT.[15]

Not only was Nat a superb contract officer; he gave thoughtful encouragement to MIT engineers conducting war research. As I have already noted, he encouaged Stark Draper to proceed with the development of the Mark 14 gunsight that was to be so decisive in thwarting Japanese Kamikaze attacks (according to Draper, he used the number 14 because he once had ill luck in standing pat on this number in the game of blackjack), and in the controversies provoked by the Whirlwind computer, he was skillful in his support of Forrester and Everett. These MIT engineers still sing his praises. His influence also extended beyond MIT, in his work with the postwar Office of Naval Research to shape its enlightened contract policy.

Horace Ford forsook a promising career in banking to come to MIT in 1914 to be in charge of its business administration. For twenty years he served as bursar and then in 1934 was appointed as the first full-time treasurer of the Institute and a member of its Corporation. During his thirty-six years of full-time and fifty-five years of total service to the Institute, he not only administered the Institute's business and then its investment affairs with great skill and foresight but he became an adviser extraordinary to the Institute community. Hundreds of students went to him with their financial problems, along with members of the staff, and invariably received his help if they deserved it. To cite but one example, Horace provided aid to a young man from Massachusetts who could not have remained at MIT without financial help. This student, Robert Haslam, after graduating in chemical engineering, went on to a distinguished and productive industrial career. He never forgot the help he received from Horace, and this inspired him to make a multimillion dollar donation to MIT.

Over the years Horace became affectionately known throughout the Institute community, by students, faculty, and employees, as "Uncle Horace," and he cherished and cultivated this role. When Compton, as president, and Vannevar Bush, as vice president and dean of engineering, were moving in their many effective ways to strengthen the Institute and widen its scope, they found in Horace an effective and imaginative associate who was creative in financing new needs and new programs and in devising budget procedures that minimized hangups in allotting funds to the several departments. Together, Compton, Bush, and Ford made an extraordinary triumvirate.

In 1939, when I first became involved with the MIT budget, Horace took me by the hand and introduced me patiently to its arcane mysteries, and later, when I was president, he was always at hand to resolve knotty fiscal problems and balance intractable budgets. He was just as effective in the care and feeding of college presidents as he was with college students, and he served five of them. Especially did he help me to learn the art of helping faculty to accept sound budget planning. He was a master tutor for me during my education as a science administrator.

In the meantime Horace was becoming widely known outside the Institute community. He was elected a fellow of the American Academy of Arts and Sciences and came to serve it as treasurer with a sensitive understanding of the aims and purposes of this house of learning. At the end of the war he received the Medal for Merit for his services on behalf of the Office of Scientific Research and Development. President Truman's citation said in part: "Mr. Ford, as Treasurer of the Massachusetts Institute of Technology Corporation, with his foresight and financial genius, provided for the unprecedented expansion of the Institute facilities that made possible the undertaking of a vast research and development program; [and] he established financial controls which he administered . . . with wisdom, skill, economy, and courage."

When he retired in 1950, he was cited by the Eastern Association of College Business Officers as "the best financial officer in American education."

Among the able staff on which the three of us so greatly depended was the Institute's registrar, Joseph C. MacKinnon, whose responsibilities included not only the keeping of academic records and the scheduling of classes but the assignment of space for both classes and research. It was he who showed me how we could shoehorn the new Radiation Laboratory into existing Institute quarters and how we could move and squeeze academic departments to meet the voracious needs of the multiplying war research projects. It was he with his great charts showing Institute floor space who provided quarters for the Army Specialized Training Program (ASTP) and the Navy training programs and kept on top of the vexatious foot-by-foot accounting of educational space required by the government in its billing for these and numerous other training programs. We ran classes twelve months a year, which the indefatigable MacKinnon, with the Commencement committee, had to fit into the calendar.

Another stalwart with infinite patience was Professor Leicester Hamilton, who served for a long period, including the war years, as the equivalent of a dean of residence as the Navy's V-12 and the Army's ASTP contingents required dormitory accommodations arranged to conform to their meticulous standards. I remember an emergency request from the Army for the Institute to house a contingent of Chinese military personnel. This required moving regular students overnight out of their residences and finding other space for them, but Hamilton managed it.

Over the life of RadLab, there was remarkably little tension between it and MIT, an achievement that attested to goodwill on both sides and the brilliant leadership of Lee A. DuBridge as director of the laboratory. I came greatly to admire him and cherished my cordial relations with him during his later presidency of Caltech and then as science adviser to President Nixon.

Some of the historians of the Radiation Laboratory have characterized Wheeler Loomis, associate director, as the tough guy or the essential SOB of the laboratory. We could argue, but in general we arrived at friendly decisions. This was certainly true when postwar, he returned to MIT at my urging to direct the Charles summer study that recommended MIT establish the Lincoln Laboratory.

At this point let me interpolate a note on human relations in a management environment where the chief executive is distinguished and at times remote. In serving under these circumstances as a surrogate for the chief executive, it becomes necessary to distinguish between one's primary loyalty and responsibilities to the chief executive and one's responsibilities to subordinates or coequals with whom one must work day to day. (Henry Kissinger, in his *White House Years* (p. 24 ff), comments on the tensions of this relationship.) This two-way pull becomes the more difficult when the chief executive is away a great deal of the time. With Dr. Compton spending frequent periods in Washington, I was not always able to handle situations requiring prompt decisions by checking with him and had instead to make the decisions myself or to reach them in consultation with immediate associates. I usually knew pretty well what Dr. Compton's views and policies were and made decisions to conform with them and thus abided by my conviction that in a situation containing possible conflicts, I must act in full accord with his policies even though some associates felt otherwise. As I reached greater maturity as an executive, I learned the art of doing this without creating morale problems with my colleagues whose access to Dr. Compton was mainly through me. The natural goodwill of Institute personnel and their overriding commitment to see our wartime responsibilities take precedence over any difference in views made my job as the in-between man much easier but not always free of tensions. The fact that my colleagues showed great forbearance led to my being entrusted with increasing responsibilities by the president and Executive Committee—and by my immediate colleagues.

I recall only one episode when the MIT administrative group, including me, felt tread upon and ignored by the OSRD bureaucracy engrossed by the glamour of the Radiation Laboratory. I don't remember the cause of the conflict, but I do acutely recall the urgent need on the part of several of us for emotional succor. In my transient indignation and miseries, I spilled over to Karl Compton. He was taken aback but understanding and moved at once to reduce the pressure. For me this was another lesson in the art of management.

Periodically Ford and I met with Wheeler Loomis to review the salaries of all the professional personnel in the Radiation Laboratory while Sage and I repeatedly traveled overnight to Washington, frequently accompanied by Phillips Ketchum, MIT's wise legal counsel, to hammer out acceptable contracting relations with OSRD and the military services. We were also responsible for the accounting for all equipment, the monitoring of contracts and subcontracts, and making sure the money was in hand to meet the payrolls. To cite but one of the more exotic but minor examples, a group in the Radiation Laboratory once asked for clearance to purchase a carousel. It was an amusing exercise to come to understand and to make OSRD understand that the laboratory had a legitimate research need for a merry-go-round to serve as an inexpensive revolving table on which the versatile V-Beam radar could be mounted for testing.

AN INSTITUTIONAL "GUINEA PIG" FOR GOVERNMENT CONTRACTS

MIT's administrative officers were concerned in making sure that it managed its OSRD contracts on a no-profit, no-loss basis. This led to extensive negotiations with OSRD for the development of a contractual procedure that was fair to both the government and the Institute, and MIT played a leading role in the development of a new kind of contract designed for government support of university research. In his oral history Bush discussed his achievement:

. . . in all of OSRD's contacts with universities we endeavored to pay the full cost, that is, we paid overhead. This was the first time, I think, that government grants for research had included overhead. When I put this into effect, I was visited by a group from the Bureau of the Budget and from the General Accounting Office, and so forth. They protested that I was subsidizing the universities, that I was giving away money. Of course, I said that I was merely paying costs. If I hadn't had the full backing of the House, I might have been in trouble on this.[16]

In an introduction to *Q.E.D.*, John Burchard's history of MIT's war effort, Compton wrote of these creative contributions of MIT's wartime administration:

In many of the civilian war activities MIT was the "guinea pig." Our facilities of personnel and laboratories, and wholehearted backing by the Executive Committee of our Corporation, made it possible for us to move rapidly to meet any new need. For this reason the first really large OSRD contract was located at MIT, and for this reason also the terms of this contract, which were set by prolonged studies and negotiations between our Division of Industrial Cooperation and our Administration and legal counsel on one hand, and the contracting office of OSRD on the other hand, set the pattern for the subsequent major contracts of the OSRD and had a very pronounced influence on all subsequent governmental contracts with private institutions, extending even now into peacetime. For the same reason it was MIT which was largely responsible for setting the policies followed by all institutions with reference to tenure and salary scale of the staffs recruited for the various research and development projects. Though this achieved little publicity, I believe that the working out of these policies on a fair "no-profit, no-loss" basis and in a readily workable manner constitutes one of MIT's most important contributions during the war.

These well-conceived contractual relations between universities and the federal government were to be threatened by inexperienced federal representatives in the 1960s and 70s. A kind of entropy came to degrade the harmonious relationships between the universities and the government—a tendency to impose upon universities procurement contracts designed for industrial organizations but unfit for universities. Faculties were to contest bitterly, for example, efforts by government auditors to use time-clock methods to measure faculty time spent on government research.

RELIEVING THE PRESSURES OF THE WAR

The great concentration of war research brought to the Institute many generals and admirals doing what comes naturally by visiting the Radiation, Servomechanisms, Instrumentation, and other laboratories as these projects invented equipment that was profoundly to change the tactics and strategies of war. These visitors, however, quite understandably added to the pressures and tension that prevailed in a situation where research activities were actively related to actions on the battlefield and aboard naval vessels.

To find relief from secrecy, guarded areas, and high pressure, several of us, including Dean John Bunker of the Graduate School and Professor Frederick Fassett of the *Technology Review*, arranged for instruction in drawing. To serve as our teacher, we had the good fortune to secure Professor John Reid of the Department of Architecture, who met with us in weekly evening sessions. One of the main issues which required extended debate was the use of a live model, but in the end we chickened and decided against such daring—afraid, I suppose, that some might think it scandalous.

Several times Wheeler Loomis, Horace Ford, Thomas Creamer, and I traveled by train and bus to the Appalachian Mountain Club's establishment in Pinkham Notch at the foot of Mount Washington. From there we climbed Washington and other nearby peaks in the White Mountains. I remember one glorious expedition in October when benign weather permitted us to scale the heights stripped down to the waist with all the autumn color in full display. Thus did we find renewal despite the pressures of war.

3
THE POSTWAR YEARS

MIT REDEPLOYS FOR PEACE

The concentration of war research on its campus, the presence here of a great assemblage of gifted scientists from hundreds of institutions, and the remarkably varied activities of its own staff in Cambridge and elsewhere all contributed to the establishment of a fresh and vigorous postwar program at MIT. After V-J Day I continued as lieutenant to President Compton and thus shared in this exhilarating task of returning the Institute to its natural and higher mission of peacetime education and research. For a young administrative officer it was bliss to take part in the Institute's move to higher ground in this dynamic environment of reconversion, bold innovation, and risk-taking spirit. Many institutions, following the war, returned to the more relaxed practices and policies of their prewar years.

The administrative organization which had functioned to oversee $100 million of war research was geared to liquidate the war program of the Institute expeditiously and to rebuild a long-term educational program. Those who served on the Institute's governing bodies during this period remember well the exciting sense of new opportunities and broadened mission for MIT that vitalized our reconversion program.

Dr. Bush made the wise decision, as the end of the war approached, that the Office of Scientific Research and Development would be demobilized, and this meant that its research projects such as the Radiation Laboratory at MIT would be liquidated. Even though there would be no continuation of OSRD, proposals inevitably arose within both government and MIT to continue the laboratory with support from other government sources. I count it one of MIT's profoundly important decisions to have rejected these proposals to continue the laboratory even in reduced form. Better ways were to be found to turn legacies of the laboratory to the highest purposes of the university MIT was becoming.

Accompanying the decision to liquidate the Radiation Laboratory was a commitment to provide funds for the publication of a series of books to be edited under the direction of Louis Ridenour which would make widely available the important results of research in the Radiation Laboratory. MIT agreed to appoint Radiation Laboratory personnel who volunteered to do the writing after the laboratory had been demobilized. The resulting volumes published by McGraw-Hill in the late forties were a major contribution to the technical literature of the period, and large numbers were sold, with all royalties being paid to the federal government.

The editor of the *Radiation Laboratory Series*, reported how MIT had to be designated as "author" of the manuscripts since the Institute was the contractor maintaining the laboratory. "This presented new problems, for the actual authors of the manuscripts for which the Institute was asked to become contractually responsible were in fact hundreds of individuals, each with his own postwar problems of relocation and readjustment. Nothing beyond the good faith of the author could be relied on as a guarantee of the satisfactory completion of the work."

Negotiations for publishing the series, said Louis Ridenour, could readily have collapsed completely at this point, had not the energetic efforts of Killian and the president of McGraw-Hill, Curtis Benjamin, surmounted every obstacle. "A contract for the publication of the series was finally signed on November 14, 1945," he said, "largely as a result of the vigor, good faith, and generous cooperation of Benjamin and Killian."

Toward the concluding period of the Radiation Laboratory operation, a Research Division was created, and Julius A. Stratton, who had served the laboratory in its early days, was brought back from his post as consultant to the Secretary of War to head this Research Division, with Albert G. Hill joining him as associate director. This division was to be reincarnated as an academic enterprise, the MIT Research Laboratory of Electronics.

Among the moves by MIT to reestablish the primacy of teaching and research at the Institute was the rapid rebuilding of both its undergraduate and graduate schools. The Institute had announced that it was prepared to readmit without red tape those of its students who had gone to war and who wished again to seek MIT degrees. As a result of this and the GI Bill, which provided educational opportunity for those who had served during the war, MIT was confronted with a tidal wave of applicants that led to an enrollment greater by 3,000 than were registered at war's end.

As the war drew to a close, the Institute also undertook to identify talent in the war research laboratories around the country and to recruit from this pool distinguished additions to its staff as well as a number from the Radiation Laboratory.[1] Important to this effort was the willingness of the Corporation's Executive Committee to set aside free funds to finance this vigorous recruiting. In fact any perceptive account of the forces that led to MIT's metamorphosis into a new kind of institution during this period must recognize the supportive role of the Executive Committee.

One of the postwar recruits was a young electrical engineer who had been on the staff of the Radiation Laboratory since 1942. Found in my files is the following letter I wrote in 1945 at the behest of Harold Hazen, offering Jerome Wiesner an assistant professorship. The last paragraph of my letter was more dramatically prophetic than I realized in 1945. Herewith the letter:

Dear Mr. Wiesner:

I wish to confirm the offer which Professor Hazen has discussed with you, a position in our Department of Electrical Engineering. We take pleasure in inviting you to join the Institute staff as an Assistant Professor for three years. . . .

The date at which this appointment starts may be determined mutually by you and Professor Hazen; but it is understood that your acceptance of the assignment in the West will in no way conflict with this appointment, although naturally we hope that you will be free to take up full-time duties as soon as convenient.

We look forward with much pleasure to having you join us at the Institute. We believe that opportunities here over the coming years in your field of interest will be of ample scope to your work.

With the support of the MIT Corporation we also quickly established a generously funded fellowship program to attract "cream of the crop" graduate students and scoured closing war establishments throughout the country to recruit them.

At this stage President Truman's approval, in 1946, of Public Law 580, the pathbreaking act that established the Office of Naval Research, played a profoundly important role by funding the re-establishment of graduate study in the research universities. A small group of Naval Reserve Officers serving in the Office of the Secretary of the Navy and working as "bird dogs" under the inspiration of Hunsaker and others has been credited with inventing the ONR concept in 1942.† Emanuel Piore is the authority for the conclusion that the late Captain Robert Conrad was responsible for the initial structure of ONR and for developing and promoting the postwar concept of support for academe by the military.

While the staff was thus throwing its released energy into reconstructing the educational and research program of the Institute, steady progress was made in demobilizing war research organizations and readapting buildings and equipment MIT needed for its expanded peacetime program. Both the temporary and the permanent buildings erected for war research were acquired by the Institute. Since the government had announced a policy of making war surplus property available without cost to educational institutions, we established a well-staffed surplus property office to search the country for items useful to the Institute. This office found in Virginia the great wooden trusses we used in building Rockwell Cage for athletic use and ceremonial assemblies.

Among the temporary buildings was Building 20, which had been constructed at a cost of $1 million to meet the needs of the Radiation Laboratory. The Institute sought to acquire this building first by purchase, but then it became possible to obtain it as a gift of surplus property. The acquisition of this building under these circumstances was of enormous value to the Institute not only in freeing space for the great influx of veterans but as a building with substantial facilities immediately useful for offices and research. The kind of research, for example, that was to be undertaken in the Research Laboratory of Electronics was facilitated by the availability of Building 20 and its equipment.

HOUSING FOR STUDENTS, INCLUDING MARRIED VETERANS

Even before the war the Institute had set for itself a program for providing new student residences and a better living environment for its students, and the postwar period provided new opportunities to achieve this goal.

First came a pioneering effort to provide housing for married veterans. As the tidal wave of admission applications from veterans poured in, the director of admissions alerted the administration that many applicants were married or planned soon to be, and some had children. How could he answer these applicants who were inquiring about housing for their families? Clearly, existing dormitories would be inadequate, as well as housing in Cambridge and Greater Boston.

I took pride in the quick response of the administration and Corporation. Let MIT build with its own funds a village of temporary houses and apartments so that it would be ready when married veterans arrived. Dean of Architecture William Wurster found more excitement and challenge in this project than he would have in a great edifice. He selected a plot for a little village on the westerly part of the campus and designed small wood houses, most of them with garden patches. Under his delighted direction the building of the village proceeded with dispatch, and as houses were completed, they were eagerly rented. Thus came into being Westgate Village, the first married veterans' housing project at an American college. The students and their families created a proud community with its own government, arrangements for neighborly babysitting, and numerous little gardens.

The students and their families came to view Westgate as a choice place to live, and when Cambridge zoning regulations properly required its removal, there were lamentations in Westgate. Later MIT was able to build permanent high-rise apartment buildings for married students, but however well designed, they lacked the simple charm of the "little one-eyed blinking sort o'place" that was Westgate.

SUMMER STUDIES

MIT's success in war research had brought it great prestige in the corridors of the Pentagon and in the staff of the National Security Council. More important, MIT possessed a large reservoir of people experienced in thinking creatively about national security and in identifying deficiences in our defenses for which these scientists saw remedies. This group constituted a kind of reserve establishment, a resource of great value to the nation, and one that all too frequently led the powers in Washington to think of MIT as the place to get a problem solved or to take the lead in organizing study groups to seek solutions to defense problems.

The group was repeatedly called on for help in the early days of my presidency. This forced MIT, while protecting itself as an educational institution, to devise methods whereby those talented faculty who had wartime experience could be helpful and still remain in residence and give primary attention to the Institute's academic program of education and research. This led to the invention by ingenious MIT academics of the "summer study" (some called it "group think"), an arrangement that made it possible for the Institute to sponsor ad hoc studies of great value to the Department of Defense and even to the Department of State.

The name "summer study" evolved as a result of the projects' being undertaken mainly in the summer, when academic personnel were more readily available, although the groups included members from industry and government as well as universities. The Cambridge academic community and the federal government provided the initiatives for a number of these projects, and their base was usually some quiet, noncampus facility.

Out of one of these studies came the initiation of the Lincoln Laboratory; from another, new communication techniques, some for penetrating the Soviet jamming of the Voice of America; from another, new concepts for air reconnaissance.

At a time when the superbomb and massive retaliation concepts were dominating much of our military policy, at least in the Air Force, these studies recognized the vital importance of other military measures—to reduce the vulnerability to surprise of our strategic air power, to keep the sea lanes open, to improve our military communications and gathering of hard intelligence, to generate fresh ideas for arms limitation. Out of one of these projects, Lamp Light, appeared the concept of an air reconnaissance system that was later to be engineered by the Mitre Corporation and given the name AWACS. Thus these summer studies, taken together, advanced our military technology in ways the superbomb, massive-retaliation boys tended to neglect.

Out of the recommendations of the Hartwell project, organized by Professor Zacharias in 1950 in association with the provost, was the building of a fleet of fast merchant ships that could outrun submarines. And one of the participants, Edward L. Cochrane, retired vice admiral of the Navy and head of the Department of Naval Architecture at MIT, was appointed by President Truman to be chairman of the Federal Maritime Board and maritime administrator of the Department of Commerce, with the responsibility—among others—of implementing this recommendation by initiating the design and construction of this new class of ships.

I was pleased to receive a letter from President Truman, dated October 16, 1950, from which I draw the following two excerpts:

I wish to take this opportunity of expressing to you and through you to all of the members of the Hartwell Group not only my very great interest in your undertaking, but also my appreciation of your fine accomplishments. As you are aware, many of the recommendations made by the Group can and will be placed in effect by the Department of the Navy alone. Such recommendations as involve other Departments will be coordinated with those Departments.

It is my hope that the individual members of the Hartwell Group will not consider that the submission of their Report completes their interest in the important project of helping to build the best possible anti-submarine structure for the Navy. The contribution made by the Group has been impressive and will, I am sure, materially increase our strength. Continued interest by all those concerned will further improve matters.

I present this sketch of the summer study projects not as a definitive account but rather to recall that as an administrator, I was in a position to encourage their initiation and later, in the Technological Capabilities Panel and through science advice at the White House, to make use of their recommendations and to be guided by the strategic and moral concepts that infused some of the studies. These studies illustrate the ways in which our government called freely on the nation's intellectual resources during the fifties and found a ready response. Those were memorable and exciting times when government, industry, and the universities felt themselves in a symbiotic relationship and achieved a powerful creative collaboration. It is urgent that once again we achieve this kind of productive interaction to prop up lagging or extravagant defense programs and to weed out fancy but impractical high technology. With characteristic pith Zacharias once proclaimed, "Summer studies and some are not." This was his way of saying that such studies must be undertaken for a sophisticated sponsor and by scientists and engineers of high talent.

PROJECT TROY

Another summer study, a quite novel one, was requested by the Department of State in 1950 and was to lead in the end to a new interdisciplinary center at MIT in the social sciences. It was named Project Troy, a name obviously prompted by Homer's Trojan horse. The problem presented for study by Under Secretary of State James E. Webb was the Soviets' effective jamming of the Voice of America broadcasts into Russia. Were technical means available, asked the State Department, to penetrate this jamming? Would MIT bring together a technical group to seek an answer?

It was the feeling of the group tentatively assembled by the Institute that the proposed charter of this study should be wider than an examination of the communication technology involved. We proposed to Webb that the project be of a scope to permit an examination not only of the technological problem but of such questions as what the United States was trying to accomplish in broadcasting into the Soviet Union. With whom in Russia did we wish to communicate? A task of this wider scope was finally agreed to, and the Institute set about to conduct the study. It seemed appropriate that a director whose experience extended beyond the technical questions involved would be appropriate, and this led to the decision to invite John E. Burchard, dean of Humanities and Social Studies, to undertake the directorship. He was an architect, not a scientist. But he had worked effectively with technical groups in his OSRD assignments, and he of course had a wide acquaintance with the social sciences and the humanities.

The group that he assembled was quite extraordinary in its variety of disciplines. It included Harvard anthropologist Clyde Kluckhohn, Nobel laureate physicist Edward Purcell, psychologists Donald Marquis and Jerome Bruner, Robert Morison, M.D., of the Rockefeller Foundation, Wiesner, Elting Morison, Millikan, Hill, Bavelas, Deutsch, and Friedman of MIT, and other scholars.

Under conditions prevailing in those days the project was highly classified, more so than was appropriate; nevertheless, it proved to be an exciting experience for the participants and a project that produced not world-shaking but useful results in both technology and new concepts for facilitating communications among peoples. When completed, its report was made to the Secretary of State, Dean Acheson, and to James Webb. In his autobiography, *In Search of Mind* (1983), Jerome Bruner made the startling statement: "For all the gravity of the proceedings, Proj-

ect Troy was the best club I have ever belonged to—so much so
that a handful of its 'old boys' set up a Supper Club that dined
together at the St. Botolph's Club in Boston the first Friday
evening of each month for the next fifteen years."[2] The success
of this supper club spun off from Troy was the result of Elting
Morison's skill as a convener and his capacity to draw men of
diverse intellectual interests to talk together.

A most significant result of the study, however, was the conclusion reached by the participants that the project had shown
the way to bring together into an effective coalition representatives of the social sciences, engineering, science, and the
humanities. This success prompted participants in the project
such as Professors Bruner, Kluckhohn, Wiesner, Millikan, and
others to advocate a continuing interdisciplinary program. I remember Kluckhohn coming to see me and Stratton to say that
this was one of the most fruitful experiences of his professional
career and that the world of scholarship would lose something
important if MIT did not turn the classified program into a continuing, interdisciplinary, unclassified research center. This we
were ultimately able to do, and we called it the Center for International Studies. The charter of this successor organization included a mandate to continue studies initiated by Troy. Max
Millikan, economist and son of the great Caltech physicist,
agreed to be director, and he brought together a potent cast,
including Walt Rostow.

The State Department wanted to finance the center, but it did
not have the necessary free funds. It suggested, however, that
funds available to the CIA could be called on with the endorsement of the State Department, and we accepted this arrangement including the continued classification of some of the work
of the center. This was unfortunate because the CIA funding
was later to bring into question the freedom of the center's
work, even though those of us who knew the individuals involved had complete confidence in their intellectual integrity. I
shared in this decision and came to regret it. Later it was possible to finance and continue the center without any CIA involvement, and today it continues as an open research center under

the direction of an able political scientist, Eugene Skolnikoff. Its financing comes in part from the Institute and in part from private sources, and it does no work that is subject to classification or that is financed or influenced by the CIA.

I had heard that Max Millikan, first director of MIT's Center for International Studies, had originated the idea of a Peace Corps. With the help of Professor Donald Blackmer, we searched without success the files of the Center for International Studies, but he suggested that the document that Millikan had written might have gone to the Kennedy Library. He was right, for a member of the staff of that institution found a twenty-four-page report entitled "Memorandum on an International Youth Service," which Millikan had presented to President-elect Kennedy on December 30, 1960. We now have this long memorandum, and indeed, it provides in considerable detail the plan for the highly successful Peace Corps which Congress created in 1961 as proposed by President Kennedy. "The problem," Millikan had written to Kennedy, "is to devise a new government instrument which can help match the apparent needs of the underdeveloped countries for trained manpower with the swelling supply of dedicated American young people eager to participate in constructive activities in the underdeveloped countries."

Project Troy and the center that Millikan created to follow it provided brilliant demonstrations of the power of a successful integration of science, social science, and technology. In a memorandum Elting Morison prepared for me on the "business of the university" in March 1984, he made this comment about Troy: "[It] didn't change the course of history—or even of State Department policy, but it gave the people who worked together in it the best possible liberal education for the world they were living in." He further noted that Troy provided a small model for how universities might develop in a time when so much of the essential structure of life is determined by technological development.

COGNATION IN A CAR POOL

An example of cognation at work among colleagues is provided by the "shop talk" of three MIT professors, a mathematician and two geologists, riding in a car pool in the late 1940s. On one ride the conversation unpremeditatedly drifted into an exchange of ideas that led to dramatically improved techniques for finding new sources of oil around the world and, at MIT, to the great benefactions of Cecil and Ida Green.

My attention was called to this cognation at a dinner in Washington when I sat beside a geologist who asked whether in my memoirs I was giving due credit to this extraordinary project that occurred at MIT in the early 1950s. What happened in the car pool discussion was that the mathematician, Professor George Wadsworth, suggested to the geologist, Professor Patrick Hurley, that geologists should seek to apply some of the ideas inherent in Norbert Wiener's esoteric mathematics, particularly his mathematics relating to time-series analysis. This suggestion and subsequent experiments by Professor Wadsworth's group in mathematics prompted Professors Hurley and Robert R. Shrock to initiate a Geophysical Analysis Group that came to be known by the acronym GAG. This interdisciplinary group of colleagues promptly saw the opportunity for a major contribution to geological exploration. It brought together a small group of exceptionally gifted and perceptive graduate students, including mathematicians but mainly geologists, to find analytical techniques for decoding these records. These students did indeed find Wiener's ideas fruitful in analyzing seismic records whose complexity had until then made it difficult to separate the useful signals from the useless noise. In oil and geophysical organizations there were bulging files of records containing buried treasure hidden in a maze.

As the research program progressed, it became apparent that the process of analysis required the use of a high-speed computer. Here fortune served them well, for MIT's great Whirlwind computer was approaching completion and was just what they needed to undertake a digital approach to exploration geophysics. MIT's Industrial Liaison Program next entered the campaign and brought together a group of representatives from the petroleum industry who thus learned of the promise of GAG's research efforts.

It took some time for the industry to build a cadre of personnel competent to use these advanced methods of analysis. A number of them were helped to acquire the necessary competence by employing the graduate students on completion of their degrees.

The long-term result of this sequence of events was the so-called "digital revolution" in exploration geophysics and an enhancement of successful exploratory activities. One commentator spoke of the petroleum exploratory groups "riding the front edge of the wave to come of communication theory and computer evolution."

One of the companies that saw greatest potential in this new approach to the digital analysis of seismic records was Geophysical Service, Inc., in Dallas, of which Cecil Green and Eugene McDermott (later Corporation members and benefactors of MIT) were leaders; their company made the most immediate use of GAG's work.

Out of this happy relationship was to grow a friendship between Cecil and Ida Green and Professor Shrock, a relationship that was to be a factor leading the Greens to provide the funds for creating the Green Center for the Earth Sciences at MIT.

It also led to Cecil Green's perceiving the possibility of inviting geology graduate students, first from MIT and later from a group of institutions, to join the field crews of GSI and thus to widen their experience and their competence as geophysicists.

Out of Geophysical Service, Inc., came the great electronics corporation, Texas Instruments, and out of the friendship of Professor Shrock and the Greens came a program sponsored by GSI whereby undergraduates and graduates could study geology as participants in field work. As Professor Shrock writes in his history of the MIT Department of Geology, the GAG project provided "an excellent example of how successive generations of scientists and engineers build on the work of their predecessors; of how a new idea or theory or formulation, that seems at first to be of little more than academic interest, is suddenly transformed into a powerful means of gaining new or deeper insight into previously unsolved problems; and of how an old theory that seems to be useless in its accepted form can take on quite novel and surprising characteristics that unexpectedly provide new means of solving old problems."

THE ORIGINS AND ROLE OF
THE LINCOLN LABORATORY

Shortly after formally assuming the presidency of the Institute in 1949, I was confronted with a major decision as to how to respond to a request from the Air Force to establish a major research project devoted to air defense.

On December 15, 1950, I received from Hoyt S. Vandenberg, chief of staff of the U.S. Air Force, a letter reporting that the Air Force felt that the time had come to set up a laboratory devoted intensively to air defense problems. He added that the Air Force felt that it was best to locate this laboratory in the Cambridge area because of the presence here of other related Air Force research programs. He stated: "The Massachusetts Institute of Technology is almost uniquely qualified to serve as contractor to the Air Force for the establishment of the proposed laboratory. . . . The problem is technically complicated and difficult. The Air Force must urgently increase its research and development effort in this area, and in this we ask your help."

MIT was understandably reluctant to undertake the establishment and management of a large research laboratory devoted to military objectives, having devoted itself so intensively to the conduct of the Radiation Laboratory and other large war projects. It was the judgment of scientists and engineers at the Institute that we should seek objective advice not only from the faculty and administration but from non-MIT personnel knowledgeable in the field as to whether there was national need for such a research program and whether MIT was the appropriate place to undertake it. In consequence we proposed to the Air Force an initial phase of the project which would be an analytical study similar to the then recent Hartwell summer study directed by Professor Zacharias in behalf of the Navy. This special study would assemble the most competent staff of scientists, engineers, and officers available and ask them to evaluate the national need and the scope of such a laboratory. In the meantime, because of the feeling of urgency in the Department of Defense, MIT agreed to undertake certain parts of an air defense study in its already established Research Laboratory of Electronics. Our decision to proceed in this way was undoubtedly influenced by the knowledge that the Russians had exploded an atomic weapon (1949), by the turn of China, under Mao Tse-Tung, to Communism, and by the tensions associated with the opening of hostilities in Korea (1950).

We further stipulated that it was our technical judgment that research on air defense must be comprehensive and that it must have the full support and participation of the Army and Navy as well as the Air Force. We further indicated our judgment as to the magnitude of the cost of such an undertaking in order to be sure that the Department of Defense and the Congress were fully prepared to finance in adequate measure so large an undertaking. We emphasized that if we undertook the project, we would expect that it would draw personnel from many institutions, as did our wartime laboratories, and not be made up of MIT staff exclusively. I reported these conclusions to General Vandenberg, and he approved our proposed procedure.

In the meantime there had been discussions with representatives of the Air Force Scientific Advisory Board, and notably with its chairman, Dr. Ridenour, who had been in the MIT Radiation Laboratory during the war. I remember sitting on a park bench in Lafayette Park in Washington discussing whether the proposed laboratory should be undertaken by MIT and why. I remember that in addition to his emphasis on the national security need, Ridenour felt that the establishment of such a laboratory would ensure that Massachusetts would become a center for electronics research and industry. His answers proved to be accurate and prophetic. We were fortunate in securing to direct this analytical study, which bore the name of Project Charles, the same F.W. Loomis who served as associate director of the Radiation Laboratory. Professor Loomis' summer study reached the unequivocal conclusion that the proposed laboratory was urgently needed and that MIT had special advantages for establishing and managing the laboratory.

Loomis became director first of the study and then of the Lincoln Laboratory that it recommended. He was aided and abetted by Jerrold Zacharias as associate director. A year later Professor Albert G. Hill assumed the directorship. As I recite in my section on the Whirlwind computer, studies by Professor George Valley, in behalf of the Scientific Advisory Board of the Air Force, had conceived of the elements of what came to be known as the SAGE system, a computerized form of air defense. In the meantime the Department of Defense, using private contractors, undertook the enormous task of creating in the Far North, the complex system of computer-linked radars recommended by Project Charles to provide early warning of any attack on the United States by Russian bombers.

During the genesis of the Lincoln Laboratory, MIT continued to press for assurance that it was an appropriate place for such an establishment. Following a visit from Secretary of the Air Force Thomas Finletter, I wrote him a letter dated December 21, 1951, which said: "I wish to be very explicit in saying that MIT is anxious to do what is in the public interest in this matter and that in writing to you at this time I am simply asking that there be at the earliest possible time an effort to get concurrence that our continuation of Lincoln is in the public interest and does justify the special arrangements and the severe problems [of administration, financing, and separate personnel policies] which it imposes upon an educational institution. . . . May I add further that if we continue it [the Lincoln Project], we do so on the contractual arrangement whereby we handle it wholly on a no-gain, no-loss basis."

Later Secretary Finletter replied, "On my recent visit with you I was favorably impressed with the future program of Project LINCOLN as outlined by Dr. Loomis. . . . The Air Force is deeply appreciative of the magnitude and the complexity of Project LINCOLN, of the tremendous burden it places on your institution, and most of all, of the fact that the Massachusetts Institute of Technology has seen fit to make available its technical talent and facilities to do this most important research study."

These carefully prepared exchanges between MIT and the Air Force proved later to be of very great importance since at one stage, reports in the public press about the Lincoln Project alleged that MIT sought the laboratory for financial gain. This led to a request from the staff of the House Appropriations Committee for documentation on the considerations that brought the laboratory into existence at MIT. The meticulous documentation that was available in our files apparently proved convincing in providing answers to all invidious inquiries.

One of the dramatic incidents that resulted from studies relating to the Lincoln Laboratory was the appearance of Professor Albert G. Hill before the National Security Council, at a meeting presided over by President Truman, to advocate the building of a distant early warning line. When expressing his approval, Truman is reported to have added, "and I hope that you will all keep your goddamned mouths shut." Like all of our presidents, he was vexed by leaks from the National Security Council.

Professor Hill's evangelical campaign to gain acceptance of the idea of early warning as a defense against Soviet bomber attack went beyond his appearance before the Truman National Security Council. He and I coauthored an article for the November 1953 issue of the *Atlantic Monthly* entitled, "For a Continental Defense." In this article we mobilized the most eloquent arguments at our command in support of a public understanding of the importance of the new and awful urgency created by the Soviets' achievement of a nuclear explosion. Before submitting the final draft of this article for publication, Professor Hill and I felt that it would be appropriate to submit the manuscript to General Robert Cutler, then Special Assistant to President Eisenhower for National Security Affairs. We wanted to be sure that the statement had adequate clearance and in addition, we wished to encourage the National Security Council to give higher priority to an adequate air defense. In writing to General Cutler, I stated that we wished him to be informed of our intention of publishing the article and to afford him an opportunity to object to any parts of the article on security grounds. Fortunately he did not propose any drastic changes in the article, and it became clear that by submitting it to him, we had introduced strong arguments in support of continental defense at the level of the National Security Council.

Thirty-four years after the decisions were reached to undertake the Lincoln Laboratory, it stands as a highly productive research center managed by MIT but located away from the campus. It thus is free to undertake classified research which would be unacceptable to the Institute were the laboratory located on campus, and it is largely a research community that in no way invades the Institute's central academic program.

There are critics of the modern university who deplore the establishment of projects or centers arranged independently of established departments. In his book, *The Degradation of the Academic Dogma: The University in America, 1945–1970*, Robert Nisbet, with a bow no doubt to Henry and Brooks Adams for his title, maintains that centers, satellites, and projects can diminish the coherence of the academic community and thus lead to the degradation of dogma which he feels to have been the heart of the traditional universities:

Why should we today expect academic aristocrats of the 1940s to have turned their backs on the vast sums of money which in the federal government, the big foundations, and large industry, in effect, lay waiting for the magic word. The magic word was, of course, *project*. And it was the project system that converted scholars into managers of research enterprises—with *research*, as a word, gradually succeeding scholarship in prestige. It was difficult, after all, to make effective use of the word "scholarship" in some of the new enterprises in the forms of institute, center, and bureau that were flooding American campuses by the late 1950s.[3]

Nisbet raises some useful red flags, but I think he lacks understanding of the way that scientific progress requires new forms of integration and organization that break across the traditional departmental lines and that contribute greatly to the academic richness and the productivity of the modern research university while still preserving the integrity of the traditional departments. For one who has watched developments at MIT since the war, reading his book prompts one to challenge many of his ideas and conclusions, but I must add that I found it cathartic to read his scholarly and informed attacks on what he feels to be the baneful influences of big projects and institutes that are not incorporated into the coherent community of the university.†

THE CREATION OF IDA

In his classic book, *Government and Science*, Don K. Price described how the U.S. government in the postwar period had improvised a new kind of federalism for the conduct of research. This development included the invention of nonprofit organizations to undertake tasks for the government, particularly the Department of Defense. The first of these independent corporate entities was the Rand Corporation, designed to undertake objective, independent studies for the Air Force. Another illustration of this federalism by contract was the request to MIT to undertake the Lincoln Laboratory. Another example, in which I was also involved, was the establishment of the Institute for Defense Analyses, inevitably known as IDA. The Department of Defense had established an agency known as the Weapons Systems Evaluation Group to undertake studies and analyses for the Secretary of Defense and for the Joint Chiefs of Staff.

In 1955 I received a letter from the then Secretary of Defense, Charles E. Wilson, proposing that MIT undertake the formation of a nonprofit corporation that would have as its members a group of universities whose purpose would be to support with their expertise the analyses of WSEG. I had earlier been asked whether MIT alone would undertake the responsibility for this study group, and I had reported back that I felt it inappropriate for a single institution to undertake this kind of responsibility and ventured the suggestion that a group of universities be brought together to sponsor a nonprofit corporation to serve the purpose.

In his letter the secretary requested that MIT "as a public service" proceed with arrangements for the support of the Weapons Systems Evaluation Group. "The need for strengthening the WSEG," he said, "has been acute for many months." He indicated that the Department of Defense had informed appropriate committees of the Congress of plans for strengthening this evaluation group, and he asked that MIT, because of the urgent need, accept an interim contract until the association of universities could be brought together to form the new corporate entity.

I reported back to Secretary Wilson that MIT would undertake this responsibility and that we would proceed at once to invite a group of universities to form a consortium to operate the nonprofit corporation. In the discussions that ensued, it became clear that under civil service rules it had not been possible to bring together enough first-rate scientists to man the evaluation group and as a result it had been unable to fulfill its mission.

We at MIT proceeded at once to invite four institutions to join us: the California Institute of Technology, Case Institute of Technology, Stanford, and Tulane. Later seven other universities joined the original group. While considering the proposal to form a nonprofit corporation to undertake responsibility for WSEG, I consulted a number of scientists and of course the administrative officers of MIT. In the pre-IDA days, Professor Philip Morse of MIT had served as WSEG's director of research. Among those with whom I talked was Harvard Professor of Chemistry E. Bright Wilson, who also had for a period been a member of the WSEG group. He described the urgent need to add scientists to the group, and he strongly supported the proposed organization that we were considering. Another person who had already accepted appointment to the staff of WSEG was Eugene Skolnikoff, an MIT graduate and Rhodes scholar. He continued with the WSEG group after the new corporation was formed and later became a professor of political science at MIT and then director of the Center for International Studies.

Among the MIT administrators who played a major role in the formation of IDA were Albert G. Hill, James McCormack, Jr., and Edward L. Cochrane. Both Professor Hill and General McCormack became officers of IDA and made major contributions in helping it discharge its responsibilities.

At the beginning the board of trustees included a representative from each of the participating universities and in addition two public trustees, William A. M. Burden and Laurance Rocke-feller. Later Burden was to become chairman of the board, and in his autobiography, *Peggy and I,* he was to write that IDA "became one of the top priorities of my life, and it came about through my friendship with Dr. James R. Killian, the President of the Massachusetts Institute of Technology."

In the buffeting winds of the late sixties, the participating universities came under pressure to cancel their ties to IDA. As a result the formal institutional membership was abandoned but the individual members of the board continued on their own. IDA continues to discharge its mission in accord with the original plans that led to its formation.

4
THE COMMITTEE ON EDUCATIONAL SURVEY

EXALTED BROODING: THE COMMITTEE ON EDUCATIONAL SURVEY

The primary postwar challenge before the Institute was of course the rebuilding of an educational program that would take advantage of lessons learned during the war and that would be appropriate for the changes that would inevitably take place in the country as a result of the nation's enormously expanded responsibilities as the leader of the free world. As vice president of the Institute, I had been giving much thought to educational policy, and in August 1946 I wrote a memorandum to President Compton proposing the appointment of a faculty committee to study the state of education at the Institute. I reported that there was a consensus in the Administrative Council that the Institute could benefit from a long-range self-study. It expressed the view that such a study in this postwar period could help to revitalize the faculty as a policymaking body (it had lost clout as a deliberative body during the war years). In addition the great increase in our research program and the fact that research is more newsworthy than educational innovation made it important that the Institute give unmistakable expression to its preoccupation with advances in its teaching and curriculum.

I suggested that this self-study committee be made up wholly of members of the faculty excluding administrative officers other than department heads and that the appropriate chairman of such a committee would be our distinguished professor of chemical engineering, Warren K. Lewis.

In appendix C I reproduce the major parts of my memorandum to Dr. Compton as an important part of the history of what came to be known as the Lewis Committee.

After careful reflection Dr. Compton presented my proposal first to the Faculty Council and then to the faculty itself. The faculty formally voted: "That the Committee on Undergraduate Courses and the Committee on the Graduate School be instructed to present jointly to the faculty a plan of organization, together with nominations thereof, to review our present educational program and to make a long-range study of our entire educational objectives, policies, and procedures."

Under this mandate John Bunker, dean of the graduate school, was charged with the responsibility of making the final selection of members for the committee. The members nominated by him and approved by the faculty were Professors Ronald H. Robnett, C. Richard Soderberg, Julius A. Stratton, John R. .Loofbourow, and Warren K. Lewis, with Professor Loofbourow serving as secretary and Professor Lewis as chairman.

After the committee outlined its task, it appointed two subcommittees, one on staff environment under the chairmanship of W. Rupert Maclaurin of economics and one on general education under the chairmanship of Thomas K. Sherwood of chemical engineering. The membership of these subcommittees had been selected with cunning care to include faculty members who resonated with each other in a way that enabled them to make major contributions to the work of the central committee.

The results of these combined committee studies, entitled "The Report of the Committee on Educational Survey," proved to be a landmark in the rethinking and updating of the Institute's educational philosophy. Winston Churchill once said that every nation needed from time to time to call on leading citizens to come together for "exalted brooding" about the problems and the future of the nation. The survey committee performed this function for the Institute with great distinction and success; it also did the grubby work of preparing a detailed blueprint of what it thought our faculty should do to maintain MIT's educational pioneering and leadership. The faculty accepted the report and started its debate on its recommendations on January 18, 1950, after I had become president.

In their lucid report, in 1979, summarizing developments at the Institute over the past fifty years, President Wiesner and Chancellor Gray expressed their estimate of the importance of the Lewis Committee report as they appraised it thirty years later. "Central to that report," they emphasized, "was the view that we should be able not only to create new science and to innovate technology but also to relate them to human values and aspirations; that we should have a certain responsibility for forecasting the impact of scientific and technical developments on society; and that we should learn how to manage the new technologies in a humane fashion."

Later in this memoir I present examples of how these views of the committee encouraged a joint program combining education in management with education in engineering and the spectacular growth of the life sciences that relate directly to man.

Most notably the Lewis Committee recommended "that a School of Humanities and Social Studies be established on an equal footing with the existing schools at MIT; we recommend further that the advancement of knowledge be considered an essential part of its program, that it assume the responsibility for planning and administering the program of general education as a part of the common curriculum, and that it offer professional courses leading to graduate as well as undergraduate degrees."

With this recommendation before them the governing bodies of the Institute quickly approved the establishment of the School of Humanities and Social Studies (now the School of Humanities and Social Science). Not only did the establishment of this school give new status to the humanities, but within its framework the social sciences—notably economics, political science, psychology, and the fields of linguistics and philosophy—flourished, aided and abetted by their graduate components.

"For the undergraduates particularly," said the Lewis Committee, "we feel very strongly that the scientific spirit of inquiry and a liberal approach to life can best be acquired by living within a genuinely creative atmosphere. Intellectual life must provide music, literature, history, philosophy . . . for students who are interested in them."

A recommendation of the Subcommittee on General Education led to the adoption of a new elective undergraduate curriculum made up of one-half science and basic engineering and one-half humanities and social science—a "double major" paralleling in depth and rigor the curricula offered in the professional fields.

Thus did the Lewis Committee emphasize the need to bridge the "two cultures" gap a decade before C. P. Snow's sensational Rede Lecture in 1959.[1] Actually the Lewis Committee dealt more perceptively with the "gap" than did Snow in his lecture. Instead of stressing sharp-edged differences between the sciences and the humanities, it sought to meld the sciences and the humanities into one great humanistic enterprise. Certainly it did much to enhance the status of the humanities and arts at MIT and to ameliorate the parochialism of both the sciences and the humanities. It dealt with the wholeness of the Institute, including its values, its environment, and its personality. Thus did the main report extend the Institute's educational writ.

THE SUBCOMMITTEE ON STAFF ENVIRONMENT
In addition the Subcommittee on Staff Environment made proposals for improving the working and living environments of staff and students, and in the years that have intervened since the proposals were made, we have seen the austerity of the original Cambridge campus steadily humanized by facilities for music and the arts and by distinguished architecture and landscaping. The Institute's growing collection of great outdoor sculpture is but one manifestation of a working environment enriched by the arts.

Other recommendations of the Subcommittee on Staff Environment included provision of adequate quarters for a Faculty Club, a large auditorium or lecture hall seating at least one thousand, and an increase in the number of seminar rooms. A master plan proposed by this committee suggested that the east campus be used for classrooms, laboratories, and administration offices, the west campus for athletics, dormitories, and other facilities contributing to student life.

I have always been puzzled by a comment that Compton made on several occasions about the Lewis Committee report. "MIT," he said, "must be very careful and not become a centipede and worry about all of its hundred legs." Some of my colleagues have speculated that Compton had a dream of an institution not unlike CalTech, concentrated in science. Certainly Compton had some misgivings about the extent to which the Institute was to accept government funds for large projects in the postwar period, and his caution in response to the Lewis Committee report is consistent with this sense of reluctance to attempt an increasingly broad agenda. Yet when Alfred P. Sloan proposed the school of management, Compton was enthusiastic.

5
INTRODUCTION TO THE PRESIDENCY

HOW IT CAME ABOUT

My career at MIT was closely coupled with the demands on Dr. Compton for national service at home and abroad.

After the surrender of Germany on May 8, 1945, the Office of Scientific Research and Development moved to establish a Pacific branch in Manila to serve our military services in the continuing war with Japan. Agreement had been reached with Generals Douglas MacArthur and George Kenney that the OSRD should create this branch under the direction of an appointee of Dr. Bush. Bush then asked Dr. Compton to be its director. Dr. Compton, in 1943, had already been appointed to the post of Chief of the Field Service of OSRD, and in this capacity he had earlier made a trip to the Pacific to find out what the needs of the theater were. General MacArthur also asked Bush to provide him with a science adviser, and MIT's dean of engineering, Edward L. Moreland, who had been serving as executive secretary of the National Defense Research Committee, was tapped for this. He and Dr. Compton flew together to Manila.

To permit him to undertake the directorship of the Pacific Branch of OSRD, President Compton requested that the MIT Corporation's Executive Committee give him a six months' leave of absence from the MIT presidency. After consultation with me he further recommended at the meeting of the Executive Committee on July 10, 1945, that I be appointed acting president to serve during his six months' leave of absence. The committee approved this recommendation.

After his early return to the Institute, in September 1945, Dr. Compton reassumed the presidency, which we had hoped he would do. I of course reverted to my post as executive vice president. Next in order came my appointment, in December 1945, as the vice president of the Institute, an appointment carrying membership in the Corporation. In the same lighthearted song for my retirement dinner in 1971, Dean Harrison used a parody from *Pinafore* to proclaim:

Though today there are nine who are called VP,
In those splendid days there was only me.[1]

I have a copy of a letter Dr. Compton wrote to his brother Wilson, soon to be inaugurated as president of Washington State University, recalling the events that cut short his stay in Manila. He wrote on October 1, 1945:

We had a decidedly thrilling two months in the Phillipines and in Japan. Happily as it turned out the job was very different and also far shorter than had been anticipated when I left on August 1. The atomic bomb was dropped the day after I reached Manila. On the following day we heard that Russia had entered the war. Two or three days after that the ships in the harbor were shooting off their flares and sky-rockets in celebration of the rumor that the Japs had surrendered. Then a little later came V-J Day. By that time the original mission for which I had come out had come to a happy end.

Then a little group of us were asked to go up into Japan with the first occupation troops to put our fingers on some of the top Jap scientists and laboratories and get all the preliminary information necessary to facilitate their later systematic study by the military technical teams which would come in just as soon as accommodations and security made it possible to do so. This new job was going on very satisfactorily indeed when I left on the morning of Monday, September 24.

Following his return from Japan, Dr. Compton resumed his leadership of MIT, but he continued to be in great demand for public service. For example, he was asked by President Truman to chair his Advisory Committee on Universal Military Training, an assignment to which Dr. Compton devoted much time and energy. He had become deeply convinced that UMT was desirable, and he and his committee fought bravely in support of it. Because of my close relations with him I was to share his deep disappointment when Congress rejected the proposals eloquently set forth in the committee's report.

And here let me briefly digress. It can be argued in 1984 that the rejection of UMT in 1947 foreshadowed the growing unwillingness of large numbers of young citizens of the United States to make the sacrifices required to maintain its once-resolute position as a bastion of peace and international decency.

In the Atomic Energy Commission's search for a general manager in 1946, it appointed an advisory panel of which Karl

Compton was a member. This panel reduced the list of candidates to about eight, and I was one of these.[2] I recall Compton coming to me to ask if I would be a nominee for the post. I, along with others, declined. My decision to decline was one of the most agonizing of my career. Under the direction of the commission the manager had the responsibility of creating an agency with tasks new in the history of the world, including the ongoing development and manufacture of atomic bombs. In accepting or declining, I had to examine my duty as a citizen, my adequacy for the post, my recognition of the fascinating virginal character of this new government institution, with terrifying necessity and immeasurable implications for the future. I recognized too that I must answer yes or no while still in a state of moral confusion about the need and terrors of nuclear weapons.

When I finally declined to be a candidate for the post, I did so with the nagging feeling that I had failed to respond to a call for national duty. But as time went on, I realized that I would always be impaled on a moral quandary if I were associated with nuclear bombs. My friend the late Carroll Wilson was subsequently invited, and I admired him for accepting.

It was not long after I had reached this difficult decision that I attended a lecture at MIT given by Robert Oppenheimer. Because of a famous statement he made for the first time in that lecture, let me recall the event. It occurred on the evening of November 25, 1947, and the title of the lecture was "Physics in the Contemporary World." To greet him and to hear his lecture, a large and prestigious audience had come together in the elegant main hall of MIT's Walker Memorial. Oppenheimer had not then suffered any of the cruel attacks that later beset him, but it was clear that in his mind and heart there simmered deep questions about the moral aspect of the development of atomic weapons. There was a hypnotic quality about his muted delivery that left the audience, it seemed, mesmerized by the man's intellectual grandeur and his brooding presence.

It was in this setting and this mood that he burst out with an acknowledgment of the moral conviction he could not suppress. What he said has been endlessly repeated and by many physicists regretted, but it was in this place and this time that he first spoke the following words of atonement to the hushed MIT audience: "In some sort of crude sense which no vulgarity, no humor, no overstatement can quite extinguish, the physicists have known sin; and this is a knowledge which they cannot lose."

It was the year 1948 that was to be the fateful year of decision for the Institute and for me. I had become aware that my name was on the "search" list circulating among institutions looking for presidents. Eventually I had exploratory overtures from three of these colleges, but I discouraged each of them. Of greater interest to me was an approach by an outstanding industrial laboratory which vigorously sought me for a post on its administrative staff. After much reflection I finally decided that I had better stay in education.

My decision not to accept invitations from government or industry did not mean that I would reject out of hand approaches from other educational institutions. For example, I was approached by a major university with which I had sentimental and regional ties. After a visit to the institution with Liz, my wife, I pretty well fell in love with its cordial, impressive people and its beautiful campus. When it extended a firm invitation that I become its president, I was on the verge of accepting when I was thrown off course by learning that a movement was afoot to keep me at MIT. While I have been writing this book, Tom Cabot, an influential member of the MIT Corporation and a friend, has given me an account of how Dean Harrison, speaking in behalf of several officers of the Institute, approached him without my knowledge to take the lead in the Corporation to keep me at MIT. This Cabot did by consulting informally with members of the Executive Committee. I had in no way initiated or encouraged this; in fact I would have viewed these moves by members of the Corporation and administration with trepidation.

It was Dr. Compton who then persuaded me to defer any decision to leave the Institute. He reported that my continuance had wide support, and he spoke words to me that left me convinced that he as chairman and I as president, the two of us working in double harness, would be a workable and effective arrangement. His generosity and his unselfishness touched me deeply, and when he asked me to let him propose to the Corporation's Executive Committee that he become chairman of the Corporation and that I be elected president, I tentatively said yes. I wanted to discuss the whole matter with Liz and our two children. I knew full well that the presidency had to be a partnership and that Liz would be accepting great responsibilities no less than I. I was acutely aware of how much I would need her help. Liz asked searching questions about our respective capacities to make the partnership successful for the Institute, but despite our apprehension and self-doubt, she agreed to our saying yes. The children concurred even though it meant a new kind of life for them. We—all four—had cherished our life in Wellesley. We had built a house there which we loved, and we had committed ourselves to a community life which we loved even more.

Our daughter Carolyn was on the threshold of four years at Mount Holyoke College, and she summed up her reaction to moving into the great mansion which is the president's house at MIT by saying, "It couldn't happen at a less disruptive time in my career!"

After this family consultation I sought the counsel of Ed Moreland, George Harrison, Horace Ford, and other close administrative associates, and of Redfield Proctor, a member of the Corporation's Executive Committee. Each urged me to accept and assured me of his wholehearted support.

And so I said yes to Dr. Compton. In doing so, I had no illusions about the difficulties inherent in succeeding so great a president as he. I was forty-four years old.

At a meeting of the Executive Committee on September 15, 1948, Dr. Compton formally recommended my election as president. At that same meeting Dr. Compton was elected chairman of the Corporation, this appointment to take effect on my succession to the presidency.

At the next meeting of the Corporation's Executive Committee, on October 4, 1948, Dr. Compton presented a letter that he had received from Secretary of Defense James Forrestal, on authorization by President Truman, urgently requesting that he accept the chairmanship of the Research and Development Board of the National Defense Establishment, succeeding Dr. Vannevar Bush, who was resigning October 15. With this information before it the Corporation of the Institute, meeting also on October 4, confirmed the actions of the Executive Committee and voted that I have the title of president-designate beginning October 15 until the time of my inauguration and that Dr. Compton as chairman of the Corporation be authorized to devote such time as he deemed proper to the chairmanship of the Research and Development Board beginning October 15.

Inevitably there were members of the MIT community, both faculty and students, who viewed my election with surprise and skepticism, so greatly was Compton admired and loved. I was aware of these reactions, understood them, and resolved worthily to meet the challenge that lay ahead.

After I became president, Virginia and Tom Cabot invited Liz and me, together with Louise and Don Carpenter of the du Pont clan in Wilmington, Delaware, to join them on their yawl, the *Avalinda*, in cruising waters off the coasts of Maine and New Brunswick. One afternoon we put into St. Andrew's for an overnight stop and on going ashore were unexpectedly hailed by a lady who was curious about the *Avalinda* and those aboard. Not put off by our bedraggled appearance, she invited us to tea the next day. While there, I was introduced to an elderly Harvard man who was, it became clear, partly deaf. When she presented me to him as president of MIT, he responded by remarking loudly, "Well, young man, when you finish there, you can expect to get a good job!"

In 1979 Tom Cabot published a memoir and asked President Nathan Pusey of Harvard and me to write testimonials for the jacket of the book. In that statement I described it as "a highly readable, lucid self-portrait of a Boston patrician of protean talents. He has marshaled his boundless energy and remarkable stamina in the service of the first-rate in education, industry, his country, and his community. In the midst of all these activities, he has lived a life of excitement, adventure, and civilized delights and drawn to himself the love and admiration of a legion of friends."

The Research and Development Board of the National Military Establishment, which Dr. Compton had agreed to head as a successor to Dr. Bush, had been originally suggested by Dr. Bush as a way of providing an organization—following the demobilization of the Office of Scientific Research and Development—that could coordinate scientific research and development in the newly unified Department of Defense. His recommendation of this board was a further expression of his lasting conviction that civilian scientists should have an independent voice in the formulation of defense policy. As a civilian he had been appointed the board's first chairman, a most difficult and exasperating assignment since the department was a caldron of interservice rivalries and budget fights. This environment brought him under great stress, and he developed torturing headaches which were diagnosed as a brain tumor. Happily this diagnosis was wrong, and his headaches may have been psychosomatic. Acting on medical advice, however, Bush resigned the chairmanship of RDB, but he was anxious that the board have the strong leadership that might make it successful. This led him to conclude that Compton had the best chance of making the organization work. I was most reluctant to see Dr. Compton, who was sixty-one, accept his invitation, even as a part-time responsibility, for I had looked forward to the two of us working in partnership in the administration of the Institute, and I was fearful of the extra load the chairmanship of RDB would impose on him.

After Bush's magnificent accomplishments as head of OSRD during the war and his preparation of the milestone report, *Science: The Endless Frontier,* he had quite understandably felt that his great prestige placed him in a position, postwar, to influence political discussions regarding national policy for science and for defense. He quickly found, however, that the power he possessed during the war flowed from President

Roosevelt, and when Truman became president, he was not drawn into the White House circle of advisers. Even when his views were sound, as they usually were, his occasional belligerency during the battles over the legislation for the National Science Foundation and the Atomic Energy Commission almost ensured his alienation from the Truman White House. As a result Bush's postwar career in Washington was a frustrating experience for him. With his welcome at the White House diminished, he lost clout even in the Department of Defense. In fact he finally lost the support of Secretary Forrestal. In addition Bush's repeated advocacy of the appointment of a scientific voice in military planning at a level no less than that of the Joint Chiefs was firmly ignored. The Joint Chiefs of those days failed to recognize their need for civilian science advisers. It was Eisenhower who adroitly met this need in 1957 by appointing a science adviser with full access to the National Security Council, where scientists could make their views known.

Although he had strongly supported Bush as his science adviser during the war, Roosevelt did not extend this relationship to diplomatic decisions that arose before his death. Apparently Roosevelt came to concur with Churchill's views that atomic energy should be kept as an Anglo-American monoply, an objective that Bush correctly considered unattainable and therefore disastrous to pursue. Roosevelt consulted neither him nor Conant about these matters involving atomic weapons. In an article written by McGeorge Bundy entitled "The Missed Chance to Stop the H-Bomb," published in *The New York Review*, May 13, 1982, he noted that Vannevar Bush at one point "became deeply seized with a concern that once there had been a true thermonuclear test, the last chance to block these weapons would be gone. Respecting the rules of secrecy, he pressed his case only privately, but he went as far up the government as he could get—to Acheson, though not to Truman. It was too late; the secretary of state would not try to change a plan whose momentum of technical success and political support he now saw— almost surely correctly—as irresistible. No one ever asked Truman to delay the decisive test of November 1952 for this purpose. Indeed even the unrelated suggestion that he should wait until after the election struck him as a proposal to let politics affect a matter of national security."[3] Nor was his Science Advisory Committee ever consulted.

In the Oppenheimer hearing Bush was asked whether he had talked with the secretary of state about the question of postponing the test of the H-bomb. Bush responded that he had but that the discussion had nothing to do with the report of the Panel on Disarmament which Dean Acheson had appointed in April of 1952 (and of which Bush was a member). During the interim while the panel participants' clearances were being processed, Bush decided to visit Dean Acheson to give him his personal opinion on the projected H-bomb test. This he did after talking with a number of his friends:

There were two primary reasons why I took action at that time, and went directly to the Secretary of State. There was scheduled a test which was evidently going to occur early in November. I felt that it was utterly improper—and I still think so—for that test to be put off just before election, to confront an incoming President with an accomplished test for which he would carry the full responsibility thereafter. For that test marked our entry into a very disagreeable type of world.

In the second place, I felt strongly that that test ended the possibility of the only type of agreement that I thought was possible with Russia at that time, namely, an agreement to make no more tests. For that kind of an agreement would have been self-policing in the sense that if it was violated, the violation would be immediately known. I still think that we made a grave error in conducting that test at that time, and not attempting to make that type of simple agreement with Russia. I think history will show that was a turning point that when we entered into the grim world that we are entering right now, that those who pushed that thing through to a conclusion without making that attempt have a great deal to answer for.[4]

Had I been in a position to speak at that time, I would have endorsed this conclusion reached by Bush. Indeed Bush echoed the statement that Enrico Fermi and I. I. Rabi had added to the main report, in 1949, of the General Advisory Committee of the

Atomic Energy Commission. They too had pointed out that any H-bomb "test by another power could be detected by available physical means."

In this and other matters after the war, Bush continued to speak with wisdom and clarity about great issues before the nation. There were times in this postwar period, however, when it seemed to many that he acted in an autocratic manner in his readiness to dispose with overweening self-assurance of the affairs of institutions and people. When he left Washington and the postwar political battles in which he valiantly fought for the freedom of science and other objectives, he returned to his old haunts at MIT, and after a period in the benign environment of the Institute, soon softened his tendency to be imperious and found himself once again revered and loved.[5]

6
AGENDA FOR THE FUTURE

MID-CENTURY CONVOCATION; PRESIDENTIAL INAUGURATION

In the spring of 1949 MIT sponsored a great international symposium devoted to the social implications of scientific progress to set the stage for a major fund-raising campaign and to provide a prelude for my inauguration, on April 2, as the tenth president of MIT. The participation of Winston Churchill in this Mid-Century Convocation together with an array of forty distinguished scholars and public figures made certain that the convocation commanded worldwide attention at the time and that it would long glow as a brilliant declaration by MIT of its role as a supranational research university sharing boldly in the worldwide advancement of learning and the humane uses of science.

The impresario of the convocation was John Ely Burchard, to whom I address a celebration later in this memoir as the first dean of the new School of Humanities and Social Studies at MIT.

Burchard was later to prepare and publish the proceedings of the convocation in an impressive volume entitled *Mid-Century: The Social Implications of Scientific Progress.*[1] I do not propose to duplicate Burchard's verbatim account, but the Compton-Killian files have provided sidelights on Winston Churchill's participation and on the convocation that are pleasant and appropriate to recall.

An airmail letter from Dr. Compton to Churchill formally invited him to speak on the evening of March 31, 1949, and reported to Churchill that President Truman had agreed to speak the following evening. Mr. Churchill cabled an accepance on February 11 and indicated his intention to sail to America on the *Queen Elizabeth* (I). On February 14, with surprising attention to practical details, Churchill cabled again to confirm his acceptance and inquire what arrangements would be made for defraying the expenses of his trip: "My party outward by *Queen Elizabeth* consists of myself, Christopher Soames, son-in-law, with one and probably two lady private secretaries and one or possibly two Scotland Yard officers. On return journey, Mrs.

Churchill and my daughter, Mary Soames, who are going out separately to Jamaica, will be with me. Cost accommodations out and home I have reserved on *Queen Elizabeth* will be two thousand and one hundred pounds sterling approximately. Let me know what contribution you feel able to make to this large sum and I will pay the rest."[2]

With prudent attention to MIT finances President Compton responded to this cable by indicating as follows: "As compromise between our desire adequately to express appreciation and our status as an educational institution supported by gifts, I suggest MIT contribute one thousand pounds, which I shall have advanced by cable." Churchill responded, saying that this was quite agreeable. He further indicated that he had not realized how prices had risen for the same accommodations since he last crossed the Atlantic in January 1946. "I have now looked into the matter more exactly, reducing my party by one secretary and one security officer. Shall be glad to know President's time-table as of course I must pay my respects to him during April 1. I should also like to hear his address that night. Kind regards." These negotiations about travel expenses were brought to a happy conclusion, apparently, by an offer from Henry Luce personally to supplement MIT's payment to Churchill.

With his unfailing attention to creature comforts, Churchill also felt it appropriate that he and his party should travel from New York to Boston and back to New York by private Pullman cars, and MIT promptly made these arrangements.

The only part of these carefully laid plans that went awry was the last-minute notification by President Truman that he had to make a cancellation of his plans. In fact the news of his bowing out was released to the press before we at MIT were notified, and we were receiving calls from reporters before we knew the score. "The cancellation," he wrote, "was not a voluntary one but was a case of necessity."

So great was the demand to hear Mr. Churchill that MIT had no auditorium on its campus large enough, and it reluctantly arranged for him to speak in the Boston Garden, which had a seating capacity of approximately 14,000. Churchill was at the peak of his popularity in the United States; so even this great space was not adequate for all who could have been legitimate guests. To accommodate the overflow, the Institute set up in its Rockwell Cage a large television screen and there projected the entire Boston Garden affair to an additional audience of 4,500.

In his speech at the Boston Garden that initiated the convocation, Mr. Churchill addressed himself to the broad topic "The Twentieth Century—Its Promise and Its Realization." He prompted laughter when he remarked, early in his speech, "Ladies and Gentlemen, I frankly confess that I feel somewhat overawed in addressing this vast scientific and learned audience on the subjects which your panels are discussing. I have no technical and no university education, and have just had to pick up a few things as I went along. Therefore I speak with a diffidence, which I hope to overcome as I proceed. . . ." He again prompted laughter when he said, "I was so glad that in the first instance you asked me to talk about the past rather than to peer into the future, because I know more about the past than I do about the future."

At the very beginning of his speech Churchill commented about the absence in Great Britain of institutions comparable to MIT. "We have suffered in Great Britain," he said, "by the lack of colleges of university rank in which engineering and the allied subjects are taught. Industrial production depends on technology, and it is because the Americans, like the prewar Germans, have realized this and created institutions for the advanced training of large numbers of high-grade engineers to translate the advantages of pure science into industrial technique, it is for that reason that their output per head and consequent standard of life are so high. It is surprising that England, which was the first country to be industrialized, has nothing of comparable stature."

Churchill, inspired by his part in the MIT convocation, later encouraged friends to found a new institution in Britain with some of the characteristics of MIT.

And then as he approached the conclusion of his address, he

emphasized that "we seek nothing from Russia but goodwill and fair play. If, however, there is to be a war of nerves let us make sure that our nerves are strong and are fortified by the deepest convictions of our hearts. If we persevere steadfastly together, and allow no appeasement of tyranny and wrong-doing in any form, it may not be our nerve or the structure of our civilization which will break; something else will break, and peace may yet be preserved. . . . Let us then move forward together in discharge of our mission and our duty, fearing God and nothing else."

Mr. Churchill's address did not command the attention of his Iron Curtain address at Westminster College, but still it re-sounded around the world. One commentator described it as "a work of art. . . . the rhythms were as solid and inevitable as those of a Beethoven symphony. . . ."

After his speech the Marine Band played the American national anthem. As it played, it was noticed that tears welled in Churchill's eyes, and he was the only one on the platform who sang the words. As Burchard was to recall, "There were those who attributed it to histrionics and to Mr. Churchill's ever-present sense of the dramatic and fitting. But Mrs. Churchill had a different explanation. When the wife of one of the committee said to her how nice it had been that Mr. Churchill sang, Mrs. Churchill leaned closer to be heard above the hubbub and said, 'He means it, my dear.' "

After the news arrived that President Truman would not speak, it fell to my lot to seek a substitute. I had come to know Harold Stassen after his election as president of the University of Pennsylvania, and at this moment he stood as a major political figure. I decided to invite him to speak in the place of President Truman. He was taken aback but vastly pleased and accepted then and there. Thus was the emergency handled by a single telephone call. And Mr. Stassen must have worked day and night to compose one of the best speeches he ever made, and one that prompted favorable comment by Churchill.

On the evening of Mr. Stassen's speech, the faculty and Corporation of MIT gave a formal dinner for the participants in the convocation. We had discovered that it was Mrs. Churchill's birthday, and in accord with custom, a birthday cake with candles was brought in while the guests sang spontaneously, "Happy Birthday to you."

During the second evening at the Garden there were ceremonial words of appreciation spoken to Mr. Churchill. The president of the MIT student body made a presentation, saying that the students would like to extend to him an expression of goodwill and fellowship.

I then stepped up to say, "Mr. Churchill, you have made a scholarly contribution to the MIT convocation. More, by your moral force and by your eloquence, you have lifted up our hearts. We are precluded by policy at MIT from awarding honorary degrees.[3] Instead, we would like to invite you to be an honorary member of the company of scholars which is MIT."

To these presentations Mr. Churchill replied with grace and wit:

I am off duty tonight. My task was accomplished as well as it lay in my power last night, and tonight I am to receive and have received kindly tokens that at any rate all friendly relations were not at an end.

I have listened with very great pleasure to the thoughtful and powerful address to which we have listened from President Stassen and I cannot conceal from you that I found myself in agreement with it on very many points of substance and on almost all points of sentiment.

Now on this occasion I have to thank you for two gifts, two presentations, which I value very greatly. The first is that I am an honorary lecturer of MIT, which means that I can come here whenever I choose and lecture you on any matter which may excite my interest. The second is the presentation to me from the student body by Mr. Kirchner of this golden key. May it always be the means of giving me the feeling and the faith that I have the key to American hearts.

If that should be so and if I may feel that in our own small island across the ocean we have reached conclusions which are in broad harmony with those of the great republic, we may indeed face the future with confidence and with hope.

And for my part, I have the strongest feeling of gratitude for all the manifestations of kindliness and friendship which I have received.

I carry away from this great gathering sentiments which will enable me for the rest of my life to view in a totally different light the Boston Tea Party, of which I heard in my youth.

And let me here express from the bottom of my heart the gratitude of the British people to the valiant, generous people of the United States for all the part that they are playing in the future world. Let me give my assurance to this great audience, one of the finest I have ever addressed, that without their aid, without their guidance and strength, all the struggles that our soldiers and sailors have made in the war might well be cast away, but that persistency along the lines which they have adopted will carry us, may well carry us, through the dangers which lie ahead and may possibly avert from humanity the fearful curse of another war.

I thank you all for the kindness which you have shown me. I don't need a microphone to tell you how deep and great is my regard for my motherland, and I will carry an inspiration from this great gathering back to Britain and I trust, indeed, that we may continue to march shoulder to shoulder along the path of truth, of justice, and of honor.

He indeed felt off duty and even frolicsome that second evening. Once during an interlude he inconspicuously crept up to the podium, peaked around it in his best cherubic fashion, and waved at Mrs. Churchill, who was seated in the front row of the audience.

After his responses to the citation, he again walked up to the edge of the rostrum and addressed words, this time with obvious sentiment, directly to the Marine Band: "I have one more favor to ask. I should not like to leave here without listening to the United States Marine Hymn . . . if I may, with your permission."

This was a high point for the Marine Band, the more so since Mr. Churchill sang lustily the lines from the hymn as the band played with great verve and obvious delight.

I think it was the wit Dean Harrison who later wrote that

Churchill once more "succeeded in stealing the entire show, which Mr. Truman's advisers may have anticipated" when they persuaded him to cancel his participation in the convocation.

Quite apart from his eloquent speech at the convocation, there were a number of memorable Churchillian incidents that should be recalled.

Mr. Churchill and his party arrived in two private cars attached to the overnight train from New York and were met by Dr. Compton and Admiral Edward L. Cochrane, who conducted the group to the Ritz-Carlton Hotel, where Mr. Churchill secluded himself in preparation for his address. As the cavalcade moved to the hotel and later when the audience was entering the Boston Garden, there was some feeble picketing by dissident or Irish groups and there were a few banners declaring "It is time to retire" and "Send the bundle back to Britain," but the pickets were largely ignored by the crowd that cheered Churchill.

At the end of Churchill's twelve-hour period of seclusion, I went to the hotel to escort him to the Boston Garden. When I arrived at his quarters, Mr. Churchill was seated alone at the dining table with a small pony of brandy before him. I presented myself and said to Mr. Churchill that I had already read the manuscript of his speech and thought it was superb. "Do you really?" he said. "I found writing the speech a labor of great difficulty since I am not accustomed to speaking to a distinguished and learned academic audience." (Mrs. Churchill later on remarked that he had not been a pleasant companion for two weeks before the speech, since its preparation worried him.)

I told Mr. Churchill that the time had come to leave for the Garden. After some delay, he, with the help of his valet, donned his coat and hat, and we moved to the elevator. As we approached the lobby floor on the way down, he removed his hat, put a large cigar in his mouth, and as the door opened, raised his arm in his famous V for victory sign and presented himself in this familiar guise to the large and applauding audience that there awaited him. We slowly managed to get to the limousine which was to take us to the Garden. The streets were lined with crowds of people seeking to get a glimpse of him; and as we got into the car, Churchill asked, "Where is the light?" It was clear that he wanted to be seen, as he appropriately should have been, by the great crowds, and we finally got the dome light of the car switched on. When we reached the Garden and as Churchill was getting out of the car, he mumbled: "The animals were being released from their cages." And as we started up the ramp that led to the stage, Churchill said something to the effect, "Here we are on the path for the elephants" (he obviously was aware that the Garden was the scene of the visits of the circus). The rostrum party entered the Garden by way of this ramp because it provided easy access to the speaking platform, not to avoid the pickets. After we were seated on the rostrum, Churchill stood to receive the applause of the great audience. His speech was preceded by a welcoming statement by Dr. Compton and an introduction by Mr. Bernard Baruch, who presented him as "the greatest living Englishman, the finest flowering of leadership and statesmanship that England ever produced. . . ."

I recall some of the meticulous arrangements that Mr. Churchill quite properly insisted on. He had asked that we arrange for a throat specialist to come midafternoon to examine his throat. It was in fine fettle. "I always have my throat examined before making a major speech," confided the orator. He had sent an emissary to the Garden to measure the height of the podium so that he could make sure that his manuscript was legible in accord with the spectacles he wore. He declined to try proffered spectacles that would reduce the glare of the television lights. When he heard about the design of the podium, which required that he stand behind it without his whole body being in view, he protested, saying that he always liked to speak with his whole body visible.

Those of us who saw the speaking manuscript of Mr. Churchill's speech noted with interest how it was typed. The "of's," the "and's," and the "the's," and other small words were largely omitted so that the substance of each sentence or paragraph could be read at a glance, and the lengths of succeeding lines in a paragraph were shorter so that they took the form of inverted triangles. This interesting arrangement enabled him to follow his text with almost total accuracy, without appearing to be reading it.

After the Churchill speech was over, the plan was for me to escort the party to the Statler Hotel Ballroom, where a great congregation of MIT guests eagerly awaited him, for it had been announced that he would appear there. When we got to the hotel, he looked about obviously mystified, and said, "This is not my hotel, this is not my hotel, I want to go to my hotel." And so I got him back into the limousine, and we returned to the Ritz. When back in his quarters there, he promptly ordered a dozen oysters and champagne. He had not had dinner, saying he disliked dining before making a major speech. After a rather lengthy pause in his quarters at the Ritz, he indicated he was ready to appear with Mrs. Churchill at the Statler, and so we again went to the Statler and seated the two of them in a box, where he and Mrs. Churchill received the greetings and applause of the audience on the floor. Churchill responded with a brief and very gracious second speech in this less formal setting.

Boston opened its heart in other ways. The Boston Symphony Orchestra offered to give a special concert for him and for those paticipating in the convocation. The producers and company of *South Pacific* with Ezio Pinza and Mary Martin volunteered to give a special performance for Mr. Churchill and all the other guests of the Institute. It was with disappointment and regret that we had to decline these generous offers because there simply wasn't time to fit them into the program.

Two days later Churchill and his party returned to New York and thence back to England. During his stay in Boston he went to a luncheon at the Club of Odd Volumes given by Henry Laughlin, head of the firm of Houghton Mifflin, which published Churchill's books in the United States. Throughout his stay he was a relaxed and pleasant guest.

Churchill arrived in New York some days before he was to speak in Boston, and he requested that Burchard come down to see him while he was staying with Bernard Baruch. Burchard reported that he found Churchill propped up in bed, in pink pajamas, smoking one of his great cigars. A lighted taper burned on the bedside table so that Churchill could rekindle the cigar when necessary. He had called Burchard to New York to review the draft of his speech, to check it for accuracy, and to make sure that nothing in it would be an embarrassment to MIT or to Washington. Before seeing Churchill again the following day, John beat it down to Princeton and gathered together several of his scholarly friends to give the speech a thorough going-over.

Before Churchill left Boston, he presented to a number of us copies of his then current book, each warmly inscribed by him. At Christmas time that year, several of us were delighted to receive Christmas messages from Churchill written in his own hand.

The convocation provided an opportunity to an industrial leader to encourage corporate grants. At a luncheon where MIT leaders presented a budget of needs "to fund its independence," the founder of IBM, Thomas Watson, Sr., inspired by Churchill, arose and announced to the large audience that his company would contribute to MIT an unsolicited $75,000. In later years IBM became one of the most generous supporters of our leading universities.

In my first report as president—the following autumn—I spoke of the transcending importance of the convocation. Imaginatively conceived and superbly carried through, it achieved an illumination and grace that made it a memorable and moving experience for all who were present.

I continued:

The Convocation prompts many other observations pertinent to education and to our objectives at the Institute. . . . Let me mention only two.

1. During the past half century, specialization has been an outstanding characteristic of scholarship and professional activity. The tactics and strategy of intellectual advance have required specialization, and specialization has moved from one triumph

to another. The tactics and strategy of the second half century will require a specialism equally strong but tempered by less isolationism among scholars and more linkages between fields of scholarship. We know that in science the boundaries between sciences are becoming less and less definable and that overlapping sciences, such as biochemistry and geophysics, reflect in their vigorous growth the interdependence of specialized investigations. We find, too, that in our university organization we must devise new organizational methods, such as interdepartmental laboratories and programs, in order to provide an integrated approach to fields such as nuclear science, international relations, electronics, and the social sciences. In his authoritative study, *The Universities of Europe in the Middle Ages*, Rashdall concluded that the true university is "a place where the different branches of knowledge are brought into contact and harmonious combination with one another." Our goal today is to achieve this harmonious combination and intercommunication.

If we can achieve such intellectual integration, the basis of the conflict between general and specialized education will have been removed. In fact, we have long passed the stage where there can be any legitimate debate over the competing effectiveness of specialized and general education. Both are essential. General education alone can result in superficiality and dilettantism; specialization alone, in narrowness and social myopia. To achieve a working partnership, however, requires an end to narrow jurisdictional differences in education. President Baxter at our Commencement exercises last June spoke eloquently of the need for flinging more two-way bridges between the liberal arts and the sciences. The colleges must bring about this two-way traffic if they are to educate men who can, as specialists, bend specialism to the broad needs of our society.

2. My second observation prompted by the Convocation is that education, if it is to serve a free society, must not only train men who can do the complex, specialized work of society; it must also cultivate in these men a reverence for the dignity of the individual. Someone has said that democracy is most effective when it tries to make all its citizens aristocrats. It might also be said that education in a democracy is most effective when it strengthens the aristocratic virtues of personal dignity, self-reliance, and self-understanding.

Men with these qualities resist all forms of statism and Stalinist totalitarianism that regiment and depreciate the individual. Men with these qualities are also more immune to fear and frustration. President Bixler suggested at the Convocation that our chief peril is a loss of faith in the power of mind to solve society's problems and a consequent tendency to pick scapegoats—as, for example, blaming science for society's ills. The education that helps men avoid these aberrations must possess a synthesis of the general and the specialistic that brings, within the limit of our knowledge, the whole of life into view.

In our educational program at the Institute these considerations have great influence, and the Mid-Century Convocation served to point up and extend this influence. The fact that an institute of technology held a convocation that inquired so widely and deeply into the social problems of the mid-century is evidence of a vigorous humanism that recognizes the interdependence, unity, and social value of all useful learning.

THE INAUGURATION

As planned by Dean Everett Baker, the last day of the convocation brought an onslaught of academic ceremony devoted to my inauguration, held in the Rockwell Cage. Seats had been arranged for delegates from 171 universities and colleges, 41 learned societies and associations, and the faculty of MIT. The ceremony was preceded by a majestic academic procession, which moved from the columned portico of the Rogers Building on Massachusetts Avenue over to the Cage. A giant of a man, Charles George Dandrow of the class of 1922, president of the Alumni Association, was chief marshal of the day and called the assembly to order. The minister of the Unitarian Church in Wellesley Hills, where my family and I had worshipped, the Reverend William Brooks Rice, delivered the invocation, and Dr. Compton inducted me into office as the tenth president of the Institute. The 4,500 seats in the Cage were inadequate to seat those who wished to attend, and to provide for the great overflow, arrangements were made to broadcast the ceremony in the Great Court of the Institute.

After my induction I delivered the customary presidential address. I said:

Education is to be found not only in the classroom and the laboratory but in the experience of living with one's fellows in an environment stimulating to intellectual activity and conducive to the development of community responsibility. We want to carry further the development of an environment at MIT which performs in the broadest sense an educational function itself, not in a passive way but in a dynamic way. Living facilities, activities, and atmosphere must be skillfully arranged to provide the kind of environment that contributes to the development of leadership, breadth, and standards of taste and judgment among our students—to give them the fullest possible opportunity to acquire, in a phrase of Sir Richard Livingstone's, a sense of the first-rate.

I next stressed an objective that I devote special attention to in this memoir. Because of their close relationship both to government and to industry, our institutes of technology have a special obligation to maintain their independence and freedom.

If our private institutions are to remain strong, they must of necessity try to avoid covering the waterfront in their programs. Their future demands restraint in numbers of students admitted. I also stressed an objective which I was pleased to note that President Paul Gray emphasized in his inaugural address three decades later. "The students who are studying to be professional men," I said, "need opportunities to reflect, to develop the intellectual maturity that comes only from self-education." I added:

It is my hope that in the years ahead we may also achieve the imaginative administration and the noble environment to give our faculty and students opportunities to contribute their full potential to the prosperity and to the peace of the world.

As we seek to broaden the education of the specialist, we must be careful to avoid overscheduling or overcramming him. Institutes of technology have always been proud of their reputation for requiring hard work of their students. I hope that they will not lose that reputation. . . . The students who are studying to be professional men need time to be resourceful, to develop judgment, to acquire a broad margin to their life. They need time to avoid what Veblen called "trained incapacity."

In noting the longevity of this presidential sentiment, I recall the answer given by the late Leo Szilard, a Hungarian scientist of legendary brilliance, when asked why so many European scientists had been so creative; he answered with one word, "leisure." Perhaps Paul Gray and I were both thinking of a witty reversal of a Veblen book title—the leisure of the theory class.

It was in this address that I described MIT as a university polarized around science, engineering, and the arts.

At the close of my inaugural address six speakers were introduced to present felicitations and greetings: Sir Richard Livingstone of Oxford University, for the Old World; James Bryant Conant of Harvard University, for the educational institutions of America; Governor Paul Andrew Dever for the Commonwealth of Massachusetts; David Allen Shepard, president of my class, 1926, for the alumni; John Thomas Toohy for the undergraduates; George Russell Harrison, dean of science, for the faculty of MIT.

In Harrison's remarks he noted with wit and accuracy that "if he [a college president] were to take an oath of office that set forth literally the requirements on his attention, the results must resemble a medley of a marriage service, the vows of a monastic order, and a research contract with the Air Force. Besides swearing to forsake all other interests than those of his institution, he must take mental vows of personal poverty, intellectual chastity, and social obedience. No bevy of medieval angels clustering on the point of a needle required such nicety of balance as a modern administrator following the curved razor edge of policy needed by present-day events." To these requirements of Dean Harrison I subsequently added another—skill in the use of inertial guidance such as my classmate, Professor Stark Draper, invented for the guidance of vehicles in outer space.

As I describe in the ongoing pages of this book, my experiences confirm the accuracy of the Harrison specifications, and I am sure that the curves of the razor edges of my successors will have become sharper and more unpredictable in the 1980s, as my memoir, in its examples, strikingly testifies.

After the ceremonial felicitations and greetings the band played the recessional, and the great assembly started its procession out of the hall. Dr. Compton and I, still in our academic regalia and dressed in cutaway and striped trousers, stopped briefly at the colonnade in the Great Court to pay greetings to the hundreds who, unable to be seated in the Rockwell Cage, had gathered there to hear the proceedings from loudspeakers.

As I left the scene of my inauguration, I could not help having indelibly engraved in my mind the words so generously spoken in the ceremony, but I could not escape the somber reflections provoked by Dean Harrison's graphic description of the duties of the modern college president. Only six days elapsed after my inauguration before I was confronted with one of the challenges inferred by Harrison.

LUNCHEON IN LONDON WITH
THE CHURCHILLS (1951)

It was not until July 1951 that I again had the opportunity of seeing the Churchills. My wife and I had gone to London at the invitation of the then rector of Imperial College of Science and Technology, Sir Roderic Hill, to visit the College, to attend the annual dinner of the English Speaking Union, and to visit Cambridge University. Sir Roderic, a distinguished air marshal during the war, had paid an extended visit to MIT and won the esteem of all by his quiet charm and breadth of mind. We both shared experiences as newly inaugurated heads of our institutions, he in 1948 and I in 1949. The dinner of the Union was the kind of occasion that the British do with such traditional color and formality, with the red coats introducing the speakers and the honored guests. Both Churchill and General Eisenhower spoke, Eisenhower having been in London in his capacity as head of SHAPE. Lord Salisbury, who presided at this dinner, aptly said that General Eisenhower was the American most beloved by the British and Churchill the Englishman most beloved by the Americans and that it was a great occasion that they both should be present.

Soon after this event Mrs. Killian and I were invited to luncheon with the Churchills at 28 Hyde Park Gate, which was the Churchills' London residence. The other guests were Lord and Lady Portal and Mrs. and Mrs. Ronald Tree. Lord Portal at that time was in charge of the British development of atomic weapons. During World War II Mr. Tree had served as parliamentary secretary to Brendan Bracken, British Minister of Information. The Trees owned a stately home, "Ditchley," which the Churchills used as a retreat during the war. Mrs. Tree, his second wife, was the charming and gifted daughter of Endicott Peabody of Groton School fame.

My wife subsequently made notes to aid our memory of this delightful luncheon, and for the sake of accuracy I resort to plagiarizing these notes with her permission.

Twenty-eight Hyde Park Gate is a typical London "city house." It is located near the Albert Memorial and was, as Mrs. Killian wrote, tastefully decorated more in chintzes than brocades and more in pastel colors than brown walnut or oak.

In the informal drawing room the guests were served sherry or tomato juice as they entered, and we noted with interest that the Churchills drank tomato juice, the Killians, sherry. Luncheon was served at 1:25 at a round table of bleached oak in a dining room on a level lower than the drawing room. The arm chairs about the table were covered in a pink patterned chintz and looked very homey in the cream and white dining room. Above the fireplace hung a large painting of the Battle of Blenheim wherein the Duke of Marlborough, Churchill's ancestor, was directing a mighty charge. At my side was one of Churchill's paintings, a pool at Chartwell, with noticeable goldfish sporting themselves. Mr. Tree with a twinkle in his eye, asked Mr. Churchill whether this was a painting by Monet. Churchill smiled appreciatively, and his lighter side was brought out by a discussion of his painting along with his love of horse racing. He mentioned that a race was to fall on Saturday at which 25,000 pounds was the possible prize. Churchill's prize horse was named "Colonist," a gift from his son-in-law, and among the six others he owned was another called "Non Stop." Earlier Mrs. Churchill remarked, he was "all agin' " horse racing. Mrs.

Churchill then wondered if his current dislike of television would change in the event that someone gave him a television set. "At present," she noted, "he thinks it just doesn't seem right for young people to gaze and gape in cowlike fashion without sufficient reading and thinking."

Also present in the dining room was Churchill's pet dog—a highly manicured French poodle. This dog had jumped up into the chair of honor pulled out for Mrs. Killian to occupy—the chair of honor which obviously was normally occupied by Churchill's poodle, who was obviously indignant about being displaced.

Everyone seemed perfectly at ease at the luncheon. Churchill was gay and communicative. The Trees told us later, in taking us back in their car to our hotel, that they had recently been there with the Chinese ambassador and his wife—a large woman who spoke only Chinese. She too, in accordance with protocol, was placed on Churchill's right and never was so much champagne drunk because they were unable to communicate.

Champagne was served toward the end of our luncheon, and Churchill noted that it came from one Odette, a French woman who kept him supplied with champagne. He described her as looking like champagne too—all foamy at the top. Many topics were talked about at luncheon, including of course the Russians. Churchill opined that a new revolution still seemed a possibility in the Soviet Union, and he then voiced one of his epigrams about the importance of being strong. "Becoming stronger does not necessarily mean becoming safer. You are safe only when you are strong enough."

He spoke of the election coming up in September at which he was again to seek the prime ministership. In preparation he said he was "only working to receive a crown of thorns." He obviously considered Eden his understudy and expressed his feeling that it was most peculiar and most unfortunate that FDR had never seemingly considered Truman or anyone else as his understudy. "It was a tragedy," he said, "that three months before his death FDR was not his capable self and three months after his death Truman was struggling with the unknown." In his judgment those six months were unusually dangerous and critical.

He wondered about the political future in America. "The usual fear," he said, "of a military man at the helm would not be valid in the case of Ike." He said that Eisenhower, Lord Portal, and a few others, together with himself, had talked until after 2:00 A.M. following a dinner the previous week. No punches were pulled. Churchill feared Taft. "He has a good mind until he makes it up." He thought MacArthur forced his own withdrawal from Korea and would have been better as a mediator in the Far East. He remarked on the inadvisability of destroying a people's symbols and pointed up his statement by remembering that there might not have been a Hitler if some relative of the Kaiser had been installed as the properly indoctrinated head of Germany. And he remarked that the British needed an organization similar to the U.S. Atomic Energy Commission.

He spoke of being at Mr. and Mrs. Tree's home, looking at a film of the Marx Brothers when news of the arrival of Hess in England came to him.

Churchill spoke of having visited practically all the battlefields connected with the Civil War in the company of Douglas Southal Freeman of Richmond, Virginia, in 1929. Churchill predicted the Depression and yet got caught himself.

Churchill had difficulty with hearing, and he said he did not hear Eisenhower's speech at the English Speaking Union dinner but read it and considered it "very sound and excellent."

Churchill recalled John Burchard and inquired about him.

THE ORIGIN OF CHURCHILL COLLEGE

When Churchill returned to England following his address at the MIT convocation, he never forgot his conviction that England should establish an institution similar to MIT. After his retirement from the prime ministership in April 1955, Churchill expressed to a group of friends his deep regret that he had done nothing about establishing such an institution while he had the power. As reported in *Footprints in Time*, a memoir by Sir John

Colville, Churchill's private secretary, Churchill said to his friends that the "most serious omission of which he was conscious," of his last term as prime minister, "left him with a sense of guilt. He should have taken steps to establish in Britain something comparable to the Massachusetts Institute of Technology . . ." by which he had been "deeply impressed. He had put the matter aside, and now it was too late." Colville reported that Lord Cherwell responded that it was never too late and that "I, having drunk enough brandy to be more than usually impetuous, volunteered to raise the money to finance such an enterprise. Churchill turned slowly toward me: 'If you will do that,' he said, 'it will be a great relief to me. You may use my name in any way you see fit.' "[4]

Colville was successful in raising funds from English industry and other sources, and he, together with Lord Todd and Sir John Cockcroft, convinced Churchill that the new institution should be a Cambridge University college. After all, there were excellent colleges similar to MIT such as Imperial College of Science and Technology. They and others were afraid that a wholly new, free-standing institution would not have the prestige of Oxford to attract outstanding fellows to prepare themselves for industry. They then suggested that this new college be called after Churchill and that it be the national memorial to him. "He did not, as I had hoped," wrote Colville, "show immediate gratification; but then he seldom reacted according to expectation. Perhaps he thought it strange that he who, apart from being Chancellor of Bristol and the recipient of a score of honorary degrees, had no connexion at all with universities, should be asked to agree that his own memorial be within one; and no less strange that it should be built in his lifetime."

"What memorial," Colville asked, "could be more lasting than a great university college? After a minute or two, he replied: 'It is very nice of them. And I ought certainly to be pleased. After all, it will put me alongside the Trinity.' "

Churchill College would be designed to embody some of the characteristics of MIT. Seventy percent of its students would study science and technology, and about a third would be graduate students. A board of ten trustees was recruited by Sir Winston, including four from the university, to undertake the founding of the college. These trustees decreed that no government funds were to be solicited or used. All monies were to be obtained in England. Funds were secured from industry, from individuals, and from foundations, and under the leadership of Sir John Cockcroft, the college was built and established.

Later all the American ambassadors to the Court of St. James, or their descendants, from the mid-1920s to the late 1970s, contributed funds to build an archival center at the college to house Sir Winston's papers. It is a British version, human and scholarly in scale, of the great, and sometimes pretentious, presidential libraries in the United States.

Another characteristic of MIT that was subsequently introduced into Churchill College was the policy of admitting women on equal terms with men. Sir John Colville, in his 1981 biography of Churchill, described the way this decision came about:

One day, in about 1958, Churchill held at 28 Hyde Park Gate one of the regular meetings of the Churchill College Trustees over which he presided. The trustees were eminent men: the Chairmen of Shell, ICI, Vickers and Associated Electrical Industries; the Masters of Trinity and Christ's College, Cambridge, the Provost of King's; and some of the most famous scientists at Cambridge, Lord Adrian, Sir Alexander Todd and Sir John Cockcroft. They were all astonished when Churchill announced that he hoped the new college, intended as the national memorial to him, would admit women on equal terms with men. No college at Oxford or Cambridge had ever done any such thing, although there were separate colleges for women.

I asked him afterwards if this had been Clementine's idea. "Yes," he replied, "and I support it. When I think what women did in the war I feel sure they deserve to be treated equally."[5]

At first the Churchill College trustees ignored Churchill's request, and it was not until 1969 that three Cambridge colleges joined to open the gates.

Sir John Cockcroft, chosen by Churchill, became the first master of the college. Churchill later wrote to the Queen asking that subsequent appointments be made by the Crown, "thus putting the new College on a par with Trinity, Cambridge, and Christ Church, Oxford." Sir John was a member of the NATO commission that I chaired in 1960–61, which recommended the creation of a European institute of science and technology having some of the characteristics of MIT. In 1965 I went to England at the request of the Ford Foundation to serve as a consultant to Lord Bowden (Vivian), who had been appointed by Prime Minister Harold Wilson as secretary of state for education. Sir John invited me to stay at Churchill College, and I was elected a Churchill Overseas Fellow.

We at MIT found much satisfaction in having played a part in the founding of this new Cambridge college. Recent resident Overseas Fellows report that the college has achieved high repute among Cambridge colleges and is intellectually robust and thriving. A recent announcement from the college reports that nine of the fellows nominated to Churchill College by the Winston Churchill Foundation of the United States, initiated by the late Carl Gilbert of Boston and of which I have been a trustee, have won the Nobel Prize. Sir William Hawthorne, a graduate of MIT, completed in 1983 a long term as master of Churchill College. In addition he has served as a visiting professor at MIT, bringing to our councils exceptional wisdom and insight. His wife is the granddaughter of President John Runkle, second president of the Institute.

7
THE TENTH PRESIDENT (1948–1959)

SHAPING AN ADMINISTRATIVE TEAM

I moved promptly after my inauguration to build my administrative team. Since I was not a scientist, I felt it essential to select an outstanding scientist or engineer to be the Institute's top academic officer and second in command, with the then unusual title of provost. One man, Julius A. Stratton, stood out as ideally qualified for this responsibility and happily accepted my invitation that he fill this post. He and his successors, Townes, Wiesner, Rosenblith, and Low, have given distinction to the title of provost.

Educated in both electrical engineering and physics, Dr. Stratton had been, as I have already reported, the director of the Research Laboratory of Electronics. He had published in 1941 a distinguished textbook, *Electromagnetic Theory*, demonstrated exceptional gifts as a teacher, served as an influential member of the Lewis Committee, and established a reputation as a scholar whose scope embraced the humanities as well as science. His doctor's degree had been awarded by Eidgenössische Technische Hoschshule in Switzerland, and at one stage of his graduate work abroad, he had studied French literature at Grenoble and Toulouse. During the war he had served as expert consultant to the secretary of war and in the Radiation Laboratory, during its concluding phase, as head of its Basic Research Division.

He was adept at applying solvents when discontents or dissatisfactions arose among his colleagues, and many went to him to find reassurance and resolution of their problems.

Urbane, humane, and prudent, he was deservedly admired and loved by both faculty and students. A gourmet, he also enjoyed adventure. Along with his friend Professor Will Allis, he once spent four weeks in the Equadorian rain forest to search for the headhunting Jivaros.

I had placed him on the winding stair to high places, for within two years he became vice president and provost; within seven years, chancellor of the Institute, and, during my absence in Washington to serve as science adviser to President Eisenhower, acting president of the Institute. With this record, and the unmistakable satisfactions he found in high administrative service, he was the logical candidate to become president of the Institute when I resigned, while still in Washington, to become chairman of the Corporation on my return to the Institute. On retiring as president, he went to New York as full-time chairman of the board of trustees of the Ford Foundation. On hearing of this Ford Foundation appointment, a friend said to him, "We trust you will keep your academic robes, because we do not like to think of you in your foundation garments."

Stratton was of inestimable help to me, and a greatly admired president of the Institute. His wife, Catherine, a woman of exceptional charm and ability, was to become a prime mover in the cultivation of a flourishing program in the arts at the Institute.

A PRIDE OF MIT DEANS
Prior to my assumption of the presidency I had participated, in 1945, with Dr. Compton in recruiting Professor Edwin R. Gilliland to serve as deputy dean of the School of Engineering during Dean Moreland's absence in Washington and Japan, and then Professor Thomas K. Sherwood, also from the Chemical Engineering Department, to become full-time dean of the School of Engineering in 1946 when Edward L. Moreland resigned to take the part-time post of executive vice president so that he could give time to his engineering firm. Moreland, Gilliland, and Sherwood were engineers of national distinction. Gilliland had won fame for his contributions to the synthetic rubber program during the war, and he and Sherwood were elected to membership in both the National Academy of Engineering and the National Academy of Sciences. As a neighbor in Wellesley I came to have close and memorable associations with Tom Sherwood. He was a blunt-speaking, frequently sardonic counselor to me when I was vice president and president. His admiration for Warren K. Lewis was unbounded, and to pay tribute to his great colleague, he edited a collection of anecdotes about Lewis entitled "A Dollar to a Doughnut." I once received a postcard from him while he was on an automobile trip through Germany. The postcard reported that he and Mrs. Sherwood had visited

the city of Wurzburg and were surprised to find a festival under way devoted to St. Kilian, who I understand is the saint who protects humans against lightning—a saint of special value to a college president! Tom Sherwood wrote on his postcard that he had inquired what this festival was all about and who St. Kilian was and added that he knew a Killian and was sure he was not a saint!

When Sherwood accepted the deanship of the School of Engineering in 1946, he asked me, then the Institute's freshly minted vice president, to give him a memorandum listing some of the problems—and opportunities—in the School of Engineering as I then saw them. With some bravura I responded with a score of items, but I was apprehensive that Tom would think I had all the answers. To my surprise, he accepted my diagnostic essay with appreciation and remarked that it was just what he needed.

Three years later I received from him, unrequested, an eight-page manuscript listing my 1946 items and after each a report on what he had done or decided not to do about them. I received this accounting with satisfaction, for it represented progress in the school under his leadership and indicated how the two of us had reinforced each other's judgments. It also provided me with reassurance that I was learning useful administrative techniques.

I have given an account of how Tom Cabot of the Corporation organized, unbeknown to me, an effort to keep me from accepting the presidency of another institution. As I found out later, Sherwood joined his predecessor, Dean Moreland, and Dean Harrison in encouraging Cabot to pursue his strategy. This I became aware of in a letter written to me by Sherwood when he became Professor Emeritus in 1969. "You have been a great friend for a long time," he wrote, "and I am proud of the friendship and of the confidence in me that you have often shown. More than any other, you are responsible for making MIT great. I'm glad I had the temerity to beat on K.T. not to let you go. . . ."

In 1952, after six years as dean of engineering, Professor Sherwood chose to return to his faculty post in the Department of

Chemical Engineering, and he was succeeded as dean by Admiral Edward L. Cochrane, who had been on leave from the Department of Naval Architecture while serving as maritime administrator and chairman of the Federal Maritime Board in Washington. I first came to know Admiral Cochrane when he was wartime head of the Navy's Bureau of Ships, and my immediate reaction was to seek ways to bring him to MIT at war's end. I reacted with the confidence of the proverbial down-Maine sailor who claimed that he could "tell a good ship by a single blow of the eye." On the appointment of Admiral Cochrane as vice president for industrial and governmental relations, we had the good fortune of gaining the acceptance of C. Richard Soderberg, head of the Department of Mechanical Engineering, to be dean of engineering. He brought rich experience in industry, in both the United States and Sweden. In all the offices that he held as a professor and administrator, he brought a quality of intellectual and moral force that was profoundly important in our academic community.

George R. Harrison had become dean of the School of Science in 1942, and he fortunately agreed to my request to continue in that post. He had come to MIT in 1930, shortly after Compton. When Compton persuaded John C. Slater, a theoretical physicist at Harvard, to head the MIT Physics Department, Slater promptly persuaded Harrison, then at Stanford but a former colleague at Harvard, to come to MIT to direct a research laboratory of experimental physics. The combination, one theoretical, one experimental, was ideal, and they proceeded with vigor to transform a service department into a thoroughbred science department. When the distinguished biologist Samuel C. Prescott retired as dean of the School of Science, Compton turned to Harrison to succeed him. It was a happy selection not only for physics but for the whole of the School of Science, which Harrison endowed with new depth and strength. He was compiler of the encyclopedic *MIT Wavelength Tables*, which today is still in demand by spectroscopists. As the American Philosophical Society was to say in its memoir, Harrison provided the conceptual leadership that brought the MIT School of Science "to its emi-

nent position among the world's foremost academic institutions." In an action long overdue, MIT in 1983 celebrated his
contributions by naming the pioneering Spectroscopy Laboratory he originally built the George Russell Harrison Spectroscopy Laboratory. He will be long remembered not only as an
able scientist but as an eloquent speaker, gifted writer, and wit.
As a horticulturist he cultivated a superb collection of orchids at
his homes in Belmont and later in Concord. He, along with
Moreland, Sherwood, and Burchard, were bulwarks of my administration.

John E. Burchard became dean of humanities on the retirement from this post of Robert Caldwell in 1948. Through an
arrangement worked out with him by Dr. Compton, Burchard
was in a holding pattern, following his war service, until Dean
Caldwell retired. During this interim he served brilliantly as
director of libraries.

In 1946 the office of dean of students became vacant, and I
joined Dr. Compton in the search for an appropriate candidate
to fill this difficult post. While living in Wellesley, my wife and I
had come to know as a neighbor an unusually attractive and
versatile minister, Everett M. Baker, then serving as executive
vice president of the American Unitarian Association. When I
mentioned to Liz our difficulties in finding the right man to be
dean of students, she ventured the brilliant suggestion that
Baker had exceptional qualifications for this post. I agreed and
presented his name to Dr. Compton. We both felt that a clergy-
man was an unconventional if not a risky candidate for the
deanship, but when Dr. Compton interviewed him, Baker's rare
qualities as a human being and his wide experience with young
people overcame all doubts. Baker had only recently accepted
the ministership of a church in Cleveland, but when invited to
come to MIT, he agreed with enthusiasm to undertake this new
career. He was on the job when I became president and winning
all with his "alacrity of spirit." What a memorably effective dean
of students he came to be! When in 1950 he died in an airplane
crash on the way home from a conference in India, the students
were deeply saddened and wanted to memorialize him in a

fitting way. This we did by naming the new dormitory, designed by the great Finnish architect Alvar Aalto, Baker House. Another expression of the widespread devotion in the MIT community to Dean Baker, both the man and his ideals, was the formation of the Everett Moore Baker Memorial Foundation with funds contributed primarily by students. This foundation makes annual awards for excellence in undergraduate teaching.

It was in the 1950s and the early 1960s that the evidence was clear that an unmistakable change was taking place in the attitude of students about their willingness to accept regulations or practices that affected their living conditions in dormitories. It was my experience that the coming of the veterans in the postwar period had initiated these changes in student attitudes. The opposition to parietal rules was inevitably growing, as Dean Baker had repeatedly reported. As this opposition became clear, the first intention of college administrators, including myself, was to oppose relaxation of such restrictions as entertainment of women in men's dormitory rooms or other activities that originally had prompted parietal rules. To maintain Victorian regulations and standards, it soon became clear, was as futile as King Canute's effort to hold back the ocean tides.

When parietal rules were ultimately liberalized through participatory efforts by administrative officers, faculties, and students acting with maturity and mutual confidence, I came to believe that liberalization has led to a better social environment in our universities.

Recently one of the faculty residents spent the time of day with me, telling me with enthusiasm and perception his observation of the temper and attitude of students he encountered. He spoke of their self-sufficiency. When I asked him whether during the summer months there would be many students still living in the residence, he spoke of how many of them seemed to make the dormitory their home for the summer. They desired to be independent and to do their own thing, he explained. It could hardly be said that they were alienated from their parents, but rather that they relished freedom to form their own living environment. Some of this mood observable in today's generation of students probably had roots in the sixties, but one can only admire their willingness to accept the somewhat limited accommodations of a university as a pleasant way to pursue further studies or to live a life of their own. Another factor has been the growing openness of our universities and the firm acceptance of equality through affirmative action.

In 1950 the dean of the School of Architecture and Planning, William Wurster, could no longer resist the pull of his native state, California, and an invitation from the University of California to be dean of its School of Architecture. Against these attractions we could not hold him at MIT. In the short span of six years he had rejuvenated our Department of Architecture, which had gone stale after Dean William Emerson's retirement. He achieved this great improvement even though he dropped from the curriculum subjects on the history of architecture, which distressed a number of us.

During his tenure as dean I found myself engaged in frequent dialogues with him about architecture and the related arts. These discussions occasionally turned into debates, and Wurster's views could be implacable when he was making suggestions about our selection of architects or the design and location of buildings. When infrequently he was overruled, he accepted the decision without pouting.

Wurster was a strong advocate of the contemporary style in architecture, but despite a brief experience with Gropius, he was too independently minded to have become a full-fledged disciple of this founder of the Bauhaus.

My architectural values were sharpened by these strenuous debates, but I came to enjoy and welcome the fresh and astringent views he brought to our community. I found full agreement too with his admiration for Professor Lawrence Anderson, whom he repeatedly described as the best teacher of design in the country. I welcomed his insistence that MIT bring into our community such fresh influences as that of Alvar Aalto and others who were not ready to succumb to the Bauhaus mystique in architecture. As I recount elsewhere, it was Aalto who designed one of our most admired buildings, the student residence Baker House.

In 1969 Bill wrote me a moving letter expressing his overwhelming sadness in the death of Horace Ford. "That he chose me as his confidant was one of the most important things in my life. I admired and loved him more than any other person." And then Bill went on to write that "the greatest thing of all was his quick and firm action to keep you at MIT and quickly to dispel the notion that you could never be president of MIT, that you could not progress above the highest status of an executive position. . . . It has been my good fortune to serve under two genius executives: the six years with you and ten years with Clark Kerr. My job at California stemmed directly from [MIT's] decision to have me as Dean of Architecture at MIT." I quote these hyperbolic statements with embarrassment, but they bespeak the generosity of a colleague I admired and loved.

In searching for a successor to Dean Wurster, I consulted with the architecture faculty at MIT and I had assistance from the beloved William Emerson. He assembled for me a majority of members of the executive committee of the American Institute of Architects, and I received from this advisory group an attractive list of prospects. Several times the name of Pietro Belluschi was proposed but usually with the warning that he was unobtainable because of his large and growing practice in Portland, Oregon.

A VISIT WITH FRANK LLOYD WRIGHT

While the search continued, I planned a trip in 1950 to southern California for alumni meetings, and it occurred to me that Frank Lloyd Wright, the great architect, perhaps the greatest of all American architects of his time, might have helpful suggestions. I was fully aware that he was reputed to have a vain and difficult personality, but anyway I wrote to ask if I could stop to see him at his winter home and studio in Paradise Valley, near Scottsdale, Arizona. To my delighted surprise I received back a cordial note indicating that he would see me. So on our way to California my wife and I stopped at Phoenix, and Wright sent a car chauffered by one of his apprentices to take us from our inn to the fabulous Taliesin West, which Eric Mendelsohn once poetically described as his "Great Fugue. A desert, a carpet, a tented camp, prehistory and the twentieth century" where "a wave from the endless desert breaks on the shore of his life. . . ."

When we arrived, the apprentice showed us around this famous place, and later Wright appeared, having dramatically positioned himself on a terrace with his profile against the sky and his great cape gracefully rippling in the wind. With courtly dignity he warmly greeted us, and we were shown around by the master himself. He then invited us to come to dinner the next evening so that we might have a leisurely discussion. We of course accepted, and he again offered to send a car. That memorable evening we dined with him, his wife Olgivanna, and his daughter just returned from Paris, where she at one time studied under the philosopher Georges Gurdjieff. After dinner, served by his apprentices (students and assistants studying under his tutelage), we repaired to the living room, one of the loveliest interiors I had seen, and we had a lively discussion of architecture and architectural education. Since I had known of Wright's relationship with Louis Sullivan, whom he called "master," I recalled that Boston-born Sullivan had attended MIT in 1872 for a brief period. When he asked about our departing dean, I stressed the merits of William Wurster. He pretended at first never to have heard of him but finally he remembered. "Ah," said Wright, "he is the architect of that shed architecture in California." He did speak knowledgeably of Wurster's wife, Catherine Bauer, an expert on housing celebrated by Lewis Mumford in his memoir, *My Works and Days*. When we finally got around to discussing a replacement for Wurster, the inference of his remarks was that he knew of no one worthy of being a dean of architecture. He did venture a couple of suggestions.

After these observations Wright excused himself, saying that he retired early and had arranged for us a showing of a recently received Russian movie which he thought would be interesting.

It was an experience to remember, this exposure to the "fire and splendor" of the great master, but we also came away surprised at the diffident, even obsequious, attitude of his apprentices. They seemed quite different from the frequently brash architectural students we knew at home.

There was nothing overbearing about the Wright we saw. He had been kind and hospitable to us, and we felt that our experience with him had been rare indeed since we had heard the many stories about his arrogance, bitterness, and ego. One of these stories recounts an incident, probably apocryphal, when he was called as a witness in a trial. While on the witness stand, he was asked if he were indeed the world's greatest architect. "I am," he said. Later his wife chided him for immodesty. "But I was under oath," he explained.

I later went to Detroit to visit with Eliel Saarinen at the Cranbrook Foundation. He had come to the United States in 1923 from Finland to establish his residence, became associated with the complex of institutions that bore the overall name of Cranbrook, designed some of its elegant buildings, and became head of the Cranbrook Academy of Art. He had won great distinction as a practicing architect not only for buildings he had designed in Finland, such as the railway station in Helsinki, but for his second prize in the Chicago *Tribune* Tower competition, a design that came to be appraised as a major contribution to American architecture, even though it was never built. Saarinen joined forces with his son Eero to practice architecture.

I recall this pleasant visit with Eliel and his helpfulness in giving me names of various people whom he thought we should consider for the MIT deanship. I recall too the sumptuous quarters, his own design, which he occupied at the Cranbrook Academy of Art. I was glad when MIT engaged Eero to do its Kresge Auditorium and Chapel.

I moved on in my search for a dean and finally decided that I would invite Belluschi to visit MIT. He came on with his wife, and to my surprise and almost everyone else's who knew about him, he accepted with alacrity the Institute's offer of the deanship. He proved to be a somewhat indifferent administrator, but he brought to the school good taste and high standards. His poetical qualities, the prestige of the deanship, and his talents as a designer brought him additional fame, and when he retired to return to the practice of architecture, he was much sought after. I loved him for his generosity in designing for Liz and me an addition to our old country house in New Hampshire while at the same time he was serving as the designer consultant or codesigner of great buildings such as the monumental Catholic Cathedral in San Francisco, the Julliard School in Lincoln Center, and a host of other distinguished buildings. He has won special fame for the many beautiful churches he has designed.

This group of deans brought exceptional strength to my administration. During their tenure and with their talents they endowed the rank of dean with heightened prestige. Without any semblance of self-serving they provided me with the administrative companionship and loyal support I needed.

I include in this goodly company, to which I owed so much, those who held several successive portfolios and finally became vice presidents for industrial and governmental relations, Admiral Edward Cochrane and General James McCormack, who also came to the Institute at my invitation after distinguished military service. Admiral Cochrane had been chief of the Bureau of Ships during the war and thus with decisive success directed the building of our World War II Navy. General McCormack, after graduating from West Point, was a Rhodes scholar. Those who came under his charismatic spell, and this included associates in major civic responsibilities in Boston, found him a general for all seasons. In his book, *Change, Hope and the Bomb* (1963), David Lilienthal gives a graphic description of how General McCormack delivered to him in 1949 the intelligence that the Soviets had set off an atomic explosion. McCormack was then an active Brigadier General and was serving as Director of the Division of Military Applications of the U.S. Atomic Energy Commission, and in this role it fell to him to deliver the grim news that the United States no longer had a monopoly of the A-bomb. As McCormack smilingly recalled upon delivering his message, in ancient times a messenger bearing bad news was usually executed. Lilienthal also notes how the AEC had been conducting round-the-clock flights of planes equipped with air filters designed to detect an atomic explosion. He notes that this procedure was first proposed by Conant of Harvard and Bush of MIT.

Military officers do not always adjust easily to the academic environment or the academic environment to them, but each of these sensitive, gifted officers came to enjoy working at MIT and to command Institute-wide admiration for their administrative skills and personal qualities.

A NEW TREASURER

Horace Ford, the treasurer of the Institute, reached retirement age (sixty-five) in 1950. I have already spoken of his key role in the Institute's administration and how his great gifts carried him beyond the narrow boundaries of finance. Since I realized my need for his wisdom, I asked him to stay on part-time for five years as a consultant to the president and for a brief period, acting director of the Division of Defense Laboratories, which had among its responsibilities the Lincoln Laboratory.

Among those in the Radiation Laboratory we invited to cast their lots with the Institute was the associate head of the laboratory's office of business administration, Joseph J. Snyder, who had come to the laboratory from the investment management firm associated with the financial interests of Edwin S. Webster, Sr., of Stone & Webster. Horace and I had gained a very favorable impression of him during the war, and at Horace's request I paved the way for Horace to invite Joe to be assistant treasurer, a new office. He won the complete confidence of Treasurer Ford, and on Horace's recommendation, I asked him to succeed Horace as treasurer when Horace retired. It was Joe Snyder who, with the policy guidance of the Corporation's Investment Committee, undertook the direct management of the Institute's portfolio, which until then had been routinely, if safely, managed by a trust company. With my support he initiated the accumulation of two financial reserves: first, the Investment Income Equalization Reserve, which was designed to even out the distribution of investment funds to the operating budget of the Institute, and next, the Research Fund, which sets aside from government overhead on research contracts an appropriate amount for the use of Institute facilities. In still another way he made an important contribution to the building of our endowment funds by his discriminating judgment in allotting unrestricted gifts to specific endowment funds and reserves. I recall with much pleasure the agreeable meetings which brought us together to debate the best allocation of these unrestricted funds.

In 1969 the president of the Ford Foundation, McGeorge Bundy, made public a report that included the suggestion that some portion of an institution's capital appreciation could be applied to current operating expenses. Mr. Snyder was not persuaded that this was an appropriate use of capital gains for the Institute; he adhered to the MIT policy adopted in the 1950s to build the funds of MIT and, through this building of resources, steadily to add to the financial strength of the Institute.

The gifted administrators I have named gave to my presidency one of the special distinctions it was to achieve. They proved that my taste in people and that of Dr. Stratton, who joined in their selection, was an important qualification for academic administration.

STRUCTURE, COORDINATION, AND MANAGEMENT

When Harvard, in June 1950, a year after my inauguration, bestowed on me its honorary degree, I was nonplussed but encouraged by the accompanying generous citation: "A genius in administration whose talents serve a pre-eminent institution; we are grateful for his emphasis on close cooperation between the two Cambridge communities of scholars." As I view my performance, my most important organizational achievement was the creation of a new management unit, the Academic Council,[1] and shaping it into an effective advisory body for policy and strategy. The council core as I recommended it to the Executive Committee included the provost or chancellor as vice chairman, the executive vice president, dean of students, the chairman of the faculty, the deans of the schools, the treasurer, and myself, as chairman. Later the vice president for industrial and governmental relations was added.

The council functioned to aid the president in long-range policymaking and to provide coherent and responsible administrative planning, decision making, and leadership sensitive to the welfare of each part of the institution and to its prosperity as a whole. When the budget pie was to be cut up to allot funds to schools and departments, the council served as a "committee of the whole," and because it consisted of the senior educational officers, including all the school deans, no part of the Institute could reasonably feel unrepresented. In dealing with appointments, promotions, and budget, we would at times witness the dean of one school arguing in behalf of recommendations originating in another school. Since all members had a voice in the strategic decisions reached, the Institute stayed remarkably free of the tensions that arise when one part of an institution becomes suspicious that another part is getting more than its fair slice of the available budget pie. The presence of the council also provided a representative amalgam of advice to the president and the Corporation while encouraging Institute-wide confidence in the decision-making process. In its weekly meetings the council dealt mainly with matters of strategy, leaving the administrative officers free to make tactical decisions on their own. One of the most remarked aspects of the Institute's administration, including my office, was its ability to act quickly and not get bogged down by indecision. In reminiscing recently about this postwar administration, former President Wiesner has spoken about the high accessibility of administrative officers and their ready reception, without red tape, of new-minted proposals from faculty members.

The debates in the council were sometimes intense but almost never bitter. Some deans were more persuasive and came better prepared than others, but each could speak his piece and did in the presence of the president, who had the responsibility of taking the appointment and budget decisions of the council to the Executive Committee of the Corporation for its review and controlling decisions. On the rare occasions when the council was split, it was fully accepted that the president had the responsibility to decide, but splits were rare and decisions usually by consensus. Some of the best experiences of my presidency occurred when vexing policy controversies arising outside the council found resolution in council debate. Its evaluations of recommendations for faculty appointments, for promotions, and tenure were searching, with each member of the council acting for the good of the Institute as a whole rather than as the parochial pleader for his part of the institution.

I had inherited another more inclusive group called the *Administrative* Council, which included nonacademic officers along with the membership of the *Academic* Council. Before this group came matters such as the management of student housing, campus planning, patent policy, the program of the Division of Industrial Cooperation (or sponsored projects), industrial and governmental relations, the business management of the Institute, and many other nonacademic items.

It was in this council, which the president chaired, that far-reaching decisions were ratified to locate in the future all student housing, playing fields, and other nonacademic facilities on the land west of Massachusetts Avenue and to reserve the land east of it mainly for academic and research activities. Concepts originating in this council led to construction of Westgate, the colony of temporary houses for married student veterans. The Administrative Council also moved to support the building of 100 Memorial Drive to provide more staff housing near MIT. This apartment house, designed by a consortium of five professors in our Department of Architecture—Robert Kennedy, Carl Koch, Vernon DeMars, Ralph Rapson, and William Brown— represented then-new design concepts, such as John Burchard and Albert Bush-Brown noted in *The Architecture of America: A Social and Cultural History:* "Apartments were entered from a corridor on every third floor from which vestibules and private stairs led to upper or lower apartments. The skip-floor elevator system reduced corridor space, provided cross-ventilation to apartments, and enabled them to have large living rooms with glass walls and large balconies overlooking the . . . river. . . . It was one of the few modern buildings with gaiety."[2]

But for a brief interlude, my wife and I have lived in this

apartment since leaving the President's House in 1959. The convenient location and appointments have provided us with a happy home.

When 100 Memorial Drive was built, it included an elegant penthouse on the thirteenth floor which has served as the official residence of the chairmen of the Corporation. The Comptons, Killians, Strattons, and Johnsons have all lived there and on retirement found suitable apartments in other parts of the house. Some wag has remarked that 100 Memorial Drive is a ghetto for retired MIT presidents, but we have all lived there comfortably and proudly.

A third coordinating group, the Faculty Council, which President Compton had effectively used, included department heads and directors of interdisciplinary and sponsored mission-oriented laboratories such as the Lincoln Laboratory and the Research Laboratory of Electronics.

To provide a unified administrative organization, a new post of director of the Office of Sponsored Research (now the Office of Sponsored Programs) was established.

As I look back on the structural arrangements put into place in the immediate postwar years, I see more clearly than ever the advantages of the multidivisional aspects of the off-campus Lincoln and, later, Instrumentation Laboratories as well as the academically integrated interdisciplinary laboratories. With administrative oversight by officers at the level of the Institute provost or vice presidency, each a member of the three councils, and with contractual and financial matters handled by the Division of Industrial Cooperation, reasonably good coordination and communication for these laboratory components were possible. As I have noted, the off-campus Lincoln and Instrumentation Laboratories provided an appropriate environment for the conduct of classified research and enabled the Institute after the war to begin the exclusion of all secret projects from its campus.

These councils and organizational arrangements have endured and in 1984 continue to be important in the administration of the Institute. In May 1979 the Institute's late vice president for research, Thomas F. Jones, long after my retirement, told the House Subcommittee on Science, Research and Technology of the Committee on Science and Technology:

One of the big differences between MIT and most other institutions is the way MIT guards itself against hang-ups which can become blinders. Rules, when they get in the way, are reexamined and reconstituted or waived for the purpose of achieving objectives that make sense. This is almost impossible in most schools. A state school will go into a fit of consternation when a rule is waived or violated. It sets a bad precedent, they say.

Dr. Jones explained that he was at MIT for his third time: "I resigned tenure in 1958 to run the Electrical Engineering School at Purdue University and went from there to the University of South Carolina as president. I have seen education from many points of view, and I have to give MIT top marks."

During his presidency Dr. Compton initiated the custom of bringing young MIT graduates into the office, each to serve as administrative assistant. In 1946 Malcolm Kispert, a graduate of our Department of Aeronautical Engineering, following his wartime Navy service, came into the office as administrative assistant, and when I became president, did yeoman work in handling the Institute budget and the minutes of the Executive Committee. Robert M. Kimball had come in 1943 and was to move on to hold a series of administrative posts. Each of these young men was to provide staff support to the Academic Council. Just before Dr. Compton resigned as president, he had called in Henry Loomis, a Harvard alumnus and son of extraordinary businessman-physicist Alfred Loomis, to serve a period as his assistant. Loomis continued with me for a brief term, moved on to accept administrative posts with the Research and Development Board and the U.S. Information Agency and then for a period was Deputy Commissioner of Education. When I went to Washington to serve Eisenhower, he took a short leave from the U.S. Information Agency to help me organize my office as special assistant to the President for Science and Technology. Later we were to come together again when I was chairman of the board of the Corporation for Public Broadcasting and he, the president.

Additional faculty members were rapidly recruited in the decade following the war, and this made it desirable to make adjustments in rules governing promotions, the award of tenure, and retirements in order to maintain an optimum "staff flow" from the lowest to the highest rank. Each year an analysis of faculty demographics was prepared and efforts were made to provide appointment opportunities to bring young people onto the faculty and to prevent a pileup in the upper age ranges. Federal funds were becoming available for new research projects, some of limited term, and this too made it prudent to avoid making permanent appointments for short-term projects. In managing staff flow, the number granted permanent tenure was carefully controlled. Not only was this a prudent budget policy, but it also resulted in setting higher standards for the selection of those awarded permanent tenure.

I must add that unanticipated increases in federal funds for research in the late forties and on into the fifties brought staff increases that overran these carefully crafted policies for the management of staff flow. The resulting increase in the permanent tenure rank led to a concentration of retirements decades later.

President Conant at Harvard had used ad hoc committees, with non-Harvard members, to advise on the selection of scholars for permanent tenure appointments. Occasionally we too used this method, believing, as did Conant, President A. Lawrence Lowell's dictum that the "surest way to ruin a university faculty is to fill it with good men" rather than the best. We found also that careful analyses of staff flow helped to prevent maldistribution among the several ranks.

These circumstances called for numerous revisions in appointment policies, and the administration sought to achieve these modifications with the full knowledge and understanding of staff. Fortunately, President Compton prior to the war had put in place a standing committee—the Staff-Administration Committee—to foster free discussion of the relationships between administration and staff. This committee, usually composed of seven officers of instruction selected by the faculty and instructing staff and seven officers of administration appointed by the president, was to prove enormously useful in the consideration of modifications in personnel policy; in fact a number of the changes affecting rules for permanent tenure decisions, for staff flow, and for retirement policy were to originate in the staff part of this Staff-Administration Committee.[3] In consequence it was possible to make needed changes in personnel policies by joint action and not by fiat. For example, the rules governing decisions on permanent tenure were changed to require consideration of the age as well as the term of service of candidates, an arrangement that departed from the national pattern recommended by the American Association of University Professors. In circumstances peculiar to MIT as it grew rapidly in staff size, this new rule helped by opening more gates for bringing in young professors.

In the period of the early 1950s the MIT administration and faculty gave extended consideration to the professional responsibilities of faculty members and their obligations as members of the Institute faculty. During Dr. Compton's presidency similar attention had been given to the consulting and other outside activities of members of the Institute's staff, and Dr. Compton with great skill succeeded in greatly diminishing any "potboiling" research undertaken by the faculty that made no contribution to their professional growth. But there was general agreement that participation in outside activities needed to be regularly reviewed and the statements of policy in our *Policies and Procedures* pamphlet kept up to date and in accord with the highest ideals of academic professional research.

POLICIES FOR PATENT MANAGEMENT
AND CONSULTING
In 1953 I appointed a committee under the chairmanship of Professor Soderberg to review policies on consulting practices and the management of patents.

In a school of engineering effective teaching in all its aspects can flourish only when fed by a continuous, active contact with research and with the realities of our industrial, economic, and social life. The Soderberg committee reasserted that these activities are a necessary and desirable part of the intellectual life of MIT but that some measure of control is essential. Like all problems of self-government, such control is best obtained by mutual agreement between the staff and the administration on well-defined canons of ethics.

The committee, in commenting on a strong statement in the published brochure *Policies and Procedures,* added its own comment that for a full-time staff member the first and foremost loyalty is to the Institute and no interpretation of tenure should be stretched beyond the point where this prime loyalty has ceased to exist. It added that there must prevail a requirement that staff members should keep their department heads informed at all times of their outside activities so that these activities could be judged in the light of whether or not they were educational within the definitions of the *Policies and Procedures* pamphlet. The committee urged that the Institute strive to keep its salaries sufficiently high so that pressure for additional income does not become the dominant reason for undertaking extracurricular activities. It further urged that there should be effective means of sympathetic administration whereby a staff member can seek advice long before the issues have grown beyond the possibility of proper correction. The position of tenure, the committee concluded, must be open to review as soon as the outside activities reach a point where the staff member can give only part-time attention to his or her duties at the Institute.

This Soderberg report was well received by the faculty. It bore the imprint of Dick Soderberg, who was held in high esteem throughout the Institute and who embodied in his own career the highest professional standards. It was a reaffirmation and refinement of principles adopted during the Compton administration to discourage any abuses of consulting. Such codification of policies and procedures governing consulting and relationships with outside industry stands side by side with policies and procedures for the handling of inventions made by members of the Institute's staff and the management of any resulting patents and the licensing governing their use. As early as 1932 the faculty and Corporation of the Institute approved a statement of patent and copyright policies and procedures that had resulted from a careful study by Vannevar Bush. This codification of patent policy had the basic aim of promoting the progress of science and the useful arts by utilizing the benefits of the established patent system. It accepted the view that patents provide for the development and appropriate utilization of discoveries and inventions, and it sought to ensure that inventions in which the Institute has an equity would be utilized in a manner consistent with the public interest. The basic concept was that inventions resulting from MIT research should not be suppressed but should be made available to industry and the public on a reasonable and effective basis that at the same time provided adequate recognition and compensation for the inventors. The original patent policy adopted in 1932 has been subsequently modified and refined, in accord with the growth of government-sponsored research and of research with increased industrial potential such as that now occurring in the field of biotechnology.

The forehandedness of the Institute in formulating these policies governing faculty relationships with industry and the management of patents has served the Institute well.[4] But recently the great achievements flowing out of research on DNA and the entire field of biotechnology have prompted widespread debate and review of how universities can appropriately handle research results of great importance to industry, to themselves, and to the public.

It is of the utmost importance that these issues be handled in a way that ensures no restrictions in communication among scholars and no inappropriate institutional involvements in commercial activities. The Institute's long experience in handling patents and their licensing and in codifying its policies relating to faculty involvement in industry has been of enormous help as it, along with other institutions, has faced the new and dramatic issues arising in the rapid translation of biotechnology research results into potential industrial use.

The wise mangement of universities' relationships to industry and commerce comes at a time when there appears to be a recurrence of attacks on universities by those whose ideology partakes of some of the views expressed in Upton Sinclair's 1923 mudslinging book, *Goose-Step: A Study of American Education.* In 1968 James Ridgeway published a book, *The Closed Corporation: American Universities in Crisis,* in which he argued that corporations were dominating the policies of universities. Surprisingly no less a radical than Thorstein Veblen countered Sinclair by asserting that such critics of the university wanted golden eggs but no goose.

I think it important to remember that these new relationships with commercial enterprises were developed in the postwar period when a spirit of entrepreneurship appeared among the faculties and graduate students of MIT and other institutions dealing with high technology. Out of research and teaching at MIT flowed a large number of graduates and ideas that contributed to the spectacular growth of the electronics industry in Massachusetts. Somehow this period when adventuresome graduate students and young alumni attracted the support of venture capital on the part of equally adventuresome financial institutions was pivotal. Massachusetts was helped to regain some of its past industrial glory. And there was no serious encroachment on the openness and integrity of our academic environment. The systematic attention given within the Institute by such studies as the Soderberg report contributed to an orderly handling of our relationships with commercial undertakings.

Under the spectacular pressures created by commercial undertakings based on university research in the broad field of biotechnology, we have witnessed in the 1980s a renewed national debate on how the universities should deal with the obvious opportunities for commercialization of research results in this field where the period between discovery and application seems so short and the potential for profiit so great.

Once again I am impressed by the way that university presidents and their associates have come together to discuss guidelines that could serve the universities in adhering to policies and procedures that represent the highest ideals of teaching and research. I find much to support and celebrate in the wisdom that has emerged from these discussions to ensure practices consistent with essential academic values. How much better they have been handled than issues arising in the commercial conduct of big-time, intercollegiate athletics! I am also proud that the long-evolving patent policies of MIT going back to the early 1930s are now being adopted by many institutions in the management of patents and faculty involvements in industry arising from university inventions. I am equally proud that the MIT of the 1980s can devise new policies and procedures that are fully in accord with the highest ethical standards and commitments to openness and freedom that must mark the true university.

In total effect these repeated self-studies and policy formulations can give powerful expression to the ethical and moral responsibilities of a university. They today stand the Institute in good stead when temptations abound to enter into commercial or governmental arrangements that occasionally tempt institutions to accept Faustian bargains in the desperate search for funds.

Now that the federal government is less free with funds so important to the research universities and their students, benign support by business and industry becomes ever more necessary. I know from experience that this support can be obtained and used without violating the freedom and independence of the universities and the high ideals society has assigned to academe.

If educational institutions cannot obtain adequate support for the advancement of knowledge and its diffusion from either government or industry, where in this society of ours can they find the support to do their rightful job?

The process of consultation between faculty representatives and administration which I have described was decisively helpful to me as it has been to my presidential successors. I have described here another example of how goodwill and interplay can be fostered in a university environment.

An example of a failure on my part to consult with faculty representatives was my premature announcement on January 4, 1956, at a dinner in New York, of the establishment of a School for Advanced Study as an "integral part of MIT's academic organization." The plan for this school had originated in the fertile mind of Professor Martin Buerger, then chairman of the faculty. I accepted his proposal with enthusiasm, but there was no adequate discussion of it in appropriate faculty committees before I reported the plan in a setting that prompted front-page stories in New York. Sensitive faculty members quite understandably reacted prematurely with alarm and made clear their reproof and objection, and not a single administrative associate stepped forward to support the proposal and defend the president. Thus did a good idea come to grief, and I dropped it like a hot potato. I found myself painfully illustrating how a hole at the center can occur. Professor Buerger and I had a good concept, but my announcement of it gained no support from administrative or faculty colleagues, leaving both of us dangling in the breeze.

This mistake and a few others I made in the hasty, onerous preparation of so many speeches led me later to a wry appreciation of historian James Froude's warning witticism that the "excitement of perpetual speech-making is fatal to the exercise of the highest powers." But in general I was loyal to my conviction that no new programs or buildings large in costs should be undertaken, however innovative, without the knowledge and advice of appropriate faculty groups.

In reporting on the achievements of the Lewis Committee, I spoke of its being an example of what Churchill once called "exalted brooding" to deal with problems in the future. One of my trademarks as an administrator was the repeated use of this technique in solving problems, mobilizing expert judgment, and encouraging innovation. I could not have achieved desirable goals during my presidency without arrangements to make available the focused wisdom, creative ideas, or criticisms of able colleagues.

One example was provided by the work of the Faculty Committee on Academic Responsibility in dealing with Communist issues in the early 1950s; another, the committee chaired by Gordon Brown on enrollment including the internal distribution of students among the several fields of study and the overall size of the undergraduate student body.

During my administration we initiated a series of out-of-town meetings of the Academic Council plus selected faculty members, most of which were at the Andover Inn in the shadow of the Phillips Andover Academy. Each of these weekend meetings usually tackled a major policy topic, with different discussion leaders, frequently a dean, the chairman of the faculty, or even the president. With good food and relaxed fellowship and much sociability, they accomplished much, contributing to high morale and collegial decisions.

When I went to Washington as science adviser to President Eisenhower, my experience with panels for exalted brooding led me to institute the panel system of the President's Science Advisory Committee. PSAC alone, limited as it was to eighteen members, could not have mobilized the expertness and talent to master the many technical and policy problems on its agenda. To do so adequately, we sought the best-qualified specialists in the nation to form panels, each to address a specialized problem or study and each with a membership qualified to do so. In this different environment the panel system I had called into service at MIT proved to be enormously helpful.

I once saw in the *New Yorker* a cartoon by Charles Adams showing a committee on a pedestal and beneath the cartoon was the ironic one liner: "There are no great men, my boy, only great committees." I hasten to add that the kinds of panels or committees I have been talking about were not administrative groups, for committees are rarely successful as managers. In speaking once about the administrative committee that administered MIT during the interregnum (1920–1923) between President Richard

Maclaurin's death and the inauguration of President Samuel Stratton, Eric Hodgins vouchsafed the comment "The divinity that doth head a committee is not much."

THE FACULTY AS THE PRIME SOURCE OF EDUCATIONAL POLICY

The administrative officers I have listed and the councils I have described constitute only one part, and perhaps the lesser part, of MIT's policymaking organization. Of course educational policy and educational decision making have always vested in the faculty, which at MIT has evolved a complex of arrangements to coordinate or exercise faculty business. At the apex of this complex is an undivided single faculty, presided over by the president in collaboration with a chairman of the faculty selected by the faculty. Among universities as large as MIT which prepare for the professions, I know of only a few—Princeton University, for example—that have preserved a single faculty structure, undivided into schools and unitary for both undergraduate and graduate studies.[5] In my judgment this unified faculty gives MIT an exceptional coherence and overall interdisciplinary character. Both science and engineering gain from their close association with each other and with the humanities and social sciences. As a result of the undivided structure of the Institute and of its unified faculty, a freshman candidate for admission applies to MIT and not to one of its schools or courses. At present he has the whole institution before him.

This unity which gives MIT a special quality and which I affirmed in the decade of my presidency was reaffirmed quite independently by President Gray in a report to the Corporation in March 1983, in talking about undergraduate education. He noted: "We do not have a separate faculty of engineering, a faculty of management, a faculty of arts and sciences. We have a single faculty with a single set of faculty committees, a chairman of the whole faculty, a committee on educational policy which has representation from all the schools and an impressive commitment of faculty energy and effort to undergraduate education." And then, in continuing his stress on the Institute's commitment to undergraduate education, he emphasized "the seamless character of the academic environment; that is, while there are twenty-three different departments, any student at MIT may take any subject for which he or she is reasonably prepared. The opportunities for changing majors, for majoring in more than one field, for taking courses outside of one's field, are rich."

MIT's single faculty is organized into some fourteen committees, each manned to carry on some specialized aspect of the faculty's work. Two committees are of very special importance—the Committee on Educational Policy and the Committee on Graduate School Policy. The first sets forth overall educational policy, sponsors educational experiments, and coordinates much of the faculty's business. The chairman of the faculty is its ex officio chairman. Recommendations made by the Lewis Committee have resulted in better arrangements for consistent faculty attention to educational policy, notably for undergraduate education.

The Committee on Graduate School Policy, as approved by the faculty, establishes admissions requirements, scholastic standards, and requirements for advanced degrees. It also grants approval of new courses of instruction at the graduate level. It reports to the faculty recommendations on policy matters requiring faculty action and recommendations for the award of advanced degrees.

I stress the powers of the faculty while believing strongly in the essential leadership role of the president and his administrative associates. Both faculty and administration must recognize their separate spheres of responsibility, but the institution depends greatly on a president who does more than coordinate and arbitrate. As President Julius Stratton once said, "he must himself be prepared to take positions on matters of eductional import." In looking back at the history of the Institute, one cannot escape the conclusion that great presidents have been at the helm during the Institute's great periods. This memoir of mine is testimony to the achievements, pre-World War II, of the Walker, Maclaurin, and Compton presidencies, with a strong faculty responding to strong presidential leadership.

In January 1970 Professor Edward Shils published an essay entitled "The Hole in the Centre: University Government in the United States," in which he expressed strong views about the unpreparedness of the machinery of university government, particularly during the period of student unrest:

The failure of American university teachers to develop the indispensable institutional structure between the president and the deans on the one side and the department on the other is the product of parochial ignorance, specialist self-preoccupation, and neglect. . . . Against the chorus of universal praise which has recently been given to the departmental system, it is necessary to speak out emphatically for the existence of an institutional counterweight of a strong president and a coherent and responsible senate or council . . . which would continuously represent the interests of the whole.[6]

Let me recall some examples where there were no holes in the center:

We had an able group in psychology, largely of the Gestalt variety and headed by a distinguished professor, Kurt Lewin. Against opposition, I made the hard administrative decision that as a result of the death of Lewin and a shortage of funds, this program should not be continued, a decision not happily received by a number of my colleagues who were involved.

The next occurred when the Hayden Library was being planned. Both William Wurster, dean of architecture, and John Burchard, dean of humanities, advocated facing this building with red brick instead of limestone. This I opposed and was subsequently supported by the Corporation.

Finally, Dean Wurster, as architectural adviser to the Executive Committee, strongly opposed locating any building in the space between the main buildings and the parallel dormitories. He fought hard to veto the placement of the Dorrance Laboratory in this area, and I had unhappily to reject his advice.

No scars were left from these administrative decisions.

I believe that MIT, by Corporation and faculty action, has so arranged its machinery as to represent continuously the interests of the whole. As I have said, the Academic Council includes all deans. Reporting to the school deans are the department heads. These department heads are not drawn in rotation from senior professors in the departments but serve as administrative officers, some with indefinite terms, some with five-year terms. They exercise great power. Since some MIT departments are larger than many independent colleges, the heads of these departments, aided by assistants or deputies, carry very major administrative responsibilities.

With the dean of the school serving as chairman, the department heads are drawn together to discuss common problems in a school council, an effective arrangement which was brought into action during the Julius Stratton administration. In talking recently with Professor Robert Mann of the Department of Mechanical Engineering, I induced him to freewheel a bit on what he felt to be the factors that make MIT work. His first observation was that MIT has relied on its traditional departments and has resisted rushing to establish new ones. It has relied more on the permeability and flexibility of the old-line departments, on taking a rib from an existing department, or on the establishment of interdepartmental centers.

This has meant that the traditional departments have occupied a secure and confident place in the faculty structure and have functioned as key elements in the achievement of a strong faculty. With large and talented peer faculty groups these foundation departments are in a position to insist on the continued quality of the faculty. Departments also provide the homes and professional identity for members of the faculty who spend part-time away from their departments by carrying on their teaching and research in the various centers and research projects. The department determines their salaries and their promotions and provides a professional sense of home and social life. As Professor Mann pointed out, most established departments have permeable boundaries that enable faculty and students to draw on the resources of more than a single department and that permit ideas to flow freely across boundaries.

In exercising their role as standard setters for professional performance, departments permit their members to embark on almost any program so long as they do it well and so long as they carry their share of departmental responsibilities. "A department," said Professor Mann, "never tells a professor that he shouldn't do something because 'That isn't done in this department.' "

The permeability of our departments and their protection of intellectual standards have been fundamental to the Institute's maintenance of a single faculty unified by a high mobility of ideas across all boundaries. Sometimes strong departments create challenges and frustrations for the deans of their schools who seek to fulfill their responsibilities for strong leadership. Even when the school councils work well, I must acknowledge that there have been departments that have resisted innovation and clung to outmoded courses of instruction. In an insightful letter to me written after his retirement, former Dean of Engineering Soderberg recognized the danger of what Shils calls "the hole in the centre":

Clearest in my memories are the years of service as Dean of Engineering—the part of this period when you were President, having succeeded Compton. It was a long one—only a part of the seven years I held that job, but our first contacts during these years stand out in my memory as the best part of the period. Professional Deans at MIT will always struggle with a complex system of leadership—the Institute was constructed on the basis of very strong Heads of Departments, into which Deans were later inserted. I do not really have first-hand information of the present state of affairs, but I suspect that the issue has not yet been resolved. Somehow, I thought we made a good start during the brief years under your Presidency, but more pressing issues of fund-raising and expansion intervened.

Twenty years earlier Dean Soderberg had commented on the inevitable blurring of the traditional professional pattern of our departments, and I quoted him in my President's Report for 1954:

As this process continues . . . the various departments will continue to respond . . . to the whole external complex of technology. They will thus tend to differ more through methods of approach and emphasis than through different syntheses of sharply defined professional fields. Most of the major subdivisions of applied science will be taught in several departments. The departments will tend to become units of administration through which the initiative of their leading personalities will find expression. This is one of the signficant by-products of the increasingly close interrelation between the members of our staff and the world of engineering. . . . It is my conviction that this tendency [as expressed by sponsored research, the Industrial Liaison Program and outside professional work by faculty members], even though it gives rise to baffling administrative problems, is a gratifying sign of strength and healthy development.

The Research Laboratories of Electronics and for Nuclear Science and Engineering in the immediate postwar period provided early recognition of Soderberg's deep-rooted views on the importance of modifying the Institute's departmental organization in order to adjust to the "whole external complex of technology."

In material prepared for a visit by the accreditation team of the New England Association of Schools and Colleges in 1979, MIT included in its list of major laboratories, centers, and interdepartmental programs nearly forty organizational units associated with but not a part of departments!

In its comment on the interdisciplinary centers at MIT, the accreditation visiting team noted that "with the large number of successful and ongoing interdisciplinary centers, it is clear that MIT has developed a style of living with them, with departments and centers cooperating and working together on many different programs." But the team also expressed concern for the problems interdisciplinary centers pose "during their formation, during their contributing life, and in their termination or conversion to new fields." "Starting these new centers," continued the team's report, "needs a continuously adaptive style, which MIT is thought to have as a distinctive strength. . . . Very clearly, members of the Visiting Team heard many views that some centers which had outlived their usefulness did have a life of their own and that it was difficult to do anything about them. Clearly, provisions for termination or change of direction should be made and enforced."

One eminent colleague of mine holds the radical view that the separation in institutes of technology of science and engineering into schools has worked to the disadvantage of both science and engineering but particularly of engineering. It has made more difficult the symbiotic blending of the two fields, especially in advanced areas where science can deepen the work of applied science. Since at MIT we are now deeply committed to the structural arrangement of a separate school of science and a separate school of engineering, he feels that the role of interdepartmental laboratories becomes ever more important for applied science. I have difficulty in accepting his objection to the separation of science and engineering into schools, but I am completely in accord with his emphasis on the importance of the interdepartmental laboratories in bringing the two disciplinary groupings together. At the same time I cannot fail to be impressed by the research successes of the Bell Telephone Laboratories, where there is no emphatic structural separation between pure and applied science.

My administrative responsibilities have spanned the period since 1944, when interdisciplinary laboratories were first introduced as a major innovation in our academic structure. I have given sustained support to these interdisciplinary arrangements, but I recognize the validity of comments made by the accreditation visiting team in 1979.

Recently, in discussing with Chairman David Saxon of the Corporation MIT's policy of avoiding the establishment of new departments, he remarked that at Berkeley, during his regime as president of the University of California, the establishment of new departments was administratively free and easy and a new department might appear with only one member. He quickly added, however, that the Faculty Senate, similar to MIT's Academic Council, exercises a strong control over the quality of faculty appointments in departments new or old, and this ensured Berkeley's great success in choosing faculty of the first rank.

Since World War II and in response to the growth of sponsored research, it has been necessary to establish new administrative portfolios for the management of large laboratories such as Lincoln and for handling relations with industry and the government. It fell to me, in the succession of presidents, to initiate and find holders for these posts, particularly the vice president for industrial and governmental relations. At the start of my administration, as we developed our alignment of administrative authority, the responsibilities for industrial and government relations, for the Division of Sponsored Research, and for interdisciplinary programs involving several departments had been the responsibility of the provost.

During the postwar years the role of the chairman of the faculty was greatly enlarged. He or she served on the Academic or Administrative Councils and was regularly invited to attend meetings of the Corporation. Thus did the administrative officers have the benefit of faculty views, and the faculty shared in the governance process. As president I found all these integrative devices a source of strength and high morale.

During my presidency the administration grew larger and more complex as the volume of sponsored research grew, although there was a determined effort to contain the bureaucracy. The growth was modest, however, compared to what has lately been required for new educational programs, multiplying services, government-imposed "affirmative actions," and increased federal regulation.

As new technologies develop, such as integrated systems and other developments associated with the silicon chip, and as biological technology and the whole DNA domain expand, MIT unquestionably will be under pressure to become what Clark Kerr has called a multiversity, but so far the governing bodies of the Institute have managed to preserve its coherence, its single faculty, and the other integrative devices I have been discussing. As a number of educators have observed, the multiversity is not likely to have a personality.

A great university must not only have a faculty of great teacher-scholars, talented students, and excellent facilities, it must possess this institutional personality, a personality that is an amalgam of tradition, past accomplishments, standards, and values. The late Karl Jaspers, an existential philosopher at the University of Basel, wrote with penetration of the qualities that make a great university. "The essence of the university," he has said, "is concerted yet unregimented activity, a life of diversity yet inspired by the ideal of wholeness, the cooperation yet independence of many disciplines."[7] I have found at MIT a clearly defined body of institutional wisdom, personality, and pervasive sense of direction. The development of an institutional personality or ethos serves to create feelings of loyalty and to give coherence to the institution.

In a seminal memorandum written in 1809 or 1810 bearing on the founding of the pioneering University of Berlin, Wilhelm von Humboldt, a great humanist and one of the inventors of the research university, similarly described the specifications of a true university.

The effectiveness of a university is preserved when those on the outside who deal with it understand its character as a sanctuary. The late sociologist Talcott Parsons, in an essay published in 1973, emphasized that the university's "relative removal from the manifold pressures of the outside world makes possible certain special freedoms, not basically different in kind from those outside, but higher in degree. With all reservations made for the ultimate importance of verification, one critical focus of academic freedom is not only the freedom to, but the encouragement of, 'playing with ideas.' Such 'play,' which may be carried out in deadly earnest, requires some immunity from immediate confrontation with consequences or objections, before the fuller implications of the new ideas can be explored. The basic spirit of tentativeness, therefore, as contrasted with 'commitment,' must be granted unusual tolerance."[8]

Another classic statement about the ideals fundamental to the quality of a great university was passionately presented by Woodrow Wilson in 1896 at the time of the Princeton sesquicentennial:

I have had sight of the perfect place of learning in my thought: a free place, and a various, where no man could be and not know with how great a destiny knowledge had come into the world—

itself a little world; but not perplexed, living with a singleness of aim not known without; the home of sagacious men, hard-headed and with a will to know, debaters of the world's questions every day and used to the rough ways of democracy. . . . A place where ideals are kept in heart in an air they can breathe; but no fool's paradise. . . . Who shall show us the way to this place?[9]

In a later chapter of this memoir I discuss the role of the Institute's top governing body, the Corporation, in reporting its response to student unrest, to the requirements of affirmative action in behalf of minorities, and to the preservation of the Institute as a "free place," a "place where ideals are kept in heart" for faculty, staff, and students.

I recall an essay by Vannevar Bush on the profession and art of management (a subject that always interested him), which he concluded by saying, "There will be managers who can be tough, on occasion, but who are always kind. They will have breadth, and recognition of their responsibilities as citizens and as fellow workers. Above all they will be men who have not only learned the technique of management, but have proceeded beyond this and learned the art.

"And, when you have learned and practiced the art . . ., you will look back and wish you could start all over again."[10]

8

COMMUNIST CHARGES AND McCARTHY HARASSMENT: WHILE OPPOSING COMMUNISM, MIT DEFENDS DUE PROCESS, INTELLECTUAL FREEDOM, AND PERMANENT TENURE

A PROFESSOR IS CHARGED WITH BEING A COMMUNIST

In commenting on the great convocation preceding my inaugural, Dean Burchard said: "Something approaching the golden sun of a miracle seemed to bathe the three days. . . . After times when many of the world's intellectuals had spoken with despair, the prevailing optimisim which flowed on the words of almost every speaker was like a cooling stream.

"But beyond the words there was something indefinable, something almost benign, something from which to take heart. It was as though spring had come again. . . . "

A new college president could hardly have imagined a more favorable climate in which to undertake his duties, and I entered into my responsibilities feeling blessed by this serene atmosphere of spring. Common sense—the comic spirit—might well have warned me not to be overconfident. In fact unexpected events were soon to becloud this sunlit beginning and to bring quickly to a close my age of innocence.

The first challenge appeared six days after I was inaugurated. On that day the *New York Times* carried a story under the headline "Professor at M.I.T. Named as Teacher of Red Revolution."

The case quickly became a cause célèbre, and MIT and its new president found themselves in a hurricane of controversy that was not quieted until October 1956. It was an insistently harassing item on my agenda for nearly seven years.

MIT sought to make clear its policy in responding to charges leveled at the professor. After extensive consultation with fellow administrative officers and members of the faculty, and wisely aided by Phillips Ketchum, MIT's legal counsel, I prepared a statement for consideration of the Executive Committee of the Corporation. The committee approved it for public release on May 3, 1949, and from then on it provided the guidelines for our subsequent actions on all other charges leveled at MIT personnel, including those intiated by the House Committee on Un-American Activities and by Senator Joseph McCarthy.

I quote from this statement as the first important publicly announced policy formulation of my presidency:

Recent reports in the public press . . . call for a statement of the Institute's attitude toward Communism and toward freedom of inquiry.

The Institute is unequivocally opposed to Communism; it is also sternly opposed to the Communistic method of dictating to scholars the opinions they must have and the doctrines they must teach. MIT seeks first a faculty and staff of thoroughly competent scholars and teachers of high integrity. Assuming this competence and integrity, it believes that its faculty, as long as its members abide by the law and maintain the dignity and responsibilities of their position, must be free to inquire, to challenge, and to doubt in their search for what is true and good. They must be free to examine controversial matters, to reach conclusions of their own, to criticize and be criticized. Only through such unqualified freedom of thought and investigation can an educational institution, especially one dealing with science, perform its function of seeking truth.

The Institute believes that [a professor] who denies that he has committed any crime should be considered innocent of any criminal action unless he is proved guilty. The Institute feels that if criminal charges are to be brought . . . they should be brought by the government and handled in orderly fashion by the courts. An educational institution has no competence to carry on a trial to determine whether a law has been broken.

Should a member of our staff be indicted for advocating the violent overthrow of the American government or other criminal acts, or if the evidence of such actions were incontrovertible, immediate action would be taken which would protect the Institute and at the same time preserve his rights. If this staff member should be convicted of this charge, he would be discharged.

The Institute also wishes to make it clear that it believes that the teacher, as a teacher, must be free of doctrinaire control originating outside of his own mind. He must be free to be critical and objective in his own way, and above all he must work in the clear daylight without hidden allegiances or obligations which require him to distort his research or teaching in accord with dictates from without. If a teacher were found to be subject to improper outside control in his teaching, the Institute would regard him as incompetent.

The Institute believes that one of the greatest dangers of the present cold war and of the present fear of Communism is the danger that they will cause America to relinquish or distort or weaken basic civil rights. This may be a greater danger than the occasional impact or influence of a Communist.

No American college or university has a more impressive record than MIT of devotion to our national welfare or of wholehearted support of the ideals of American democracy. It has been the training ground for thousands of alumni who serve and strengthen our system of free enterprise and who vigorously uphold the principles of our free society. Its faculty serves the community, the state, and the nation in a spirit of complete dedication to the public service. I need only cite the Institute's war record and the major contributions it made through research and training to the national cause.

I believe it is equally true that it would be hard to find an educational institution in which the [U.S.] students are so unanimously devoted to American ideals. They are too critical and independent to be easy marks for any special pleaders. The overwhelming majority of our students are so thoroughly imbued with their democratic heritage and with their responsibilities and privileges as American citizens that there is no danger of their being corrupted.

The Institute proposes to deal with all charges of Communism or other ideologies in the light of these considerations and convictions.

The government of the Undergraduate Association endorsed the policy as did the Alumni Council. Later the statement was reprinted as the lead chapter in the book *Primer of Intellectual Freedom* edited by the late Howard Mumford Jones, Harvard's distinguished scholar in literary studies.

As I knew it would, the statement provoked controversy and heated attacks, but it was also praised. President Conant of Harvard on June 10 wrote me: "I have just had a chance to read the statement from your office dated May 3, 1949, which I understand was published in the Technology Review. I am sending this note to offer my heartiest congratulations. I think it is a magnificent document and will do a great service both to the Institute and all American education."

Senator Ralph E. Flanders of Vermont, a member of the MIT Corporation, wrote that the statement "gives evidence of clear thinking on the part of Dr. Killian." It was Senator Flanders who later courageously initiated the debate in the Senate which led to the censure of Senator McCarthy.

Robert Oppenheimer was also moved to write: "From Dr. Zacharias I have had a copy of the statement that you have made on the policies of the Institute with regard to academic freedom in these present most difficult times. I wanted you to have a word from me saying how much I appreciate the temperate spirit of what you have written and the loyalty it implies to the American tradition."

These favorable reactions were reassuring to a new college president who was coming under fire for defending tenure and freedom of inquiry. In the late 1940s a popular play, *Goodbye My Fancy* by Kay Kanin, appeared in New York which depicted a college president who had become intimidated by "reactionary trustees." I was not intimidated by critical attacks prompted by the case and in addition, with the exception of one member, I had the strong support of a board of trustees that was not reactionary.

In all of its decisions the Executive Commitee had the benefit of advice from members of the faculty, and every effort was made to prevent any cleavage in the MIT community. A faculty committee was appointed to formulate a statement concerning the rights of faculty members in testifying before courts of law or legally constituted investigating committees. In substance the faculty committee concluded:

A policy of openness and of honesty is a proper one for every member of our society, and particularly for teachers [italics mine] . . . . The Faculty expects its individual members, by their actions, to contribute to this atmosphere in every way. Furthermore, the Faculty expects its members to bear in mind that anything short of complete candor may reflect adversely upon the individual, the Faculty, the Institute, and the academic profession as a whole.

In spite of these considerations, it is conceivable that a member of our Faculty, on being asked to testify before an investigating committee, might decide to rely upon his rights under the Fifth Amendment rather than testify. . . . In the event that a faculty member refuses to testify, neither the Faculty nor the Administration of the Institute should draw any conclusions from this action without knowledge of the underlying facts. . . .

The MIT professor who was indicted as being a Communist was never brought to trial; and when the indictment against the professor was dropped, MIT restored him to full status, his tenure remained intact, and he returned to teaching and to the collegial community of the Institute.

AN INVESTIGATION BY SENATOR McCARTHY

On December 15, 1953, a story attributed to Senator McCarthy appeared in the *Boston American*, from which I quote the following excerpts:

The projected probe of MIT's Project Lincoln by Sen. McCarthy's subcommittee will "blow the top off spying in high places," it was reported today. The Wisconsin lawmaker said in New York that his committee was forced into the new probe. . . .

"I would not be surprised at all if some Project Lincoln personnel are suspended within the next few days—or before we get up to Boston," McCarthy went on. "We have uncovered some very interesting information there."

As a probable prelude to McCarthy's arrival in Boston Thursday, his two committee probers held a secret conference with President James R. Killian Jr., of MIT. . . .

Except for the paragraph reporting that I had a conference with the two investigators, the article, in pernicious McCarthy fashion, was outrageously reckless and injurious.

The two McCarthy staff men did come to see me and explained that the senator had asked them to inspect MIT's personnel files. I told them in unmistakable words that the Institute did not permit examination of its personnel files by outsiders.

They had sought separately to obtain information from other Institute officials, who gave them some of what they requested but refused to give them a hunting license to inspect our files.

They appeared again the next day, and by then I had consulted MIT's legal counsel and asked him to join me in confronting the two probers. They promptly spread on my desk a batch of subpoenas signed in blank by Senator McCarthy. They were prepared, they said, to fill the blank spaces with the names of MIT staff members if we refused to open our files to them. Phillips Ketchum and I did not blink in the face of this raw exercise of power and angrily told them that we would publicly protest their improper and high-handed use of subpoenas signed in blank as a means of frightening us to open our files to them. That, we said, was all that we had to say, and we would not discuss the matter further with them. Apparently they were unwilling to face a public exposure of their shocking and illegal use of subpoenas signed in blank to persuade us to open the Institute's files. Sheepishly they departed, and we never heard from them again. There were no suspensions by the Lincoln Project, and no evidence came to light of "spying in high places." We were horrified to learn that a young engineer from the Voice of America who was visiting MIT to consult about the location of a VA transmitter station committed suicide after reckless charges made by Senator McCarthy. Apparently McCarthy's investigation of the Army Signal Corps had directed his attention to the Lincoln Project, one of whose sponsors was the Signal Corps.

PROFESSORS BEFORE A CONGRESSIONAL COMMITTEE

During the 1940s and 1950s the House Commitee on Un-American Activities included on its agenda investigations and hearings designed to identify persons who might be communists or engaged in subversion.

In 1953 four other MIT professors were called before the committee to be quizzed about organizational attachments of their green days. One of these shortly left the Institute and the state, and we did not become involved in his case; but the other three professors, members of the faculty honored for their integrity and their scholarship, testified freely without resorting to the Fifth Amendment. Their appearance inevitably, of course, resulted in sensational reporting in the press. In its response the Institute once again was governed by the statement of policy that had been formulated in May 1949. In accord with this policy the Executive Committee examined the position and recent conduct of these professors and reached a firm conclusion that the Institute had no cause to change their status, and it reported this conclusion to the press: "Commenting on the action of the Institute's administration, Dr. Jerrold R. Zacharias, speaking as Chairman of the Committee on the Responsibility of Faculty Members, said: 'The Committee concurs with the decision of the Institute's Executive Committee and believes that the three members of the faculty concerned acted with integrity, courage, and candor.' "

These episodes required the expenditure of an enormous amount of time and energy by the administration, the Corporation, and leading members of the faculty. The sensational press coverage of these events quite understandably caused segments of the public and groups of alumni to be concerned over whether MIT had been infiltrated by crypto-Communists and members of the fifth column. That it had not we diligently sought to make clear. There was never a shred of evidence of spying, and, there was no group at MIT remotely similar to the group of "moles" at Cambridge University, England, including Maclean, Burgess, Philby, Blunt, and others, who were recruited for espionage by the Soviets.

We felt it our responsibility to answer all letters of criticism, to explain the Institute's philosophy in dealing with such matters, and to defend the integrity and loyalty of the Institute community. We sought to answer every letter of criticism as well as every letter of praise. A statement on the case was sent by me to all alumni, and I appeared countless times before alumni groups to report and explain the Institute's method of handling these episodes and to defend the actions it took in response to them.

I have recalled in some detail the Institute's handling of these episodes because I believe it was guided by the great and humane traditions of free inquiry and individual rights on which our American educational heritage has been built. The decisions reached in those days reaffirmed and clarified the Institute's common law for the handling of all challenges here to academic freedom.

9
KARL TAYLOR COMPTON

THE IMMEASURABLE DEBT WE OWE HIM

On June 22, 1954, at age sixty-seven, Dr. Compton was felled while in New York by a heart attack. So massive was the attack that it was beyond the skills of the medical profession to come to the rescue. There had been forewarnings. In 1932 he fell or fainted on a stairway at the President's House. At an MIT commencement he had experienced angina, with chest pains and shortness of breath. In October 1948 he went to Washington to accept the chairmanship of the Research and Development Board of the Department of Defense. While serving in this post, he experienced chest pains and had to be taken to a hospital. In August 1949 he and Mrs. Compton went to a luncheon in Washington with four friends, and during the meal he suffered a stroke, which temporarily paralyzed his throat.

It became clear even to Karl, who had repeatedly refused to say quits, that he should not continue in the chairmanship of the Research and Development Board, and on November 2, he wrote a letter of resignation to President Truman and then returned to Cambridge with his wife, Margaret. Five years later came the fatal heart attack.

His loss was a tragedy of stunning sadness for the MIT community. He had always seemed so strong and tireless and so possessed of exceptional powers and endurance.

On June 25, 1954, a memorial service was held in the Great Court before Bosworth's portico. Forty members of the string section of the Boston Symphony Orchestra provided the solemn music. The tribute was spoken by Theodore Ferris, Minister of Trinity Church and member of the MIT Corporation. "He leaves us," Dr. Ferris said, "the perfect example of the kind of human being we are trying to educate, a man with one eye continually and honestly on the facts and the other on the stars." And in his prayer, Dr. Ferris added:

We thank thee, O God, for the men and women who rise above the confusion of their time and think clearly and speak fearlessly. Especially for the life of thy servant, Karl, we do thank thee now. For the extraordinary diversity of his interests and talents; for his unmistakable honesty and his humility in the face of facts; for his broad human concern and for his loyalty to his friends and whatsoever cause he thought worthy of his support; for the beauty of his face in which the fineness of his character was so clearly revealed; for the things he has accomplished and the milestones he has set; for the strides he made in education and for the multitude of men and women he served in one way or another; and for the serenity with which he approached every situation; for all these we are grateful, O Lord.

Immediately after his death it fell my lot to compose and deliver a memorial broadcast and to prepare resolutions for the Corporation, and I draw on those spontaneous expressions of grief and tribute and other biographical material of the time to add to the eloquent testimony of Dr. Ferris. I worked for Karl and with him for nearly a quarter of a century and because of the generous opportunities he gave to me, I had the privilege intimately to know his ways, his mind, and his luminous personality. He of course appears many times in this memoir of mine; yet there is so much more to be said. No full-scale biography of him has yet come to publication, and I express the hope that some gifted biographer will be inspired to give full-dress attention to a great American.

If for no other reason than his unmatched contribution to the advancement of university education in his time, his life warrants study as a part of any adequate history of American education during the twentieth century.

When he became president, MIT, as I have said, was a leading school of engineering. He left it a great technical university. In a tribute to Compton, Physics Professor Philip Morse spoke of his immediate impact on the Institute when he became its president:

Within two years the newly built Eastman Laboratory of Physics and Chemistry began to attract graduate students and post-doctoral fellows. Under the guidance of the new Chairman, young John Slater from Harvard, the physics department expanded, reorganized its undergraduate curriculum, and instituted a complete new graduate program. Other departments changed, too, in response to Compton's gentle prodding. Engineers were given more solid education in basic science. Pure scientists were exposed to engineering subjects and were encouraged to visit industrial laboratories. As a result engineers were graduated who went in for research and pure science graduates went on to industrial research.

It is a striking fact that under Compton's leadership, the Great Depression in the 1930s was one of the periods of greatest advance for the Institute.

Dr. Compton's courage in moving decisively to reduce the deadwood in MIT's curriculum is revealed in a letter he wrote to Gerard Swope in 1938, stating the changes he was recommending to the Executive Committee:

. . . that our courses in Mining Engineering, Electrochemical Engineering and Sanitary Engineering be discontinued as soon as students now enrolled in the courses shall have graduated, which will mean in each case not more than two years.

As to Sanitary Engineering, the number of students is very small, Harvard is doing a better job than we are, and we believe that the content of the Civil Engineering course on the one hand and the Public Health course on the other, together offer a more important preparation for the types of jobs which will be open in the future.

We think that Electrochemical Engineering as such has outlived its usefulness and that this interest can be better served by introducing some fundamental study of Electrochemistry as one of the "unit processes" around which Chemical Engineering is built, and also providing for a little more attention to electric furnace work in the Metallurgical Engineering course.

As to Mining Engineering, we believe that it also has outlived its usefulness, at least so far as MIT is concerned. Most of the present mining engineers are being trained in the state-supported schools in mining territories . . . .

For what he accomplished in bringing depth and coherence to the Institute's educational program and for his contribution to its humane and spiritual endowment, Compton has been justly canonized in the annals of the Institute. So great were his scientific contributions to the winning of the war that his Medal of Merit citation by President Truman included the extraordinary statement that he personally was responsible for shortening the duration of the war. In honoring him for his achievements as president of the American Physical Society, another distinguished scientist, Henry G. Gale of the University of Chicago, said to him: "Sir, there is in America no physicist more beloved than you."

In the appendix of this memoir I publish a memorandum Karl wrote in 1945 explaining why he accepted the presidency of the Institute. He recognized the need to transform a distinguished engineering institute into a great technical university, strong in science as well as engineering and engaged in research and graduate study of the highest order. This objective he fully accomplished, and the timing was fortunate for the nation: the research university he created was ready to make a major contribution to the winning of World War II. It is no exaggeration to say that Compton's feat in transforming the Institute into a world-class university was an achievement of educational leadership that should place him in the pantheon of America's greatest university presidents.

Compton's colleague, Dean George Harrison, in speaking at the dedication of the Karl Taylor Compton Laboratories at MIT in 1957, reported that during his life Dr. Compton served as adviser, trustee, or director of more than seventy-five foundations, government organizations, and industrial companies.

Karl's wife, Margaret, contributed greatly to his achievements as president of MIT. She survived him for twenty-six years and during her long widowhood she kept alive his influence.

Margaret was invited to give the invocation at the MIT centennial convocation in April 1961:

We bow in reverence before the beauty and majesty of that universe whose myriad intricacies and vastness are being made known to us, bit by bit, by the work of so many minds. We acknowledge humbly our incalculable debt to all those who through the ages have extended knowledge or have deepened our understanding of ageless values.

But especially this afternoon we give thanks for all those individuals who have poured their lives into the building of this great university. Many of their names are forgotten. Others rush quickly to all our minds. Yet each has added a little to the sum and from this assembled whole there *has* arisen a certain grandeur.

At the request of the Compton family, I had the honor of speaking words of tribute to her at her memorial service in the MIT Chapel.

Several years before she died Margaret confided her vivid recollection of an incident that occurred in the formative days of the NDRC and the decisions to undertake the atomic bomb. I recorded what she told me in the following memorandum because I think it should not remain unpublished:

August 19, 1977

Yesterday in visiting Mrs. Karl Compton at Jaffrey Center, New Hampshire, she spoke of an incident in connection with the decision to proceed with the development of atomic weapons that is important and I would like to check it out.

What she said was that she had never mentioned this to anyone but that in the early days of the group in Washington that eventually became the NDRC and then the OSRD, a group came together to advise President Roosevelt on a letter he had received from Albert Einstein. This was a famous letter which suggested that it would be possible to develop bombs using nuclear fission.

When Bush was asked to advise on whether this was a program that the Government should undertake, he drew together a group, largely engineers, which decided that it was not a worthwhile undertaking. Subsequently he saw Karl Compton and told him about this decision, and as Mrs. Compton said, for once in his life, Karl Compton blew his top. He said to Bush that he should have called together a group of scientists who had a better understanding of nuclear matters. He came home obviously upset and spent a sleepless night fearing that he had broken his good relations with Bush by his outburst. Subsequently, however, Bush did call together a group of physicists including Arthur Compton as well as Karl and others, and they strongly recommended that the United States proceed with a research program looking toward the development of atomic bombs.

Subsequently Bush did not show any signs of anger at the intervention of Karl Compton, and the two worked together very harmoniously throughout the war.†

A FOOTNOTE: GERARD SWOPE'S ROLE

In his account of how he became president of the Institute (appendix A), Dr. Compton made clear the central role played by Gerard Swope, President of the General Electric Company. In 1945, at the request of Compton, I undertook to assemble all the records of events and negotiations leading up to Dr. Compton's appointment and obtained from Mr. Swope his records describing the role he had played. Among this material, loaded with important MIT history, was a memorandum written by Mr. Swope in 1938 describing his efforts as a member of the MIT Corporation to strengthen pure science at the Institute, to introduce an honors program for gifted students, to establish a student loan fund, and to recruit Dr. Compton.

Mr. Swope's interest developed during a period when he was chairman of the Visiting Committee for MIT's Department of Electrical Engineering, from which he had graduated. In his memorandum he described how in 1925, while in England, he had visited two eminent physicists, Sir Ernest Rutherford—later Lord Rutherford— and Sir J. J. Thomson at the Cavendish Laboratories of Cambridge University:

I had long discussions with them in regard to the essential difference between scientific and engineering education in England and the United States. Lord Rutherford made the sweeping statement that in the training of scientists and engineers, the average of our graduates was far above those in England, but then he said, "But your graduates cannot touch the graduates of our Honors Course, which is about the first quarter of the class. These are the men to whom we direct our attention; we don't pay much attention to the other 75% of the class, although they do get something from the atmosphere." I came back much impressed with this and thought if we could still keep up our standard of attainment in scientific and engineering work for the average graduates of Technology, and then allow liberty to those men of special attainments, by forming them into an Honors Course, we might retain our high average for all students and emulate England with men of special qualifications and ability. I spoke of this before the Corporation on March 11, 1925, and I remember the idea was warmly seconded by Dr. Lowell [President of Harvard University].

After this visit Mr. Swope succeeded in getting the Institute to establish honors programs, primarily in electrical engineering.

Mr. Swope also concluded that the Institute should plan for a successor to President Samuel Stratton, then approaching his seventieth year. He noted that the Institute had encountered difficulties three times in securing new presidents, first in obtaining a successor for Francis Amasa Walker, then for Henry Pritchett, and then for Richard Maclaurin. "In corporate enterprises, in industry and business, it is good organization and good administration, while the organization is going along well under the leadership of its administrator, that thought be given to training the man who will take over the responsibility at some time in the future."

While serving on the Executive Committee of the Corporation, to which he was elected in 1926, Mr. Swope pursued his various objectives and in 1928 proposed that the Institute arrange for the presidential succession to follow the regime of Samuel Stratton. He found other members of the Executive Committee in full accord, and they began to plan for a successor to President Stratton. He also gained their support for establishing a very large student loan fund, for which he would personally undertake to raise the money. He described how he approached Edwin Webster while they were walking across Boston Common, and Webster said he would be very glad to be the first to subscribe by committing $500,000. "I hugged him right there on the Common," recorded Mr. Swope, "much to the amazement of the passersby. After that I talked to other members of the Corporation and men interested in Technology, seeking subscriptions to the Technology Loan Fund." He found a ready response, and a multimillion-dollar fund was secured, at that time the largest student loan fund in any American educational institution. Among those who subscribed to the fund were Alfred Sloan and George Eastman. He visited Mr. Eastman, telling him of the decision reached to invite Dr. Compton to become president and asking him for his help in raising the loan fund. "Well, how much do you want me to give?" asked Mr. Eastman, and Mr. Swope mentioned the $500,000 contributions others were making. Mr. Eastman promptly said he would be glad to contribute this sum.

Mr. Swope and his fellow members of the Executive Committee arranged matters so that the creation of the loan fund occurred at the same time that Dr. Compton was announced as the new president of the Institute. He also introduced for the first time the plan for a chairmanship of the Corporation, a post to which Dr. Stratton was appointed on Dr. Compton's accession to the presidency. Mr. Swope further recorded that on March 12, 1930, the matter of Dr. Compton as president "was laid before the Corporation of the Institute and the faculty, with Dr. Compton in attendance." Dr. Stratton died in October 1931, and because of the provision that had been arranged largely by Mr. Swope, the administration and organization of the Institute went along smoothly and without any break.

In the material from his files that Mr. Swope sent to me in 1945, he included copies of letters he personally wrote, inviting a number of distinguished figures to attend the inauguration of Dr. Compton. Among these was Lord Rutherford (Compton and Rutherford were both associated with Allied research on antisubmarine warfare in World War I), who responded with the following note dated April 7, 1930:

Dear Mr. Swope:

Just received your letter at my cottage in Wales where I am on holiday. It was news about K. Compton and I hope he will prove a successful president.

It is very good of you to ask me to attend his inauguration. If time and space were unimportant, I would gladly do so but I am bound to the whirl of my duties. However, I much appreciate your kind thought and proposals for a possible journey.

We are all very well and I am avoiding writing letters but make yours—even if brief—an exception.

E. Rutherford

K. Compton should do well—a good choice.

10
TRAILBREAKING IN EDUCATION: TWO EXEMPLARS

A TWENTIETH-CENTURY COMENIUS: PIONEERING CURRICULUM REFORM IN SCIENCE

I come now to the saga of Jerrold R. Zacharias, physicist, humanist, and entrepreneur of innovative programs for the improvement of education at both college and precollege levels.

He was among those recruited from the wartime laboratories who became principal postwar faculty members at MIT. He was brought to the Radiation Laboratory by I. I. Rabi, who had been his mentor while he was a graduate student at Columbia; after playing an important role in the research and development of this laboratory, he was recruited for Los Alamos, where he spent the closing days of the war as head of its Division of Engineering.

Zach quickly became a highly visible figure at MIT. He carried on important molecular beam research, thus continuing work he had participated in at Columbia in Dr. Rabi's laboratory, and he invented the first useful atomic clock. He was alert to the fact that research universities had entered a new period after the war when science was to command unprecedented government support, and he quickly developed relationships with the Office of Naval Research and other sources of government funds for worthy programs at the Institute.

An MIT wit, impressed by the bold solicitation of funds in those uninhibited days, coined a unit of grant-making dubbed the "Zach," $250,000, the smallest amount Professor Zacharias felt was appropriate to request for a worthy project. He raised all our sights.

Zacharias joined John Slater in promoting and organizing the Research Laboratory for Nuclear Science and Engineering and for a period served as its director. This laboratory joined the Research Laboratory of Electronics in demonstrating the power of interdisciplinary research and teaching.

In the late 1940s and early 1950s he directed several summer study projects dealing with urgent defense problems. His leadership of Project Hartwell, a study of undersea warfare and the security of overseas transport, was dramatically successful and brought to a high art this method, originated at MIT, of bringing outstanding talent from industry and academe into an ad hoc format for the intensive study of a problem in defense technology. In 1951 he participated in Project Charles for research on air defense and electronics, and in 1952, in the Lincoln study that resulted in the decision to build the Distant Early Warning Line.

I write of Zach now, however, especially to recall a significant educational initiative for which he was responsible. In 1956 I received from him a memorandum entitled "Movie Aids for Teaching Physics in High Schools." This classic document contained the basic ideas that were to lead to the Physical Science Study Committee (PSSC), out of which was to come a revolutionary physics course for high schools, and in fact a curriculum reform movement with worldwide impact in which first-rate scholars in our universities turned their creative attention to the development of better teaching in precollege schools. I had the privilege of participating in this process by enthusiastically supporting Professor Zacharias's initial concept and by running interference for him in launching and funding the PSSC program.

As the curriculum reform program attracted the participation of many distinguished physicists, it became clear that its full development would require contracts with publishers, manufacturers of laboratory equipment, and other commercial organizations which were difficult for an academic institution to handle. This led MIT, during Dr. Stratton's administration, to sponsor the establishment of a spin-off institution to handle the PSSC program. This was known as Educational Services Incorporated (ESI), a nonprofit corporate entity devoted not only to the innovative physics program for secondary schools but to other curriculum reform activities. When I returned from Washington, I was recruited to serve on the board of this interesting institution and in fact for a period served as its chairman. For many months Professor Zacharias, executive officer Gilbert Oakley, and I held frequent meetings, working off the corner of my desk as we sought to keep this fledgling organization alive and to find the means to realize its full potential as a seedbed for new, modernized curricula, instructional materials, and teacher training programs. In 1967, through an association with the Institute for Educational Innovation, ESI was recast as the current Education Development Center Inc., one of several such centers sponsored by the Office of Education.

In the development of the high school physics program, Zacharias enlisted the creative gifts of his scholarly colleague in the MIT Physics Department, Professor Francis L. Friedman, who undertook, out of his exceptionally deep learning, to direct the preparation of a wholly new kind of text for this new physics course. Under Friedman's leadership this turned into a remarkable collaborative effort commanding the participation of some of the nation's most outstanding physicists. This textbook became the heart of the PSSC course, as I noted in an introduction to the textbook when it was completed.

Physics was presented, as I wrote, not as a mere body of facts but basically as a continuing process by which men seek to understand the nature of the physical world.

Besides the writing of the textbook, the new course required the preparation of a laboratory guide, a set of new inexpensive apparatus, a large number of films, standardized tests, and a comprehensive teacher's resource book directly related to the course.

Associated with Zach in the preparation of this high school course was the gifted producer of film, the late Kevin Smith. Working with scientists and engineers, he produced more than three hundred films for a dozen curriculum programs in physics, engineering, mathematics, and the social sciences. These films set a new standard for educational movies.

The PSSC physics course ultimately involved the work of several hundred people, mainly school and college physics teachers, over a period of four years. It involved an expenditure of over $6,000,000, with the funds coming mainly from the National Science Foundation and, in lesser amounts, from the Ford Foundation and the Alfred P. Sloan Foundation. The new program was tried out in eight schools in the fall of 1957. In the following year it was introduced into 630 schools, and by 1970, over 220,000 students in 5,000 schools were learning modern physics from the program.

The PSSC textbook has been translated into seventeen languages and used in schools around the world. At last report over a million copies have gone into use. In recent years the editing of the revisions and extensions has been carried on by Uri Haber-Schaim of Boston University, who has carried through revisions reflecting reactions and suggestions from physics teachers in many schools. It has become a classic textbook and has achieved the largest circulation of any coming out of the MIT environment except George B. Thomas's *Calculus and Analytical Geometry* and Paul A. Samuelson's *Economics*.

I gained great satisfaction from my small part in encouraging this PSSC enterprise by running interference and helping to find support in the early days for those who were doing the creative work.

I also came to benefit from my associations with Zach. By his example and pungently persuasive advocacy, he convinced research scholars in our universities that research in education, long neglected by first-rate scholars, was worthy of their insights and best talents. While fathering the curriculum reform movement in secondary schools, he has also helped to enhance the effectiveness of MIT undergraduate education by chairing a faculty committee on curriculum content planning and by sponsoring such innovations as the Unified Science Study Program for freshmen and a center for education research.

In convincing the National Science Foundation that it should sponsor and fund teacher institutes where high school teachers could prepare to teach the new physics course, Professor Zacharias showed his appreciation of the primary role of the teacher and his concern that schools of education were inadequate for this job of teacher training. One of my vivid recollections of the PSSC days was watching Zach demonstrating in his fetching, aphoristic manner his impedance match with these teachers who were on the firing line. He might have appeared a haughty university scholar, but no. He was one of them, humanely seeking a joint understanding of the teaching job. As a "teacher of teachers" he was superb. In addition he brought together in his office during the PSSC days and the debates about independent study courses for freshmen a number of ingeniously contrived, inexpensive bits of laboratory apparatus for illustrating the principles of physics, and in this fascinating environment he led discussions of new ways of teaching that might release the creative and self-reliant instincts of students. He engaged his guests in conceptualizing new courses and new ways whereby students could educate themselves. In much the same way he resonated with students during the dire days of the late sixties. He regularly arranged in his home a kind of seminar bringing together troubled students and staff for exploring common concerns.

In the 1970s he turned his attention to learning problems at the elementary school level, with special attention to mathematics. He served as the original project director for the design and funding of the *Infinity Factory,* a Public Broadcasting series aimed at the improvement of mathematics teaching for Black and Hispanic children, ages eight to twelve.

During his work on *Infinity Factory* he became concerned about the effectiveness of mass-administered standardized tests. His conviction that better tests were needed, especially for mathematics, has helped to stir much of the current controversy about standardized tests.

I have touched on only a selection of Zach's efforts to invent ways to mobilize the best talent of the nation for the hard work of solving difficult problems, whether they lie in education, research, or defense. So many times I have heard him say "Get the subject straight," or "Get it right." I think of his insistence that current educational movies were atrociously bad and his persistence in presiding over the production of PSSC movies in which great physicists were inspired to "Get it right." Even in ordinary conversation his ideas were expressed with vivid exactitude.

I find satisfaction in the fact that MIT, a large research university, found this man, a twentieth-century Comenius (Moravian educational reformer, 1592–1670), encouraged his unusual, unconventional proposals, and bore with the idiosyncratic conduct and entrepreneurial determination that marked his pursuit of new educational initiatives.

For me, Professor Zacharias has been at one time a goad, at another time a friendly, uninhibited, and often provocative counselor (we have often disagreed, but not on the great goals), at still another time a tireless companion-in-arms fighting for educational causes. It continues to be a happy and stimulating privilege, in his retirement and mine, to be the friend of this delightfully charismatic scientist, teacher, and humanist who has so enriched and enlivened the MIT fellowship of scholars, young and old.

Let me emphasize that the Zacharias-PSSC curriculum reform was launched in 1956, a year before Sputnik. It deserves to be celebrated as the initiative that marked the return of the university scholar and scientist to direct concern with the teaching of their subjects at all levels of the learning scale. It also had great influence in persuading foundations to make grants for curriculum reform. One of the major achievements of the National Science Foundation was its bold grants in support of curriculum reform.

As the PSSC demonstrated its success, other disciplines found its courage contagious. With the aid of the NSF, the School Mathematics Study Group (SMSG) started in 1958; the Chemical Education Material Study produced the first of a series of course materials for high schools between 1960 and 1963, with distinguished chemists providing vigorous leadership; the American Institute of Biological Sciences, inspired by the PSSC, in 1959 started on the preparation of an impressive series of course materials; and even the American Council of Learned Societies pondered how it might follow suit. One of the most widely adopted programs, Introductory Physical Science (IPS), was sponsored by Uri Haber-Schaim based on his experience in helping prepare the PSSC.

Under the gifted leadership of the late Harry Kelly, MIT graduate, who headed what came to be called the National Science Foundation Education Directorate, the NSF became the principal funder of a gloriously creative group of educational projects for the improvement of teaching, many of which originated in Educational Services Incorporated. The innovative teaching materials that ESI resources made possible—particularly its Educational Film Division—were illustrated by the *Educational Films in Fluid Mechanics,* which were produced under the direction of Professor Ascher H. Shapiro at MIT. Professor Shapiro's mastery of photographing fluid mechanics phenomena led to a whole new approach to the teaching of fluid mechanics and to the formation of a National Committee for Fluid Mechanics films. These remarkable films stand as another example of the educational innovations to which ESI contributed.

Back at Educational Services, the sponsor of PSSC, pioneer work on new curricula for the social sciences was undertaken with brilliant guidance and insights provided by Elting Morison, Jerome Bruner, and Franklin Patterson. Included in the first part of this new curriculum was a section "Man: A Course of Study," which included some startlingly explicit Canadian motion pictures of Eskimo life. These movies and related material were to prove a disaster when they came under attack by textbook watchers and excessively puritanical observers in Congress. The result was an outcry that led to congressional action that was to inhibit support by the National Science Foundation of further imaginative programs for the teaching of the social sciences. The effects of this censorship have proved to be long lasting by circumscribing the ability of the National Science Foundation to support highly innovative curriculum reform programs.

In 1965 I was moved to write an article published in the December 1965 issue of the *Atlantic Monthly,* "Teaching Is Better Than Ever," based on what I had witnessed in the decade of the fifties. Later the reform movement faltered, except in the best of our precollege schools and colleges. In these schools excellence still prevails. But in many other precollege public schools there has been a dismaying deterioration in recent years, as emphasized in 1983 and 1984 by the dramatic Gardner report *A Nation at Risk* and a spate of other studies. The evidence accumulates that we who feel the importance of education to the quality and prosperity of our society have reason to be despondent. Federal funds for public schools are opposed by the president, and there is no visible leadership in government to speak for educational excellence that matches the leadership of the forties and fifties.

There are many reasons for the deterioration of our public school education, but one is the red tide of regulation. In an article "Private Schools, Public Schools, and the Public Interest," published in the *Public Interest* (Summer 1981), James Coleman concludes

Public schools have become an over-regulated industry with regulations and mandates ranging from draconian desegregation to mainstreaming of emotionally disturbed children, to athletic activities that are blind to sex differences. It is in part these regulations imposed on the community and the school which are responsible for the slackening of academic demands and the breakdown of disciplinary climate that many public schools have experienced in recent years.

Physics Professor Philip Morrison of MIT was right when he said, inspired by the curriculum reform launched in the fifties: "Only when the universities recognize that all learning is partly their business can a self-sustaining system not cursed by obsolescence come into being!"

EDWIN H. LAND: HIS ROLE IN INITIATING THE UNDERGRADUATE RESEARCH OPPORTUNITIES PROGRAM

I come next to a legendary figure with whom I have had unforgettable associations for over thirty years. I introduce him principally to celebrate his largely unrecognized contributions to higher education, some of which have found deep roots at MIT and others which found expression in his research and in his public service, where he put daring ideas to work in behalf of national defense. In these several aspects of his multiple careers I have been a close observer of his genius at work and an adviser to whom he turned as he maneuvered, at times agonizingly, to realize his dream of devoting his life wholly to pure science unencumbered by corporate responsibilities.

I first came to know Edwin ("Din") Land through his participation in summer study projects undertaken in 1951 and 1952 by

MIT for the Department of Defense. His original contributions to these projects and his gift for teaching led me to invite him to join a task force being formed in 1954 by the president's Science Advisory Committee to make a study of ways to protect the nation against surprise attack. I asked Land to head that part of the task force devoted to the acquisition of hard intelligence, and out of this group under his leadership came spectacular advances in reconnaissance, including the concept of the U-2 plane and other technology, still classified.† When President Kennedy appointed an advisory board on foreign intelligence under my chairmanship, he included Land at my suggestion. Through these associations with presidential advisory panels, Land continued to make major contributions to the sophisticated technology of gathering hard intelligence and to the art of using it benignly and well. Even in these public service activities he achieved success by virtue of his unique gifts for melding teaching with research. He was able to excite the occupant of the Oval Office about the value of science.

In Washington, when we were engaged in our work for President Eisenhower's Technological Capabilities Panel task force, a group would frequently come together in a nearby bistro before going back to the Executive Office Building for an evening of intensive work. These relaxed interludes afforded me an opportunity to freewheel with Land on a number of common interests, including the state of university education. As a result I became aware of his convictions about the failure of universities adequately to develop creative potential.

His provocative ideas about new ways of teaching led me to ask him whether he would accept appointment as a part-time Visiting Institute Professor at MIT. He readily consented and inaugurated his professorship by spending several hours meeting with MIT faculty and students in preparation for the 1957 Arthur Dehon Little Memorial Lecture at the Institute, which he had been invited to give to inaugurate the professorship. It was in this lecture, entitled "Generation of Greatness, the Idea of a University in an Age of Science," that he exposed in detail a program for the enrichment of undergraduate education by offering freshmen the opportunity immediately to engage in research, to become the working colleague of a senior research scholar, and in these ways to open gates to their latent creative powers. The following excerpts include parts of this memorable lecture:

In the two weeks during which I was your guest here at MIT, I have had some twenty meetings with groups of the faculty and with groups of undergraduates. . . . Nothing which I saw changed the latent conviction that I brought with me, that the freshmen entering our American universities have a potential for greatness which we have not learned how to develop fully by the kind of education we have brought to this generation from the generations of the past. What do I mean by greatness as I have used it in the title of this lecture? What do I mean by the Generation of Greatness?

I mean that in this age, in this country, there is an opportunity for the development of man's intellectual, cultural, and spiritual potentialities that has never existed before in the history of our species. I mean not simply an opportunity for greatness for a few, but an opportunity for greatness for the many.

I believe that each young person is different from any other who has ever lived, as different as his fingerprints; that he could bring to the world a wonderful and special way of solving unsolved problems; that in his special way, he can be great. Now don't misunderstand me. I recognize that this merely great person, as distinguished from the genius, will not be able to bridge from field to field. He will not have the ideas that shorten the solution of problems by hundreds of years. He will not suddenly say that mass is energy; that is genius. But within his own field he will make things grow and flourish; he will grow happy helping other people in his field, and to that field he will add things that would not have been added, had he not come along.

. . . The great contribution of science is to demonstrate that a person can regard the world as chaos, but can find in himself a method of perceiving, within that chaos, small arrangements of order; that out of himself, and out of the order that previous scientists have generated, he can make things that are exciting and thrilling to make, that are deeply spiritual contributions to himself and to his friends. The scientist comes to the world and says, "I do not understand the divine source, but I know, in a way that I don't understand, that out of chaos I can make order, out of loneliness I can make friendship, out of ugliness I can make beauty. . . ."

But not many undergraduates come through our present educational system retaining this hope. Our young people, for the most part—unless they are geniuses—after a very short time in college give up any hope of being individually great. They plan, instead, to be good. . . .

One feels, when among our young students, that they are honest and honorable and full of ideals; that they come to the door of our universities with the dream of being our colleagues, that if we could provide them intimate leadership there would be no discipline to which they would not subject themselves and no task so arduous in the pursuit of knowledge and science that they would not devote themselves fully to it. But if we imply, as I believe we do by our present attitude, that we do not have this kind of faith in them, then their own strength wanes and they cannot believe the best of themselves. . . .

I believe each incoming freshman must be started at once on his own research project if we are to preserve his secret dream of greatness and make it come true.

It was indeed a dramatic lecture, and when Dr. Land finished, there was clearly a feeling in the audience that words of lasting educational importance had been heard.

Academic audiences are generally case-hardened when subjected to lectures, especially lectures on pedagogy, but this time the ideas presented by Land at MIT fell on fertile ground. As large government funds became available in the postwar years, there occurred a growth in graduate study and research at MIT that might have resulted in the serious neglect of undergraduate teaching. Instead, the increasing number of research projects made it possible for undergraduates, if they so elected, to participate in "hands on" research as early as their freshman year. The critics who were proclaiming that the system of education in research universities was "rigged against good teaching" overlooked the opportunities for undergraduates to combine research with formal courses and thus to add a new dimension to their education—to realize Land's vision of working with their professors as colleagues.

As the Land ideas took root at the Institute, other experimental programs for undergraduates were conceived and initiated by Institute teachers. Each was designed to enable freshmen to depart from the prescribed curriculum with a high degree of freedom for self-education. These programs originating within the Institute excited Land, and he later wrote me to say that he had created a trust instrument, the income from which would be available to MIT.

"Through this trust," he wrote, "I wish to assist MIT's current program for the advancement of teaching and learning and its program in providing its students with opportunities more fully to realize their inherent creative capacities."

Members of the faculty had launched four experimental programs alternate to the fixed curriculum from which each student could select the one that appealed to him most. There was a ferment, happily encouraged by the availability of the Land funds and the leadership of Chancellor Gray, out of which grew these alternate programs for freshmen, representing significant departures in style from the standard curriculum. As Chancellor Gray was later to point out, these programs differed subtly in educational philosophy and methods of practice, but they all provided students with greatly increased contact with the faculty, with the opportunity to make full use of MIT resources far earlier than students in the regular curriculum were permitted to do. These alternate courses, two of which have survived as regular offerings, call for independent work at an early stage.

It was in 1969 that a program took shape incorporating many of the suggestions that Land had made in his Arthur D. Little Lecture, and it has become a celebrated feature of undergraduate education at MIT. This is the Undergraduate Research Opportunities Program, better known as UROP. To build and direct the program, the administration found in the Physics Department a young talented teacher, Margaret MacVicar, who demonstrated just the right taste, rapport with staff and students, and administrative skills to ensure UROP's success. As the Report of the President and Chancellor was to note in 1979, "This year marked the tenth anniversary of the founding of the Undergraduate Research Opportunities Program. This unique program . . . has had a significant effect on the educational climate of the Institute as it is perceived by both students and faculty. It is, we believe, the most important single development in education at MIT in the past several decades. . . ."

Later Clark Kerr, in the postscript to his classic book, *The Uses of the University*, identified the UROP program which grew out of Land's lecture as one of the few reforms undertaken by the universities in the sixties.

I shall always remember those Washington days in 1954 and 1955 when the members of the Eisenhower science panel dined together, when minds ran free and conversation was wide ranging and my antenna picked up the frequencies of Land's ideas about education, which were to lead in part to the events I have described.

Land's activities in the service of national security benefited greatly from his concurrent contributions to the art and technology of instant photography and to the unique company designed to undertake the research and the manufacturing to put cameras and films for instant photography into the hands of the amateur. As Polaroid grew, he created a novel corporate entity where research was central and where new concepts were developed to create a corporate environment shaped by values that made it possible for the employees of all ranks to find personal growth and educational opportunity.

Land believed that the management of a modern company should be infused with a spirit of research; in fact he went further and reiterated with an occasional touch of exaggeration his conviction that the management of a company appropriate for modern society was one in which the chief executive officers were deeply involved in science and research. In his career as chief executive officer he confirmed his belief by making inventions that resulted in over 500 patents.

When I returned to MIT in 1959 after serving my term as science adviser to President Eisenhower, Land promptly asked me to become a member of the Polaroid Board of Directors. My admiration and affection for him made it easy to say yes, and so I became involved and still am in one of the most interesting of all the directorship assignments I have had over the years.

So deeply did he envision corporate responsibility and opportunity that he once proposed to me and to the dean of the Sloan School of Management that the school should establish a model company—a practice school—to explore other ways to create other noble prototypes of industry. One of my failures as president of MIT was to think of all the ways Land's proposal could not be carried out!

My service on the Polaroid board brought me even closer to Land as he turned, in the early seventies, to several of us board members for consultation. Clearly his interests were tilting less to Polaroid and more to pure research. As his friend I was aware how long he had suffered the conflict I have mentioned between his inner world—his tropism toward pure science—and his outer world—the creation and management of a major, original, research-oriented company with "mass cultural impact."

It was not an easy transition for Din, but as Polaroid grew into the big company he loved, he found increasingly onerous the housekeeping chores that were imposed by law, necessity, and precedent on him as chief executive officer. Subconsciously, perhaps, he was disappointed that he and the directors together could not find another Land to succeed him. All along he had been buttressed by a devoted managerial team headed by William McCune, exceptionally able but of quite different management style. Instead, McCune was the kind of chief executive Polaroid needed at this juncture. After intimate and extended discussions with a few of us, Land concluded, obviously not without a wrench, that he should yield the CEO of his beloved company to McCune while he himself remained as chairman of the board.

Land had long hungered for an opportunity to devote himself, without let or hindrance, to pure research; when he saw a way to be relieved of the burdens of corporate management, he moved rapidly at age seventy-three to launch a new career wholly devoted to science.

On the morning of July 26, 1982, he called me during my breakfast at home and urgently said he would like to see me that morning at my office. When he came, accompanied by Polaroid's President McCune, he showed me drafts of a contract arranging the details of his withdrawal from Polaroid and of a news release reporting his decision, both to be presented for approval at a regularly scheduled meeting of the directors the next day. He had crossed the Rubicon, and all that his close friends and associates could do, not without sadness and emotion, was to cross the t's and dot the i's of these formal statements of his plans. Actually we who were close to Land knew that he had formulated his plans earlier when the Rowland Foundation, a family charitable entity, sold some of his Polaroid stock to permit him to create the Rowland Institute for Science in 1980 and start the construction of a private laboratory to house it.

I felt it was symbolic that nearly coincident with Land's retirement from his company, a Polaroid team appropriately succeeded, at the invitation of the Vatican Museums, in reproducing Raphael's last masterpiece, the *Transfiguration*. Using methods developed under Land's guidance, the team carried to the Vatican a room-sized camera to use $3\frac{1}{2}$- by 10-foot sheets of the remarkable color film Land had brought to perfection. Land could only be proud that the photographic revolution he achieved could thus be brought to culminating aesthetic and educational use when the reproduction was exhibited in Rome, then at Harvard's Fogg Museum, before being exhibited in various parts of the world. This great camera has also proved useful to artists seeking to restore the badly deteriorated *Last Supper* by Leonardo da Vinci in Milan. The National Gallery in Washington has proudly exhibited a dramatic, large-scale reproduction of the *Last Supper* which the Land process made possible.

These are examples to illustrate the aesthetic uses of his film, but on another occasion, Din arranged, in a spontaneous act of friendship, for the distinguished photographer Yousuf Karsh to make 50th Wedding Anniversary portraits of my wife and me, using the huge Land 20- by 24-inch camera.

The announcement of Land's withdrawal from Polaroid to spend full time at the Rowland Institute for Science, his career, his accomplishments, and his blithe, creative genius prompted deserved encomiums in the media.

11
VITAL EDUCATIONAL GOALS

ACHIEVING NEW GOALS FOR ENGINEERING

As I have already reported in describing the Servomechanisms Laboratory created during World War II, Professor Gordon Brown was inevitably drawn into administration, first as head of the Department of Electrical Engineering and then as dean of the School of Engineering. He was positioned to instigate far-reaching advances in engineering education. He and his colleagues junked the large rotating machines that had squatted for many years with antedeluvian arrogance in the laboratories of the department, substituting for them small, more useful and generalized apparatus.[1] He induced the faculty to write a series of novel textbooks devoted to more scientific, more modern electrical technology based on revised courses in electrical engineering and science that had been in preparation for five years. Then with financial support from the National Science Foundation he and his associates of the engineering school faculties organized a Curriculum Workshop for Electrical Engineering Education that in September 1957 brought to MIT professors from more than one hundred colleges to appraise the handiwork of Brown and his colleagues and then to spread their dispensation across the land. Each guest professor was presented a stack of manuscripts of the yet-unpublished textbooks authored by the MIT faculty and urged to express his views. During the workshop I said: "Many of us feel intuitively that we may be on the verge of an advance in professional engineering education not unlike the advance in medical education which followed the Flexner report and the revivification of legal education that followed the innovations of Langdell."

To that Brown self-assuredly replied: "It already is launched!"

In his Killian Faculty Achievement Award Lecture in April 1983 Professor Hermann Anton Haus commented on these advances in the teaching of electrical engineering that took place in the Department of Electrical Engineering in the late 1950s. "The goal," he said, "was to provide the students with a firm understanding of the fundamental physical laws and mathematical methods of electrical science and engineering. These fundamentals were perceived as invariants, accompanying students through their later professional careers in a rapidly changing technology. The technological developments in the intervening years have exceeded even the most sanguine expectations. Yet, the undergraduate teaching within the department still adheres to this principle—twenty years later—and, I believe, properly so. Professor L. J. Chu, who died ten years ago, was at the fulcrum of the undergraduate curriculum reform."

In the spring of 1957 the Ford Foundation was shaping a program on behalf of engineering education, and Henry Heald, then president of the Foundation, indicated that he would welcome informal suggestions. I sent to him, after consulting various draft proposals already prepared by several of my MIT colleagues, a long letter dated March 12, 1957, outlining the philosophy of engineering education then under discussion at MIT and interspersed with my own views and hopes. In the manuscript of his history of the Department of Electrical Engineering, Professor Karl Wildes describes this document as a "ten-page letter setting forth with lucidity and conviction the thinking at MIT. . . ."

Let me present a precis of this letter as a condensation of the ideas on engineering education that were evolving during the Killian-Stratton presidencies:

We believe that engineering education has today an unprecedented responsibility and opportunity to bring about this much-needed advance in the professional excellence and constructive influence of engineers. In the second half of the past century when engineering education was establishing itself in the United States, it was marked by bold educational experimentation and innovation, and in this period it was influential in shaping the national pattern of higher education. In the first half of this century, while growing in competence and scope, our system of engineering education, except in a few specific fields, has not kept pace with the rapid advance of technology and the expansion of our industrial society.

Now, in response to national needs, there seems to be a renaissance in the making. We may well be on the threshold of a transformation or new embodiment if we can realize upon the current upsurge of ideas in our leading engineering schools.

In seeking to meet the enlarged responsibilities of the engineering profession and to capitalize on the emerging ideas of its faculty, MIT has been evolving, in accord with a "grand plan"— a plan to achieve in scope, excellence, values, and spirit a new kind of university where science and engineering are cultivated at an advanced, innovating, humanistic, professional level, . . . but embracing as essential partners the social sciences and the humanities, each interpenetrating the other and all working with the double objective of advancing engineering and of using it for the creation of a better society.

This institutional concept, built upon the tradition of engineering education in the United States, requires bringing into intimate relationship and interaction the basic sciences, the applied sciences, the social sciences and humanities. It requires a closer articulation and interaction of postdoctoral, graduate, and undergraduate studies with the spirit and example of research infusing all of these educational levels. Our goal and our emerging program call, in fact, for a *new* degree of articulation of undergraduate and graduate study and of general and professional education, all moving in concert toward higher standards and deeper penetration. This goal seeks to achieve education that is adequate for modern social needs both with respect to its high scientific and technical level and with respect to the breadth of knowledge and interests it engenders.

We also see a growing opportunity and need to bring elements of our School of Engineering into close association with our School of Industrial Management. Already engineering students are choosing more management subjects as professional electives in engineering courses. We seek to multiply the opportunities for doing this, but of more importance, *we wish to formulate and try new courses and research programs which achieve an amalgamation of the management and engineering points of view.*

We need to strengthen the older and long-recognized fields such as Mechanics and Thermodynamics, but we wish to go much further and define more clearly those syntheses which are emerging as new engineering sciences, as for example, solid state technology. The success of our Electrical Engineering Department, in formulating conceptual groupings such as Energy Conversion to bring together a wide range of scientific and technological knowledge, suggests the possibility of formulating other conceptual schemes such as Energy Processing, Materials Engineering and Processing, and Information Processing.

Two years later, in July 1959, MIT submitted to the foundation a formal proposal on behalf of engineering education at the Institute which was prepared under the direction of C. Richard Soderberg, the retiring dean of the School of Engineering; his successor, Gordon Brown; and other senior administrative officers and faculty members, including, preeminently, President Stratton. The foundation responded with a munificent grant for engineering of $9,275,000. Thus Professor Brown's founding of the Servomechanisms Laboratory had led him to new initiatives in engineering education. This record-breaking Ford grant was one of the payoffs.†

THE ORIGIN AND RISE OF PROGRAMS IN ECONOMICS AND MANAGEMENT

My experience as an undergraduate in Course XV, Business and Engineering Administration, and later my association, when a tyro president of the Institute, with the transformation of Course XV into the Alfred P. Sloan School of Management have given me an abiding interest in the origin and rise of management education—and of economics—at the Institute. I also wish to pay further tribute to Francis Amasa Walker, third president of the Institute, leading economist of his day, and the progenitor of today's program in the social sciences at MIT.

Actually in the founding of the Institute it was predestined that social science, particularly economics, would ultimately occupy an important place in the curriculum of the new institution. In his original plan "for a Polytechnic School in Boston" (1846), William Barton Rogers, the founder, visualized "a polytechnic college on the most ample plan" which would provide professional education in science and engineering along with a "wide general cultivation."

In a report of President John Runkle's dated 1876–77 I find a fascinating statement by MIT's professor of english and history, William P. Atkinson, boldly suggesting a need for a course of study to prepare young men who rejected liberal arts colleges "requiring the study of the ancient languages" but who would be attracted to a college—a polytechnum—in which they could prepare "for an active business life by an education in the study of the modern languages, the experimental study of natural and physical science, and in English subjects, including History and Literature, the elements of Law and Political Science, Political Economy and Statistics and Commercial and Industrial Geography." The statement continues:

There is a large and rapidly increasing class of young men in the community who, for various reasons, are not prepared, on the one hand, to invest their school years in the study of the ancient languages which is required for admission to our colleges, and on the other hand, have no taste or talent for engineering, or the other technical professions, but who yet do desire something beyond the education which our high schools give. By a not expensive addition to our teaching force, as at present organized, and by proper modifications in the course in 'Science and Literature"—such modifications as shall give it a character as distinctly individual as the course in Chemistry, or the courses in Engineering—that course might be made to meet exactly this want. As at present arranged, it fully meets no want, and consequently attracts few students.

Although the specific program of studies suggested by Professor Atkinson was probably never seriously considered, he did teach some economics, and his advocacy of a program to prepare young men for active business life was startling, the more so since the advocate was a professor of english and history who prophetically recognized the importance of economics and the other social sciences in an education for management.

In England during the 1860s it took a "select committee," a kind of Royal Commission, to present a convincing argument that instruction in theoretical and applied sciences should not be limited to the "industrial classes." It was not just the artisans who needed education in applied science, said this committee loud and clear, but the managers.[2]

This conviction was implicit in Rogers' plans for the polytechnum drawn in 1846, and certainly from its very beginning MIT was pitched at an educational level, university in standards, that realized the importance of a polytechnum educating managers and other professionals and not just "artisans."

Perhaps this provides another explanation of why MIT educated so many great industrial leaders even before the turn of the century.

My solicitation of facts about the introduction of political economy or economics into the Institute curriculum made clear that economics would prepare the way for the broader reaches of the social sciences.

In the introduction to his famous economics textbook, Paul Samuelson, in describing economics as "the queen of the social sciences," concluded: "Economics borders on other important academic disciplines. *Sociology, political science, psychology,* and *anthropology* are all social sciences whose studies overlap those of economics."[3] I hasten to note that in proof of Samuelson's thesis, all of these subjects have come to appear in the Institute's program of education in neighborly association with economics.

In addition to founding and launching the new Institute in 1861, Rogers, in 1881, made another major contribution to MIT by finding and recruiting as its third president, Francis Amasa Walker, professor of political economy and head of the department in Yale's Sheffield Scientific School. Walker had served in the Civil War with a bravery and distinction that had been recognized at war's end by his being breveted, at the age of twenty-five, brigadier general of the Union Army. In the immediate years following the war he engaged in a variety of activities including helping his father prepare his publications on political economy and in his teaching at Amherst. He spent a period on the faculty of Williston Academy and served as a journalist for the *Springfield Republican* in the heyday of that influential newspaper. From there he was called to Washington to become chief of the Bureau of Statistics of the Treasury Department and in 1870 of the Ninth Census. When funds ran out in the Interior Department to complete Walker's work on the Ninth Census, the department had the wit to arrange an appointment for him as Commissioner of Indian Affairs so that he could receive a salary for the time he needed to complete his work on the census; in fact he fulfilled both assignments with great distinction. In his autobiography Henry Adams mentioned several times his friendship with Frank Walker and spoke of the article they prepared for the *North American Review* on the history of the Legal Tender Act.

Walker started his teaching career at Yale and while there was persuaded to become unsalaried superintendent of the Tenth Census by taking leaves of absence or operating from his home. His acclaimed accomplishments in these census posts brought him fame among statisticians and social scientists of the day. He accepted the presidency of MIT in 1881. As Samuel C. Prescott was to write in *When MIT Was "Boston Tech,"* "General Walker not only assumed the arduous duties of president, but also plunged into work as an enthusiastic teacher, and gave a course of lectures on the principles of political economy, attended by all third-year students and many 'specials.' These lectures were very popular, and students soon realized they were listening to a master of the subject."[4] He also found time to prepare his textbook, *Political Economy*, published in 1883. A century ago Walker had international fame as America's leading economist. When he agreed to join the new, controversial *American Economic Association*, its viability was ensured, and he was made first president. In 1968 Bernard Newton, in his book *The Economics of Francis Amasa Walker: American Economics in Transition*, wrote that Walker's text "became the most widely used work in college economics from 1883 to the turn of the century." In his introduction to Newton's book on Walker, Professor Joseph Dorfman of Columbia University summed up the Walker story:

The name of Francis A. Walker is known to the present generation of economists only because it graces the most coveted honor an American economist can receive: the Francis A. Walker medal which is awarded by the American Economic Association, at intervals of no less than five years, to a "living American economist who has in the course of his life made a contribution of the highest distinction to economics." Until very recently he was rarely mentioned in the influential, let alone popular, histories of economic thought. Yet General Francis A. Walker played a leading, creative role in the molding of modern economic science during its formative period in the 1870's and 1880's; and men whom the histories salute as seminal figures in the reconstruction of economics, such as Alfred Marshall, F. Y. Edgeworth, and John Bates Clark, have acknowledged his powerful influence.[5]

Walker's achievements in the public service, his scholarship in economics, his contributions to national policies for precollege education, and his success in the advancement of MIT to national status clearly certify him as one of the great American college presidents.

In 1886 President Walker brought to MIT a young instructor in history and political science, Davis R. Dewey, a Vermont Yankee, the brother of philosopher and educational reformer John Dewey. After graduation from the University of Vermont Davis served as principal of the Hyde Park High School in Chicago, where years later a young student named Paul Samuelson prepared for college. Before Walker brought him to MIT, Dewey had studied in the graduate department of economics at Johns Hopkins and won his doctorate in 1886.

Here at MIT he joined President Walker in teaching subjects in political economy, and their combined impact led to economics' becoming a required subject for all students. His courses in economics were located for a number of years in Course IX, a kind of catchall for subjects not in the main professional courses in science, engineering, and architecture.

While Henry Pritchett was president (1900–1907), the Executive Committee of the Corporation handed down to the faculty a decree discontinuing Course IX in the form then offered and substituting for it an elective course in general science. Although not documented, legend has it that this action to cancel Course IX was taken in anticipation of a merger of MIT and Harvard University then under intensive consideration by the Corporations of the two institutions. It has been alleged that the MIT Executive Committee held the view that if the merger of the two institutions were achieved, the appropriate arrangement would be to have MIT concentrate on engineering and science while Harvard would provide the equivalent of the general studies in Course IX. The record does not make clear what motivated the Executive Committee of the MIT Corporation to request the faculty to discontinue Course IX, but I have found no other example of the Executive Committee's preempting the educational prerogatives of the Institute faculty.

Legend further has it that Professor Dewey was angry, even heartbroken, on learning that his cherished Course IX, containing his general study in economics, would be discontinued and possibly would be taken over by Harvard.

Of course the absorption of MIT by Harvard never occurred despite the fact that President Pritchett and a majority of the MIT Corporation were in favor. The MIT faculty and alumni were determinedly opposed. What really blocked the merger, however, was a court decision that the conditions under which the Commonwealth had given the land in the Back Bay to the Institute prevented the sale of the land except under conditions the Institute was then unable to meet. The sale of this land was calculated to provide funds to pay for new buildings near Harvard where MIT would be located when the merger was a reality.

In a Rede Lecture in 1929, John Buchan, Lord Tweedsmuir, discussed the "pregnant trifles," the momentous accidents in history when "destiny does seem for one moment to have trembled in the balance." The inclusion by the General Court of a brief clause preventing the Institute from selling the land given it by the state without the consent of abutting property owners might well be considered one of these turns of chance with tremendous consequences. Had the Institute been free to obtain the funds to acquire land for a merger with Harvard, MIT in its present independent glory would not exist nor would there be an array of the social sciences, MIT style, nor any Alfred P. Sloan School of Management. At least I find it interesting thus to speculate about the consequences of the time, the time in 1905, when a merger with Harvard was near.

Parenthetically, it was not until 1938 that MIT was able to sell the Back Bay land on which the historic Rogers Building stood. The funds received from the sale were used to build a new Rogers Building in Cambridge and to provide a new home for the Department of Architecture, which had been left in the old Rogers Building when the Institute moved to Cambridge in 1916.

It was in Professor Dewey's department that ideas developed for a course in engineering administration, which led in 1914 to the formal establishment of Course XV. In every sense Dewey was the father of this course, and he took great pride in it. The decision to establish it came about not only through the initiative of Professor Dewey but at the insistent recommendation of a group of alumni.

The first dean of the Sloan School, who was also the first graduate (1917) of the Department of Business and Engineering Administration, E. P. Brooks, has recently written for me a fascinating account of the origins of the school. He speaks in his letter of an Alumni Council meeting when an announcement was made that Dr. Dewey had been chosen to head Course XV:

The story is (and I believe I had it from Dr. Dewey himself) that without introduction he rose to his feet and said, "This is the happiest day of my life."

The nonengineering subjects of Course XV began with the fall term of 1914. As I remember some 40–50 students previously registered in some other department applied for transfer to the new course to be known as engineering administration.

Being the first group to enlist, we were in on the shaping of the course and had many long discussions with Dr. Dewey and other members of the new faculty. (There were only 2, 3, or 4 at the most.) A few of us were called into Dr. Dewey's office for long discussions. It was a great experience.

Dr. Dewey became a hero to us all. For over 60 years I have had his autographed picture on the wall of my office.

As a student in Course XV some of my subjects were taught by Dewey, and I learned much under his tutoring. He had long been immersed in academic affairs, and I found him a stately, sagelike figure, crowned by a great thatch of white hair. Following in Walker's footsteps, he was at one time president of the American Economic Association and edited the association's journal for twenty-six years. He also wrote prolificly and consulted widely but was always available and warmly friendly to his students, for MIT commanded in his mind a loyalty above all other professional activities. Despite his imposing presence there was a twinkle in his eye and in his manner.

Horace Ford once reported that after sending Dewey a copy of his annual treasurer's report, he had asked Dewey for his opinion of it. "It ranks," said Dewey, "with the best current fiction."

In 1917 Dewey brought into the Department of Economics a young MIT alumnus, Erwin Schell, '12, who had had a varied experience as engineer or manager in a number of companies. Under Dewey's tutoring he rapidly developed his academic bona fides and became so effective as a teacher of management that in 1930 he was selected to succeed Dewey as head of Course XV.

Schell moved rapidly to initiate a pioneer program of fellowships to bring to the Institute men from middle management for a year's program of study. After various viscissitudes this program was securely established and attracted the support of the Alfred P. Sloan Foundation for a number of years. As developed in Course XV these Sloan fellowships were trailblazing fellowships in management, the first year-long fellowships in any university. They rapidly became known as the flagship of all management school programs for men and women from middle management in business and industry. By the time these fellowships were conceived and plans made for them, Dr. Dewey was on the verge of retirement after forty-seven years of service, and the Department of Economics he had headed was being established as a freestanding professional department independent of Course XV.

Both as student and, later, as an administrative officer of the Institute, I developed a sustained admiration for Professor Schell, and I sought to explain why in my "Tribute to a Teacher" presented at the memorial service for him in Christ Church in Cambridge on January 17, 1965. In the classroom, I said, he was a skillful expositor of the knowledge, art, and doctrine of professional management. But his teaching transcended mere classroom craftsmanship. He was an enthusiasm-amplifier and an optimist, a spur, a person of exceptional force, warmth, and light. This luminous style of his, I always felt, was a greater accomplishment than his professional achievements.

His practical sagacity in the techniques of management and his emphasis on the human factor were blended with a personal philosophy and a strong feeling of moral responsibility. In a day when so many avoided commitment, he was a *committed* man. He also had other kinds of unexpected commitments. One of these was to the enlargement of the sports program at MIT. Together with Walter C. (Jack) Wood he raised the funds to build a sailing pavilion and to acquire for student use a fleet of "Tech" dinghies designed by George Owen, Professor of Naval Architecture. Schell and Jack Wood together had a major hand in initiating intercollegiate sailing and in giving MIT a prominence in North American sailing. I have the pleasure of living in quarters where I can obseve the beautiful spectacle of scores of sailing dinghies on the Charles. It is an aesthetic experience which is one of the most attractive amenities of the Boston scene.

Schell's philosophy was illustrated in the letters he wrote to alumni of Course XV. This series of communications ran from 1920 to 1956. Even though some were bromidic, many were astute and pungent, and they served to create and cohere a fellowship that spread round the world. This society of Course XV graduates came to have a sense of relatedness unmatched in any other large college group I have known. Like such other great MIT teachers as Bush, Dewey, Draper, Hans Mueller, Warren K. Lewis, Stratton, or Weisskopf, Schell was an experience and an influence not to be forgotten. These teachers drew students together into a lasting professional companionship.

ENTER THE SLOAN SCHOOL

Alfred Sloan's interest in management education obviously was stimulated by the success of Erwin Schell's fellowship program. He expressed this growing interest to Dr. Compton, and as a result of their joint discussions Mr. Sloan took the initiative in proposing that MIT greatly extend its work in the field of industrial management and administration. That Mr. Sloan took the initiative that led to the transformation of Course XV into a formal School of Industrial Management at MIT is indicated in a letter that Dr. Compton wrote to Mr. Sloan in December 1950:

In our press conference the other day, I commented on the fact that this gift from you to MIT *had come unsolicited* [italics mine] and was over and above the fact that in my twenty years at MIT you have never failed to do all and more in any situation in which I have come to you for help for the Institute.

As early as September 1950 Mr. Sloan had indicated his willingness to come to Boston to outline his concept of a School of Industrial Management to the governing bodies of the Institute.

It fell to my lot as president to develop, at the suggestion of Mr. Sloan and with faculty advice, a detailed proposal to the Sloan Foundation and on December 15, as requested by Sloan, I wrote as follows:

Mr. Alfred P. Sloan, Jr., has discussed with the officers of the Massachusetts Institute of Technology the possibility of the Institute's greatly extending its work in the field of industrial management and administration. He has asked specifically whether the Institute feels it appropriate and desirable to create a center of research and education in the field of industrial management which would embrace both a graduate and undergraduate program and which would stand as a strong and well-defined entity within the structure of the Institute.

In response to Mr. Sloan's queries, the Executive Committee of the MIT Corporation has carefully studied the advisability of the Institute's embarking upon the kind of program suggested by Mr. Sloan and has concluded unanimously that such a project would be in full accord with the objectives of the Institute, that it would enthusiastically accept funds to create a strong center of industrial management, and that it is prepared to accept the responsibility of establishing and carrying on the project.

In this letter I reported that the Institute had explored various ways of providing adequate housing for the proposed school and that a conclusion had been reached that this could best be done by the purchase of a building at 50 Memorial Drive, Cambridge, formerly occupied by Lever Brothers Company, which had decided to move its headquarters from this building to a handsome new building in New York. With the help of Mr. John Hancock, a member both of the MIT Corporation and of the Lever Brothers board of directors, we moved to negotiate the purchase of this building to house the Sloan School. We were prompted to execute a purchase agreement even before the completion of the arrangements with the Sloan Foundation because the Lever Brothers Company, we heard, had under consideration the sale of the building to the government, thus making it probably forever unavailable to the Institute. I remember during these negotiations Mr. Sloan came to Cambridge and he, Dr. Compton, and I walked down Memorial Drive to have a look at the building as a possible home for the School. Mr. Sloan's reaction was immediate. "What are we waiting for?" he asked.

After we were assured by Mr. Sloan that his foundation would make a grant to MIT of $5,250,000, we moved at once to recruit a dean, a corporate administrator with industrial experience. Faculty members of Course XV strongly endorsed a candidate we already had in mind, the Edward Pennell Brooks I have already mentioned as a graduate of Course XV, an admirer of Dr. Dewey's, and at that time a vice president of Sears Roebuck and a former member of the MIT Corporation. Our negotiations with him revealed him as hesitant to give up his important post at Sears, but his abiding enthusiasm for Course XV and his admiration for Dr. Dewey were factors that finally won him.

A meeting of alumni in Chicago, at which I had been invited to speak, provided an appropriate setting for announcing his appointment as first dean of the school. In his response, Penn, as he was called by his friends, expressed his enthusiasm for Mr. Sloan's vision of a new kind of management education. Then with a light touch he noted that "this was the first time Sears had ever been asked to ship a dean."

In planning the foundations for permanent structures, conditions sometimes appear that require modification in the design as the preparation of blueprints proceeds. This occurred in the founding of the Sloan School. Questions arose about the relation of the Sloan Foundation to the School. These questions principally were directed to the proposal that the Sloan Foundation would have a right to submit to MIT its point of view regarding the eligibility of those appointed to the faculty of the school as well as the policies adopted by the school. A second question arose as to arrangements for an Advisory Council to the school to be chaired by Mr. Sloan. These questions, though amicably answered in the end, involved issues fundamental to the preservation of the freedom of a university, its trustees, and its faculty. My participation, along with Dr. Compton's and Dean Brooks', in the resolution of these issues was a fascinating learning experience for me in the early days of my presidency. In a skillfully written letter to Mr. Sloan, Dr. Compton emphasized the principle that an educational institution should be just as careful to maintain its freedom from domination by private financial interests as from government or any other group that might provide financial support. In regard to the Advisory Council, a question had been raised within the Sloan Foundation as to the foundation's role in selecting members of the council. Again we expressed our preference for an alternative arrangement whereby the Advisory Council would be selected and appointed by the Institute with four members out of twenty-five proposed by the Sloan Foundation.

It was my responsibility, as chief executive officer of the Institute, to write to the foundation accepting the Deed of Gift as modified. As I said in this letter, the purpose of the Advisory Council would be, as its name suggests, to advise the Institute and the dean of the school on major policies and plans. And then I concluded with the following statement:

While the Institute will seek the advice and counsel of the Advisory Council . . . and in fact will be most anxious to secure such advice, final decisions on all policies, procedures, and appointments must rest with the Executive Committee of the Corporation in accordance with the charter and bylaws of the Corporation. In accordance with long-standing custom, the Executive Committee will be governed on matters of educational policy by recommendation of the Institute's Faculty.

As you know, we already have a preliminary list of names from which to draw the membership of this Council. Mr. Brooks, who participated in drawing up this present list, I suggest should participate in the final choice of the Council.

Being the sensitive and broad-gauged man that he was, Mr. Sloan accepted these views as they affected the Deed of Gift. In one of his letters, however, he somewhat wryly made the comment: "Being schooled in business—as I of course have been—my approach naturally is to take what position seemed desirable as an objective and then get the objective. I realize that educational institutions perhaps cannot work directly as business can, especially in the present state of the art, I might add."

I must add that in all of these discussions concern in the business community about Keynesian economic doctrines doubtless resulted in some of the proposals that were inappropriate for an educational institution. The Advisory Council took some time to find its role. Only in one instance did it act in a way that resulted in a minor bouleversement. One of the advisers Mr. Sloan had used in his decision to sponsor the school and who served for a brief spell on the Advisory Council made highly critical comments to Mr. Sloan about the policies of the school. Dr. Compton calmed the waters with a letter that explained some of the limitations of college administrative officers. He recalled that General Eisenhower had consulted with Dr. Vannevar Bush about the advisability of his accepting the presidency of Columbia University. In his accustomed pithy way Dr. Bush said to him: "The first thing that a college president has to know is that he issues no orders and maybe that will be hard for you to take."

The formal Deed of Gift and Agreement signed for the foundation by Mr. Sloan and for MIT by me stated:

Industrial management is a field of rapidly growing importance in a society with many industrial enterprises presenting problems of a complex technological and human relationship nature. The Foundation and the Institute agree that there is an urgent need for a center of research and education which would embrace an extensive program of scientific research into the problems connected with the management of industrial enterprises and an academic organization for dealing with the subject at both the undergraduate and graduate levels. The Foundation desires to see an adequate program worked out in this field and desires to make contributions that will permit the development and carrying out of such a program. The Institute desires to accept the responsibility for carrying out the program by establishing and operating a fifth school which would be a well-defined entity within the structure of the Institute.

The Deed of Gift was based on a memorandum which specified that the school be a separate entity in the MIT academic organization and that it would stand coordinate with MIT's four other schools, that the school would be so housed that its staff and its activities would not be dispersed so that the total program could work as an entity with unanimity of purpose, that it should include an active research program in the field of management, and finally, that it should take the fullest possible advantage of the engineering and scientific resources of MIT. It was emphasized that the school should not unduly duplicate existing schools of business administration or of commerce.

When funds for the new school were ensured, Dean Brooks moved to merge the Course XV staff and program and to recruit additional faculty from outside the Institute. One of the outstanding professors in Course XV was Ronald H. Robnett, professor of accounting and a teacher admired throughout the Institute. He had been a member of the Committee on Educational Survey, and during the war he devoted his skills to assist the administration in negotiating the novel research contracts that were invented. Brooks had the good fortune to get Robnett to accept appointment as associate dean of the new school, and he proved to be a great help in those early days.

In all of the appointments Brooks was committed to his goal "to find a better approach to management education and to make research a fundamental part of the program." Although admiring the way the Harvard Business School had made the case system central in its teaching, Brooks and his colleagues felt strongly that an exclusive pedagogical reliance on the case system was not right for the Sloan School. As the current dean of the school, Abraham Siegel, was to say much later:

Our own design efforts were cast neither in such singular ideological molds nor intended to be delivered in any uniform pedagogical style. In our research and in our teaching our bent was from the start pluralist and pragmatic and has so remained.

There was, however, a "faith" of a different sort which underlay our early efforts at research and teaching and still does. In essence, that design put its faith in the power of ideas—in the power of disciplined thought and analysis—and in the import which the generation and dissemination of ideas deduced from such disciplined analysis could have for the practice of management and, indeed, of our lives. We did not seek to replicate worldly experience in the classrooms but to build on and prepare for more of it by trying to analyze it scientifically. The strategy was clearly influenced by the then prevalent descriptor of MIT as a "university polarized around a core of science."

In addition to Dean Brooks the school has had the leadership of three successive deans, Howard W. Johnson, William F. Pounds, and now Dean Siegel. Of these three deans one was to be selected, in 1965, as president of the Institute.

As Siegel has written, "The MIT Sloan School of Management has become and has been recognized as one of the leading management schools in the world." One of the contributing factors to this achievement has been the close association of the school with other academic programs at MIT. Happily the Sloan Building was large enough at the start to permit bringing into it the Economics Department from its quarters in the Hayden Library Building, thus avoiding any weakening separation of economics from management; to this day the Sloan School faculty includes a group of distinguished economists who also hold appointments in the Department of Economics. To serve the increased needs of American industry and technological leadership, the School of Management has joined forces with the School of Engineering to offer the first joint master's degree program between the two schools. It entails a full-time, twelve-month curriculum developed jointly by faculty from the two schools. The joint program is responsive to the interests of students who want to study the highly specialized, critical area of the management of technology and technologically based innovation. I note with satisfaction that I advocated such a joint program in my letter to the Ford Foundation in 1957, which discussed my views about engineering education.

Recently the MIT faculty approved a five-year experimental program leading to a new Ph.D. in health policy and management. The program will be conducted in the Whitaker College of Health Sciences, Technology, and Management in conjunction with the Departments of Economics and Political Science and the Sloan School of Management.

ECONOMICS AT MIT
Let me now return to the concurrent evolution of a great Department of Economics.

In 1931 Ralph E. Freeman, Professor of Economics at the University of Western Ontario, accepted an appointment in Professor Dewey's Department of Economics and in 1934 became head. His coming set the department on a course to greatness, primarily because of his rare good taste in the selection of teachers who were not just good but the best. And the best found in him qualities of sensitive leadership that had an impedance match with their talents.

It was Professor Harold Freeman who called Ralph Freeman's attention to a young economist at Harvard, Paul Samuelson, whose future at that institution was uncertain. Ralph Freeman promptly offered Samuelson a post at MIT. In considering the offer, Samuelson consulted "my revered teacher of mathematical economics and statistics," E. B. Wilson, long a distinguished figure at MIT and later at Harvard, who advised Samuelson to accept the MIT offer rather than others he had received, and Samuelson chose MIT.

So brilliant had Samuelson's record been at Harvard and so immediately productive was he at MIT that he soon became a magnet drawing still other able economists to the Institute, who together were to help build a department famous the world over. Another member of the department who helped to identify promising young economists, including Samuelson, was Rupert Maclaurin, son of the sixth president.

The economics staff now in the department like to emphasize that the freestanding department of "pure" economics started with the appointment of Ralph Freeman in 1934. Accepting that view, I note that the department was under the direction of but three heads over fifty years. This almost unmatched continuity of leadership is one source of the great strength and high morale of the department. Freeman, Bishop, and Brown are as renowned in their domain as Tinker to Evers to Chance became in theirs. The presence of this array of outstanding economists in turn enabled the department to introduce in 1941 a Ph.D. program which quickly attracted graduate students who further enhanced its fame.

During Freeman's chairmanship and with his support, Professor Maclaurin led the formation in 1937 of an Industrial Relations Section as part of the Department of Economics and Social Science. It became one of the five earliest centers in the United States for the systematic study of labor relations and related fields of economics and behavioral science. Under the direction of Maclaurin and Douglass Brown, the section brought together such seminal figures as Douglas McGregor, Charles Myers, and Joseph Scanlon, the latter, father of the Scanlon Plan, coming from the United Steel Workers of America. When the Sloan School matured, both Economics and Sloan concluded that the Industrial Relations Section should be in the Sloan School but with continuing close relations with Economics.

The growth to greatness of the Economics Department, and in fact the impressive development of the entire field of the social sciences at MIT, can be attributed to the prestige of Samuelson and other outstanding scholars in the department such as Robert L. Bishop, Richard M. Bissell, E. Cary Brown, Charles P. Kindleberger, Charles A. Myers, Evsey Domar, Max Millikan, Walt Rostow, and Robert M. Solow, who found satisfaction in being members of a team that included Samuelson. To this list of distinguished economists should be added Lester C. Thurow, Franco Modigliani, Sidney Alexander, and Abraham Siegel, who have appointments in both Economics and in the Sloan School of Management. Thurow has come to command a wide public audience through his speeches, television appearances, and books, notably *The Zero-Sum Society* followed by *Dangerous Currents: The State of Economics.* In this latest book of his, Thurow discusses the discordant views observable in the economics profession and the current public loss of confidence in economic forecasts. He further says, however, that "if you criticize a discipline, you can easily sound too negative. A critic tends to see what's wrong, not what's right. In any case, nothing I have to say will deny the fact that in their 200-year history, economists as a group have advanced our understanding of economic behavior. In fact, the problems with economics are no more serious and the disagreements no more prevalent than those in other fields. They are just more visible—being reported on daily, and more important, affecting the immediate economic well-being of everyone. So even as I criticize the economics profession, let me say at the outset that I am myself proud to be called an economist."

John Kenneth Galbraith, in his book *The Age of Uncertainty* (1977), said: "Generations of students have learned their economics from Paul Samuelson, the pre-eminent teacher of his time, whose textbook in the face of sharp initial attack, instructed millions." It became in fact for an extended period the largest-selling textbook in economics.

It is said that Samuelson at first reluctantly undertook, at the request of his department, to prepare a set of notes for the teaching of elementary economics. His associates were dissatisfied with the pedestrian texts then available and were sure that a Samuelson-composed textbook would be far better. Samuelson finally consented, and it was this set of notes that grew into the textbook that was "to instruct millions," that along the way won worldwide fame, and that helped to develop a favorable environment for other social sciences at MIT.

In his preface to his textbook Samuelson expressed his ambition to write a memorably distinctive book. "Why does a scholar interested in the frontier of research write a textbook?" asked

Samuelson. "In my case for two reasons: I sensed that there was coming to be a widening *gap* between the technicalities of advanced economics and what the intelligent non-professional has to know about the subject if he is to be a good citizen, a competent statesman, an effective businessman or a cogent critic or defender of the modern mixed economy. And like economists here and abroad, I lamented the fact that in our generation we did not have any great introductory treatise like those which have become classics in other subjects—*The Principles of Psychology* by William James, *Differential and Integral Calculus* by Richard Courant or *Pure Mathematics* by G. H. Hardy, and in the present age *Lectures in Physics* by the Nobel laureate Richard Feynman." Samuelson well knew that Walker—America's leading economist a century ago—just after becoming president of the Institute, had also published a textbook, *Political Economy*, that educated an early generation of college students in economics. It is a striking fact that two MIT economics texts, published sixty-five years apart, achieved great influence and acclaim.

Samuelson's fame and influence did not derive alone from this famous text. His prodigious work as a scholar resulted in an enormous output of papers and contributions to the general literature. Except for his highly technical or mathematical papers, many of his publications are marked by an exuberant, spritely style peppered with wide-ranging allusions, anecdotes, and skillful use of the current argot.

Despite its great success and its wide use, Samuelson's text was not without critics, some vehement and persistent. In his report to the president for the academic year 1947–48, Professor Freeman, the head of the department, included this statement:

The Visiting Committee of the Department made a study of our undergraduate curriculum directing their attention especially to Economic Principles (Ecll). They recommended the use of additional material to supplement the textbook. Acting on this advice, we plan to introduce a set of readings presenting points of view somewhat different from that taken by the author of the book, Professor Paul A. Samuelson. We believe that this device will improve our instructiton in this important subject. Incidentally, the textbook, which was published last spring, has already been adopted by more than fifty universities and colleges.

Obviously the department was acting with equanimity while seeking a sensible way to meet the criticism without drawing back from Samuelson's masterful text. It was understandable why Samuelson smarted under letters sent to him by the chairman of the Corporation Visiting Committee, but he reacted with cool dignity and maintained an unswerving belief in the integrity of his scholarship.

The objections to Samuelson's text were prompted by his views on Keynesian economics. Obviously many of those attacking Samuelson's book pressed their views on Compton and Killian. We took no position for or against his economics, but we strongly insisted on his scholarly integrity and his achievements as a leading scholar. The voluminous correspondence that flowed to our offices was answered with care, based on wise guidance from our colleagues and with stout defense of Samuelson.

In a lecture he gave in March 1971 Samuelson frankly discussed with forbearance and maturity his response to the early attacks, now mostly subsided, on his text. After describing the effects of the criticism on himself and on his book, he said:

When I felt I was wrong, I uncheerfully made the change; but being a bumptious fellow I fear that not very often did I find that I was wrong. . . . More often when I felt that my point was not wrong, I carefully rephrased the argument so that its logic and empirical cogency would stand out. . . . In a sense this careful wording achieved its purpose: at least some of my critics were reduced to complaining that I played peek-a-boo with the readers and didn't come out and declare my true meaning.

Nevertheless, such defense writing weakens the elan of a book. And I reread today, say the fifth edition of the book, with certain irritation for the care with which many matters are formulated.

The initial objection to Samuelson's text and to Keynesian economics was paralleled at Harvard, as James B. Conant reported in a chapter entitled "Much Ado About Economics" of his book *My Several Lives: Memoirs of a Social Inventor* (1970).

In 1970 Samuelson was the first American to receive the Nobel

Memorial Prize in Economic Science, and we at the Institute noted this recognition of his talents with pride and joy. I have already reported that President Walker and Professor Dewey both served as presidents of the American Economic Association. So did Samuelson (1961), Franco Modigliani (1976), and Robert Solow (1979), and now comes the announcement that Professor Kindleberger is president-elect of the association. Recently Samuelson has pointed out in an essay for *Technique* that the MIT department has been reconfirmed as number one in the nation, which today means number one in the world.

Having reached the age of seventy, Samuelson retires from his MIT professorship at the end of the academic year in 1985. His *Economics* has been called the most durable text ever published, having sold over three million copies. As he approached retirement, he faced the question of whether he would prepare a twelfth edition or let the classic gradually die. He finally decided that he "owed it to the book not to."

Together with his publisher he sought a coauthor and his first choice was Professor William Nordhaus of Yale, who had received his doctorate under Samuelson. Nordhaus agreed to join in preparing a twelfth edition to appear in 1985, this revision to reflect "the shifting contours of economic thought" since Samuelson prepared the first edition in 1948.

In an article in the *New York Times* (February 19, 1985), the coauthors quoted the adage " 'Let others write a nation's laws if I can write its textbooks.' These words were not written completely in jest. Textbooks reflect the state of a science. They also help shape the development of a science, and indeed of a nation."

It may appropriately be said that the initiatives of President Walker in the 1880s were prophecies of what education in the social sciences and management have become at MIT.

My exploration of early Institute history, particularly relating to economics and management, has helped to sustain my view that it was the manifest destiny of MIT to become a research university, a "university limited in its objectives but unlimited in the breadth and the thoroughness with which it pursues its objectives."

USHERING IN A NEW ERA IN BIOLOGY

When it was reported in January 1983 that MIT's graduate programs in biochemistry, microbiology, and cellular and molecular biology had been ranked first in the nation by the Conference Board of the Associated Research Councils, I recalled how a new era in biology at MIT was opening in the early 1940s when I was learning to be an academic administrator.

At that time biology and food technology were joined together in one department, but it was becoming clear that each group saw a future independent of the other. I remember Bradley Dewey of the Corporation, as chairman of the Visiting Committee on the Department of Biology and Food Technology, roaring into the president's office waving a paper containing a strong proposal that food technology be made a free-standing department independent of biology. He doubtless remembered how chemical engineering found itself uncomfortable when embedded in the Department of Chemistry and how it had taken a great leap forward when it was released to become a free-standing department.

Actually, the separation of biology and food technology was to advance the fortunes of both fields. Under the leadership of Samuel Prescott and his successors, William L. Campbell and Bernard E. Proctor, food technology had a running start in becoming renowned in its field.

Even before our Biology Department began to turn quantitative and embrace molecular biology, its work had been turned to great purposes. It educated many students for medicine and provided training in applied fields such as sanitation and in pioneering education in public health and food technology. But in the 1930s and even earlier, scientists in the department were beginning to perceive opportunities in quantitative biology and the need to direct it toward more basic research in fields that would bring it into association with physics, chemistry, and technology. In the mid-1930s Compton, Bush, and Professor John Bunker had formulated a proposal that MIT undertake a program in biological engineering. In 1938 Compton presented a paper to the American College of Physicians which discussed in detail his vision of the opportunities before biology to make use of the physical and engineering sciences. In that paper he said:

. . . In conclusion, I would like to make one comment lest, in my effort to present the case for biological engineering, I may have given the impression that I believe the physical and engineering sciences can step blithely in to lead the biologists to a quick solution to their problems. I do not believe this at all; I only believe that there may be an opportunity now for us all to get together more effectively along some such line as I have tried to suggest. The main avenue of advance is, and will continue to be, the direct approach through biology, physiology, and medicine. But these problems are so complex, so vast in scope and human import, that every promising avenue of approach to their solution should be followed. And I believe that this avenue of biological engineering shows some real promise of leading in the desired direction.

The proposal that MIT develop biological engineering arose independently of concepts that the Rockefeller Foundation had been developing under the leadership of Warren Weaver. In the early thirties he became a strong advocate of applying the techniques of physics and chemistry to biology. Under his leadership the foundation had made grants to programs evolving at MIT and in other leading institutions in support of what Weaver was to call "molecular biology" in a letter he wrote in 1938. The same year Compton presented his paper on biological engineering. While continuing to support the physical sciences, the foundation sought in addition to encourage those fields of science making use of the physical sciences but mainly biological in their application. Under Weaver's encouragement grants began to flow toward the science of man and to the biology of the cell, its components and precursors.

Thus Compton's concept of biological engineering and Weaver's concept of molecular biology were both concerned with the application of physics, chemistry, and technology to biology at the molecular level. These visions were to lead to significant appointments that were belatedly to usher in a new era, the era of molecular biology at the Institute. During this period when the move had begun to raise MIT biology out of the dull period into which it had drifted, Dr. Weaver's colleague at the Rockefeller Foundation, Alan Gregg, head of its grant making in medicine and other aspects of the life sciences, was asked by Compton to review our program in biology and food technology. I remember joining Dr. Compton at the President's House for the meeting in which Gregg reported his appraisal of these fields at the Institute and made recommendations for the future.

One of the first moves that Compton made was to recruit biophysicists to join the faculty of the Biology Department. The approaching retirement (in 1942) of Dean Prescott, who had been a major figure in the department at the Institute in the days when it had programs in public health and food technology as well as in general biology, provided an opening to recruit a distinguished professor whose research and teaching interests were in biophysics. This man, Francis O. Schmitt, was found at Washington University in St. Louis, and Dr. Compton lured him to MIT to help build biophysics and bioengineering and thus to build a foundation for molecular biology. Professor Schmitt has often reminded me that since Dean Prescott would be continuing for a year or so as dean and also as head of the department, he, as a new MIT professor and scheduled to succeed Prescott as head of the department, would need an administrative connection to afford him independence from the biology of the past as he undertook to build a strong program in biophysics and to introduce the biology of the future. Under these circumstances Dr. Compton, knowing that he himself would be often in Washington, had asked him to come to me for any matters on which the president's office might be helpful to him as he built a program of research under his own direction and started staffing the department for molecular biology. For a brief period I thus served, in effect, as a dean to Professor Schmitt, and we came to have a relationship that provided a way of affording freedom to his new undertaking and incidentally gave me valuable experience in the art of academic administration as well as some knowledge of modern biology.

A second biophysicist who joined the department was John R. Loofbourow. During the war he served as technical aide to Division 14, which supervised for the government the activities of the Radiation Laboratory and other NDRC radar projects. He continued after the war, in his successive roles as professor of biology, executive officer of the Department of Biology, and chairman of the faculty, to make great intellectual contributions both to biology and to the Institute's educational program.

My next association with the development of a new kind of biology at MIT was in the early days of my presidency, when Schmitt, knowing that biophysics and molecular biology had deep roots in biochemistry, concluded that we must have a first-rate biochemist on the team. He quickly found the man, Professor John Buchanan, and asked me to join him and Dean Harrison in attracting Buchanan to the Institute from the School of Medicine at the University of Pennsylvania. I recall, as does Professor Buchanan, the meticulous list of needs he expected us to meet, including a spacious laboratory, in order for him successfully to pursue his career at the Institute. Together, Professor Schmitt and I found ways to meet these requirements.

We did not realize then how important the acquisition of Professor Buchanan was to be to the development of molecular biology at MIT. Not only did he initiate a program that has now been rated the best in the country in biochemistry, but he became a magnet drawing other outstanding scholars to the Institute. I am told by Professor Salvador Luria, the eminent microbiologist who came to MIT from the University of Illinois in 1958, that his interest in the Institute originated through his friendship with Professor Buchanan. The acquisition of Professor Luria under Professor Irwin Sizer's leadership was a great coup for the Institute, for Luria had achieved research results that were to bring him the Nobel Prize in 1969.

After his achievement of turning the department toward biophysics and biochemistry and thus forward to molecular biology, Professor Schmitt asked to be relieved of the headship in 1955 to accept the distinguished post of Institute Professor. His interests were turning to the neurosciences, an emerging field that both he and the Institute were anxious to cultivate—a field that Schmitt recognized as promising.

In the early days of Professor Buchanan's tenure, biochemistry was concentrated in the Department of Biology, but in recent years the Department of Chemistry has made strong biochemistry appointments. In fact the current head of chemistry, Christopher Thomas Walsh, is professor of both chemistry and biology and in addition, Uncas and Helen Whitaker Professor in Whitaker College. Still another link between the biology and chemistry departments is provided by Har Gobind Khorana, the Nobel laureate who holds professorships in both departments. I cite these joint appointments as another example of the synergistic relationships which my memoir identifies as a hallmark of the Institute.

Professor Schmitt was succeeded in the headship of the Department of Biology by Professor Sizer, and it was under his talented leadership that the department, given the contributions of his predecessors, was to become one of the leading centers in the world for molecular genetics and cell biology, with a stellar group of scholars in molecular biology coming together as a team in the department. Included in this group are Professors Alexander Rich, Herman Eisen, and Phillip Sharp.

To provide for its expanding programs in food technology and biology, the Institute in 1950 sought funds for a new building and was successful in obtaining a grant from the Campbell Soup Company to honor John T. Dorrance, the founder of that company and an MIT alumnus. I remember the president of Campbell Soup, James McGowan, Jr., inviting me to meet with him in New York to discuss the gift and his decision at that meeting to recommend to his company a grant of a million dollars to the Institute. This was my first experience in having a million dollars from a corporation dropped into my tin cup.

It was in this period too that we attracted the enthusiastic attention of Uncas Whitaker. He and his wife, Helen, were to become princely contributors to the life sciences at MIT. Living memorials to them are the Whitaker Building for the Life Sciences and the building that houses the Whitaker College of Health Sciences, Technology, and Management and the Whitaker Health Sciences Fund (a private foundation headquartered at MIT). Also included in this building is the Health Services Center. I think Whitaker's interest in the life sciences was prompted by his long-standing interest in developments in medicine, notably at the Cleveland Clinic, and what he learned as a member of the Visiting Committees on the Medical Department and the Biology Department at MIT. The Whitakers came greatly to admire Professor Sizer, and their confidence in him was to prompt Uncas at one time to say that Sizer had become their "window" on MIT. It might be added that another "window" for the Whitakers was Dr. (M.D.) George Thorn of the MIT Corporation, who became through his Visiting Committee assignments an adviser and enthusiastic advocate of biology and the whole range of the life sciences and medicine at the Institute.

Professor Luria and his associates—including Professor David Baltimore, who was awarded the Nobel Prize in 1975—proposed in 1971 that the Institute should establish a Center for Cancer Research, which would require an additional building. I initiated successful negotiations with the Seeley Mudd Fund for a matching grant to provide this building. Still later came the creation of the Whitehead Institute for Biomedical Research financed by Edwin Whitehead with funds in excess of $100 million. Although independent of MIT, this much-debated Institute was to be associated with it in terms of personnel, objectives, and programs, and it was to be headed by Professor Baltimore.

So far I have spoken of developments in biology at MIT which came during the period I was serving the Institute as an administrator, first as an aide to Dr. Compton and, later, as president or chairman. It is appropriate, however, to recall some of the important achievements of biology in the days when it was devoted mainly to work in fields other than molecular biology, including public health and food technology. Its achievements in this era were distinguished. William Barton Rogers, the founder of the Institute, considered that the institution he envisioned should embrace "natural history" as one of its major programs, Lamarck's word "biology" not yet having come into general use. Rogers himself taught biology under this title in the early days of the institution to show his conviction of its importance, and he was so determined to have a biologist on the staff of the fledgling Institute that he took $2,500 out of his own salary to pay the salary of the new man. I suspect that this is the only example in MIT's history of a president using his own funds to pay the salary of a professor. It was also interesting that this biologist, Dr. Samuel Kneeland, appointed by Rogers was actually a medical clinician who also taught paleontology, physiology, and related subjects. Another figure of these early days was Professor Alpheus Hyatt, who taught paleontology at the Institute and later founded the Marine Biological Institute at Woods Hole.

One of the great events of those early days is to be credited to President Walker. It was he who brought William Thompson Sedgwick from Johns Hopkins, having known him when they both were at Yale. After coming to MIT, Sedgwick pioneered the application of biology to public health problems and took national leadership in initiating premedical programs. He came to be recognized as the founder of the public health movement and the father of epidemiology in the United States. His contributions to these fields anticipated what belatedly became primary activities undertaken in the leading medical schools. As President Walker and Professor Sedgwick were promoting the study of biology at the Institute, budgetary problems led some members of the Corporation to suggest that work in this field be dropped because it was in no sense "a necessary factor of an engineering school!" President Walker and Professor Sedgwick determined that they would fight "for the continuance of the work and did not intend to be defeated." Later on, what Sedgwick did and what he stood for led to action by the medical profession belatedly to embrace public health as a professional field of inescapable importance. Out of Sedgwick's achievements and his evangelical zeal for improving the public health came in 1913 a joint program between the Harvard Medical School and Sedgwick's group under the rubric Harvard-MIT "School for Health Officers," later called the "Technology-Harvard School of Public Health." A joint committee served as the administrative board for the school, with Sedgwick ("The Chief") presiding as chairman.

Recently I was reading the tercentenary edition of Samuel Eliot Morison's *The Development of Harvard University* and noted with satisfaction that he had provided a chapter that gives fair credit to this joint MIT-Harvard program. "It was a pioneer organization," read the statement by Dr. David L. Edsall, dean of the school, in Morison's history, "without funds, dependent for existence and activity upon the devotion of a group of persons interested in improving public-health training, and who asked little recompense except the opportunity to influence public welfare.

"The establishment of the Harvard School of Public Health in 1922 was in large part due to the effective work that the joint School had done"—work, it could be added, in which Sedgwick had played a leadership role.

When Harvard received a grant of funds from the Rockefeller Foundation to establish a free-standing school of public health with an all-Harvard public health program carried out in association with its medical school, MIT, which largely had pioneered the development of the discipline, felt it was under pressure to withdraw.

In 1924 the Yale University Press published a volume of tributes to Sedgwick under the title *A Pioneer of Public Health*. This almost forgotten memoir reveals Sedgwick as one of the greatest humanitarians in MIT's pantheon of its great scientists and teachers.

Another major contribution that came in the early days of the Department of Biology was the development by Samuel C. Prescott of a scientific basis for the canning of foods. Usually this achievement is ascribed to Appert in France, who indeed had developed cut-and-try methods for the canning of foods. His work, however, was undertaken before Pasteur had made the discoveries that were necessary to the scientific understanding of food preservation based on the destruction of contaminating bacteria by sterilization. Working with William Underwood, Prescott brought to bear on the canning process the essential scientific understanding and the technology that now makes possible huge industries based on methods devised by Prescott, Underwood, and their successors. Thus the Biology Department was to become the home of a great contribution to nutrition and food technology, and it was out of the pioneer work of Prescott and Underwood that would ultimately come the MIT Department of Nutrition and Food Science.

Many of the advances that have given great distinction to the life sciences at MIT came after my retirement and during the presidential regimes of Stratton, Johnson, Wiesner, and Gray. Projects in the life sciences were being launched in many parts of the Institute. Professor Bernard Gould has identified for me nearly thirty departments, laboratories, or projects at the Institute currently undertaking research addressed directly to the needs of man as a living organism. In identifying this extraordinary array of teaching and research activities in the life sciences, Professor Gould has concluded that MIT is probably the largest bioengineering research center in the United States, perhaps in the world.[6] The Institute of Biology which had been in the back of Sedgwick's mind has thus found fruition in this array of programs.

In Mechanical Engineering Professor Robert Mann heads a laboratory devoted to Human Mechanics and Rehabilitation. An associated laboratory is the MIT Sensory Aids Evaluation and Development Center directed by Professor Derek Rowell. A dramatic example of institutional partnership and of the synthesis of technology and medical science is provided by the development of artificial skin. In 1969 Dr. John F. Burke of the Harvard Medical School and the Shriners Burns Institute at the Massachusetts General Hospital enlisted MIT's participation in this important project. Ioannis Yannas, professor of polymer science and engineering in the Department of Mechanical Engineering at MIT, in response to their call for help, volunteered to participate in this program. Yannas, together with a group of graduate students in mechanical engineering, working in partnership with Doctor Burke's group at Harvard, were able by April 1981 to make the "stunning announcement" that the new synthetic skin had been used successfully in treating ten patients who had sustained third-degree burns over fifty to ninety percent of their bodies.

These two programs to aid the handicapped and injured have flourished in the fast company of a department that has repeatedly been rated the best in the country.

An important program jointly conducted by the Harvard Medical School and MIT is a division devoted broadly to the health sciences, technology, and management. The genesis of this Harvard-MIT Program in the Health Sciences, Technology, and Management came in a proposal that was presented to MIT by Dr. James Shannon, then head of the National Institutes of Health, and Dr. Colin MacLeod, deputy director of the Office of Science and Technology in the White House. They came to MIT to propose that it undertake to build a medical school. They were strongly of the view that the United States was lacking a medical school that benefited from a close relationship with research and teaching in technology, and they presented their view that MIT was the place for such a medical school. Their visit to the Institute to discuss their ideas came in 1966, just as Howard Johnson was assuming the presidency of the Institute, and I, as chairman of the Corporation, together with Johnson, Jerome Wiesner, and Irwin Sizer, met with them in the Emma Rogers Room. We were startled by their suggestion that they would be able to put together about $50 million toward the necessary funds to start a medical school.

It happened that about this time Dr. Wiesner had been having discussions with Dean Ebert of the Harvard Medical School and learned of the discussions taking place there about the creation of a Department of Engineering and Technology in the Medical School.

It was clear that MIT, although deeply committed to the life sciences and with a large enrollment of post-M.D.'s in biology, would find it difficult to raise funds beyond the $50 million offered, particularly since there were a number of other major projects requiring funding at this time. As a result of what Wiesner had learned in his meeting with Dean Ebert and MIT's careful consideration of the Shannon proposal, the idea developed that the two institutions might come together. Harvard was not anxious to undertake a program of its own in technology at the Medical School, and MIT, as I have indicated, drew back from undertaking a medical school with its accompanying hospital. Why not, the question was asked, bring the two institutions together, with MIT providing its resources in science and technology and Harvard, the clinical resources needed for medical education? The answer proved to be agreement between the two institutions jointly to undertake an educational program as well as to conduct joint research projects. As the plan developed, an education program was undertaken in which students seeking medical degrees, primarily those holding S.B. or A.B. degrees, would come to MIT to work in science and technology and then go on to Harvard Medical School for their clinical work. The plan also included a parallel doctoral program leading to the Ph.D. degree for a new breed of MIT-Harvard-educated engineer devoted to medical and related fields.

The Harvard-MIT program has been a success. The students admitted to the program leading to the M.D. degree have proved to be extraordinarily able and, on completing the program, greatly in demand. It was fortunate that the two institutions were able to engage Dr. Irving London to head the program and to occupy a professorship that provided him permanent tenure in both institutions. It was agreed that in the beginning the program should have an endowment of at least $10 million, and I, together with Dr. George Thorn, began the solicitation of funds for this endowment.

Mrs. Whitaker (through the Whitaker Foundation) gave funds that matched a large grant from the Pew Memorial Trust which made it possible to finance that part of a building complex designed to handle the aggregation of biomedical sciences, including neuroscience.

In the 1970s, when I was a trustee, the Sloan Foundation undertook a program of grants to encourage research and teaching in the neurosciences. MIT had already launched a program in this field which was in part inspired by Professor Schmitt and by research in the Department of Psychology initiated by the late Professor Hans-Lucas Teuber, who created MIT's Department of Psychology. The program of the Sloan Foundation in support of the neurosciences (later including the cognitive sciences), was not unlike the pioneering program undertaken by the Rockefeller Foundation in the 1930s to advance work in the field of molecular biology. Initially aided by grants from the Sloan Foundation and from the growing interest in the brain sciences, MIT today offers strong programs in these fields, including the cognitive sciences. A formal course in the latter field has now been established, leading to a degree.

Dean John Deutch of the School of Science has defined technology as science plus engineering. Biology, he emphasizes, presents two perfect examples—biotechnology (genetic engineering) and molecular pharmacology—of the fruitfulness of this combination. Already molecular biologists are specifying the opportunities opening up in neurobiology! And I am told that the brain sciences will usher in a revolution in science similar to the revolution created by molecular biology and that MIT is well positioned to make major contributions to plant biology.

Recommendations and judgments of Corporation Visiting Committees to the Department of Biology in the 1960s were influential in shaping the future of the department. One committee (1961–62) reported its consensus that "for the reasonably forseeable future specialization in molecular biology was entirely appropriate" but added "that this should be viewed as a temporary posture and the Department should be prepared to enlarge its interests into other aspects of biological research." Another visiting committee (1963–64) continued "to wonder whether it is appropriate to base biology at MIT entirely on molecular biology." Committee members, especially from biology departments in other universities had not encountered elsewhere the uninhibited concentration that they saw in this vigorous and growing program.

A third visiting committee (1965–66), this one chaired by Dr. Bush, cast aside the concerns of previous committees. "The report of the Visiting Committee several years ago," noted the

Bush report, "had raised the question of whether there existed in the department an undue concentration on molecular biology. Your committee feels strongly that no such undue concentration exists at this time." This unequivocal endorsement of the frontier field of molecular biology was a decisive takeoff event in the department's climb to great distinction. Recently Professor Boris Magasanik, for several years head of the department following the release of the report, reviewed for me the growth to greatness of MIT biology and identified the Bush report as a watershed event in the Institute's program of molecular genetics.

I was a kibitzer at these three visiting committees, and my conviction about the value of strong Corporation Visiting Committees was enhanced. I recalled the visiting committee report that resulted, as I have noted before, in the separation of biology from food technology and realized that two visiting committee reports had been hinge events in moving MIT biology into a new era. In addition they demonstrated how visiting committees have made significant contributions to MIT's advance to a position of renown as a research university.

Professor Buchanan, now retired as John and Dorothy Wilson Professor Emeritus, has called my attention to other important influences that helped biology to flourish at MIT and that illustrate several of the themes that run through my memoir. One factor of importance was the decision that all related disciplines would remain within the single Department of Biology. This integration has provided an environment where professors can move into new areas of scientific endeavor quite different from their earlier training. These several circumstances moved the department, said Professor Buchanan, "from a collection of disciplines into the integrated field of molecular biology."

A notable example of the exciting discoveries that continue in molecular biology at the Institute and elsewhere was described in an eloquent lecture by Professor Robert A. Weinberg of MIT's Center for Cancer Research, a lecture prepared especially for the 1983 annual dinner meeting of the MIT Sustaining Fellows. Those who heard Professor Weinberg's lucid lecture came away enthralled by his exposition and by its revelation of the startling and promising discoveries that are occurring in molecular research laboratories. Professor Weinberg's lecture derived from his discovery, together with a group of associates, of a clue at the molecular level to explain how certain genes—called transformed genes or oncogenes—trigger cancer in the cells in which they are found. Later was to come the exciting announcement that work done in the Center for Cancer Research and the Department of Biology under the direction of Professor Eisen and Professor Susumu Tonegawa has achieved a long-sought immunological goal, "the identification of the receptor molecules by which T cells recognize antigens." These achievements, for me, brought into brilliant focus the story and the potential of biology in the setting of an institute of technology transformed into a research university.

This brief statement summarizes what I observed and learned as MIT moved aggressively to share in one of the most profound revolutions in the history of science.

In this sketch of the history of biology at the Institute, I have noted two programs that brought Harvard and MIT into effective collaboration. The first was the Harvard-MIT School for Health Officers; the second, the Harvard-MIT Health Sciences and Technology Program. These and other joint programs are instructive as case histories of how two institutions, one venerable and comprehensive, the other younger and specialized, both preeminent in their respective fields, have created an environment benign to cooperation. What has been achieved in Cambridge is a commonwealth of scholarship. Two strong, independent, individualistic institutions, vigorously competitive where need be, have forged an intellectual federation that makes Cambridge one of the great centers of learning and research in the world. Even though the two institutions remain jealously independent, they have been creating together a University of Cambridge—an entity that is the more effective because it has no corporate existence except as a willingness to collaborate among a community of scholars. The progress of MIT has been greatly aided by this collaboration.

THE ARTS AND HUMANITIES IN EVOLUTION

A School of Humanities and Social Studies was established in 1950 in response, as I have already reported, to a recommendation of the Committee on Educational Survey. Prior to this structural move to give the same professional status to the humanities and social studies as that afforded science, engineering, and architecture, these studies had been grouped under the less prestigious title of Division, but the division was headed by a dean. By the time that I came aboard there had been two deans of this division, first Edwin Burdell and then Robert Caldwell. Professor Burdell was to move on to become president of the Cooper Union in New York. An historian, Dean Caldwell had come to MIT at the request of President Compton after a period in the foreign service as a cultural attaché.

Under the more exalted title of School, the departments devoted to the humanities and social studies were able more rapidly to continue the development of a faculty of distinction that had been achieved in the divisional arrangement and to undertake graduate programs as well as undergraduate. Professor John E. Burchard had been told, to my delight, by President Compton that he would recommend him to be the first dean of the new school. My associations with Burchard and my cordial relations with him were an assurance to me that we could work together effectively in the development of the new school.

Burchard made lasting contributions to the new school and in other ways to the greening of the Institute. The Department of English and History in the new school became the Humanities Department and remained a faculty mainly for teaching undergraduates, and John and his successors concerned with the humanities as distinct from the social sciences experienced from time to time periods of discouragement in maintaining harmony, high morale, and motivation in a department without graduate students. Furthermore the requirements for study in the field by all undergraduates brings to the department's classrooms some who tend to view the humanities as dillettantish, and the teaching of whom seems to be a process of "entertaining strangers." If it has been difficult to maintain the same faculty spirit that prevailed in the days of Aydelotte, the fact remains that MIT is currently blessed with an array of distinguished humanist-scholars in its Humanities Department, which includes about one hundred members who, during the deanship of Harold J. Hanham, were skillfully grouped in six autonomous sections: anthropology and archaeology, foreign languages and literature, history, literature, and music, plus a writing program.

The School of Humanities and Social Science includes of course not only the Department of Humanities but strong departments in political science, psychology, linguistics and philosophy, and one of the world's great economics departments.

Burchard might well have been appointed dean of the School of Architecture because he had a scholarly interest in this field when he studied architectural engineering at the Institute and when he headed the Bemis Foundation, which had been created by a bequest from Albert Farwell Bemis, '93, to stimulate research in the field of prefabricated housing and which possessed small funds that could be allocated to other objectives. Associated with him for a brief period on this project was a brilliant young graduate in architecture, I. M. Pei, '40.

Burchard served as dean for fourteen years, and during this long tenure he continued his devotion to both the arts and the humanities while developing his scholarship in architecture. He thus brought to the deanship experience in a great variety of fields; in fact he was to affect profoundly the whole domain of the liberal arts and architecture at the Institute. There is no better way for me to discuss my relationship with the humanities and the arts at MIT than to describe Burchard's manifold activities, which I draw from a tribute paid to Burchard at the dedication of a plaque in his honor in 1979.

His first full-scale assignment at MIT was to be director of libraries, a shrewd appointment by Karl Compton, who recognized the need for what Burchard was to accomplish—a new type of university library building and a new philosophy of humane library management that placed books within easy reach of the users of libraries. This new approach did much to humanize and to quell the tendency to build monuments rather than active, easy-to-use, attractive libraries. His work and the Charles Hayden Memorial Library at MIT attracted national attention, and it was not long before John was called in as consultant by other universities in the building of new libraries and was asked to serve as a member of a Rockefeller Foundation-sponsored Cooperative Committee on Library Building Plans, which prepared a monograph, "Planning the University Library Building." In 1949 John was invited by the Australian government to consult on the building of the Australian National Library in Canberra.

As the first dean of the school of what was then called the Humanities and Social Studies, John, moved by the recommendations in the Lewis Committee report, initiated Course XXI and, along with Professors John Blum, Giorgio de Santillana, and Roy Lamson, demonstrated the value of this double-major program combining the humanities with engineering or science.

As he presided over the new school, John encouraged doctoral programs in political science, as the Lewis Committee had recommended, and established a political science section. He created a psychology section which was ultimately to become the distinguished department we now have. He ran interference for Professor Morris Halle in the start of a Ph.D. program in linguistics, which has become, together with its academic partner, philosophy, a distinguished department and a world center in linguistics. John also found satisfaction in the assistance he was able to give to Professor Joseph Everingham in recreating the Student Dramashop. He was responsible for including in the design of the Hayden Library a gallery for the exhibition of art. He contributed directly to the design of the gallery and initiated visiting shows with the diligent help of Professor Herbert Beckwith. He made seminal contributions to the Institute's program in the visual arts. He organized a distinguished committee under the chairmanship of Bartlett H. Hayes, Jr., to prepare a study of the visual arts at MIT. The committee's report, entitled "Art Education for Scientist and Engineer," contributed importantly not only to the treatment of the arts in the School of Humanities and Social Studies but in architecture and to the developing interest in the arts throughout MIT. His long-time interest in music had brought him into association with the Boston Symphony Orchestra, and at one time he audaciously negotiated with the manager of the orchestra to see if it were possible to have Boston Symphony concerts brought to MIT by direct cable. This didn't come off, but he exerted influence in leading the symphony to start public rehearsals and to undertake Youth Concerts. And it was he who initiated the MIT Humanities Series concerts, which continue today to bring great music to MIT. He deserves much of the credit, by backing Dean Everett Baker's recommendation, with the support of students, of Klaus Liepmann as music director and by supporting such distinguished appointments as those of Ernst Levy and Gregory Tucker, who provided the foundation for our present musical glories.

All of these enduring innovations occurred under his leadership as dean, but there were others.

I think of Burchard's influence as director of the Technology Press in its early days and his later chairmanship of the Technology Press Board; he deserves credit for helping to make the Press one of the distinguished university presses in the nation.

John served a period as president of the American Academy of Arts and Sciences and once remarked that the publication achievement that he was proudest of was the leadership he provided, with the help of the late Harlow Shapley, Howard Mumford Jones, and others, in establishing the academy's journal, *Daedalus*. He had the concept, brought to realization by Gerald Holton, of a quarterly intellectual journal that went beyond the quality of anything then published in the United States. Under the successive leadership of great editors this distinguished journal of interdisciplinary scholarship has come close to achieving the ideal John had in mind and is one of the glories of the American Academy of Arts and Sciences.

Although John received his degrees in architectural engineering at MIT, he never practiced architecture or engineering. Throughout his career, however, he cultivated his insights and skills as architectural critic and historian. This resulted in his sustained influence on the School of Architecture and on the architectural environment of MIT. He was influential in the decision of the MIT Building Committee to invite the firm of Anderson & Beckwith to design our elegant swimming pool, which was to become the first contemporary-style building on the campus, in fact the first modern university building in Cambridge. Because of a funds shortage we almost omitted the walled garden which had been planned as an integral part of this pool. But John Burchard was determined to see this unique feature kept. He solved the problem by persuading his class of 1923 to give the garden.

As head of the Bemis Foundation he made funds available to the School of Architecture to bring to MIT a series of great modern architects from abroad. Similarly, in his role as dean of the School of Humanities and Social Science, John brought distinguished lecturers here in the humanities, including such figures as Sir Richard Livingstone, Jacob Bronowski, and Aldous Huxley. We who were here remember the rapport between John and Huxley and how the Huxley lectures drew overflow audiences from all over metropolitan Boston.

John Burchard had still another career, this time in the defense research during World War II, for which he received the Medal for Merit awarded by President Truman.

John was the impresario and later the reporter of two great convocations at MIT which involved participation of scholars from around the world and some distinguished political figures, notably Winston Churchill and then Prime Minister Macmillan.

John was a prolific writer. He was the author of *Q.E.D.*, the history of MIT's participation in World War II, and editor of *Mid-Century: The Social Implications of Scientific Progress*, the proceedings of that great assembly in 1949. He wrote extensively on architecture and was the author, with Professor Albert Bush-Brown, of *The Architecture of America: A Social and Cultural History*, a volume that was undertaken under the auspices of the American Institute of Architects to commemorate its centennial in 1957. He joined Oscar Handlin in editing *The Historian and the City*, and he wrote a book-length essay, *The Rise of the Phoenix*, an account of West Germany's brilliant architectural reconstruction from the rubble of war. He worked with Mr. Bemis in writing *The Evolving House*, one of the early publications of the Technology Press. I worked with them both in seeing this through the press. Bemis, a socially minded Boston industrialist, had a vision of simplifying and rationalizing house construction.

Together with Mrs. Burchard, John, over his married career, visited practically every distinguished architectural monument in accessible parts of the world. This "architectural travel" was to lead him in the end to the writing of his magnum opus, the encyclopedic, unconventional, 600-page volume, *Bernini Is Dead? Architecture and the Social Purpose*. This book reached me after John's death and carried the following inscription written by Marjorie, his wife:

For Liz and Jim

This book was important to John, and in giving it to you he meant to express his deep appreciation for Jim's staunch and generous support and for the years of friendship we have enjoyed with both of you.

September 1976

In his major architectural books, as the subtitles indicate, there is preoccupation with social purpose and moral values. In the conclusion to his introduction to Kenzo Tange's beautiful book on the Ise Shrine in Japan, moved by this architectural masterpiece, Burchard noted that for himself, the priceless ingredients of any great architecture anywhere are repose, serenity, and silent space. "Perhaps these can be fully achieved," he wrote, "only if one believes in something very much—and if the something is greater than architecture."[7]

Following his retirement from active leadership of the school, John accepted invitations from several other institutions, notably from the University of California at Berkeley, where he was a visiting professor and, for a period, acting dean of the College of Environmental Design. Later, while serving as Thomas Jefferson Memorial Foundation Professor of Architecture, he received the University of Virginia's Thomas Jefferson Memorial Medal in Architecture, the second person to receive this distinction. The dean of the university's School of Architecture paid tribute to this versatile man by describing him as "an all-around person—a generalist, critic, and socially conscious man," and "a consultant to everybody about everything."

John was no pedant, far from it. He enjoyed the companionship of interesting people and was a conversationalist who elevated the level and vigor of social discourse and who caused delight by his rich collection of anecdotes and oddities. He was a baseball fan. He liked good food and had a scholarly knowledge of wines supported by a sharp palate. He was a walking Michelin guide to European restaurants. When my wife and I occasionally traveled in Europe, we asked his advice about hotels and restaurants and carried with us his copious suggestions. For a brief period he found his recreation in playing tournament bridge. His mastery of this kind of professional bridge led him momentarily to consider a career in it.

Although not a mountaineer, he was charmed by mountains. He once scrambled up the Matterhorn, but his love for the poetry of mountains was expressed mainly in ways other than climbing. Once while in Pakistan he and his wife undertook a rashly adventuresome, even dangerous, trip northward through the rugged country along the Afghanistan border in order to have a look at the wildly beautiful Hindu Kush range of mountains.

Long ago, when we were young and lighthearted, John gathered several of us to join him for an evening at a now-defunct but respectable Boston rathskeller to sing the antiphonal variety of German drinking songs, such as "Ein Heller und ein Batzen." I can still hear his reverberant voice when the singing reached a crescendo. What a lusty, exhuberant companion he could be!

I must add that this man of Renaissance versatility was no unflawed paragon beyond criticism. He had his crotchets, his frailties, and his shortcomings, but he admitted them and sought correction. He had his discouragements and severe disappointments, but he bore them bravely.

I have presented but a few facets of the colleague I remember and loved, but I would feel this tribute incomplete did it not, in conclusion, celebrate two other qualities—his teaching and his central vision of beauty.

While he was dean and after he retired, John taught undergraduate courses in the humanities. In a long letter that he wrote to me from France in May 1973, he spoke movingly of how illness had curtailed his teaching. In paraphrase: the last two years have been murder for me, he wrote, incapable of summoning the strength to undertake the routine of teaching which I loved so well, and the rewards I experienced in my last class when it was apparent that I could still be on such easy and pleasant terms with the young, who still write and call and often ask for advice. In these years near the end of his life, Burchard had also been deeply disturbed by the politicization of a few humanities teachers at that time. In fact radical teachers grievously disoriented humanities teaching in many institutions, including MIT, during those unhappy years.

John never ceased to urge the Institute to engage the great architects and to erect buildings that recognized beauty as well as commodity as indispensable to education.

In the lines of W. H. Auden:

To us he is no more a person
Now but a whole climate of opinion.[8]

As I conclude my appreciation of John Burchard and his accomplishments as the first dean of the School of Humanities and Social Studies, let me affirm some of my own views about the humanities based on my experience at MIT.

In his Arthur D. Little Lecture at MIT in 1951, Sir Henry Tizard recalled a statement I made in my inaugural address in 1949. "President Killian," he said, "has recorded that when he was returning with Mr. Churchill, after the latter's great speech in this city at the Mid-Century Convocation, Mr. Churchill leant over to him and said, 'As you advance science at your great institution, don't neglect the humanities.' Mr. Killian told him that you [MIT] have not, and will not. Had I been Mr. Killian, I should have been sorely tempted to add: 'Will you, Mr. Churchill, use your great influence to persuade the humanists not to neglect the sciences?' "

I believe that the modern research university offers unique opportunities to cultivate many new integrations between the liberal arts and the sciences. In addition I have witnessed in my time the emergence of a number of new fields such as the neurosciences, the cognitive sciences, computer science, artificial intelligence, and molecular biology, which in spirit and method can and must be both humanistic and scientific. Inevitably they make inventions or achieve discoveries that raise ethical questions, whose handling could be aided by the insights of humanists. In fact these fields more and more need cognate relations with the humanities. The rapid discoveries occurring in genetic research and in biotechnology create many developments that would benefit from the guidance of humanists. This is true of course in technology as it changes our environment for good or ill and in medicine as shown in spectacular fashion by the introduction of an artificial heart into a human being and the prospect that biotechnology can create animals larger than their normal size.

In listing examples of the many ways the humanities appear in productive partnership with intellectual undertakings not usually thought of as humanistic, I hope that this commerce with other domains can give the humanities new confidence, wider scope, and unrealized consequences *for all learning* by the ordering of its boundaries.

Nationally the humanists seem deeply worried as science thrives and invades territory that once was the property of the humanities. A distinguished humanist at Harvard recently wrote for the *Harvard Magazine* a refreshingly candid article about "The Crisis in English Studies," and many other humanists are stressing the need for reform.

In the 1950s, when university physicists, chemists, and biologists were undertaking major curricular reform programs in the secondary schools, many of us hoped that the university humanists would join the effort. Only the social scientists were energetic enough to launch a program of their own, although they failed to see it through. This indifference was a great pity since in those years the government and a few major foundations were moved to appropriate large funds for the preparation of new and better teaching materials and for teacher training institutes for secondary teachers.[9] This failure by the university humanists is felt today in the weak preparation of many students entering college. The humanists today have an even greater opportunity than did the scientists in the early 1950s to aid curriculum reform in precollege schools—and in the universities as well.

Although I am glad to see the current efforts to quantify and computerize the humanities, I think we in the universities must be alert to prevent the attenuation of those subjects that draw their power from the free spirit of the *litterae humaniores*. I do not favor a kind of scientific humanism, nor do I suggest that we develop the humanities in the image of science and technology or overwhelm them with computer software, however brilliant. I believe, as did Jacob Bronowski, that "every cast of mind [especially the humanities] has its creative activity which explores the likeness appropriate to it." There are exciting new methods arising from computer programs such as Athena, but there are no substitutes for the humanities in their basic pristine forms.

Isaiah Berlin, in a collection of his essays published in 1978, concluded that in the domain of abstract ideas, a divorce between the sciences and the humanities was effected in the early eighteenth century by the ideas advanced by the Italian philosopher Giambattista Vico and his contemporaries.[10] Is it not possible that a reunion may soon be achieved by the multiplying linkages of the humanities with science and other disciplines we see today, especially in research universities, where powerful computer systems are being integrated with teaching and research?

AFFINITIES AND INTERSECTIONS IN SCIENCE AND THE HUMANITIES

While living and working in a hotbed of science and technology, I have found occasional recreation in searching out what Adam Smith called "ingenious similitudes" connecting science, the humanities, philosophy, and other fields of knowledge. Adam Smith not only wrote the classic *Wealth of Nations* but an essay, *Principles which lead and direct Philosophical Enquiries, illustrated by the History of Astronomy*. In this discussion on the philosophy of scientific discovery he gives priority not to *utility* but to the intellectual or aesthetic sentiments of *wonder, surprise,* and *admiration* as the principal motives of "philosophical research."[11]

At this point in my memoir let me pause to provide a few examples of the less recondite sort where metaphors and equations meet, and where the arts have impressively contributed to science and technology.

In the fall of 1970 *Daedalus* published an essay by Gerald Holton which explores the roots of Niels Bohr's concept of complementarity and cites Bohr's view that "in other fields of knowledge we are confronted with situations reminding us of the situation in quantum physics." Bohr, for example, had apparently been stimulated in thinking about complementarity by a "little book" written by the nineteenth century poet and philosopher Paul Martin Møller. In addition Bohr once made clear his indebtedness to a chapter, the "Stream of Thought," in William James' *Principles of Psychology*.

An unusual contribution of science to the humanities has been called to my attention by Sissela Bok—Johann Wolfgang von Goethe's little-read romantic novel *Elective Affinities*, published in 1809. The structure of this fiction dealing with individual and social conduct was suggested to Goethe by a concept originating in studies by the Swedish chemist Torben Bergman. In fact this concept of elective affinities is still familiar in modern chemistry.

At MIT Cyril Stanley Smith, a distinguished metallurgist and materials scientist, has devoted himself in the years of his seniority to searching out ways in which the artists and craftsmen in ancient times were frequently the precursors in the processing of materials and at times the originators of technological and scientific advance. In his introductory essay for an exhibit, *Aspects of Art and Science*, at the National Museum of History and Technology and later at MIT, Cyril Smith noted: "The rich diversity of the properties of materials was discovered, primarily in the Middle East, centuries before there was any attempt to analyze this diversity or explain it in philosophic terms. Almost all materials used in engineering prior to the present century were known in the decorative arts before 2,000 B.C." As organized by Dr. Jon B. Eklund, this exhibit illustrated the concepts of Professor Smith by showing dramatically that "the qualities and nature of the materials to which the artist responded sensually are inherently the same as the properties and structures that are measured and explained by the scientist."

Among the talented teachers and scholars in the humanities at MIT of my time was Giorgio de Santillana, historian of scientific ideas and author of the distinguished study *The Crime of Galileo*. In his essay, "The Role of Art in the Scientific Renaissance," he agreed with art historian Erwin Panofsky that "the discovery of perspective and the related methods of drawing three-dimensional objects to scale were as necessary for the development of the 'descriptive' sciences in a pre-Galilean period as were the telescope and the microscope in the next centuries."[12] De Santillana also emphasized that the great architect-artist Brunelleschi created his theory of perspective by experimental means.

The syncretic relations of science and the arts are coming to be more widely understood. In a very deep sense they are interdependent, and they spring from the same act of imagination. Dr. Wiesner is fond of quoting a comment made by the poet, Stanley Kunitz, at a meeting of the MIT Council for the Arts. "There are many disciplines," said Kunitz, "but only one imagination." At another time Wiesner, in discussing the theme of creativity in science education, said: "We must explicitly encourage the development of habits and skills in looking for, and using, analogies, similes, and metaphors to juxtapose, readily, facts and ideas that might not first appear to be interrelated."

In his posthumously published Pegram Lectures, André Maurois recounts an anecdote told to him by the poet Saint-John Perse. (Alexis Saint-Léger Léger). Once while he was living in Washington, Einstein called Perse from Princeton and asked him to come to see him. "I have a question to ask you," said Einstein. Saint-John Perse did visit Einstein, and the great physicist put to him the question: "How does the poet work? How does the idea of a poem come to him? How does this idea grow?" Saint-John Perse described the vast part played by intuition and by the subconscious. Einstein seemed delighted: "But it's the same thing for the man of science," he said. "The mechanics of discovery are neither logical nor intellectual. It is a sudden illumination, almost a rapture. Later, to be sure, intelligence, analysis, and experiments confirm (or invalidate) the intuition. But initially there is a great forward leap of the imagination."

The late George Sarton, historian of science, concluded that "one of the truly great events of the Renaissance" was the cultivation by pioneering German botanists of a class of draftsmen and woodcut artists to make accurate illustrations of plants directly from nature. "Art and science came together and great was the result."[13] These drawings were beautiful as well as accurate.

Over the years I have observed the remarkable success of the Research Laboratory of Electronics in projecting information theory and cybernetics into many fields of technology and the humanities. Out of it have cascaded many new ideas to start new river deltas in other parts of the Institute. Among these we may count the MIT brand of linguistics, which found encouragement in the Research Laboratory of Electronics.

I have also observed from a grandstand seat the identification of new intersections where the humanists and the social scientists find common ground. In econometrics, mathematics, literature, music, and philosophy, for example, there appear to be rigorous and versatile methods of analysis that can provide humanistic scholars with new and sharper tools for their research and teaching. In his distinguished study of elites in Mexico, political scientist and historian Peter Smith successfully used quanitative methods to dig deeper into his subject.

Historians especially are finding increasing opportunity to take advantage of techniques in other fields. I recall the use of statistical inference by Frederick Mosteller and David Wallace to identify the authorship of certain of the Federalist Papers, an identification that over the years baffled historians. The work of these two scholars reaches back to that of the British mathematician Thomas Bayes and draws on other methods of discrimination useful to the historian. For those who do not know the story, these two statisticians reached the firm conclusion that Madison was the author of those papers whose authorship had been uncertain. Many institutions contributed to this statistical work, including MIT's Computation Center.[14]

The work of Mosteller and Wallace on the Federalist Papers followed the lead of the earlier studies by the Swedish scholar, Alvar Ellegard, on the so-called Junius Letters, a series of letters that appeared in the *Public Advertiser* under the pseudonym Junius. Ellegard published a book on his work under the title *Statistical Method for Determining Authorship*. One of the objectives of the study was to determine whether a Sir Philip Francis was an author of some of the letters. Ellegard never reached a firm conclusion about the authorship, but he did find many features of writing style and vocabulary that resembled closely those of Sir Philip.[15]

In the last two decades the application of computer technology to linguistic and literary data has been steadily increasing. One example of exceptional interest is the analysis of the Greek (Koine) New Testament text by Timothy and Barbara Friberg at the University of Minnesota.[16]

B. L. Vercoe, associate professor of Music and Technology at MIT and himself a composer, has made his Experimental Music Studio a noted center for experiments in computer-generated and computer-processed sound, including the use of the computer for musical composition. The MIT Press publishes the *Computer Music Journal*, the most comprehensive publication to concentrate fully on the skills, technologies, and promises of computer-processed and digital audio sound.

In the preface to his famous textbook in economics, Paul Samuelson recalls C. P. Snow's lament about the separation of the two cultures. "Economics," wrote Samuelson, "is part of both those cultures, a subject that can combine the attractive features of both the humanities and the sciences. For two centuries, educated men have found in it the human interest of life itself, while at the same time economic principles display some of the logical beauty of Euclid's geometry."[17]

A program in anthropology and archaeology, with a staff of six, has prospered at MIT by drawing together the social sciences, the humanities, the arts, and materials science and engineering. Heather Lechtman, for example, has recently introduced me to her archaeological studies of prehistoric metallurgy in pre-Colombian Andean societies. Through a feat of scholarship she has brilliantly illuminated Andean prehistory through her sensitive demonstration of how sophisticated technology gave subtle expression to the Andean value system. Her colleague, Arthur Steinberg, trained as a classicist, has studied ancient bronze and copper-working in Middle Eastern digs.

This program in archaeology, conjointly with the Department of Materials Science and Engineering, has founded a center that serves eight universities and cultural institutions in metropolitan Boston, with MIT accepting the coordinating responsibility for the group.

Nobel laureate and MIT alumnus Richard Feynman in his famous physics textbook known as the *Feynman Lectures* ends a discussion of symmetry in physics by introducing a charming aesthetic metaphor:

. . . Why is nature so nearly symmetrical? No one has any idea why. The only thing we might suggest is something like this: There is a gate in Japan, a gate in Neiko, which is sometimes called by the Japanese the most beautiful gate in all Japan; it was built in a time when there was great influence from Chinese art. This gate is very elaborate, with lots of gables and beautiful carving and lots of columns and dragon heads and princes carved into the pillars, and so on. But when one looks closely he sees that in the elaborate and complex design along one of the pillars, one of the small design elements is carved upside down; otherwise the thing is completely symmetrical. If one asks why this is, the story is that it was carved upside down so that the gods will not be jealous of the perfection of man. So they purposely put an error in there, so that the gods would not be jealous and get angry with human beings.

We might like to turn the idea around and think that the true explanation of the near symmetry of nature is this: that God made the laws only nearly symmetrical so that we should not be jealous of His perfection![18]

Whether the progress of science is shaped to some degree by the larger cultural movements is more uncertain and more difficult to argue. Yet I remember well a conversation I had some fifty years ago with Norbert Wiener, who expressed to me his own conviction that *mathematics,* at least, "has been an active participant in the larger aesthetic movements." Later Wiener set these ideas down at my request in an article on "Mathematics and Art" in the *Technology Review.*[19] He essayed to show how mathematics is a fine art as close to that of music, literature, and painting as these are one to another and that it has shared in the characteristic style of the philosophy and aesthetics and general culture that differentiates, more or less, one period from another in the history of Western civilization.

Wiener's humane influence on our academic community was enormous and lasting. Today's great humanists in nonhumanistic disciplines are typified by physicist Victor Weisskopf, metallurgist Cyril Smith, and numerous others, to which I must add without apology a succession of Institute presidents.

GYORGY KEPES

Another distinguished teacher and artist at MIT, a cherished friend and colleague of mine, Gyorgy Kepes, has written and spoken eloquently about the syncretic relationship of science to the arts; in fact he was among the first faculty members to stir significant interest at MIT in the kinship of science and the arts. His classic book, *The New Landscape in Art and Science* (1956), was a definitive statement of his views.[20]

In 1978 a volume of tribute to Professor Kepes and reproductions of his work was published as a monograph prepared by Marjorie Supovitz in behalf of the MIT Committee on the Visual Arts.[21]

This monograph provided me with an opportunity to make clear that Kepes too had been for several decades, perhaps without knowing it, a broadening influence in my life.

I really came to know him first through his paintings. In 1953 I acquired for my office one of his paintings, *The Nest*, and as I carried on my day-to-day duties, I found inspiration and delight in the way this painting captured something of the essence of nature's poetry. Sometime later I went to the Whitney Museum of American Art to see the annual exhibition of works by American artists, and there was a Kepes painting bearing the title *Blue Reflections*, which was so compelling to my taste that I acquired it for my home. Still later my wife and I were able to add to this early collection two other paintings of his, *Smiling Horizon* and *Sunscape*, which were generous gifts from Professor Kepes and his wife Juliet. Thanks to the generosity of Kepes and his Fellows at the center for Advanced Visual Studies, we subsequently were honored to be presented with a pure light sculpture, an expression of the relationship between art and science conceived by Kepes and executed by Gary Rieveschl. We also possess a large bronze sculpture executed on commission for our home by artist Professor Richard Filipowski, a striking three-dimensional constructivist piece.

I have come to know Kepes well as a teacher and as a friend. I recall, not long after he arrived at MIT, visiting his photographic studio in the Department of Architecture. I then began to understand the provocative ideas Kepes was bringing into architecture at MIT, indeed into all of the Institute. His fundamental belief in the symbiotic relationship of art and science had already been eloquently set forth in his books, lectures, and teaching, and I saw his influence spreading through all parts of MIT. I came to agree with the statement made by Dean Wurster in a letter to me in 1969 that "on the educational side at MIT, my great gift was to get Gyorgy Kepes."

From time to time I sought to find for him some modest support for his programs and those of his associates and I greeted with much satisfaction the initiative taken by President Stratton to reconstruct a building to house his Center for Advanced Visual Studies. During this period others at MIT were encouraging the development of the arts and the acquisition of art not simply as an embellishment but as an essential part of the task of educating men and women for the kind of society we aspire to in this country. Kepes's presence provided inspiration and assurance to this group that has given MIT an indigenous role for itself in the arts. His catholicity as an artist and his lucidity as spokesman for the arts have thus played major roles in this development of the arts at MIT. Both as writer and speaker Kepes has shown an artistry that greatly enhances his impact. Although his native language is Hungarian, he has a mastery of English, yes an eloquence, that is brilliantly expository and evangelical in expressing his ideas and ideals.

In addition to admiring these ways in which Kepes has advanced the arts in a scientific setting, I came to count him as a friend in whose bright company I found intellectual delights.

One of his great accomplishments has been the way in which he has quite unconsciously achieved a magnetism to draw friends to him and to refresh the air about him. Contributing to these qualities and sharing his interests stands his wife, Juliet, a delightful woman and herself a talented artist.

I count it fortunate to have this opportunity to speak of two master teachers of immense personal charm, Kepes and Burchard, in the domain of the arts and humanities.

A CHAPEL FOR ALL AND
A RELIGIOUS PROGRAM FOR MIT

The Committee on Financing Development included in its campaign objectives funds for a chapel and an auditorium and secured from the Kresge Foundation large grants to help in financing these buildings. To design these two structures, we engaged the distinguished architect, Eero Saarinen, and he came forward with two dazzling designs, an auditorium enclosed by a thin-shelled concrete eighth of a sphere and a round chapel surrounded by a moat to reflect dancing sunshine onto its interior walls. Both designs, especially the chapel, provoked controversy. "Whoever saw a round church," asked an MIT Corporation member, but we soon made available to the Corporation photographs of numerous round churches in Europe, one of which I had photographed in Cambridge, England. In the end a brave Corporation approved the designs. But when the chapel was built, the controversy about its design broke out again in the local press. Those who had not experienced the reverential quality of the chapel's interior and its lovely altar and Bertoia screen crudely described it as a "gas tank." Today it is on the itinerary of sightseeing buses, and the soaring Bertoia screen and the bell tower designed by Theodore Roszak were to whet the appetite of the MIT community for additional sculpture of distinguished quality. In an article in *Time* magazine (May 7, 1984) architectural critic Wolf von Eckardt described Saarinen's chapel as "one of 20th century architecture's greatest triumphs." I often have thought of the chapel and other buildings on the oval common as providing MIT, in the traditional New England sense, a meeting house.

In the decision to build a chapel, the administration of the Institute was sensitive to the importance of avoiding the introduction into the Institute community of any bias for or against any denomination or religion. Unlike several institutions in the Boston area, MIT had never been associated with a particular faith. Rather, as a secular institution MIT had been wholly ecumenical in its attitude toward religious activity and it had welcomed the appointment of chaplains by the different denominations and provided offices for them.

I sought advice, notably from a member of the MIT Corporation, the Reverend Theodore P. Ferris, the memorably eloquent minister of Trinity Episcopal Church in Boston, and he expressed the wise hope that in proceeding with the chapel, the Institute would not encourage any arrangement that would stir religious controversy. This led us to recognize that the design of the chapel itself should not express commitment to any particular tradition, and in its design, Saarinen skillfully fulfilled this requirement, creating a meeting place adaptable to almost any kind of religious service, funeral, wedding, or meditation. If the chapel had been Gothic, for example, it would not have been acceptable in the way that his final design proved to be. Still it provided an interior exalting and reverential in spirit.

When we showed our chapel design to the Catholic chaplain at the Institute, he regretfully expressed the view that his church was unlikely to make use of any house of worship unconsecrated by the Catholic church. I was unwilling to be governed by this view, and so I went to see Archbishop Richard Cushing, later to become cardinal, whom I had come to know and for whom I had great respect. I told him of our desire to have a chapel that would be used by all religious groups and made clear that the Institute had no commitment in its history to any denomination and no prejudice regarding his great church. After some reflection he said: "Jim, this is the only policy for MIT to follow." He then told me that he would instruct the Catholic chaplains who provided service to the MIT community to use the chapel without hesitation. He further said that on completion of the chapel he would come and offer the first Mass, which he did. Later on he made a gift to the chapel of a set of ceremonial "furniture" to be used in the Catholic services. As matters worked out, the Catholics conduct Mass several days a week, and the chapel is available to every authentic religious group, including the Vedanta Society and Hillel. Two other institutions in the Boston area had found it necessary to build three chapels in order to provide for all religions.

During these discussions I sought to express the policy of the Institute and the spirit of the chapel in my President's Report of 1954, and my statement on the chapel won wide acceptance. I wrote:

An institution which embraces general as well as professional education must give attention to man's spiritual life—to the place of religion in man's history, in contemporary society and in the life of the individual. It also must encourage an understanding of those postulates which underlie our society's concept of virtue—the unifying ideals and standards, the moral and ethical beliefs which men in general agree upon but reach by diverse paths of faith, philosophy or social pressure. The responsibility to deal with these great matters is inherent in any program to educate young people adequately and broadly. Their all-round development requires a growth of the spirit as well as the mind.

How does a secular institution such as MIT handle this responsibility properly? It does so by maintaining an atmosphere of religious freedom and, within this environment of freedom, by providing adequate opportunity for its students to deepen their understanding of their own spiritual heritage and freely to pursue their own religious interests and to worship God in their own way. Certainly it must avoid advocating any creed or theological doctrine. While partaking of the Judeo-Christian traditions and postulates of American society, a private secular institution must at the same time embrace our tradition of religious tolerance by being equally hospitable to all genuine religions, creeds and personal convictions. Its institutional policy must be one of equal opportunity for all beliefs and outlooks, which means not only that it must express no bias toward any creed but also that it must not exhibit any bias toward religion itself. A private secular institution should be hospitable to religion and to the pursuit of spiritual matters by men of all creeds and differing outlooks, but it should not as an institution permit itself to be used to advocate or deny any theological doctrine or any philosophical position toward religion. Our responsibility is to provide opportunity, in a manner wholly elective, for the development of spiritual maturity and the exercise of spiritual interests.

The small devotional chapel which we are building at MIT has been conceived and will be used in accord with these principles. It will be in the completest sense non-sectarian, equally available to individuals and groups of all faiths. Its purpose is two-fold:

First, to stand as a symbol of the place of the spirit in the life of the mind and as a physical statement of the fact that MIT has a right and a responsibility to deal with ideals as well as ideas and to be concerned with the search for virtue while we become proficient in the search for things.

Second, to provide ready opportunity for students and other members of our community to worship as they choose, to have on campus a building, beautiful and evocative of reverence and meditation, where those who wish may enter and worship God in their fashion.

This two-fold purpose of course includes the provision of opportunities for the separate faiths and groups to use the chapel each in its own way so long as this does not require special privilege. It also means that the chapel will be available for appropriate ceremonies such as marriages and other rites. The chapel will not embrace the full responsibilities of a church and thus will not compete with the neighboring churches which serve members of our community.

I share the hope, I said, that the chapel may serve to encourage a creative approach to matters of the spirit. As I have already suggested, an institution of science may well be an environment especially favorable to deeper spiritual insights. More important than its practical achievements are the spiritual contributions of science, its emphasis on the importance of truth and of the value of brotherhood and its revelation of the beauty, the order and the wonder of the universe. Through these contributions it shares with the great faiths opportunities for furthering man's spiritual understanding; and creative minds and spirits, availing themselves of the resources of both science and religion, may advance man's search for virtue and understanding with new vigor and in new ways.

The chapel is in this sense but a part of a broader spiritual program long evolving at the Institute. The future direction and method of this program must rest upon community acceptance and desire, and coordinate with our developing program in the humanities and social sciences. It should grow naturally out of the spiritual values which are inherent in our institution. We should remember that MIT was founded by unselfish men for altruistic purposes and that it has always been an implicit expression of high moral purposes and standards. As a consequence we have a community held together by a humane and tolerant spirit of mediation, reconciliation and reverence for the individual, a community governed by a passion for truth, freedom of inquiry and a preoccupation with ideal aims. We have a community generous in its opportunities to live and let live; a community where men of many faiths and backgrounds are free to interact on each other; a community committed to the ideals of professional service, of ministering to the public, of advancing learning and creating beauty.

These are the spiritual bonds that hold together our society of scholars. Our developing spiritual program, to be valid, must embrace them, exalt them and be consonant with the environment they have created.

This policy for the chapel, as well as its architectural design, placed the chapel firmly and unambiguously in the liberal position of being fully nondenominational. Thus we avoided the controversy that at one time arose over the uses of Harvard's Memorial Church.

At the time the chapel and the Kresge Auditorium were dedicated, I made a brief statement about my attitude toward untraditional or modern architectural designs. In the design of the Anderson and Beckwith swimming pool and of the Aalto dormitory MIT had taken the lead in the Boston university community by introducing the contemporary style to its campus. Harvard too was to become a seedbed of the modern style,

Bauhaus version, beginning with its recruitment of Walter Gropius for its design faculty. MIT's acceptance of modern architecture provoked criticism, but we felt that an institute of technology, especially one that had established the first School of Architecture in the nation, had a responsibility to accept the vernacular of the currently most creative architects in the design of its new buildings in the same spirit that it seeks scientific innovations in its research. Its intellectual resources and outlook, I felt, permitted it to be bold and advanced in the design of its buildings. In fact an architectural critic made the comment that only MIT had the self-assurance to build its domed auditorium and its round chapel.

I am persuaded that we have a great obligation to cherish and preserve all that is fine in the world, but we also should have the courage and freedom to undertake the new. Instead, then, of our campus's becoming "a museum of caution and paralysis," its buildings should seek to express the best methods and materials and the best aesthetic ideals of the periods in which its buildings are built, all subject to the firm discipline of a master plan constantly reappraised.

After I had recalled for this chapter words spoken at the dedication of the Kresge Auditorium and the MIT Chapel, I became aware of an exhibition called "Boston: Forty Years of Modern Architecture" at the Institute of Contemporary Art in Boston. In an article in the *New York Times* reporting this exhibition, the distinguished architectural critic Ada Louise Huxtable generously wrote: "Most of the buildings [in this exhibition] were brought to Boston by something else that the city's intellectual leadership has specialized in—enlightened patronage. Strictly speaking, Boston's great educational institutions, Harvard and the Massachusetts Institute of Technology, were the real crucible in which American modern architecture was formed. . . . It was in the Harvard-MIT crucible that several generations of architects were trained who became the leaders of the profession and the setters of the style."

Architectural innovation is accompanied by controversy and

reveals deep divergencies in taste—and here I speak knowingly. This is the price of creativity in the arts, and we should be willing to risk the controversy in order to achieve a mutation in beauty or to afford the searching, creative minds of our time an opportunity to try new solutions.

In the 1940s and 1950s, beginning with the contemporary alumni swimming pool, the Aalto serpentine dormitory,† and Saarinen's Kresge Auditorium and round chapel, MIT began to break away from Bosworth's Beaux-Arts architecture and plan. As Joseph Hudnut once said, a university is a "live and unpredictable creature" and cannot be contained in any grand composition conforming to a single style. A look at MIT today confirms this judgment.

When the architect of the Chapel, Eero Saarinen, died, his family arranged to have his memorial service in the MIT Chapel as he had requested. Later I received from Mrs. Saarinen this note: "I appreciated the kindness of everyone at MIT in letting us use the chapel for the memorial service. It seemed right. I thank you, too, for giving Eero the opportunity to work at MIT. It meant much to him. Those two youthful works were foundation stones for much that came afterwards . . . and I am consoled that they will be there as long as this world lasts."

The new-style buildings of the late 1940s and the 1950s at MIT aroused latent interest in the arts in the Institute community, and they were the precursors of a rapidly growing commitment to the arts during the regimes of my presidential successors.

I have always admired the architectural splendors of the Oxford and Cambridge colleges. By a passionate commitment to "firmness, commodity, and delight" and by a skillful adaptation of the vernacular of their times, these colleges, with few exceptions, have achieved buildings human in scale and in plan that place architecture brilliantly at the service of humane education. I hope MIT is well on the way to achieving in the style of its time a similar architectural achievement in which nobly humane buildings, bold in design, serve to enrich its education. This can be achieved, I am sure, without resorting to the current slavish vogue of gable roofs.

A VISIT WITH HENRY MOORE

While in England in October 1972 I arranged to see Henry Moore, the British sculptor, at his home and studio in the pastoral village of Much Haddam. He had already been approached by Jerry Wiesner and by Wayne Andersen, chairman of the Committee on the Visual Arts, to do a large work for the Institute. I was delegated to encourage him to accept such a commission.

When I arrived, he was attending to another client who had already arrived, and he invited me to roam around the adjacent garden and fields, where a variety of his great pieces were displayed, and to visit the work under way in his studio sheds, where several pieces were being burnished or completed. This was a revelatory experience that helped me better to understand the achievement of Moore's unique sculptural style and how it combines the purely abstract with the obviously realistic—"the exact point," as Professor Wayne Andersen was to say at the dedication four years later, "between 'made by nature' and 'made by man.'"

Moore later proposed a piece that was promptly approved, after he had submitted a maquette and suggested a title *Three Piece Reclining Figure, Draped*. Now in place in Killian Court, it seems beautifully right and naturalistic for this environment.

Some time after the dedication of Moore's sculpture, I was browsing in Professor William H. McNeill's *The Rise of the West: A History of the Human Community* and read his penetrating insights into the relationship of the arts to the evolution of men and their societies. In concluding his discussion of the visual arts, he devotes a full page to one of Moore's earlier versions of his reclining figures series and observes that "presumably the artist intended to penetrate beyond optical appearances in order to achieve an imagery capable of resonating within the observers' subconsciousness." And then he adds: "In such a statue . . . our twentieth-century scientific emancipation from the cultural parochialisms of the past finds concise visual embodiment." How apt a statement about Moore's reclining figure at MIT!

The Moore sculpture was a superb addition to the arts-in-the-environment program at MIT which the energetic efforts of President Wiesner were furthering. May the Institute in the future find continued fulfillment of its intent to achieve an environment where distinguished art, architecture, and landscaping are not just embellishments or luxuries but an essential and natural part of the process of education and growth.

COLLEGE ATHLETICS UNDEFILED

In 1954 MIT's varsity lightweight crew, who had an impressive winning record, journeyed to England to race in the Henley Royal Regatta, the world's most renowned crew races. There it won the Thames Challenge Cup for being first in its class. The crew invited me to accompany them to Henley. And as I watched the race, I overcame my normal reticence and urged them on with a display of uninhibited cheering that would have astonished my colleagues back in Cambridge and indeed did shock the great gathering of English spectators, the men wearing straw boaters and rowing blazers and the women in elegant haute couture dress. My conduct and the ambiance, I am sure, were as gauche as Eliza's in *My Fair Lady*, when she broke through all restraints to urge on her favorite horse at Ascot. The MIT lightweight crew brought the cup back from Henley again in 1955.

Recently an MIT alumnus, H. W. McCurdy, made gifts to the Institute to endow rowing. He proudly bears the title "Father of Crew" at the Institute and over the years has frequently contributed new shells for our rowing program. He does this because, as he said in the deed for his endowment gift, "In creating this fund, it is my purpose to provide an endowment for the permanent benefit of rowing at MIT. I have long felt crew to be an ideal college sport. It tends to attract students of exceptional quality, offers special benefits to those who participate, and provides a form of intercollegiate competition that fulfills the highest ideals of amateur athletics. . . . I further wish through this endowment to express my enthusiastic support for the Institute's athletic policies and programs."

In another letter McCurdy extolled the noncommercial aspects of crew and by inference decried the commercialization of big-time televised intercollegiate sports. "Crew," he wrote, "is the last of the major intercollegiate sports that remains amateur. All the rest are training camps for the professionals. It will stay that way. No one will ever make a dollar pulling an oar."

A second example of the pride taken in our athletic program occurred in 1955. A student, David Flett du Pont, was killed in an automobile accident shortly before he was to return to the Institute for his senior year. One week before his death, on attaining the age of twenty-one, he signed a will that provided a trust for the benefit of a number of charitable causes and institutions including MIT, and this trust included $1 million for the improvement of our athletic facilities. He said that he was prompted to do this because of the pleasure he had experienced in playing on intramural teams as a representative of his fraternity.

Alumni contributed funds before World War II for the Alumni Pool and Briggs Field House and, in the late 1970s, for a fine new track, the Steinbrenner Stadium, and a magnificent Athletics and Activities Center, which includes a hockey rink and indoor 200-meter track. Earlier the Harold Whitworth Pierce Charitable Trust, by making a grant of $300,000, made possible the building of one of the nation's finest facilities for rowing. At the dedication of this boathouse, I said: "A thousand years ago, when I was an MIT undergraduate, the athletic facilities at MIT were meager indeed. There was then no swimming pool, no Briggs Field House, no Rockwell Cage, no Sailing Pavilion, no playing fields on West Campus, no Armory, and no du Pont Athletic Center. Having experienced those austere conditions, I have found special satisfaction in the opportunity to share in the dedication of every one of these facilities we didn't have in 1926."

MIT refuses to offer or grant a single athletic scholarship or to recruit a single applicant whose athletic ability takes precedence over scholastic ability. Its sports and recreation program is totally free of commercialism. The Institute charges no admission to any athletic events, nor does it accept a share of gate receipts collected by host institutions when visiting them.

The percentage of the student body participating in athletics at the Institute is probably unmatched in any other American institution. The program for men includes varsity and subvarsity teams, and there are eleven sports for women. It has had the good fortune to have great directors of athletics such as Ivan Geiger, Richard Balch, and Ross Smith, who exercised national influence through their devotion to integrity in college athletics. Smith helped in finding his able successor, Royce N. Flippin, Jr., who came to MIT from Princeton in 1980. Highly competent coaches for both men and women are available not only for intercollegiate teams but for all students and members of the MIT community interested in achieving skills for lifetime use in sports such as sailing, tennis, and sculling, to mention but a few. A high-spirited intramural program for student residences and fraternities continues to attract a large number of students. MIT fields excellent teams in such glamorized, high-pressure sports as basketball, track, and hockey without their being infected by commercialism. There is football, but it is low-key "club" football and played for fun.

Originally inscribed above a now-dismantled gateway to an old MIT athletic field and now on a prominent plaque in the new athletics center are these lines of an MIT alumnus of the class of 1887, the late Gelett Burgess (who also wrote of *The Purple Cow*, and regretted it, and who coined new words for the English language in use today, such as bromide):

Not the quarry, but the chase
Not the laurel, but the race
Not the hazard, but the play
Make me, Lord, enjoy alway!

In a day when mottoes are out of date and sentiments are inhibited, this inscription is still appropriate for MIT's athletic program.

Among those who were ardent supporters of MIT's athletic system in its early days were three whom I wish to commemorate. John A. Rockwell, '96, whose name was given to the Cage, for many years lent time and energy to the furtherance of the athletic program. The field house next door to the Cage bears the name of Frank Harrison Briggs, '81, who along with President Walker initiated MIT's athletic policies.

Finally, I especially delight in celebrating the late biochemist, Dr. Allan Winter Rowe of the class of 1901, to whom I was deeply indebted for many personal reasons. To those who did not know him, he must have appeared a boulevardier who had wandered by mistake onto the playing fields of MIT. His waxed mustache, his spats, his elegant clothes most certainly would lead to this impression. To those who had the privilege of knowing him, however, he was a memorable figure in the life of the Institute in the decades of the twenties and thirties. This figure who appeared so incongruous among those who normally gathered at a track meet or at meetings of the Alumni Council, the Medical Department, or the MIT Corporation is etched in my memory as one of the most loyal and useful members of the MIT community, and he left his imprint on many aspects of MIT life.

It was my good fortune to become his friend, and I recall happily dinners with him and Dean Lobdell at the old Engineers Club on Commonwealth Avenue, where his advice and counsel to the chef produced Lucullan meals. I remember the evenings we spent with him in his bachelor apartment in that club, where conversation ran free and where we were surrounded by the evidence of his preoccupation as a bibliophile and his collections of exotic artifacts. It was good for a young graduate such as I, who had tendencies toward the conventional, to come into contact with a man whose character was marked by determined individualism and scorn for a standardized world. During the early years of our marriage he was counsel and friend to my wife and me, and soon after we set up housekeeping in a tiny apartment in Cambridge, we recall him as the adventurous first man who came to dinner.

DESIGNING A BROADER SUMMER SESSION

While I was vice president, I became convinced that the Institute's summer session was unacceptably routine and financially unproductive. It could hardly be otherwise since it mainly served students who wished to make up deficiencies or take courses for advanced standing. Although it offered a few teachers an opportunity in an unexciting way to augment their nine-months salaries, it served a restricted number of both teachers and students and contributed little to making our rich educational resources available to a wider and more mature audience. Neither did it add to the "technology transfer" that many were already advocating in those days.

When I became president, I turned to an able and persuasive colleague, Professor Walter Gale, of the Department of Aeronautical Engineering and later secretary of the Institute, and gave him carte blanche to design a broader summer session with conferences, seminars, and courses for representatives from industry, government, other institutions, and the Institute itself. He promptly did. The summer session he designed has prospered. In 1984 about 1,800 individuals from the U.S. and abroad attended sixty-seven separate programs.

ATOMS FOR PEACE AT MIT

In 1953 President Eisenhower delivered his memorable "Atoms for Peace" speech before the United Nations and in that same year the United Nations started to plan the First International Conference on the Peaceful Uses of Atomic Energy to be held in Geneva in 1955. Professor Walter Whitman, head of MIT's Department of Chemical Engineering, was named to be secretary-general of the conference. His success in persuading all the nations with nuclear programs, including the Soviet Union, to declassify sufficient information to ensure a meaningful conference received worldwide applause. The conference was a breakthrough in opening a large chest of secrets for public discussion and unclassified exploitation in the spirit of Eisenhower's "Atoms for Peace" speech.

As early as 1946 the Laboratory for Nuclear Science and Engineering under Professor Jerrold Zacharias was a seedbed for academic initiatives in nuclear engineering, and in 1948 the Chemical Engineering Department established an Engineering Practice School at the AEC's Oak Ridge center.

The major advance came in 1952 when Manson Benedict came to MIT as a full-time faculty member to teach the first courses in nuclear engineering at MIT, and soon enough ·the field had progressed so effectively that he became the first head of the newly established Department of Nuclear Engineering in 1958. Benedict, a chemical engineer of widely recognized talents, had been in charge of developing the gaseous diffusion process for separating uranium-235 for the Manhattan Project and later had been appointed the first engineer on the AEC's Advisory Committee on Reactor Safeguards. Other moves came fast, including decisions to offer a doctor's degree in nuclear engineering and to build on, or near, the campus a nuclear research reactor.

I was an active member of the group that concluded that a research reactor was needed for both teaching and research, and in my President's Report for 1954 I said in part: "Among the many reasons leading to the decision to build an unclassified nuclear reactor is the conviction that the development of atomic energy for beneficent use is important to the spirit of America. . . . Is it not possible that bold and imaginative acts by Americans to demonstrate the moral purpose and the non-military use of science and technology can contribute to our own reassurance and to our leadership in a world seeking peace?"

In a recent paper on the beginning of nuclear engineering at MIT, Professor Benedict has written:

In this spirit Dr. Killian and the MIT Corporation directed that a safe, versatile research reactor be built as close to the MIT campus as possible, that the reactor be free of security restrictions, and that it serve all MIT departments and other New England schools and industry. . . . A one-megawatt heavy-water reactor, to cost an estimated $1.5 million, was selected. Dr. Killian approved the recommendation, allocated $1.5 million from MIT funds and gave administrative responsibility to Dean C. Richard Soderberg of the School of Engineering and to Whitman. . . .

The MIT Administration felt that the proposal to build a nuclear reactor in the heart of Cambridge needed review by and concurrence of our Cambridge neighbors.

The plans won complete acceptance. And there has been safe operation of the reactor for over twenty-five years.

James and Elizabeth Killian with son, Meredith, and daughter, Carolyn, in 1948. Photo by Fabian Bachrach

At MIT's Mid-Century Convocation in 1949, Killian awards honorary lectureship to Mr. Churchill. (MIT has never awarded honorary degrees.) In the background, Compton, Burchard, and Governor Dever.

Above: At Killian inauguration as president of MIT. First row: Killian, Compton, Dr. William Rice, minister of Unitarian Church in Wellesley; second row: James Bryant Conant, Harvard president, and Sir Richard Livingstone of Oxford. *Top right*: Karl T. Compton accompanying Winston Churchill at the Mid-Century Convocation, 1949. *Bottom right*: Honoring Alfred P. Sloan, Jr., at successful completion of Mid-Century fund-raising campaign in 1951. Sloan served as honorary chairman of the Committee on Financing Development and Marshall B. Dalton (seated at left) as chairman. Marshall Dalton won renown among MIT alumni by his leadership in enhancing the Institute's financial independence, and the Corporation Development Committee has established the Marshall B. Dalton Award, annually presented, to memorialize his leadership.

The author (second from right) and other members of the President's Communications Policy Board meet with President Truman in 1951. Irvin Stewart, chairman, is at the President's right. In 1951 Truman appointed the author a member of the first presidential science advisory committee.

Philip Morse, Vannevar Bush, Killian, and Thomas J. Watson dedicate MIT's first major computation center, donated in 1957.

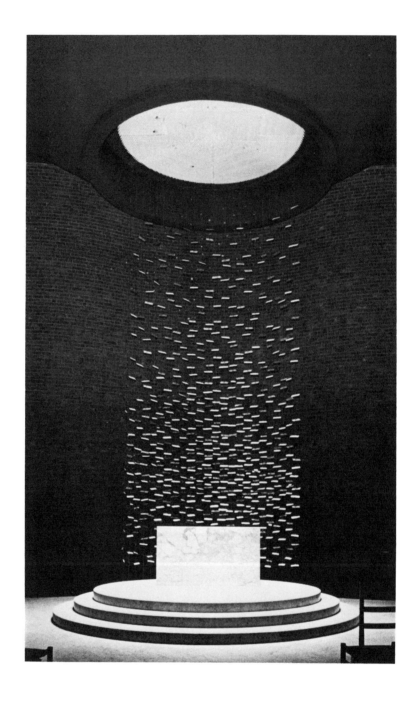

The MIT Chapel and Kresge Auditorium, both designed by Eero Saarinen. The screen behind the altar in the chapel was the work of sculptor Harry Bertoia and the chapel's bell tower, of Theodore Roszak. The thin-shell concrete dome of the auditorium was one of the first in the United States. Interior view of chapel by Calvin Campbell; exterior view of chapel and auditorium by Balthazar Korab

Life magazine photographer Gjon Mili records Killian during evening with students at MIT fraternity house. MIT Museum collection

MIT crew dedicates shell, "The Liz," in honor of Elizabeth Parks Killian. *Overleaf:* To include in his brochure "MIT Revisited," master photographer Gjon Mili, in 1960, took this photograph of hundreds of senior class members massed in the lobby of the Rogers Building. Almost all the students in this picture are wearing coats and neckties, and there is no evidence of anyone affecting the long and uncombed hair so prevalent later. The change in dress styles apparently came almost suddenly in the mid-1960s.

12
A NEW STRATEGY FOR FUND RAISING

During World War II the Institute had committed itself almost entirely to research and training programs in behalf of the nation's war effort. As a result it was diverted for an extended period from undertaking the fund raising that in peacetime would normally have engaged its attention and that did indeed receive attention from some major institutions that were not so heavily burdened with war responsibilities. Of the greatest urgency was the need for funds for increasing faculty salaries. As industry turned from war to peacetime production and sought scientists and engineers experienced in World War II high technology, it offered salaries that the universities could not meet. Especially was the Institute faced with requirements to increase its faculty salaries in order to hold the talented faculty members already on its staff who were qualified, out of their war experience, to introduce new fields and new technology that had resulted from war research.

In recognition of these needs the faculty and administration formulated a list of high-priority projects for presentation to the Corporation in 1947. It responded immediately by sponsoring a study of the Institute's financial resources that would list its needs in priority order, with higher salaries at the top of the list.

I seek in this section to describe the process of organizing the largest fund-raising campaign the Institute had undertaken up until that time and to describe the novel and creative methods that were devised to increase faculty salaries as rapidly as possible. The postwar salary emergency faced by the Institute and other universities was not unlike the emergency of the 1980s.

At the suggestion of Dr. Compton, Mr. Joseph Snyder, the assistant treasurer, and I visited with investment banker John R. Macomber of the Corporation's Executive Committee and sought his consent to chair this study committee. He manfully accepted and in three months came forward with a bold report recommending that the Corporation organize to raise $20 million to "fund MIT's independence as a private institution" and outlining what the fund-raising organization—the Committee on Financing Development—should be.

The Macomber study made two additional recommendations:

that we should have an honorary chairman and a volunteer chairman of the proposed Committee on Financing Development and that the ideal men to fill these important chairmanships were Alfred P. Sloan, Jr., and Marshall B. Dalton, respectively. Under their leadership 600 alumni and friends of the Institute were mobilized to participate in the development effort, and with great energy and devotion, Mr. Dalton proceeded to draw a plan that was to include the Mid-Century Convocation and Winston Churchill's speech. These events set the stage for an arduous solicitation, national in scope, of individuals, corporations, and foundations.

The launching of the CFD campaign was later limned by a parody from *Pinafore* sung at my retirement dinner:

Since we needed cash on a grandiose scale,
I soon was going round with a big tin pail.
Those tall new buildings which are now going up
Have arisen from the tinkle in my little tin cup.
Though they seem to be built of cement and glass,
They were brought into existence by a tower of brass.

The Institute had not undertaken a major fund-raising effort since 1918, when George Eastman—publicly identified for several years as "the mysterious Mr. Smith"—offered to make a spectacularly large capital gift to the Institute on condition that others would contribute an equal amount. This matching challenge, together with a crisis in the Institute's financial condition, made it necessary for President Maclaurin to move boldly to secure additional funds. Plans were developed to solicit industry by an arrangement with industrial companies called the Technology Plan and the creation by the Institute of a new agency entitled the Division of Industrial Cooperation and Research. Professors of chemical engineering had earlier provided a prototype of this division by the conduct of the Research Laboratory of Applied Chemistry, which undertook sponsored research for industry with great success.

The Technology Plan to secure corporate support was the first large-scale effort by an American university to establish extensive ties with industry not only to attract funds but to encourage technology transfer.

In the beginning the Technology Plan appeared to be successful. One hundred eighty corporations subscribed or pledged retaining fees exceeding $1 million. Despite this auspicious start the plan—which involved the Institute's making available to the participating corporations consultation with qualified members of the faculty, the offer of assistance for the planning of new research and improved industrial procedures, and the services of the Institute library—was later to come under criticism. There was a feeling that the Institute was entering into competition with the private practice of its alumni and that the participating corporations were being asked to pay for services hitherto obtained gratuitously. There was further criticism that the plan inevitably would represent an unacceptable overcommitment of the faculty to provide consulting services. Perhaps if Dr. Maclaurin had lived, he could have corrected these faults and made the Technology Plan a success, but without his leadership the plan had to be severely modified. The Division of Industrial Cooperation established to manage the plan ultimately was altered by Compton to handle special contractual relationships with corporations and in addition with agencies and departments of the federal government. He saw it as a vehicle for providing increased support to departments and programs and for doing so in an orderly way. The division proved to be the only lasting achievement of the Technology Plan, and it was fortunate that it was well developed in time to handle the war research program.

THE INVENTION OF THE INDUSTRIAL LIAISON PROGRAM

In 1948, thirty years after the Technology Plan, the Institute's administration again pondered how support could be obtained from industry and how the benefits of closer relationships with corporations could be achieved without the faults and overcommitments of the Technology Plan. An MIT alumnus, E. V. Murphree, then head of Esso (now Exxon) Research and

Engineering, proposed to me that the Institute solicit from a selected group of industrial corporations annual grants identified as a business expense and that these annual grants be used by the Institute as unrestricted funds essential to maintaining and advancing its research and educational programs. In return the Institute would staff an office to provide the corporations with a valuable quid pro quo consisting of conferences, one-day symposia, advanced copies of papers to be published, and other techniques for keeping the corporations informed about basic research at the Institute. The Institute would maintain a staff of liaison officers who would identify faculty members working in an area of interest to a specific company and make arrangements for company personnel to meet with those faculty and staff at the Institute. In addition they would encourage and sponsor visits by faculty and staff to the company premises. The objective of these various liaison arrangements was to accelerate technological transfer and bring industry into close relationship to the Institute's basic research program without in any way committing the faculty of the Institute to do consulting or special research for the companies.

This plan, shaped with faculty advice, was one of the creative achievements of this campaign. In the beginning, companies were successfully solicited to commit themselves for five years to make annual grants of at least $50,000. Later, as the number of companies increased, this threshold amount was established at $30,000 a year for five years. By 1984 the program had yielded a cumulative total of $72,400,000 and a membership of 300 companies. This pioneering method of soliciting corporate support, promoting technology transfer, and enhancing communication between academe and industry was later adopted by other research universities.

The success of the Industrial Liaison Program suggests other beneficial relationships that might be arranged between corporations and universities for the exchange of scientific ideas of mutual intellectual interest and the training of talent. As I prepare this memoir, there is widespread apprehension that the vigor and creativity of U.S. research and the productivity of the American economy are threatened. The scientific resources of both the corporate world and the university world must be pooled more effectively to counter these risks.

The Industrial Liaison Program has demonstrated one of the ways to benefit science and education by bringing universities and corporations into partnership in a mutually beneficial relationship, but new, and yet to be conceived, arrangements must be invented to take full advantage of the university-industrial connection.

In addition to the invention of the Industrial Liaison Program another important achievement during the CFD campaign was the successful effort, independent of the Industrial Liaison Program, to secure large corporate gifts. MIT was the first major institution to secure such large corporate donations, and it was greatly assisted in this successful solicitation by the powerful advocacy of corporate grants to universities by a group of industrial leaders including Alfred Sloan.

In an article in the Spring–Summer 1982 special centennial issue, *The Lamp*, a journal published by Exxon, gives an account of the legal test case promoted by Standard Oil of New Jersey to determine whether corporations could legally make gifts to universities.

In this article it is reported that the first education grant made by the company was a grant that went to a handful of MIT graduate students in 1919. The article notes:

That gesture turned out to be prophetic as well as wise, for within less than a decade a group of young MIT men had set about revolutionizing the company's research and development operations in Louisiana.

A more sweeping revolution in corporate support for higher education was instituted by Frank W. Abrams. When he assumed the chairmanship of Jersey in 1940, Abrams brought along a gnawing dissatisfaction with state laws that gave rise to legal uncertainties about business contributions to colleges and universities for general education, rather than business-related, purposes. He frequently said that aid to higher education was essential to the survival of many private institutions.

Abrams wanted Jersey to test these restrictive laws in court, but the board of directors declined. With the encouragement of Abrams and Courtney Brown, who was Abrams' assistant, the board of A. P. Smith Manufacturing Company, a maker of industrial valves, declared its intention to give $1,500 for general education purposes to Princeton University. A Smith stockholder sued the board, and a case testing the law was under way. "We got two other men interested," Courtney Brown recalls, "Irving S. Olds and Alfred P. Sloan . . . ."

The state judge, too, realized he had a landmark case before him. "On the day he was to hand down his decision," says Brown, "he peered over his glasses and asked 'Is the press here?' The press wasn't. 'I want them here,' he said. 'Case adjourned until ten o'clock tomorrow morning.'"

Next day, with reporters assembled, the judge ruled for the Smith Company. Frank Abrams declared that a corporation should not be prevented from "voluntarily discharging its high obligations as a constituent of our modern social structure." The U.S. Supreme Court declined to review the decision, and in 1953, the way was clear for corporations to make [without legal challenge] unrestricted gifts for higher education.[1]

I remember a fund-raising dinner for bank executives when the head of a Boston trust company, a prominent lawyer, argued, with positive self-assurance, that it was clearly illegal for a corporation to "give away stockholders' money." The outcome of the case in New Jersey changed his mind.

Corporate contributions to educational institutions were further encouraged by the formation, with support of several foundations, of the Council for Financial Aid to Education in 1952 by a committee of five business leaders which included Alfred Sloan and Frank Abrams. This council of corporate executives was certainly stirred by demographic predictions in the mid-1950s that "war babies" would rapidly increase college enrollments in the 1960s with the result that more space and equipment and more student aid would be needed from corporations and all other sources. President Eisenhower's Commission on Higher Education forcefully pointed this out.

MIT was no exception. The goal originally set for its CFD fund campaign was $20,000,000. The total raised, including $5,250,000 given by Mr. Sloan came to $26,000,000, an amount that stated in terms of the purchasing power of today's dollars (Bureau of Labor Statistics) is equivalent to approximately $100,000,000. Twenty-six percent of this total was contributed by corporations. With but one exception this was the largest amount raised by any university, and the unprecedented total of corporation gifts ushered in a new era of corporate support for higher education.

In our pioneering efforts to attract funds from corporations, we stressed MIT's remarkable record in educating many great industrial and business leaders, particularly those who graduated in the 1880s and 1890s who fell in the category Schumpeter described as having "the defining characteristic . . . the doing of new things, and doing things that are already done, in a new way (innovation)."[2] A quick check turns up the names of Alfred Sloan, Gerard Swope (General Electric), who was in Mr. Sloan's class of 1895; Charles Stone, '88, and Edwin S. Webster, '88 (Stone and Webster Corporation); Godfrey L. Cabot '81 (Cabot Corporation); T. Coleman du Pont, '84; Henry B. du Pont, '94; Irenee du Pont, '97; Pierre S. du Pont, '90 (du Pont Company); John T. Dorrance, '95 (Campbell Soup); Charles Hayden, '90 (Finance); James C. Kimberly, '94 (Kimberly-Clark); Frank W. Lovejoy, '94 (Eastman Kodak); Paul W. Litchfield, '96 (Goodyear); William C. Potter, '97 (Banker).[3] It is worthy of note that all of these were students during the presidency of economist Francis Amasa Walker (1881–1897).

Eleven of the industrial leaders I have mentioned were later to serve at one time or another on the MIT Corporation. Out of their wisdom and experience they contributed importantly to the governance of the Institute. In later years their influence and leadership contributed to the rapid transformation of MIT from an institute of technology to a university polarized around science. In my introduction to this memoir I have indicated my hope to identify the forces that led to this emergence of the Institute into a world-renowned university. The influence of Gerard Swope and Elihu Thomson of General Electric, of Frank

Jewett of the Bell Laboratories, and of Alfred Sloan of General Motors clearly played a major role in creating the institution that MIT has become.

In addition to educating a stellar group who created the modern corporation, MIT also produced in this end-of-century period pioneers in the development of industrial research, including Arthur D. Little, '85, and Willis R. Whitney, '90, who was recruited by Elihu Thomson to organize and direct, while on part-time leave from MIT, General Electric's Research Laboratory—the same Elihu Thomson who was to serve for a brief period (1920–1923) as MIT's acting president. Whitney turned to MIT to recruit for his laboratory William D. Coolidge, '96, who combined engineering and science to achieve the tungsten filament for electric light bulbs. Historian Daniel J. Boorstin described Whitney as an American Heraclitus, preaching and teaching that only change is real.[4] Boorstin also recalled that when General Electric was importuning Whitney to come to Schenectady, Whitney expressed his reluctance to leave MIT by saying, "I would rather teach than be President!"

The moves that Gerard Swope made to strengthen science at the Institute no doubt were inspired by his knowledge of what Whitney and Coolidge and their colleagues had achieved in their General Electric research. Whitney also was to make clear to his former colleagues at MIT how important it was for them to read "the countless uncut pages of science" along with their preoccupation with engineering.[5] It is my surmise that it was he, and perhaps Coolidge too, who called to the attention of Swope the name of Karl Compton, the Princeton physicist who was a consultant to the General Electric Research Laboratory in the 1920s. Both of these pioneers in industrial research—Whitney and Coolidge—continued throughout their lives to cherish their days when they were teachers at MIT. It was as late as January 1971 that I had the pleasure of welcoming Dr. Coolidge to MIT. He had come to see some of the work of Professor Robert Mann in the field of bioengineering, but obviously he was happy to return to his alma mater at age ninety-seven.

The CFD fund drive laid the basis for the Second Century

Fund campaign a decade later, which again broke records by raising $98 million, and the Leadership Campaign, completed in 1980 with a record take of $250 million. As a result of a steady inflation, successor campaigns have had to achieve returns much larger than previous campaigns in order to maintain equivalent purchasing power.

The funds made available by the CFD campaign in the early fifties enabled the Institute to take advantage of opportunities and new visions that grew out of its war program and gained high visibility during the Institute's redeployment for peace. They also contributed to the implementation of the recommendations that had been made by the Lewis Committee. It should also be noted that the worldwide prestige of the Institute has been greatly enhanced.

Although the total of funds raised by the CFD campaign was substantially larger than the original goal, it did not yield funds to meet one of the stated objectives—a much-needed building to

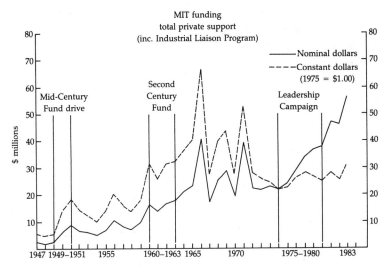

Chart prepared by the MIT Development Office expressing in both nominal and constant dollars the annual amounts received since 1947 from private sources as a result of hard campaigning.

house the new Research Laboratory of Electronics and the Laboratory for Nuclear Science.

At a luncheon at the President's House following the memorial service for Dr. Compton in 1954, Mr. Sloan suggested that the Institute should consider immediately a fitting and permanent memorial for its great and beloved president. The luncheon group agreed that such a memorial might appropriately take the form of a laboratory and educational building to serve those fields of science in which Dr. Compton had worked as a practicing scientist. It was finally agreed to design the Compton memorial to house the Research Laboratory of Electronics and the Laboratory for Nuclear Science.

Following this discussion Mr. Sloan moved at once to set in motion an effort to bring about the memorial. He himself offered to contribute a million dollars and to seek contributions from others.

As the planning progressed, it became increasingly clear that the Institute should have a really adequate computation center. A faculty committee under the chairmanship of Professor Philip Morse had surveyed the Institute's needs and brought to Dr. Stratton and to me and to an interested officer of IBM, Cuthbert Hurd, a proposal that MIT seek the means to provide at the Institute the most advanced and versatile research computer available. Here again we found that when the Institute was faced with a need and an opportunity, understanding and generous friends responded. I visited Mr. Thomas J. Watson, Jr., president of IBM, and described our urgent need. Mr. Watson's response was sympathetic, and as a result IBM shortly offered to provide as a part of the Compton Laboratory complex the most advanced of its research computers. In addition IBM volunteered to defray the cost of a building adjunct to the Compton Laboratory to house the computer. It is interesting to recall that the Institute agreed to make the computer available to other institutions and thus to create at MIT a regional computing center for the use of all interested educational institutions in New England. MIT's soaring needs for computer capacity soon made this arrangement obsolete.

The successful completion of the CFD campaign and of these several minicampaigns that followed it still left unfulfilled an urgent need of the Institute to increase faculty compensation. Clearly this was to require another innovation in fund raising if the Institute were to achieve a level of faculty salaries adequate to meet the competition of industry and other first-rate institutions. The way that we found to do this in the face of all the previous efforts to secure new funds is described in the following letter written to me by Alfred Sloan, dated October 30, 1956. I include this as an exhibit of his meticulous style in arranging for grants to the Institute.

My dear Dr. Killian:

This letter has reference to conversations I have had with Dr. Kelly and yourself as well as the discussion which took place recently at the Finance Committee meeting of the Institute.

It relates to the fact that I have been informed by you that more or less of a critical situation is developing in the Institute because the level of salaries of the faculty and related personnel is abnormal as measured by existing competition. The result is that it is difficult to attract into the Institute's service, talent of the highest order. And again, it is difficult to retain in the Institute's service, similar talent.

Nobody recognizes any more than I do, the basic fact that to maintain the leadership of the Institute, we must have personnel of the highest order for both talent and experience.

I further understand that to adjust the present level of salaries more adequately to meet competition would involve a yearly increase of approximately 20% and an annual operating increase of approximately $1 Million. To capitalize this at 4% would require $25 Million in capital. This certainly is something that could not be contemplated in the immediate foreseeable future.

I have suggested that if a Fund of $5 Million could be obtained for adjusting the level of salaries and related personnel, the Institute might feel justified in making such an adjustment without delay—let us say at the beginning of the academic year of 1957. This would be based upon the belief that the urgency of the situation would justify the acceptance of a certain amount of risk, supported by business judgment as to what the future might bring forth.

Having all the above in mind, and desiring to do what I can to help, I offer the following:

1. That I would be willing to recommend to the Board of Trustees of the Alfred P. Sloan Foundation, Inc. that they make a grant to Massachusetts Institute of Technology to establish what might be called a "Faculty Salary Adjustment Fund," subject to the following conditions:

(a) That the maximum amount of the proposed grant on the part of the Alfred P. Sloan Foundation, Inc. over a maximum period of five years, would be $1,250,000.

(b) That the maximum grant would be contingent upon the Institute obtaining subscriptions to the Fund over same period, in the amount of $3,750,000.

(c) That the contributions made under both "a" and "b" would be restricted to the purposes of the Fund; viz., raising the compensation of the faculty and related personnel.

(d) That the Alfred P. Sloan Foundation, Inc. would match for every dollar contributed to the proposed Adjustment Fund, thirty-three and one-third cents ($.33⅓) up to the maximum specified in "a" over the five year period.

(e) That the Alfred P. Sloan Foundation, Inc. participation in the Fund would be final and would not be contingent upon the full amount contemplated to be raised under "b."

(f) The Alfred P. Sloan Foundation, Inc. would have the privilege of matching its pro rata contributions to the Fund as they develop, or of extending same over whatever there remains within the five year period.

2. It is definitely understood that the purpose of making this suggestion is to determine whether the Institute would feel justified in taking action contemplated on the basis of the proposal.

It remains, therefore, for you to advise me whether the Institute would be interested in such an idea and, if so, whether formal action could be taken?

We promptly accepted Mr. Sloan's concept of a wasting fund, and as a result the Sloan Foundation approved a grant of $1,250,000 on the condition that the Institute obtain $3,750,000 to provide a total of $5,000,000. The matching effort, under the leadership of Corporation member Walter J. Beadle, vice president of the duPont Company, and others, was successful. And we promptly undertook the program of utilizing the concept of a wasting fund for five years to ensure that we would add at least a million dollars a year to the Institute's faculty salary budget.

As a final example, prior to making the proposal for a wasting fund to enable the Institute quickly to start raising faculty salaries across the board, Mr. Sloan, together with his wife, had offered to provide funds to enable the Institute to make special "Faculty Achievement" awards to selected members of the faculty for high performance. The idea of these awards was similar to the bonuses paid by corporations. In my tribute to Mr. Sloan in Chapter 13 I describe in detail this unique arrangement for helping the Institute to attract and hold a faculty of the highest talent.

These successful special efforts to supplement the $26 million raised by the CFD were greatly encouraging to the Institute's president. As I have said, the decade of the 1950s was a good time to be a university president despite the harassments of Senator McCarthy. The earlier creation of the Office of Naval Research and the launching of the National Science Foundation in 1950, together with other government programs in support of research, brought federal funds in amounts far larger than anyone dreamed of prior to the war. These federal funds along with the growth in corporate grants enabled not only MIT but other major research universities to make great strides ahead in their education and research.

13
MY DAYS AS CHAIRMAN OF THE MIT CORPORATION

FROM PRESIDENT TO CHAIRMAN VIA WASHINGTON

When the Soviets orbited Sputnik I, the world's first man-made satellite, on October 4, 1957, the American people reacted with near hysteria, and President Eisenhower realized that he must reassure the jittery nation. After consultation with a number of scientists, he delivered a nationally televised address on November 7 in which he announced that he had "created a new office called the office of Special Assistant to the President for Science and Technology. This man will be aided by a staff of scientists and a strong advisory group of outstanding experts reporting to him, and they will have the active responsibility of helping me follow through on the program of scientific improvement of our defenses.

"I am glad to be able to tell you that the position has been accepted by Dr. James R. Killian, President of the Massachusetts Institute of Technology. He is a man who enjoys my confidence, and the confidence of his colleagues in the scientific and engineering world, and in the government."

This invitation to me by President Eisenhower and my acceptance occurred at a breakfast with him at the White House. I agreed to undertake the post but emphasized that I must gain the assent of members of the MIT Corporation Executive Committee and provide adequately for the administration of the Institute during my leave. In pressing his invitation, the president offered to write personally to members of the Corporation whom I wished to name. He immediately did just this by writing to Vannevar Bush, then chairman of the Corporation. As I suspected, my selection for this new post in government had been prompted by my chairmanship of the Technological Capabilities Panel, which undertook a classified study for President Eisenhower in 1954. This was verified when General Robert Cutler, special assistant to the president for national security affairs, wrote me that "We all . . . wanted you after your wonderful service on the TCP."

After I had discussed the invitation with the Executive Committee, I was promptly granted a leave of absence because it was felt by the committee as well as by me that Eisenhower's emergency call could not be denied. In granting the leave, the Executive Committee set no terminal point but, at my recommendation, invited Chancellor Julius Stratton to serve as acting· president during my absence. There had been precedent for this in my appointment as acting president during Compton's absence in the Far East to serve as chief of the Pacific branch of OSRD in 1945.

I was acutely aware that my leave for the full-time post in Washington would inevitably throw heavy burdens on the able backs of Stratton and other administrative officers of the Institute. In discussions with Stratton I moved carefully to make sure that no presidential duties would be left unattended. I undertook my duties at the White House on November 15. On arriving, I quickly agreed to chair the President's Science Advisory Committee and became deeply involved in matters of urgent importance to the President and to the nation. In view of the reaction to Sputnik, it was necessary to move dramatically to formulate a civilian space program and to design an agency to manage it. Eisenhower made clear that he was ardently seeking ways to encourage progress toward nuclear test ban agreements and would look to his science advisers for assistance, and there were many matters of defense policy that commanded the attention of our group. By July 1, 1958, the president had reached an agreement with Khrushchev to convene a Conference of Experts at Geneva to undertake technical studies looking toward the limitation of nuclear testing. I shared in the appointment of the American delegation to this Geneva conference and served on the Committee of Principals appointed by the president to which our delegation of experts reported.

These and other urgent matters occupied my office, and my preoccupation with these duties made the date of my return to the Institute difficult to determine. As the months of 1958 rolled on, the uncertainty became unsettling to the Corporation's Executive Committee and to my administrative colleagues. The question appropriately arose as to whether the Institute was approaching an expedient time to rearrange its administrative organization. Was it not appropriate to select a new president and to open the way to my election as chairman of the Corporation, which would permit me to remain in Washington until such time as I could return to MIT without prematurely resigning my Washington post?

It was also well known that Dr. Stratton was receiving invitations to fill posts at other institutions, as I did when serving as vice president of the Institute, and there was widespread desire to anchor him at MIT. It was recognized that he possessed ideal qualifications for the presidency, including his distinguished record of achievement as a scientist-scholar. I had brought different attributes to the presidency, but they did not include high scientific achievements. They did include special qualifications for the chairmanship as that post increasingly grew in scope.

Prior to going to Washington, I had in fact privately reached a conclusion that I would welcome transferring to the chairmanship, having become, like Compton, so deeply involved in activities external to the Institute and recognizing the urgent need for a Corporation chairman free to concentrate on fund raising and public relations increasingly important to the Institute.

Under these circumstances the Executive Committee, after consultation with senior members of the faculty and officers of the Alumni Association, decided that the Gordian knot be cut by my resigning the presidency and accepting election to the chairmanship of the Corporation (as had Dr. Compton in 1948).

The Executive Committee on November 30, 1958, formally voted to accept my resignation as president effective as of January 1, 1959, and approved my appointment as chairman of the Corporation (on leave) as of that date. At that time Dr. Bush was part-time chairman of the Corporation, and he indicated his intention to resign from the chairmanship so that I could take the post.

The Executive Committee, having gained Stratton's acceptance of its invitation to be president, then formally voted to recommend his appointment. These actions were unanimously approved by the Corporation at its meeting on December 1,

1958. In accepting Dr. Bush's resignation as chairman, the Corporation enthusiastically elected him as honorary chairman.

And so I returned to my post as special assistant to President Eisenhower and continued in that role until July 15, 1959, at which time I resigned with Eisenhower's understanding approval and returned to MIT to assume its post of Corporation chairman.

Prior to these changes I had put my thoughts into a memorandum that stated my conclusions about the presidency for presentation to the Corporation and subsequently to the faculty of the Institute. I concluded this memorandum with the statement: "It is hard to imagine a better time for the Corporation to select and hopefully to gain the acceptance of a successor who is ideally qualified. It is one of the principal responsibilities of a chief executive to set the stage for the succession. I am happy and confident that I have accomplished this. . . ."

I confess that I found some of my responsibilities as president to be vexing and at times intimidating experiences, but they also had an annealing effect that later stood me in good stead as chairman. As a result my twelve years as chairman were happy, confident years, years that afforded me full opportunity to serve MIT and to fulfill my deep sense of commitment to public service. My emotions in returning from outer space to MIT find apt expression in the last two lines of Robert Frost's poem, "Directive":

Here are your waters and your watering place.
Drink and be whole again beyond confusion

From time to time I hear with incredulity that I am listed on the totem pole as one of the Institute's great presidents. I would not myself dare to venture such an appraisal, but I do agree that the challenging combination of presidency and full-time and honorary chairmanships lasting for over thirty years was a regime unprecedented in the history of the Institute.

There was ample precedent for an MIT president to devote time to public service, and the opportunity to do so had increased greatly in the postwar period. Certainly Dr. Compton had found it appropriate and in the public interest to accept a succession of assignments. Throughout my own presidency I was subject to a never-ending series of requests to accept assignments away from the Institute.

William Barton Rogers carried a great burden of public service during his period at the University of Virginia and as the founding president of MIT. So did Francis Amasa Walker, the third president. So did Richard Cockburn Maclaurin, the sixth president. So did, beyond all others, Karl Compton.

In a tribute to Walker for the annals of Boston's venerable Saturday Club, Judge Francis Cabot Lowell, a friend and fellow member, is quoted as having made an observation that might be applied to all these MIT presidents: "Walker," he wrote, "seemed unable to refuse an opportunity of public service. He had, indeed, the faults of his temperament. . . . His reputation might have gained if he had somewhat limited his undertakings, but to his generosity limitation was impossible. Happily for him, 'No pale gradations quenched his ray.' "

The pressure to undertake many public service assignments led to Dr. Compton's move to the chairmanship of the Corporation, and similar pressures also led to my move from president of the Institute to chairman of the Corporation. Indeed, the need for Compton in Washington had been a factor in my move to the presidency of the Institute.

It is appropriate to note here that twelve years after I became chairman of the Corporation, Dr. Bush, with a twinkle in his voice, asked the Corporation to accept his resignation as honorary chairman of the Corporation, and at that time nominated me to be his successor in this honorific role. Both Dr. Bush and I laughingly agreed that anybody's deliberate resignation from an honorary post was an unusual if not whimsical act. But he obviously enjoyed making this proposal, and I accepted the nomination with affectionate appreciation.

MIT has been almost unique in having both a president and a Corporation chairman as senior administrators. The arrangement has worked well because the process of selection has ensured that the two officers be congenial associates. In addition the concentration by the chairman on outside affairs has ensured that there would be no encroachment on the president's responsibilities as chief executive officer and that he be free of much of the burden of fund raising. Most important has been the continuity in management and policy provided by the arrangement. In my judgment this arrangement where two senior officers share the administrative burdens has been uniquely successful, and I frequently hear the overburdened presidents of other universities speak of the MIT arrangement with envy.

To permit me to serve as full-time chairman beyond my normal retirement date (June 1970), the Corporation in 1968 by acclamation requested that I continue in the post for three additional years, until June 30, 1973. Actually I resigned as chairman and became honorary chairman in June of 1971, at which time Howard Johnson succeeded me as chairman, on the election of Jerome Wiesner as president.

THE CORPORATION ADJUSTS TO CHANGE
Our governing body, the Corporation, has demonstrated its high sense of trusteeship responsibility by aiding the Institute's adjustment to pressures of many different kinds—those of World War II, the cold war, and the student strife of 1969–70. As I have recounted, during World War II the Executive Committee of the Corporation accepted financial risks so that MIT could get on with its war research and, in the postwar period, set aside special funds for reestablishing its graduate school by adding a brilliant group of new faculty members and recruiting an impressive array of graduate students. During the unhappy days of the McCarthy era and the cold war a small group of Corporation members kept in touch with those alumni who were actively critical of the Institute and did much to provide staunch support to the administration. Similarly it worked in close harmony with the administration in 1969–70, when student radicals were rampant, and again in supporting Howard Johnson in the complex moves to divest the Draper Laboratory with minimum

damage to the laboratory and to the Institute. In that stressful period the Corporation kept its cool magnificently, and only one member melted under the heat of the fray.

During my chairmanship it also adapted to changing conditions. In the 1960s it elected its first woman member, Mary Penney Wagley,[1] and first black American, Jerome H. Holland, and later elected additional women and minorities. It also put into place a plan for adding to its ranks a group of very young alumni fresh from their experience as students. It established at my suggestion the Corporation Joint Advisory Committee, a standing committee made up of students, faculty, and Corporation members. This committee is still available to the Corporation to keep it in close touch, when needed, with sensitive matters arising in the student body and in the faculty. This modified form of participatory democracy has served the Corporation well, and for this, much credit goes to the committee's student-oriented chairmen, James Champy, Gregory Smith, and Claude Brenner.

Another addition to the structure of the Corporation was a committee with nationwide membership of MIT alumni to aid in fund raising. This Corporation Development Committee, formed in 1965, was invited to help in identifying new donors, to cultivate them, and to serve as ambassadors of the Institute. The members who agreed to serve over the years have brought both wisdom and new resources to the Institute, and among the reasons for the Committee's success has been the stalwart staff support it has received year in and out, first by Vincent Fulmer and later by Nelson Lees. I came to have a very close rapport with this group and found satisfaction in their friendship.

THE ART AND PRACTICE OF TRUSTEESHIP

In his book, *Servant Leadership: A Journey into the Nature of Legitimate Power and Greatness*, my friend and sometime neighbor in New Hampshire, Robert K. Greenleaf, has written with great wisdom of the servant as leader and of trustees as servants. His philosophy has captured the character of MIT's top governing body, the Corporation.

During the years I served on the Corporation I came to appreciate the immense contribution of this board of trustees. It gives to its Executive Committee great powers, and this committee, in its frequent meetings, has exercised these powers with diligence and wisdom. The Corporation has discharged with success its responsibility to conserve and raise funds. It has maintained a large and adequately staffed visiting comittee system of exceptional influence in governance.[2] It has brought to our councils continuity and the long view, the assurance of stability, and a strong representation of the public interest. When the going has been rough, as well as when it has been smooth, it has been a firm sheet anchor. Central to this effectiveness has been staff work of Vincent Fulmer, talented, tireless, and alert to the individual and collective needs of members. With gratitude the Corporation has elected him secretary with full membership.

The visiting committee system which I have mentioned in my brief history of the Biology Department has been profoundly important in acquainting Corporation members with the policies and personnel of the Institute, and some of the Corporation meetings devoted to visiting committee reports have been exciting as a demonstration of the contributions that devoted trustees can make to the governance of an institution. Among the visiting committee procedures established during my chairmanship was the scheduling of meetings by these committees with students planned in a way to afford the students an uninhibited opportunity freely to express their views without administrative officers or faculty being present.

In addition the Corporation has successfully discharged its responsibility to select presidents of the Institute—and a chairman—by appointing search committees made up of Corporation members. In the postwar years these committees were chaired twice by James Fisk and twice by Carl Mueller, and their nominations were enthusiastically received by both Corporation and faculty. Although preserving to itself the final decision for the appointment of presidents and chairmen, the Corporation has also in recent years called on the wisdom of faculty advisory committees, as have most other universities, to share in the selection.

It is interesting to note that as late as 1948, the Corporation's Executive Committee selected presidents without formally consulting faculty members. In an earlier chapter I have noted that the invitation to Dr. Compton to accept the presidency of the Institute largely resulted from the recommendation of one member of the Executive Committee, Gerard Swope, then president of the General Electric Company. I need not dwell on the superlative wisdom of that selection.

The search committee that chose Howard Johnson as its nominee for the presidency had been instructed to undertake a comprehensive review of the top organizational structure of the institution, and it was consequently designated as a Committee on Succession, with a more comprehensive responsibility than "search" implies. I had suggested to this Committee on Succession that I was prepared to retire as chairman of the Corporation on the election of Johnson as president, but the formal report to the Corporation of this committee overrode my suggestion and expressed the view, not without embarassment to me, that "the Institute's best interest would be served by asking Dr. Killian to remain indefinitely, with a change in the Bylaws if later necessary, to continue his brilliant leadership of the Corporation."

The next search committee, the one that nominated Jerome Wiesner to become president and Paul Gray to become chancellor in 1971, continued to base its recommendations on consideration of the entire structure of the Institute's presidency. Those who were present for Dr. Wiesner's inauguration as president of MIT vividly remember Archibald MacLeish's "Speech on a Public Occasion," which gave a poetic certification of those rare Wiesner qualities which we are proud to have perceived when we induced him to accept an appointment to the MIT faculty in 1945:

A good man! [said MacLeish with an exclamation point]
Look at him there against the fog!
He saunters along to his place in the world's weather,

hitches his pants, lights his pipe,
talks back to accepted opinion. . . .
Advisor to Presidents, the papers call him.
Advisor, I say, to the young. . . .
I love this man. I rinse my mouth with his praise
in a frightened time. The taste in the cup is of
mint, of spring water.

In his assignments as professor, director of the Research Laboratory of Electronics, dean of science, provost, and president, Wiesner has served the Institute with acclaimed brilliance.

When President Wiesner retired from the presidency in 1980, the Corporation made no recommendation for the appointment of a chancellor. The search committee, in recommending Gray as president-elect, suggested elimination of the chancellor's office he had held in view of Paul's wish to make other administrative arrangements in the office of the president.

In 1965 the search committee of the Corporation chaired by Fisk decided, after considering many candidates and after several of its members had visited with Howard Johnson, to invite him to accept the presidency. Johnson had already resigned the deanship of the Sloan School of Management and accepted a post with Federated Department Stores with headquarters in Cincinnati. He had even bought a home there and had bidden farewell to his MIT colleagues.

The committee then declared that clearly the chairman of the Corporation (meaning me) should formally convey its invitation to Howard and persuade him to remain at the Institute. I undertook this assignment with zeal and retain a vivid recollection of the episode. Howard was later quoted as saying: "When Jim Killian asked me on behalf of the Corporation, I said 'yes.' I didn't even say 'I'll call you back.' " The next morning I met with Professor Charles Kindleberger, then chairman of the faculty, and reported Howard's acceptance. He appeared startled, although I now know that Dr. Bush had given him a hint the evening before. At the inaugural ceremony Professor Elting Morison, in his remarks, drew spontaneous laughter when he said that something had happened to Johnson on his way to the forum.

During his presidency it fell to Howard Johnson to lead the Institute through the period of student discontent and disruption. This he did valiantly, rejecting the actions of radical extremists and staunchly reaffirming those qualities of civility and consensus so important to a university and to the maintenance of a decent and appropriate environment for the pursuit of truth.

Perhaps the most difficult problem that faced him during his presidency was the attacks that were made on the Instrumentation Laboratory, a laboratory under the direction of near-genius engineer Stark Draper, whose record I have given in some detail in the section on the Instrumentation Laboratory.

After the war Draper had mastered the technology of inertial guidance, which was to be a key, first to the development of ballistic missiles and then to the guidance of our space vehicles, including the spectacular Apollo project that landed men on the moon and brought them safely back.

The fact that the Instrumentation Laboratory was a center of guidance technology for ballistic missiles prompted attacks on it as a weapons-oriented laboratory inappropriate for a university. These sustained attacks on Draper and his laboratory in 1969 made it necessary to bring to bear the best judgment available in the Institute's governing bodies, including of course the faculty. This Howard did in full recognition that here was a laboratory of great value to the national security of the nation, a source of new technology for industry and for the generation of funds through indirect costs and overhead paid under the contracts between the Institute and the government. It was also important to protect the interests of those who worked in the laboratory and to devise changes that would permit it to continue its service to the national security. Under Johnson's direction these problems were remarkably well handled.

The divestiture of the laboratory was not accomplished without great cost to the Institute and hurt to Dr. Draper. But the separation of a large and creative institution from the Institute itself was accomplished by the skill of Johnson, Vice President Albert Hill, and others in a way that both protected the public interest and relieved the Institute of its difficult burden of managing and justifying the laboratory.

It was Johnson's good fortune that Al Hill was available to share in the planning of the independent Draper Laboratory and skillfully to conduct the negotiations with the Department of Defense that ensured appropriate financing of the laboratory, although at considerable expense to MIT. Under Johnson's quarterbacking my own participation as chairman of the Corporation was to invent a two-stage arrangement whereby a division was formed to provide a board of directors independent of MIT; this temporary board was to serve until all arrangements had been completed to give the laboratory independent status as a nonprofit institution. Putting in place this arrangement required my recruiting a majority of the members of the divisional board, all of whom fortunately later accepted membership on the board of the formalized corporate entity. It was the good fortune of the divested laboratory that Al Hill was appointed chairman of the board and carried through this role magnificently.

Later, as chairman of the Corporation, Howard directed the Leadership Campaign that raised $250 million for the Institute. Notable also, in his presidency, was the successful exchange arrangement with Wellesley College whereby students in one of the institutions can, without complicating red tape, elect to take courses in the other.

At a time when the Museum of Fine Arts in Boston faced difficult problems of policy and management, Johnson agreed to be its president, and in this role he ushered in a new era for this great museum.

In its final report (1980) the Carnegie Council on Policy Studies in Higher Education included high on its check list of imperatives for universities during the next two decades the encouragement of strong leadership by the institution's chief executive officer. "We also see the need," said the council, "for more authority in the hands of the president and for longer presidential terms." I share these recommendations and add that it has been the good fortune of my institution to have among my fellow presidents leaders of this quality and endurance. With the carefully crafted organizational structure I have described and the kind of Corporation chairmanship arrangement I have reported, MIT presidents have been free to be strong chief executives and not merely mediators. They have not, however, resorted to the stern policy of the great Benjamin Jowett, master of Balliol College, Oxford, who advised: "Never retract, never explain. Get it done and let them howl."

In recognition of the growing supranational character of the Institute, the Corporation in the postwar period added to its membership distinguished international figures: Luis Ferré from Puerto Rico, C. D. Howe, Robert H. Winters, and Allan J. MacEachen from Canada, Virgilio Barco from Colombia, Sir William Hawthorne from England, and Yaichi Ayukawa from Japan.

I was constantly on the lookout for other men or women of exceptional distinction to serve the governing body of the Institute. Unlike several sister institutions, MIT has not limited the membership of its governing bodies to alumni but has reached out to attract nonalumni trustees equivalent in talent to the able alumni and alumnae who constitute the main body of the Corporation. William B. Murphy, Wisconsin alumnus and CEO of Campbell Soup, is a conspicuous example.

My presence at the dedicatory naming of new houses in the student residence complex on Memorial Drive has led me to reflect on the fortuitous ways my extracurricular associations have paid off by enabling me to recruit new members of the Corporation who have subsequently served MIT with devotion and wisdom. I could name a number of these but let me cite three who have been justly memorialized by having student residences bear their names.

First, there is James B. Fisk, whose service to the Institute has already been suggested by his chairmanship of two successive search committees for new presidents.

Following his graduation at MIT in 1931, Jim started his professional career at the Institute as a research assistant in aeronautical engineering, where he worked with Charles Stark Draper at the beginning of that eminent engineer's career. He received a traveling fellowship that took him to Trinity College, Cambridge Univeristy, and then came back to MIT for a brief period as a teaching fellow in physics. But wider recognition rapidly came. He was invited to membership in the Society of Fellows at Harvard and later on served for two years as Gordon McKay Professor of Applied Physics there.

My associations with Dr. Fisk go back to the Science Advisory Committee first appointed by President Truman in 1951. Service on this committee led to Jim's participation as deputy director of the Technological Capabilities Panel, a task force that I chaired for President Eisenhower beginning in 1954 to study our military and intelligence technology as requested by the president.

Later Eisenhower's arrangement for a Science Advisory Committee reporting directly to him brought Fisk and me together again. As a result of findings reached by PSAC in 1958 on the possibility of detecting nuclear tests, Eisenhower wrote Soviet Premier Khrushchev, suggesting technical studies and indicating his view that diplomatic negotiations working toward a test ban agreement would certainly follow if the technical experts reached an agreement on a detection system. This letter was drafted for the president by the State Department, which unfortunately had failed to consult the Department of Defense, the Atomic Energy Commission, or the CIA. While I think it was right for the president to move promptly and aggressively on the basis of information provided him by PSAC, this lack of internal consultation was to aggravate differences in our own government in later discussions.

Within twelve days Khrushchev replied, agreeing to the proposal, and in a subsequent exchange of letters he and the president agreed that a Conference of Experts should be convened to start meetings in Geneva on July 1.

The president asked me to suggest a head for the American delegation, and I suggested Dr. Fisk. Admiral Lewis Strauss of the AEC suggested Ernest Lawrence, and I added the further name of Robert F. Bacher of PSAC.

The negotiations were to include British representatives, and these proved to be Sir John Cockcroft and Sir William Penney, both distinguished British scientists, and Penney came to be one of Jim Fisk's closest and most admired friends.

I have given a detailed account of these negotiations in my previous memoir, *Sputnik, Scientists, and Eisenhower* (The MIT Press, 1977), and I will not repeat the details here. Let me only reiterate that Fisk did a brilliant job, an appraisal shared by a number of eminent judges who were close to the negotiation. British Prime Minister Macmillan, for example, wrote in a letter to President Eisenhower his admiration of Dr. Fisk's performance:

The recent expert conference at Geneva on suspending nuclear tests was clearly an outstanding success. This has been underlined by Khrushchev's willingness to open substantive talks with us on the subject on 31 October.

I feel that a great deal of the credit for this success should go to your scientists led by Dr. James B. Fisk. Under his leadership the whole Western team worked in harmony and effectively. I think that Dr. Fisk is to be commended for the way he managed the Russians, who, I am told, were proficient and pertinacious on both technical and political matters. Sir William Penney [now Lord Penney] described Dr. Fisk's performance as magnificent. If it is in order, I would be glad if you would convey my personal thanks to him.[3]

Fisk returned after the end of the negotiations, and there was much jubilation, particularly in the scientific community, over the agreement reached with the Soviets. The extent of this agreement was greater than in any other disarmament discussions our American government has had with the Soviets.

Events following this successful negotiation, however, were tragic in that a concerted effort was made, particularly among segments of the nuclear missile research community, to discount and discredit the findings of the Geneva conference. New seismic data and new concepts for conducting tests underground were advanced by the antagonists of the Geneva conference conclusions, and the use of these came to be fatefully destructive in further discussions with the Soviets. I count it the major failure of the President's Science Advisory committee not to have made clear that science involves the process of progressive checking and rechecking and testing and retesting and that this process would be an appropriate way to continue to negotiate with the Soviets. Instead, in the diplomatic discussions that were arranged as planned to follow the Conference of Experts, the Soviets clearly were embittered and full of suspicion that the Americans were not sincere in their attitude toward the results of the Geneva conference.

Not long before he died of a heart attack, Dr. Fisk and I reminisced about the Eisenhower days, and he suggested that it would be important, should there be further discussions about the ratification of the SALT II agreement, that leaders in our government should be informed about the extraordinary agreement reached in this Conference of Experts in 1958, particularly the agreement that there should be a limited number of on-site inspections in circumstances where seismic signals were ambiguous. Dr. Fisk and I agreed that at no subsequent negotiation with the Soviets on arms limitation had the Soviets expressed such willingness to permit on-site inspection. In the 1958 negotiation they also agreed to a global network of seismic stations, a good many of which would be in the Soviet Union and at all of which there could be manning by multinational personnel. The conclusion of this conference also approved aerial overflight of a suspected test site.

In recalling Dr. Fisk's extraordinary leadership in 1958 at the Geneva Conference of Experts, I feel a sense of deep satisfaction in having recruited him in 1959 to serve on the MIT Corporation, of which he became a life member in 1963, and on its Executive Committee. Jim was eminently qualified to be president of MIT, and on one occasion this possibility was discussed with him at length. But this prospect faded when his colleagues in the telephone company convinced him that his obligations as president of the Bell Labs were overriding. After serving on the Corporation for almost twenty-two years, he died on August 10, 1981.

Dr. Fisk stands in my memory not only as a gifted scientist but as a good man—a man free of guile and instinctively devoted to intellectual and moral order. In every setting where he served, he commanded the confidence of his colleagues not only by his intellectual powers and moral values but by a personality marked by patrician qualities of grace and considerate courtesy. Lest I paint him in colors too formal and austere, let me add that he was a boon companion, notably in the setting of a good tavern, where his bounding wit and good nature became manifest. He was a connoisseur of German beer and of fine cigars. In a period when I too was addicted to cigar smoking, he repeatedly presented me with one of his, asking for my appraisal of it.

Next is William A. Coolidge, whom I came to know when we both were members of the Board of Trustees of the Boston Lying-in Hospital (now called the Brigham and Women's Hospital).[4] In 1952 he visited a group of his friends, starting with President Pusey of Harvard and me, to ask if we and our wives would be interested in coming to his home on the Ipswich River in Topsfield for Sunday lunch once a month from September through April. He made clear that the plan was an experiment. More than thirty years later the luncheons continue, the original group having suffered a few defections and gained some additions, and the plan is a happy success. The regular group includes a distinguished judge, several lawyers, museum curators, sculptors, university corporation members, journalists, and other interesting people, including members of the Coolidge family. As Bill suggested in the beginning, its members on occasion bring their children, grandchildren, and house guests. Some of these young folk are grown up and married, but they return to partake of Bill's infinite welcome, bountiful luncheons, fine art, and beautiful flowers. Occasionally he invites special guests to his luncheons, and frequently there are students from Oxford's Balliol College, which Bill attended, who are in this country on traveling fellowships provided by Bill.

Always at these affairs the talk is lively and wide ranging, and we all find delight in the gentle hospitality of our host. We have come to feel that these luncheons achieve the best of social life in our time.

While on the Corporation Bill Coolidge served on its Executive Committee and also accepted membership on the Corporation Joint Advisory Committee, where students, faculty members, and Corporation members came together to discuss current issues. In this assignment as well as in his work on the Executive Committee, he demonstrated a sensitive understanding of student views and thus made a contribution to the resolution of the student discontents of those difficult days.

Along with the late Erwin D. Canham of the *Christian Science Monitor*, I served under Bill's chairmanship on a committee of the Boston Museum of Fine Arts that was charged with the delicate task of extricating the museum from a tangle of international legalities that resulted when two staff members acquired what was hailed with much hullabaloo as a Raphael painting, a work of art which the Italian government felt determined to take back to Italy. Because the painting was brought into the United States without being declared, U.S. Customs felt justified in confiscating the painting. Our assignment required us to engage in a dramatic series of conferences with the Italian ambassador, the head of U.S. Customs, the secretary of the treasury (then George Shultz), and an emissary from Italy. As a result the museum escaped a threatened indictment but sent the painting back to Italy.

At one of his Sunday luncheons Bill somewhat casually said to me that he wanted to offer his real estate properties to MIT. This was the first intimation that Bill was considering such a generous gift to the Institute. I reported this to the Institute's administration, and the outcome was a formal plan for the Institute to receive the real estate. Bill wrote President Gray:

I do hope that over the years the Institute finds a way to make use of the property in the furtherance of its own purposes. It is a lovely place, and over the years, with the addition of my own land on this side of the river—which I intend to leave to the Institute—might well be able to play an important part in some development of the Institute's activities. . . .

I feel indebted to the Institute for the many hours at breakfast meetings that I enjoyed during the past years of meeting with the Executive Committee. They were always stimulating and gave me a feeling of considerable confidence that the Institute was well run.

The Coolidge luncheons are but one example of numerous dining clubs to be found in Boston. My membership in several of these, notably in the Library Society, has been an enriching experience. These groups also serve to build bridges between the academic community and other walks of life.

In its early days members of the venerable Saturday Club, for example, took specific actions to protect and enhance the quality of life in Boston. In the *Later Years of the Saturday Club*, edited by M. A. DeWolfe Howe, appear biographical sketches of those who were members of the club from 1870 to 1920. A sketch of member William Barton Rogers, MIT's founder, written by another member, President Pritchett, appears in this volume. It notes: "Amongst the memorials in favor of the proposed institution [MIT], was one from Benjamin Peirce, himself a distinguished member of the Saturday Club. Others of the Saturday Club, more identified with classical studies and interests, also lent Rogers their aid and support."

Rogers and his brother Henry had close associations with Philadelphia, and Rogers might have succeeded in founding MIT there. The support he found in Boston is but another item that E. Digby Baltzell might have recorded in his *Puritan Boston and Quaker Philadelphia*, in which he alleges that the first families of Boston—and Cambridge—have contributed more to the intellectual, educational, and political life of their cities, state, and nation than have comparable families of Philadelphia. "It is to the everlasting credit of Boston," wrote Pritchett in his Saturday Club sketch of Rogers, "that it understood and accepted this man and enabled him to realize his conception."

Gertrude Stein said even more, in writing about education: "In New England they have done it they do do it they will do it and they do it in every way in which education can be thought about."

It was at the Coolidge luncheons that I came to know Dr. George Thorn, a gifted physician whose talents, I recognized, could make a great contribution to MIT at a crucial period in its development of the life sciences. There was about him in addition a grace, warmth, and gentleness that touched the hearts of his associates and made his companions feel better simply by being with him.

On his retirement from the Harvard Medical School Thorn was saluted in the *New England Journal of Medicine* as "one of the few physicians living today who can claim such a consistent pattern of service and excellence in teaching and clinical care." His versatility was also acclaimed when he was described as a rare "medical triad": outstanding as teacher, clinician, researcher, and he was widely admired for his personal attributes. He might now be described as a rare quartet to recognize his services to Whitaker College and the Whitaker Health Sciences Fund at MIT and to the Howard Hughes Medical Institute.

In 1946 he was attracted to the possibility of making an artificial kidney, which had first been accomplished by a European researcher. He and his colleagues were the first in the United States to construct an artificial kidney and the first to initiate an active dialysis program. In 1951 he collaborated with the Peter Bent Brigham Department of Surgery in the initial trial of a kidney transplant.

In addition to his work at Harvard, George undertook the post of director of Medical Research of the Howard Hughes Medical Institute. In this he administered a program of scientific research in which the Institute laboratories were associated with research activities in several major hospital-medical centers.

As the health sciences were moving into a great period of development at MIT, he obviously was among the Corporation members specially qualified to bring to the trustees the knowledge and vision that could support the talented faculty being assembled. He also readily made himself available for important committee assignments during his sixteen years of active membership. For twelve years he served without interruption on the Corporation's Executive Committee, and he was a member of the search committees that nominated first Jerome B. Wiesner and then, on his retirement, Paul E. Gray to be presidents of the

Institute. He took a special interest in the Biology Department and came to be one of its most enthusiastic protagonists.

He next served as co-chairman of the National Sponsoring Committee for the Harvard-MIT Joint Program in Health Sciences and Technology, which raised $10 million in endowment to launch this program. For a period he and I joined forces in travel about the country, seeking understanding and support of this unique interinstitutional program for bringing to medicine the resources of science and technology.

The Whitakers, who contributed so generously to the life sciences at MIT and notably to the creation of Whitaker College, developed a special admiration for this remarkable physician, and he had great influence in leading them to decisions to make large contributions to the advancement of the health sciences at the Institute and to the creation of Whitaker College.

I could go on and on in presenting this extraordinary record of service and of professional leadership, for he so admirably fulfilled the goal of bringing talent and vision to the Institute's government.

I also delighted in the companionship that grew out of our meetings at Bill Coolidge's luncheons and out of George's manifold services to MIT.

I was attracted, too, to George's horticultural program. Both of us had an interest in shrubs and trees, he at his summer place on Coolidge Point in Massachusetts and I in Sharon, New Hampshire. Over the years he has created an impressive arboretum in which he has himself planted four hundred trees. He once remarked: "I have always thought that growing trees is a good thing for a physician to do. Trees will get along by themselves if the physician gets busy and has to leave them alone for a couple of weeks, and planting trees is also a good thing because it means that you also intend to be around for a few years to watch them grow."

For the information of students in Thorn House, I have to report that he played a hot banjo in the Peter Bent Brigham jazz band. Now that MIT appropriately and happily has dedicated to him one of its new dormitories, he will have an opportunity once again to display another talent to the students who have the good fortune to live there.

Carl M. Mueller, '41, is another member who joined the Corporation during my chairmanship and became one of its most energetic and influential life members.

Let me note a few of his services to MIT. As I have said, he chaired two of the Corporation's committees on succession. The first was to fill the vacancy in the presidency resulting from the retirement of Dr. Wiesner, and the second was to nominate a chairman of the Corporation to take the place that Wiesner normally would have filled had he not chosen to become a professor again. An earlier search committee, of which Carl was a member and which was chaired by Dr. Fisk, had nominated Dr. Wiesner to be president and also recommended that the post of chancellor be reestablished and that Paul Gray be chosen for that post.

President Wiesner reached the age of retirement as president while Howard Johnson was still serving as chairman of the Corporation. Wiesner had let it be known during his presidency that he wanted to return to his Institute professorship on completing his service as president. Thus the chain of continuity, president to chairman, that had prevailed over the years was broken and Howard Johnson later chose to retire from the chairmanship.

It had become public information that President David Saxon of the University of California had chosen to retire from the Cal presidency and return to teaching physics at UCLA. The committee quickly determined that this MIT alumnus could be interested in replacing Johnson as chairman of the Corporation, which provided a happy solution by continuing a man of presidential experience in the chairmanship. With skill and sensitivity to opinions within and without the Institute, Carl brought about this happy arrangement, and Saxon agreed to accept the post.

In addition to these important roles in the selection of members of the Institute's administration, Carl, a banker and financier, has served as chairman of the Institute's Investment Committee.

I have a sense of special and cherished relationship with Carl. Both of us served together on the board of the Cabot Corporation, and when that institution invited its directors and their friends each autumn to an elk hunt in the Sangre de Cristo Mountains of Colorado, he almost always participated and I, who was not a hunter, occasionally joined the hunters for fellowship and good conversation. On one occasion I joined Carl in going by jeep high into the mountains in search of elk, and he fortunately encountered one of the great beasts grazing in one of the high mountain meadows. With a shot of extraordinary skill he brought the elk down. Under these circumstances I found myself serving as his assistant in the required ritual of eviscerating the elk so that it could be carried down to the camp by jeep. His readiness and skill in undertaking this butcher's task impressed me. In between hunts in those spectacular mountains we would get off to a quiet place to discuss MIT and its people, and I came to realize how deeply devoted Carl was to the institution and how broad was his concept of the role of the trustee.

One other aspect of this urbane man is the felicitous way he embroiders his ideas by expressing them in picturesque idiom or metaphor.

All four—Fisk, Coolidge, Thorn, and Mueller—came to be appointed life members as well as hard-working members of the Executive Committee, where they could bring to bear most effectively their wisdom and their devotion to the Institute.

THE SECOND CENTURY FUND CAMPAIGN

In my capacity as chairman of the Corporation, I undertook to provide the executive leadership of another campaign for funds ten years after the CFD campaign. With the devoted help of volunteers from the Corporation and alumni body, I was able to do this and thus relieve President Stratton of many onerous fund-raising tasks so that he might devote himself with fewer interruptions to the academic administration of the Institute.

In commenting later on this campaign, Dr. Wiesner said that "across the length and breadth of this land, there are many who speak affectionately of Jim Killian as their 'most expensive friend.' " For this campaign a program of goals developed largely under the direction of Dr. Stratton and the Academic Council was priced at a total of $66 million.

Once again we had the leadership of Alfred Sloan as honorary chairman of the drive and as general chairman, John J. Wilson. Walter Beadle, still generous with his time, took the responsibility to chair the effort to secure leadership gifts from individuals; Mervin J. Kelly, former president of the Bell Telephone Laboratories, the chairmanship of leadership gifts from corporations; and Philip Peters of the John Hancock Company, chairman of the committee on area organization. Marshall B. Dalton, who had led with skill and rare devotion the Committee on Financing Development ten years before, again provided oversight and inspiration as chairman of the Corporation's Committee on Development. We had the assistance of an able staff, with Vincent Fulmer, at a sacrifice to his professional career as an economist, giving me highly efficient personal assistance. To senior administrators he came close to being the indispensable man.

Spread over three years, it was a grueling campaign, requiring the team to travel throughout the nation. It fell to my lot to work closely with Mervin Kelly, who was not an MIT alumnus but a very influential member of the MIT Corporation. By virtue of having been president of the Bell Labs, he brought to our corporate solicitation a special persuasiveness in arguing that industry had an opportunity and responsibility to support the programs set forth by the Institute. With Fulmer, he and I together boxed the compass with carefully prepared charts relating specifically to each corporation we were soliciting. Our general policy was to present our case to the chief executive officer. The technique worked, and once again MIT broke records by raising more than $20 million through corporate donations. I also spoke to many local groups, sometimes under bizarre circumstances. I recall holding forth at noon beside the swimming pool of an athletic club where our local development staff felt I could reach the largest number of potential donors in that city. The alumnus who was presiding had dropped my written sales pitch into the pool; my waterside speech was better for being dampened down. Other recollections include an appointment that led me deep into the purlieus of the Chicago stockyards and still another, by way of contrast, the episode that was contrived by the prospective donor so that my presentation had to be made in the midst of a fashion show, which added a piquant, stylish touch to what might have been an "otherwise bald and unconvincing narrative."

After three strenuous years the Second Century Fund campaign was brought to a successful conclusion. "In the glitter of the Waldorf-Astoria's grand ballroom," recorded the *M.I.T. Observer*, "more than 1,000 business leaders, scientists and educators gathered at a festive dinner to honor Alfred P. Sloan, Jr." The guests assembled from all over the country heard a special tribute by me to Mr. Sloan, and as he rose to reply, he received a standing ovation, which he termed "truly the crowning event of my long life." And then came the general chairman, John Wilson, with a sensational announcement: "Since the Second Century Fund was launched three years ago," he said proudly, "the total of gifts, grants, and pledges received by MIT—all from private sources—has amounted to the magnificent total of $98 million!" More than 4,300 volunteers across the country had worked tirelessly and loyally to achieve this success.

The campaign financed the largest construction program in the Institute's history up to that time. It included a women's residence, McCormick Hall, the Green Center for Earth Sciences, the Center for Materials Science and Engineering, a Student Center, a Center for the Life Sciences, and a Center for Space Research.

Fourteen new professorships were endowed, including the Abby Rockefeller Mauzé Chair to be filled by a succession of distinguished women scholars, and $30 million was allocated to teaching and research programs. Another $10 million was contributed for scholarships, fellowships, and student loan funds.

As this is written in 1984, MIT has completed the third major campaign that I have observed in my years at the Institute. This time, encouraged by the breakthroughs made in the first two major campaigns—and in the intervening efforts to raise capital funds, including funds to finance the Compton Laboratory, the Faculty Salary Fund, the Dreyfus Chemistry Building, and the Sherman Fairchild Electrical Engineering Building—the Institute boldly set out to raise $225 million, and that total was exceeded, as I have indicated, with more than $250 million raised or pledged, although no comprehensive solicitation of alumni was undertaken. This campaign was led by two senior administrative officers, Howard Johnson as chairman of the Corporation, and President Wiesner, who made the unprecedented decision late in 1977 to take leave from the day-to-day duties of the presidency to maintain a more flexible calendar in order to work with the chairman of the campaign, an arrangement which Dr. Wiesner characterized as a shared duty roster in the office of the president and the chancellor. Since his retirement from the presidency in 1980 he has continued single-handedly to solicit funds for additional projects, including a boldly conceived arts and media technology center.

The day following the great victory dinner in New York, in 1963, the Killians left for Greece in response to an invitation they had received from the royal family of Greece, Paul and Frederika. The origin of this invitation is of interest. Queen Frederika,[5] a woman of both brilliance and charm, had come to the United States during the period when I was special assistant for Science and Technology to President Eisenhower. She had a great desire to promote science and technology in Greece, and her trip to this country was for the purpose of learning about atomic energy technology. She had included MIT in her itinerary, and I first met her at a dinner given in Washington by the Chief of Naval Operations, Admiral Burke, and Mrs. Burke, where the queen and her daughter Sophia were the honored guests. Admiral Burke had come to know her when he was Commander of the Sixth Fleet in the Mediterranean. Her daughter Sophia, incidentally, is now the wife of the King of Spain.

Frederika was aware of the NATO study, which I had chaired, exploring the feasibility of an International Institute of Science and Technology, and I rather think that she had hopes that this institution or some parts of it might be located in Greece. I received the invitation from the royal family through Professor Elias Gyftopoulos of MIT, a native of Greece and a very able nuclear engineer. In Greece we not only visited the royal family in their country home, but under their auspices we visited the Greek Islands, Delphi, and other famous places in Greece. Queen Frederika or her staff had selected as a host during our stay in Greece a retired air force officer, Mr. C. Potamianos, who undertook a variety of assignments in behalf of the royal family. He escorted us on our travels in Greece and proved to be a host that we shall always remember for his courtesy and careful arrangement of our visit.

I was invited to speak on several occasions, including an evening address at the University of Athens. On this occasion two tall and very royal-looking chairs were placed in the hall directly in front of the podium, and just as I was to start, they were occupied by the king and queen, perhaps the most unusual setting I had ever experienced in presenting an address.

A CONSTELLATION OF GREAT BENEFACTORS

In 1968 I was disturbed about the trend of national discussion which suggested that private education may become economically unsustainable, and I turned pamphleteer by writing an essay, "Don't Sell Our Private Colleges Short." It was in this pamphlet that I made an appeal that the federal government, individuals, corporations, and foundations give a higher priority to those kinds of gifts and grants that enable the private institution to strengthen the heart of the enterprise, else the grantors of funds may end up supporting the side shows while the main tent is falling down:

I do urge that in this period of stress a larger share of the philanthropic dollar go into . . . unrestricted grants that the private institution can use in behalf of its core needs. Happily, a few of the major foundations have been making grants of this kind in recent years.

Every institution must have adequate funds for salaries, for student aid, for venture capital and the enhancement of quality, and for other basic needs, and it must have adequate buildings in which to carry on its work. It must have those kinds of funds that give it stability, flexibility, and independence. It has exceptional need for those kinds of funds that are unrestricted and that can be applied broadly to the core strength of the institution. And it also must have endowment funds that are in proper balance with increasing levels of operating and program costs. Endowment, moreover, as the late Alan Gregg once emphasized, "becomes the one type of valuable aid which the government cannot give. Furthermore, endowment gives an institution independence of government; indeed, it would be claimed that adequate endowment of a private institution not only makes it independent of government—it makes government dependent on the private institution's dependable resources."[6]

Grouped together in this section are sketches of several great donors to MIT whose private benefices illustrate the goals that I stressed in my pamphlet. In addition they brought to the object of their giving a creative intellectual contribution to accompany their gifts of funds. All of these donors became involved in the programs they were aiding and found satisfaction in their participation and in the opportunity to share their ideas with the faculty and administration of the Institute.

I speak of Alfred P. Sloan, Jr., of the class of 1895, Katharine Dexter McCormick of the class of 1904, Cecil Howard Green of the class of 1923 and his wife Ida, and Uncas A. Whitaker, also of the class of 1923, and his wife Helen. Together with Edwin H. Land, whose portrait as an innovator and benefactor I have already sketched, their donations to the Institute approximated $120 million.

Alfred P. Sloan, Jr. became MIT's greatest benefactor, greater in total of gifts than George Eastman's spectacular donations which began in 1912 and which enabled MIT to leave its cramped quarters on Boylston Street in Boston and build its new home in Cambridge. George Eastman was not an alumnus, but he was grateful to several of our alumni, including Frank Lovejoy, for their skilled contributions to the management of Kodak.

Mr. Sloan's interest in MIT was greatly enhanced by his admiration of Karl Compton. As a result he invited Dr. Compton to become a public member of the General Motors Board of Directors and a member of the Board of the Sloan Foundation. After Dr. Compton's death Mr. Sloan continued to feel that these two boards would benefit from an MIT presence and that such a presence would also be of benefit to MIT, so I accepted his invitations to serve on both. One of Sloan's characteristics was his deep loyalty to the institutions he admired and considered first-rate. MIT was one of these institutions.

Sloan had some baffling notions about "professors" except those, fortunately, at MIT and a few other institutions who had won his respect. He assigned strange characteristics to this professional tribe. They never really worked hard, he thought. During the period that Warren Weaver served as an adviser to the Sloan Foundation, he asked Sloan how he could hold such views about academics and still so greatly admire that academic institution, MIT. His reply to Weaver was: "MIT is not an academic institution! It is a technological institute!"

Almost all his gifts to MIT were for programs he himself initiated. In his direction of the Sloan Foundation he scorned handouts—giving away money for the sake of giving. He wanted to make available funds to support creative undertakings, usually those he himself had conceived.

At MIT Sloan initiated in 1938 the Sloan Fellowship Program, which made it possible for young business executives in corporations to take leave of absence to attend MIT for a year to acquire new skills and new perspectives. He later established a similar program at Stanford. And as I mentioned earlier, with a gift of over $5 million he founded the Sloan School of Management at MIT with the goal of cultivating the "science" of management in new ways and also provided it with $1 million for research. Encouraged by the success of the Sloan Fellowship Program for corporate executives, he proposed that MIT establish a Center for Advanced Engineering Study to provide opportunities for midcareer engineers to return to the Institute to modernize their skills and acquire a deeper understanding of advancing technology or to take widely distributed self-study extension courses for these purposes. In writing to me in April

1963 about the wording of the announcement of this center, he said: "It is the ideas phase of it that I would like to emphasize rather than the funds, although the latter should be mentioned, I believe, incidentally."

Sloan's experience at General Motors had convinced him that superior performance should be rewarded by liberal bonuses. During a discussion MIT officers had with him about our urgent need to increase faculty salaries, he proposed to me that MIT should experiment for a trial period with incentive compensation by making monetary awards above their normal salaries to faculty members of high achievement. To my knowledge, special compensation of this kind to a number of faculty members had never been tried in any university. In fact academic communities have generally preferred compensation policies adhering to academic democracy and nondiscriminatory compensation based on standard salary scales with variations for outstanding members. Nevertheless, we agreed to conduct a cautious experiment, and for two years we made special Sloan awards to outstanding faculty members financed by funds provided by Mr. and Mrs. Sloan and the Sloan Foundation.

Fortunately we were able so to manage these unique awards without criticism by making it clear that they came not from Institute funds but from funds given specifically for this purpose. The experiment was a great success during the two years the awards were made. Faculty morale was raised, and Mr. Sloan received many letters of thanks from grateful recipients. Both Mr. Sloan and the MIT administration had considered the plan as interim, and after we had made modest progress in securing funds for financing more adequate salaries for the entire faculty, we were able to discontinue the bonuses after two years without any adverse reaction.

In March 1965, at his request, I wrote Mr. Sloan a long letter in which I sought to be responsive to his interest in helping to promote outstanding excellence in personnel. Because he wanted to keep our discussion very personal, I sent my letter marked "Personal and Confidential" to his home rather than to his Sloan Foundation office. I excerpt parts of this letter below because it influenced the contents of the later deed of gift by which he hurriedly provided, seven months before his death at ninety, for a personal gift of $5 million to help maintain at MIT as its highest priority, in Ashley's phrase, that "thin clear stream of intellectual excellence."

When I called upon you recently, you spoke of your conviction about the overriding importance of MIT's attracting and holding superlatively able members of its faculty and administration. You commented, in effect—and I fully agree—that MIT's greatness in the final analysis depends upon its success in recruiting great people. And you spoke in confidence of some ideas you were turning over in your mind about how you might assist the Institute—should certain conditions obtain—in finding, encouraging, and keeping outstanding personnel.

First, MIT is now on the highest plateau in its history of responsibility, size and scope of activities and effectiveness. To hold this new position and to be responsive to the leadership expected of it, it must constantly maintain a faculty of front rank, but it must do something more. It must find and hold rare and exceptional personnel—men who stand out as towering peaks in the educational and research world, who make the major breakthroughs in their fields and give a quality of world-recognized excellence and leadership to the institution.

We have people of this quality at MIT but not yet enough of them.

Second, MIT finds itself today in the main stream of events and its fields vital and relevant in relation to major national needs. As a result, its faculty has a special strategic importance and visibility, as well as exceptional qualifications. Many of them are the kinds of people that industry needs as well as other universities, and in consequence, many of our people are offered positions elsewhere, frequently at salaries substantially higher than we pay them (and probably out of line with others at the institution making the offer).

As I write these words about Sloan's vision and generosity in 1965, I find myself brooding about circumstances when inflation and the acute needs of industry for engineers make it unprecedentedly difficult for universities to match the salaries offered by industry and thus to retain enough "seed corn" talent to educate the talent of the future, which industry will surely need.

To complete this account, let me emphasize that the Institute formally agreed to Sloan's request that "MIT shall include in its solicitation of funds a proper appeal for a fund for faculty advancement, which fund shall be added to the Fund he proposes to establish."

The crown piece of Mr. Sloan's assistance to MIT was an endowment to support basic research in the physical sciences, which he started in 1960 and formally defined by a deed of gift dated December 18, 1963. He and I spent many meetings in discussing the appropriateness and management of such a fund. In this deed of gift he meticulously explained what he meant by basic research. He defined it as the "quest for knowledge for knowledge's sake" or the "search for new knowledge—discovery in contradistinction to development." He said that he had come to understand the vital importance of basic research and the "necessity for a far greater effort in that regard, if the country were to keep ahead in the competitive race for survival, as well as in the interest of providing a better life for people generally." He wrote that there must not only be greatly increased funds for basic research, "but there must be the most thoughtful and imaginative management of such funds."

By a combination of personal gifts, Sloan Foundation grants, and a bequest, he provided the munificent total of $25 million for this purpose, bringing the total of all his donations to MIT to $57 million.

The "inner endowment" represented by the basic research fund in effect provided within MIT a foundation administered by three of its senior officers, and the subventions it made possible have enabled the Institute to stimulate and carry on research on a scale and with freedom generally beyond the restrictions that government or foundations imposed on their grants. The succession of MIT presidents that followed me relied greatly on this innovative endowment to give a lift to young scientists of promise and to start projects that later grew to attract government or other support. It became a major resource for supporting emerging scientific talent.

Mr. Sloan provided funds to a number of institutions other

than MIT. He founded the Sloan Foundation and the Sloan-Kettering Institute for Cancer Research. He made major contributions to the California Institute of Technology, New York University, Stanford University, and numerous other institutions, and in all these he provided not only funds but a philanthropy of creative ideas.

He was a pioneer advocate of corporate contributions to institutions of higher learning at a time when there were few grants to education by business firms. He wrote an article in the June 2, 1951, issue of *Collier's Magazine* entitled "Big Business Must Help Our Colleges." In addition in an article in *Philanthropy*, he stated: "In its own interest, corporate enterprise should support the sources from which fundamental knowledge flows."

My association with Alfred Sloan was one of the most intellectually rewarding in my MIT career. For a number of years I kept in close touch with him, at periods calling on him almost monthly. In all these meetings I found him always reaching for quality and for innovative ways to contribute to the strength of American society. I will never forget his long period of almost uncontrollable grief following the death of his wife. He was one of the greatest men I ever knew, and when he died at age ninety, I experienced such a sense of profound loss that it led me uncharacteristically to weep.

Katharine Dexter McCormick, '04, gave MIT by gift or bequest more than $30 million. When she became of age, she at first devoted herself to the usual activities of a Boston debutante—but not for long. Once, in reminiscing about her youth, she recalled that she had grown up on French and music. She soon decided that she wanted an educational career not then generally of interest to debutantes—in fact she wanted to study biology. She visited several of the recently established women's colleges such as Wellesley and Smith but lost interest in them because they then had no adequate laboratory facilities in biology. With determination and pioneering spirit she decided to seek an MIT degree in biology, but she could not be admitted as a regular student because she lacked the requirements for admission. This difficulty did not deter her resolve: she attended MIT for three years as a special student to prepare for its entrance examinations. And when she had passed them, she attended the Institute for another four years to achieve her degree in biology. We have in the MIT Library a copy of her thesis entitled "Fatigue of the Cardiac Muscles in Reptiles."

While at MIT she came to know Stanley McCormick of Chicago, a Princeton student and son of the inventor of the reaper, Cyrus McCormick. A young man of many talents, he had been a varsity tennis player at Princeton and demonstrated abilities as an amateur painter. Even as a student he had successfully served as comptroller of his father's company. In September 1904, following her graduation and his, they were married. The couple had many common interests. They loved sports, became engrossed in art, and possessed exceptional taste. It is reported that on their wedding trip they began collecting Monets and Manets. It was a lyrical marriage, but tragedy lurked ahead. Two years after their marriage Stanley became mentally ill, and this illness was to prove incurable despite his wife's effort over a period of forty years to provide him with a benign, calming living environment and to find a cure for his schizophrenia. In 1909 Stanley was declared legally incompetent.

Under these circumstances and in her loneliness, Mrs. McCormick took up some of the latent interests that she had acquired while a student in biology at MIT, and in addition she began to devote herself to the advancement of women's rights, including suffragism and population control. For an extended period her husband's estate was administered by the courts, and she, with the distinguished Cleveland lawyer Newton Baker and his partner William Bemis, was forced to conduct a long legal battle to gain control of her husband's estate. Once she had control of the estate, she was financially able to make substantial grants to agencies that had prompted her interest and support. In exercising her interest in women's suffrage, she marched in parades with Carrie Chapman Catt and served as an officer of the National American Women's Suffrage Association.

It is reported that at MIT, notices put up by suffragists were torn down by male students, but as an alumna of MIT, she carried the flag for her fellow coeds. With Carrie Chapman Catt she founded the League of Women Voters.

More dramatically she joined Margaret Sanger in a campaign to gain acceptance of population control. It was this relationship that brought her into the orbit of Gregory Pincus of the Worcester Foundation for Experimental Biology. She had been sending funds to the Planned Parenthood Foundation's research fund, and her intense interest in contraception motivated her to provide directly or indirectly for the research of Dr. Pincus. The record indicates that she was pressing hard for advances in birth control techniques, and she became perhaps the principal supporter of the research of Dr. Pincus, supplementing what he had received from the G. D. Searle Company. When Pincus gained the support of Dr. John Rock, Harvard gynecologist, Mrs. McCormick provided Dr. Rock with support for the testing of the pill, which was to be the ultimate development of Pincus. Scientific work at two pharmaceutical houses, Syntex Corporation and G. D. Searle Company, contributed importantly to Pincus's achievement. In an article in the *Boston Globe* about Dr. Rock, Loretta McLaughlin makes the statement that Mrs. McCormick contributed financially to every step of the pill's development including "massive field trials in Puerto Rico. Not a single government dollar went into its creation, but McCormick donated $2,000,000."

Throughout her exciting career Mrs. McCormick maintained an abiding interest in women students at MIT. In 1945, persuaded by Margaret Compton and a group of MIT faculty wives, the Institute established a small experimental residence for women on Bay State Road in Boston. Mrs. McCormick was a close observer of this effort, and she provided a helping hand in a variety of ways. One of her concerns was for the transportation, in bad weather, of these young women back and forth from their Bay State Road dormitory to the Institute. Having mushed my way across the bleak reaches of the Harvard Bridge for three winters, I fully understood and sympathized with Mrs.

McCormick's concern. At one time she speculated on the possibility of a conveyance with some of the characteristics of a modern people-mover, but in the end she made available a taxi fund so that the girls could use cabs when the going was rough.

The success of this house for women students undoubtedly encouraged Mrs. McCormick's ultimate decision to provide funds for an elegant women's residence at MIT, Stanley McCormick Hall. During the planning of the first unit of McCormick Hall, for which she had provided the funds, we received information that it might be possible for MIT to purchase the Sancta Maria Hospital building, which was located adjacent to the site of McCormick Hall. Were this building to be sold by the hospital, it might have been used for some purpose that would be inappropriate for a building adjacent to a women's dormitory on the MIT campus. We wrote to Mrs. McCormick explaining the situation, and she very promptly committed herself to a gift to cover the purchase of the hospital building. This was also advantageous for the hospital, for MIT's payment for the building was a major contribution to the cost of an enlarged and modernized hospital facility in another Cambridge location.

The last call which I made on Mrs. McCormick, in November, 1967, at her home on Commonwealth Avenue, took place just a month before she died. When I arrived at her house, I was told that she would be a little delayed in seeing me. Her staff had assumed that I would see her in her private third-floor quarters, but Mrs. McCormick had decided otherwise. She explained that she considered it inappropriate to receive a senior officer of the Institute except in her reception room. Consequently she wished to be brought down from her private quarters. She must be properly dressed, she decided, and wearing hat and gloves. Thus gallantly and with an exquisite sense of decorum did she pay homage to the Institute and hold fast in the face of illness to her turn-of-the-century dignity and style. The gesture was typical of her. She was a great lady, self-disciplined, steadfast in principle, decisive in judgment, firm in adhering to her own ideas and taste, and withal instinctively gracious and generous. (I am sure that President Julius Stratton and Vice President

Philip Stoddard, who worked with her so closely on the planning of McCormick Hall, would concur with these evaluations.) In our talk she expressed her satisfaction that the second part of McCormick Hall was approaching completion. She wanted to know whether we were still certain that the new room arrangements were right. She reaffirmed her belief in the role of women in the professions and MIT's commitment to the professional education of women. And finally, she expressed satisfaction in the fulfillment of her plans for McCormick Hall. And so I bade her good-by, the last visitor, I am told, she was able to receive. I shall always cherish my remembrance of this meeting.

In her will, in which Mrs. McCormick named MIT as her residual beneficiary, she included a gracious statement about her special interest in the Institute—a statement which touched us deeply at MIT. "Since my graduation in 1904," she wrote, "I have wished to express my gratitude to the Institution for its advanced policy of scientific education for women. This policy gave me the opportunity to obtain the scientific training which has been of inestimable value to me throughout my life."

The completion of McCormick Hall, the finest dormitory on the MIT campus, did much to stimulate an increase in the number of women applicants to the Institute. Despite the opposition of a few faculty members Dr. Stratton and I had earlier come to a firm decision to encourage the admission of more women. It was a prophetic decision. By 1984 the number of women students at MIT had exceeded 2,200.

This story about Mrs. McCormick recalls to mind how another young woman, Ellen Swallow, a Vassar graduate, refused to accept no for an answer and gained admission to MIT in 1871. She did it by first getting a job in one of the Institute's laboratories. Ellen Swallow gave the Institute a claim to having been the first Eastern men's college to admit women. This was a year before Cornell formally became a coeducational school and launched the first substantial demonstration that coeducation was not a dangerous undertaking for an institution traditionally male—a discovery that MIT had similarly made.

Cecil ('23) and Ida Green, husband and wife, of Dallas, Texas, are two other masters of what John D. Rockefeller once called "the difficult art of giving." In turning their cultivated benevolence greatly to benefit MIT and many other institutions, they have conducted their art of giving in an unusually personal way. It has consistently been marked by a distinctive decision making that reflects a true marriage of the ideals and judgment of both.

Cecil's education in MIT's cooperative course in electrical engineering placed him at one stage as a candidate working for his master's degree in the research laboratory of the General Electric plant at Schenectady. While there he met Ida Mabelle Flansburgh, a GE industrial statistician, and ultimately they were married. After winning his degree, Cecil tried several different jobs, requiring cross-country travel, before he settled, with Ida's help, on what he wanted. What he wanted proved to be a job as chief of a seismic field party operated by a young Texas company, Geophysical Service, Inc., in Dallas. There were interruptions in his job there, but in the thirties he found steady employment in "doodlebugging," and in the fifties, his career with Texas Instruments, Inc., became a permanent lifetime affiliation. Important to this story was the close partnership of Ida and Cecil and the great benefits to him of her steadiness and good judgment as his career evolved.

Cecil's relations with his alma mater, MIT, were enhanced by his admiration for Professor Robert Shrock of MIT's Geology Department and by an internship program for selected students of the department arranged by Green and Shrock. Out of these relationships over the years grew the Greens' decision to contribute of the order of $6 million to construct a building as the center for the earth sciences, erected, as the plaque reads, "through the generosity of Cecil Howard Green and Ida Flansburgh Green" and testfying "to their interest in the study of the earth and its surroundings and their deep devotion to education."

When the building was being designed by architect I. M. Pei, the Greens made clear their desire for a distinguished architectural result. They supported the Institute in its effort to achieve outstanding aesthetic distinction for the building.

The Greens brought within the MIT orbit Cecil's Texas Instruments partner, now deceased, Eugene McDermott and his wife Margaret. Gene came to be an active member of the MIT Corporation, and he and his wife gave funds for the McDermott Scholarships and for McDermott Court and its great Alexander Calder stabile. Calder and McDermott were classmates at Stevens Institute of Technology. Since Gene's death, Margaret has continued generously to support the arts at MIT by endowing a professorship and by aiding the purchase of the Henry Moore sculpture in Killian Court. Back in Dallas, her home city, Margaret was to play a very major role in the combining of two museums into one and making the one a very distinguished museum of art.

The Greens' benefactions in behalf of MIT have continued over the years. They have endowed nine professorships and provided support for student aid and other purposes—in total, in excess of $13 million. Today Cecil and Ida continue as life members, emeriti, of the MIT Corporation and are beloved members of the MIT community.

Over the years their philanthropy has become highly diversified geographically and in terms of different kinds of institutions. They have given funds for buildings, laboratories, professorships, scholarship funds, and other resources important for the advancement of education and research. Cecil was born in Manchester, England, and with his parents moved to Vancouver, where he grew up and attended precollege schools. It was appropriate therefore for him and Ida to make contributions to institutions in England and Canada (and also Australia); in fact a recent benefaction was their donation to Oxford University to share in the funding of a postgraduate college. This "society of the university" has been named Green College, the primary purpose of which is to serve the needs of students whose interest is in clinical medicine.

In November 1978 the presidents, chancellors, and other officials of more than thirty colleges, hospitals, museums, secondary schools, scientific associations, and universities in Australia, Canada, England, and the United States came together to pay tribute to the Greens. The dinner and convocation of tribute had been convened at the National Academy of Sciences in Washington by a committee headed by President Wiesner of MIT.

Cecil and Ida were the first joint recipients of the Public Welfare Medal of the National Academy of Sciences in 1979 "in recognition of distinguished contributions in the application of science to the public welfare." The names of Cecil and Ida stand unique in the roster of recipients of this distinguished award—the only example to date of husband and wife being honored together. They also became joint honorary members of the American Institute of Architects in 1983—the first couple so honored in the twentieth century. Separately from Cecil, Ida has received many recognitions and honors for her contributions to community life and to education. MIT's residence hall for women graduate students, completed in 1983, appropriately bears her name. There are also Ida Green Fellowships for Women, in Texas and at MIT, and other programs and facilities named in her honor.

The Greens' spectacular and well-conceived program of international philanthropy stands as one of the great demonstrations of discriminating personal generosity. Their gifts have beneficially affected the lives of hundreds of thousands of young people.

With an extraordinary blending of personality and purpose they today live their lives with taste, informality, and simplicity. This has given their generosity a special quality of humility and grace that endows it with a gift beyond dollars.

Uncas ('23) and Helen Whitaker. Uncas Whitaker, a farm boy from Missouri, acquired great wealth by applying his entrepreneurial engineering skills to founding and building AMP Incorporated (at first called Aircraft Marine Products, Inc.) a "growth" company that came to be numbered in *Fortune*'s list of the 500 largest American companies. This company today would be described as a "high technology" company, but Whitaker, in his earthy Missourian lingo, said it achieved success by "engineering the hell out of the product." Built around an ingenious technique for making electrical connectors, the company's trademark finally emerged as "Precision Engineering at the End of a Wire."

After obtaining his S.B. degree at MIT, Whit (he detested the name Uncas and sought in vain to be called Whit) worked first at the Westinghouse Air Brake Company and while in Pittsburgh, by attending night school, won a degree in electrical engineering from Carnegie Tech. Later in his career he obtained a third degree, this time in law, again by night study.

As his company developed, Whit, too, developed an idiosyncratic management technique that worked. Through his relations with MIT and particularly through the assistance provided him by Nathaniel Sage of the Division of Industrial Cooperation at MIT, he was able to recruit a number of first-rate engineers, and at the same time he became impressed by the effective technology transfer existing between MIT and a number of industrial companies. His biographer W. H. Cohn, in a biography posthumously published, wrote:

Whitaker found in his commitment to and association with MIT a new challenge and a new outlet [for his] energies in the later years of his life. Whitaker's visits to MIT, according to one of his intimate colleagues on campus, served to recharge his mind, leaving him refreshed after a demanding period of work in Harrisburg. Perhaps of equal importance was the comfortable feeling he had with the group of people he associated with at MIT. Whitaker liked President James R. Killian as an individual and for his progressive view of engineering. He was impressed with Killian's broad educational perspective and was especially pleased when Killian added a strong humanities segment to the MIT curriculum. . . . In fact, Whitaker's high opinion of Killian led him to ask the MIT President to serve on the board of directors of AMP Incorporated, a request Killian had to turn down on account of other commitments.

Whitaker did not marry until he was in his late forties. Over the years he had kidded all of his associates about the viscissitudes of married life, and when he himself secretly married Helen Fisher, whom he had come to know while working at the Hoover Company, his associates and his family were astonished, particularly because he did not announce the marriage for several years—for two years even to his family.

Two years after they were married, Uncas's sister in Missouri died of cancer, leaving two young daughters. So strong was his sense of family that Whitaker and his new wife made the decision to adopt the two daughters, and so the former bachelor, with Helen at his side, achieved a happy family life. He had become fascinated by sailing and acquired a forty-six-foot boat. He and Helen developed the navigational and sailing skills to handle this craft alone. Their joint skill and independence in handling their boats found another expression in their philanthropy.

In 1961 Whitaker was invited to accept a term membership on the MIT Corporation and did, a pivotal point in the story of a series of philanthropies. While a member of the Corporation, Whitaker threw himself fully into its activities. For fourteen consecutive years he was a member of the Corporation Visiting Committee for the Department of Biology, and he also served eight years as chairman of the Medical Department Visiting Committee. During this period he and his wife established the Whitaker Professorship of Biomedical Engineering. His membership on the Department of Biology Visiting Committee brought him into contact with Dr. Irwin Sizer, then head of the department, a relationship that developed and proved decisive in encouraging the Whitakers' support of the life sciences.

The changes that were taking place in biology at this time appealed very much to Whitaker. Sizer was moving it, as I describe elsewhere, into molecular biology and to a new emphasis on quantitative biology, which had grown out of the ideas of Bush, Compton, and Bunker to develop biological engineering as a new field at the Institute.

As the interest of the Whitakers in the new biology at MIT grew, Uncas helped to finance a building specifically for biology. They later established the Whitaker Health Sciences Fund, with Irwin Sizer as president and George Thorn as vice president, for the purpose of supporting doctoral candidates at MIT and faculty members doing research in the health sciences at

MIT, the Harvard Medical School, and the Boston University School of Medicine.

Uncas did not confine his contributions to biology and the health sciences. He made other generous donations to the Institute, one for a faculty salary fund, another for research in mathematics, and still another for a large building to provide an adequate home for electrical engineering and electronics.

In the life sciences bold plans were afoot, but Uncas did not live to see them brought to fruition. He died in 1975. Mrs. Whitaker, succeeding him as a member of the MIT Corporation, continued her interest in the health sciences, notably the Harvard-MIT Program in the Health Sciences, Technology, and Management and in plans to create a major center and symbol of the health sciences at MIT. As she responded to the persuasive information provided her by Sizer, Thorn, Wiesner, and Johnson, she agreed to make a major contribution (through the Whitaker Foundation) of $10 million toward a two-building complex designed to house a new aggregation of health activities. Her generosity and that of the Pew Memorial Trust, originally established as the Glenmede Trust by the late J. Howard Pew, a graduate of MIT, permitted the Institute to proceed with the development of Whitaker College of Health Sciences, Technology, and Management to be housed in a center (together with the Medical Department and Infirmary) costing $30 million. After the death of Uncas, Mrs. Whitaker discharged her responsibilities as a member of the Corporation and trustee of the Whitaker Health Sciences Fund with diligence and commitment. Using her own resources, she proceeded to set up a chair in Whitaker College. Together with grants by the AMP company to supplement their personal gifts, the Whitakers brought to MIT and related Boston institutions a total in excess of $17 million.

Whitaker College is another example of how MIT has extended opportunities for interdisciplinary collaboration. It transcends the activities of any single department or school of the Institute, and in recognition of its uniqueness and the fact that the Institute was running out of names for designating interdeparmental programs, the term "college" was used for the first time in the history of MIT.

The program of Whitaker College is directed toward gaining a more comprehensive understanding of the structure and development of the nervous system. This inevitably has brought it into close working relationship with the Institute's pioneering work in artificial intelligence.

In reporting the Whitaker and Green benefactions to MIT, I would point out how MIT's education and environment have produced many alumni who have used high technology to create companies that had spectacular growth in the postwar period. One of my Harvard friends, in commenting on the fundraising successes of MIT, has pointed out how this entrepreneurship and "habit of success" have facilitated MIT's fund raising.

Despite these successful fund campaigns and the generosity of major donors, the Institute, in my judgment, remains dangerously short of endowment, and I am heartened to note that members of the Corporation and of the Institute administration are likewise concerned about our inadequate capitalization. One outstanding member of the Corporation has walked up to the problem by concluding that the central funding challenge of the Institute is to augment its capital resources by several hundred million dollars. I concur fully in his conclusion. Only by setting and achieving such bold goals can the Institute be sure of maintaining its position in the forefront of the world's leading institutions. To paraphrase Mr. Churchill's MIT convocation speech, let us then move forward together in discharge of our mission and our duty, fearing God and nothing else.

FOR THE BENEFIT OF POSTERITY
AND GOOD LEARNING

When George Eastman, Alfred Sloan, Mrs. McCormick, Cecil and Ida Green, Uncas and Helen Whitaker, Edwin Land, and many others gave "tokens of affection" to MIT, they joined that great society of donors who over the ages have been moved by an "affection . . . for studies of good learning." Let me recall by way of an early example Sir Thomas Bodley, who, in 1598, wrote in language quaint to modern ears the following letter to the vice chancellor of Oxon:

Sir, although you know me not, as I suppose, yet for the furthering of an offer, of evident utility, to your whole University, I will not be too scrupulous in craving your assistance. I have been always of a mind that if God, of his goodness, should make me able to do anything for the benefit of posterity, I would show some token of affection that I have evermore borne to the studies of good Learning.

Bodley followed up by providing funds and other support for the refounding of the library at Oxford University which was to bear his name and become an enduring resource for "good learning."

PORTRAITS AND TRIBUTES CONCLUDED

Sprinkled throughout these pages are vignettes of tutors, associates, and companions in arms who influenced my days and enlarged my vision. Many more should be presented, but I conclude with four to round out a company that can best be described by recalling what Yeats said in his *Last Poems:*

Think where man's glory most begins and ends,
And say my glory was I had such friends.

Viki Weisskopf: The Joy of Insight

Professor Victor Weisskopf once said in an interview, "I often tell my students that two things make my life worth living: Mozart and quantum mechanics." This remark presents one facet of this distinguished physicist, but let me describe a number of others.

He was born in Vienna in 1908 and became professor of physics at MIT at the end of World War II. He was among the group of brilliant scientists that MIT diligently recruited from defense research establishments at the end of the war. While at the Institute, he has grown to be a physicist of worldwide distinction, and the range of his contributions both to physics and to the public service has made him one of the most admired and influential members of the MIT community. Although he taught mainly graduate students, he enjoyed teaching undergraduates, including freshmen. For a period he served as head of the Department of Physics and with his enthusiastic support the department recruited a number of brilliant young physicists and, under his leadership, gave powerful encouragement to the Center for Theoretical Physics. As his career developed, he achieved supranational fame that led him to be called on for an international array of services. He served with distinction as director general of CERN, the great high-energy physics center in Switzerland. In 1980 he was awarded the National Medal of Science, the highest distinction an American scientist can receive. I was present by invitation at the White House when the medal was bestowed and at the dinner honoring the medalists in the elegant Diplomatic Functions Area of the Department of State. During the presentation Viki whispered something in President Carter's ear, which prompted a smile and an affirmative nod. Perhaps Viki said something in support of SALT II, the ratification of which he strongly supported at that time.

Earlier he had served as president of the American Academy of Arts and Sciences and had been elected a member of the Pontifical Academy of Sciences, an international advisory body to the Vatican with a membership of about seventy, many non-Catholic, representing all of the major sciences. In 1980 the president of the academy convened a working group of scientists to discuss the consequences of nuclear war and to offer suggestions concerning possible statements and actions by the pope. As a result Pope John Paul decided to address an apostolic message to the heads of the four nuclear powers: France, the United Kingdom, the Soviet Union, and the United States.

For the approach to President Reagan, Professor Weisskopf was selected to head a group consisting of Professor David Baltimore (Nobel laureate) of MIT, Marshall Nirenberg of the National Institutes of Health, and Howard H. Hiatt, dean of the Harvard School of Public Health. On December 14, 1981, this group representing the Vatican met at the White House with President Reagan to present him the statement of the academy, together with a copy of a personal letter which the pope had sent two weeks earlier. As Wiesskopf was to report in his NOVA broadcast, "We came to the White House, and we had to wait a little and then we were ushered in and we weren't even asked to sit down. And we had only very little time to present our ideas. And when I, who was the spokesman . . . said, 'Mr. President, you've received a letter from the Pope,' the President couldn't even remember that he did. And after ten minutes we were shoved out of the room."

I cite this episode in Viki's career to illustrate his deep commitment to disarmament and his leadership in mobilizing world opinion in support of reducing the threat of nuclear war. Former President Jerome Wiesner, Professor Henry Kendall, head of the Union of Concerned Scientists, and Weisskopf have been among the group of conspicuous advocates of efforts to reduce the threat of a nuclear holocaust. As Gerald Holton did of Einstein, one can appropriately emphasize with equal force Viki's "untiring efforts . . . for peace and international security."

In October 1974 the American Institute of Physics sponsored a symposium at MIT in honor of Viki. Most of the dozen participants spoke in the arcane language of their specialties but included in their abstruse papers engaging words of wit and tribute for Viki. Despite a slightly bemused sense of being a "shabby curate among dukes," I enthusiastically opened the symposium with words of welcome on behalf of the Institute and used the occasion to continue my campaign to see a science adviser once again in the White House.

The climax of this joyful occasion of tribute was a gala evening of chamber music by participants in the symposium or their friends who were competent musicians as well as scientists. Mustered from their group were those who played the piano, violin, cello, viola, and clavichord cembalo, the last being played by Provost Francis Low. Included in the program were Trio in E^b major, op. 1, No. 1 (Beethoven) and Brandenburg Concerto No. 3 in G major (Bach). It should be added that Viki and the great pianist, Rudolf Serkin, were boyhood friends while studying in a Vienna gymnasium.

Professor Herman Feshbach, in his preface to the published volume of the symposium papers, said just the right thing when he noted that the style and spirit of Viki had been beautifully captured by his own phrase, "the joy of insight." "He more than satisfied," said Professor Feshbach, "Milton's definition of a great man: 'He alone is worthy of the appellation who either does great things or teaches how they may be done, or describes them with a suitable majesty when they have been done.' " When Harvard awarded Weisskopf an honorary degree in 1983, the citation noted that he is "justly called the conscience of the American physics community."

I conclude this tribute to Viki by excerpting an observation on science that he made in his NOVA broadcast, "The World According to Weisskopf." He said:

. . . at the target of our accelerators, where the particles hit matter, we create more or less the same situation as was in the first millionths or even billionths of a second in the universe. . . .

When I first heard and read about all this evidence, I was sort of really impressed by it. It made me shudder. A kind of uncanny feeling that there should be a beginning. That things started out with a big explosion of light hits me very deeply, and I think must hit everybody very deeply. But it hits me especially because I always remember Haydn's oratorio *The Creation*, where he describes this beginning in so wonderful music with a big strong C major chord which describes this first creation of light by God.

The more I begin to comprehend how the universe has developed from a hot gas to the earth and the sun and life, animals and human beings, the more I see . . . some sense in it, a development from the primitive to the complicated, and I feel we—I see where life comes from, where I come from, where my origins are.

That means here we see a creativeness of nature that even random processes can create new forms, new shapes, new animals and humankind, and in this I find a deep sense, a satisfaction and also I would say a source of a certain moral attitude.†

Herbert York: Should Truman Have Approved Proceeding with the Development of the Superbomb?

Herbert York was a star of the first magnitude whom I promptly recruited for membership on the President's Science Advisory Committee. At that time he was director of the Livermore Laboratory of the Atomic Energy Commission and had been deeply engaged there in research and development of the superbomb and therefore was a close colleague, if not a disciple, of Edward Teller. He also had been a member of the von Neumann committee, which was so influential in the planning of our intercontinental ballistic missile program.

The orbiting of Sputnik and the "mythology of terror" it created in the minds of the American public had a great impact on York and certainly were factors in his ready decision to come to Washington to spend full time. When he made this decision to join our group at the White House, I don't think he realized that he was leaving Livermore forever. But as events worked out, the excitements of Washington launched him into a new and, to my mind, more important career.

Herbert possessed a charming, boyish, and almost cherubic manner but a whiplash mind and courage. He was a refreshing tonic for all who found themselves within his orbit.

One of his first contributions to help the president deal with the panic provoked by Sputnik was to join George Kistiakowsky in accurately appraising the merits of the U.S. space vehicles then under construction or proposed. He quickly became a much-sought-after expositor of the mysteries of space and a debunker of the hard-sell technologists who he felt were trying to exploit Sputnik and the missile-gap psychosis.

In 1958 the secretary of defense, Neil H. McElroy, in consultation with myself, York, and others, decided to establish in his office the Advanced Research Projects Agency known as ARPA, and when he came to recruiting personnel for it, McElroy chose York, at my urging, as chief scientist. This assignment was short because in December 1958 the president appointed York the first director of Defense Research and Engineering in the Department of Defense, an office in the same echelon as the secretaries of the services and which had been recommended to Eisenhower by several of us of PSAC. When I asked York recently what he considered to be among his major achievements while holding high office in the Department of Defense, he identified first his steady and persuasive support of Eisenhower's adherence to a test ban policy and a continuation of a moratorium on American testing. The second contribution which he recalls with similar satisfaction was his part in achieving the transfer of the big space program from the Army to NASA.

When ill health forced him to resign from this arduous assignment, York returned to San Diego, where he served for a brief time as chancellor of the University of California there and then continued as professor of physics.

I shall always feel indebted to him for the enthusiasm and the wisdom that he brought to the work of the President's Science Advisory Committee and his encouragement of me as chairman. Given his mastery of defense technology and his close accord with the views of the president, it was not surprising that he became one of the PSAC group that was especially close to Eisenhower.

I remember the occasion in 1958 when the two of us were invited to breakfast with the president to discuss various defense matters. As we were leaving, the president mentioned that the Republican National Committee, he understood, had complained that the scientists he had selected were not out campaigning and whooping it up for the Republican Party. "Don't you know, Mr. President, that all scientists are Democrats?" said York with his tongue in cheek. "I don't believe it," said Eisenhower, "but anyway, I like scientists for their science and not for their politics."

Later on York spent several periods on leave from the University of California to undertake special assignments. He helped me when President Johnson assigned me to a committee to study how technology could be mobilized for the benefit of the Latin American countries. During the Carter administration he became a close adviser of Harold Brown, the secretary of defense, and at the recommendation of Brown he was appointed by the president to represent the United States at the Geneva conference to negotiate a comprehensive test ban. In that role he held the rank of ambassador.

As York became involved in Washington affairs and in the domain of national security, it became clear that his views on the wisdom of the superbomb were undergoing a sea change. In a few years he was to become one of the most ardent and persuasive advocates of disarmament. He wrote three books, *Race to Oblivion: A Participant's View of the Arms Race*, which he published in 1970, followed by *Arms Control* (1973), and *The Advisors: Oppenheimer, Teller, and the Superbomb* (1976), in which he brilliantly presented an account of the debate on whether the United States should have undertaken to develop this hydrogen-fusion or "H" bomb. The first of these books, *Race to Oblivion*, was a lucid discussion of Eisenhower's warning about the dangers of the military-industrial complex followed by an account of many of the excesses that characterized American armament activities in the 1950s and 60s, including proposals to develop a nuclear-propelled airplane, the missile gap mania, and the antiballistic missile program so ardently supported by President Nixon and Henry Kissinger. The third book presented his brilliantly written account of the decision "that changed the course of modern history," the decision to proceed with the development of the hydrogen bomb. In this book, *The Advisors: Oppenheimer, Teller and the Superbomb,* he wrote: "It now seems clear to me in retrospect that Truman *should* have taken the advice; he should have held back on initiating the development of the super while making another serious try to achieve international control over all nuclear arms, including especially the super. The benefits that could have derived from forestalling the super altogether were incalculable; the odds of succeeding in doing so were small, but so were the risks in trying. . . . There can be no doubt that Truman would have found it very difficult to promulgate and conduct a policy of thermonuclear forbearance, but it might well not have been impossible."[7]

Later in this book York added:

In making such assertions, I do not charge that the United States bears the major part of the blame for the existence of either the cold war or the technological arms race; in my view the responsibility for these is widely shared among the major powers of the world. However, I do believe that the United States has pursued policies which caused the technological arms race to advance at a substantially faster pace than was really necessary for America's own national security. . . . Rather, the reason is that the United States is richer and more powerful, and its science and technology are more dynamic and generate more ideas and inventions of all kinds, including ever more powerful and exotic means of mass destruction. In short, the root of the problem has not been maliciousness, but rather a sort of technological exuberance that has overwhelmed the other factors that go into the making of overall national policy.[8]

These last comments now seem more appropriate than when York first wrote them because of the disturbing exuberance which seems to be preparing us technologically for war in space.

Walter A. Rosenblith: What Is a Provost?

Dr. Rosenblith, bless him, looked in on me in my retirement from time to time as a pure act of generous friendship to bring me morsels of news about MIT affairs or some significant piece of intelligence about the world of science. His gentle civility made these visits a delight, and his encyclopedic knowledge, an exceptional learning experience.

In close coupling with President Wiesner, Walter earlier played an entrepreneurial role in the development of the health sciences at MIT. It was Norbert Wiener who attracted him to MIT, and over the years he has kept alive and creatively useful the fertile ideas and magic influence of that great mathematician.

Walter is a member of a very exclusive club of polymaths who have been elected to the major American academies, including the National Academy of Sciences, the National Academy of Engineering, and the Institute of Medicine. The Sciences Academy has chosen him to be its foreign secretary, a post to which he has brought a cosmopolitan wisdom and the benefits of his extraordinary array of worldwide contacts.

One of Walter's prized possessions is a three-volume first edition (1771) of the *Encyclopedia Britannica,* a rich mine of distinguished scholarship, which Walter has frequently and entertainingly used as an intellectual benchmark to show where science in America has moved since the founding of the nation.

When he yielded the title of provost of the Institute, Walter received the plaudits of the MIT Corporation at its June 1980 meeting. In response he reported on his search for the meaning and origin of "provost," and this is what he said:

As I look back over the nine years that I have been Provost, and even the two additional years that I carried the title of Associate Provost, the questions that people have asked me most often have been: What is a Provost? What does he do? What are his responsibilities? I thought I knew the answer, but I was puzzled as to why did people have so much trouble with the term "Provost."

Most university titles relate to titles from older institutions such as the military or the church. Perhaps not all of our deans are aware of the fact that originally a dean was a military person with authority over ten people. That is the origin of the term. Later, dean became the senior cardinal bishop and finally, in some British foundations, as they are called, even a provost. For an answer to my query I went to my customary source of information—the first edition of the Britannica, 1771, printed in Edinburgh—and I read the following entry: "Provost of a city or town is the chief municipal magistrate in several trading cities, particularly Edinburgh, Paris, etc., being much the same as mayor in other cities. He presides in city courts, and together with the bailiffs, who are his deputies, determines in all differences that arise among citizens. . . ."

Unless you went to the University of Pennsylvania in times gone by when the University was run by the Provost, whose monuments, by the way, are found on the campus, the Provostship is an institutional invention that was born out of the needs that Dr. Killian perceived around the midcentury when he took over the leadership of MIT. The Provost came together with the formation of the Academic Council and responded to the needs of a university polarized around science which was more than a holding company for the disciplines. What was needed was both an academic officer whose task would be to deal with the Lewis Committee Report, with the five Schools, and the interdepartmental laboratories, and who could act both as an academic convener and as a guardian of the integrity of our academic processes, and who would never let the institution forget that no matter what the research achievements, no matter what the service to our society, MIT is, above all, an institution with a unique commitment to a unity of educational programs based on science and technology.

Albert O. Seeler and a Precept from Hippocrates

During his service as director of the MIT Medical Department, Dr. Albert O. Seeler, to my good fortune, served as my personal physician. Not only was he a physician of exceptional talents, but he possessed a warmth, wit, and generosity of spirit that gave an extra dimension to his professional skill.

In 1969, during a routine examination, he called for tests to determine whether I had an incipient case of the gout or just an attack of rheumatism. Dr. Compton had suffered from gout in the late forties, and later Dean Burchard and Professor Zacharias were sorely afflicted. Was gout an occupational disease of academicians? This question was implicit as this list grew. The possibility no doubt prompted Dr. Seeler to mail me an editorial from the *Journal of the American Medical Association* entitled "Uric Acid and the Psyche" with a note saying he thought it might amuse me. It did. Wrote the editorialist:

Literary satire and pictorial caricature have been adding for centuries insult to the injury caused by gout. . . .

Belying the popular image is the impressive list of prominent men who had gout. Alexander the Great, Charlemagne, Bacon, Milton, Newton, Darwin, Harvey, and Hunter were victims of the disease. Sydenham—himself a sufferer from gout—noted that the disease tends to afflict the upper social strata. In his *Study of British Genius*, Havelock Ellis submitted that the association of gout with so many famous men could not be ascribed to chance. More recently Popert and Hewitt have noted uncommon frequency of high social class among gout patients attending their clinic. . . .

In a study of serum urate levels of 51 University of Michigan professors, Brooks and Mueller found a positive association with drive, achievement, and leadership. Not to be outdone by professors, high school students manifested a similar relationship of serum uric acid levels to achievement-oriented behavior. In a study of 62 male high school students, Kasl et al. found higher serum uric acid values in those who were highly motivated to obtain further education. Kindergarten pupils have as yet not been investigated.

I wrote a note to Dr. Seeler, thanking him for the editorial and adding: I must conclude that my diagnosis is doubtless wrong if the data, both historical and currently statistical, are correct. I am further led to this conclusion by the following observation that Lord Chesterfield made in a letter to his son dated November 28, 1765: "Gout is the distemper of a gentleman; whereas the rheumatism is the distemper of a hackney-coachman, *or chairman* who is obliged to be out in all weathers and at all hours."

To this letter I promptly received Dr. Seeler's impish reply: "I must disagree with the conclusion you draw from Lord Chesterfield's clinical comments. While indeed you, as Chairman, are obliged 'to be out in all weathers and at all hours,' you occupy the Chair rather than carry it. It is, therefore, my opinion that Lord Chesterfield would have regarded your distemper as gout rather than the rheumatism."

I cite this pleasant byplay to recall two later episodes, the first a cardiac attack as I was getting ready to go to Washington. A call by my secretary brought Dr. Seeler on the run to my office, and he promptly insisted that I go instead to the Massachusetts General Hospital.

Later, in 1973, I had been admitted to the Mt. Auburn Hospital for some simple treatments for cervical spondylosis, for which I had been wearing a collar. One night while there I was found on the floor in a deep coma. How I fell to the floor is still a mystery.

With Dr. Seeler in charge, a team of doctors was assembled and unanimously concluded that I was the victim of a cranial blood clot, or subdural hematoma, and that it was necessary to undertake major surgery involving trephining of my skull and other measures to remove the clot. Complications ensued, requiring in addition a tracheotomy. For a period it was touch and go, and the prognosis was doubtful as pneumonia threatened.

In the weeks of convalescence that followed, Dr. Seeler visited me in the hospital practically every day, cheering me on by his wondrous capacity to inspire and to heal.

There was a speculation about the cause of the clot, but I attributed it to a bad fall in New Hampshire several months before the clot produced the coma.

After I was fully recovered, I came upon an elegant edition of Harvey Cushing's biography of Sir William Osler, which I sent to Dr. Seeler with the following note:

This book about a great physician who was also a great human being is a sincere though inadequate way of expressing my heartfelt gratitude for what you have done to bring about my recovery through your professional skill and judgment; it also expresses my delight in our friendship. In his *Precepts*, Hippocrates wisely said that ". . . some patients, though conscious that their condition is perilous, recover simply through their contentment with the goodness of the physician." I have been recovering through both professional skill and this kind of contentment.

With appreciation and affection.

Three years later, in February 1976, when only sixty, Dr. Seeler was felled by a mysterious respiratory attack, the cause of which his physicians were unable to identify and against which there seemed to be no defense. About six months later came the great attack of Legionnaire's disease at a convention in Philadelphia. Would this provide a clue to the cause of Dr. Seeler's death? The distinguished expert on infectious diseases at the Massachusetts General Hospital speculated that it might, and he was able to find a specimen of tissue still stored at the MGH that had been taken during the effort to diagnose Dr. Seeler's illness. In his postmortem examination he discovered that what caused the Legionnaire epidemic had been the cause, almost six months before, of Dr. Seeler's death.

John J. Rowlands: Letters from Cache Lake

John J. (Jim) Rowlands, who died in 1972, served as director of the News Service at MIT for thirty-two years. Edward A. Weeks, long editor of the *Atlantic Monthly,* in 1950 wrote: "In my judgment the best public relations in the college world over the past twenty-five years have been those maintained at the Massachusetts Institute of Technology." I believe it is true that Jim was the first person to reach Vice President Calvin Coolidge in Vermont with the news that President Warren G. Harding had died. At that time he was manager of the United Press for New England and eastern Canada, and in this post he arranged an ingenious communication circuit to get the word to the vice president.

Jim's gifts as a journalist and in public relations were but one expression of his many talents and rare qualities as a human being. He was born in North Carolina and attended Staunton Military Academy, Fishburne Military Academy, and the Meisterschaft School in Toronto, Canada. Although born in the South, Jim was deeply loyal to Canada, the country of several of his distinguished ancestors. In his early life he became a gold prospector and mining surveyor for a company operating in Colbalt, Ontario, Canada. This left him with an abiding interest in the North Woods of Canada, and he was later to write extensively about experiences in this far country. Whatever his principal job was at the time, he wrote over a period of years what he called the "Cache Lake Letter" reporting for his friends his recollections of his North Woods experiences. In 1947 these were supplemented and collected into a successful book entitled *Cache Lake Country.*

After he retired from his post as director of the News Service at MIT, he acquired a house on the seashore in Cohasset, Massachusetts, and his observations and experiences there prompted him to bring together a further collection of reminiscences under the title *Spindrift.* In addition from time to time he contributed articles to the *Atlantic Monthly* and other magazines.

Both of his books were illustrated by my friend and colleague Henry B. Kane, whom I had invited to come to the Institute from industry to be director of the Institute's Alumni Fund when it was launched. During his undergraduate days Kane had demonstrated exceptional skill and imagination as a cartoonist on the staff of MIT's humor magazine, *VooDoo*, and this ability flowered into his highly regarded professional talent in pen-and-ink drawing. His delightful illustrations were called on for many trade books, and the drawings he did for the books of Jim Rowlands, new editions of Thoreau, and a collection of poems by David McCord added to his reputation as an illustrator. Rowlands had developed similar talents as a skilled craftsman, particularly as a builder of ship models and as a wood carver.

Jim was one of my closest friends and candid advisers, and I still delight in reflecting on all the many memorable times I shared with him, times when we worked together and celebrated together, times when he introduced me to new crafts, new experiences, new friends, new insights into the world of nature he loved. At times when I found myself beset with problems and needing advice on weighty matters, I turned to Jim both for solace and for sound counsel, and he responded in terms large-minded, direct, and frank.

Far beyond his professional responsibilities and his personal relationships with me, he brought a rare quality of spirit to the MIT community. Indeed the combination of Jim and Laurie, his wife, each enhancing the other, made them memorable members of our academic fellowship. To paraphrase John Buchan, once governor-general of Jim's beloved Canada, Jim and Laurie possessed the power to rediscover for us life's forgotten graces.

PUBLIC SERVICE AT HOME AND ABROAD

My maiden presidential assignment in Washington after becoming president of MIT was membership on the President's Advisory Committee on Management. In its brief report to President Truman in December 1952, this committee made recommendations bearing on the organization and work of the executive branch. It stressed the need for further implementation of the recommendations of the Hoover Commission, proposed that the president should be granted permanent reorganization authority (which he was), and urged that the permanent management staff facilities of the president and of the heads of departments and agencies should be strengthened.

Service on this committee was a learning experience for me, and through it I gained knowledge and insights in regard to the functions and work of the office of the president and particularly of the Bureau of the Budget. It also brought me into association with Frank Pace, Jr., who was then secretary of the Army and who in 1967 was to be recruited for the chairmanship of the Corporation for Public Broadcasting. James E. Webb, another member of this Committee on Management, had served as under secretary of state and had been the principal liaison officer in government with Project Troy at MIT; and later of course he was to become administrator of NASA. The executive secretary of this Committee on Management was William F. Finan, with whom I later worked, while presidential science adviser, in drafting a design for President Eisenhower to propose to the Congress for the National Aeronautics and Space Administration (NASA).

Next came membership on President Truman's Communications Policy Board (the Stewart Committee). This brought me into a working relationship with Irvin Stewart, whom I had come to know when he was executive secretary and later deputy director of OSRD, and with Lee DuBridge, who had been director of MIT's Radiation Laboratory in World War II. The board made recommendations touching many complex aspects of the federal government's telecommunications policy and practice, including the proposal that the president should include in his office a telecommunications advisory board. This recommendation was rejected by President Truman. Ultimately President Nixon did appoint a unit in his office that had essentially the responsibilities that we had recommended in 1951, but Nixon used this board to attack public broadcasting, and I could not but rue the day when I, as a member of the Truman board, had joined in proposing such a unit. The Stewart Committee study, however, was relevant and helpful when I came to be involved in the establishment of the public broadcasting system.

My third and most important assignment by President Truman came in April 1951, when he appointed me a member of the original Science Advisory Committee (first located in the Office of Defense Mobilization). This committee had been planned in accord with recommendations made by William Golden for the establishment of a science advisory committee and a presidential science adviser, each reporting directly to the president, but opposition within the Truman palace guard resulted in placing this advisory arrangement in the ODM, where it had little to do and was called on hardly at all by President Truman. At the end of the Truman administration, the committee was on the verge of recommending its dissolution, but happily its members decided to wait to see whether the committee would be continued by President Eisenhower. On the recommendation of Henry Cabot Lodge, chairman of Eisenhower's transition team, it was, with ultimate results of such moment that they warrant special emphasis later in this account.

At this point let me recall that it was at a meeting in November 1952 of this ODM Science Advisory Committee, of which Oppenheimer was a member, that I had the distasteful responsibility of reporting on the rumors I had been hearing, through contacts with the Air Force, that Dr. Oppenheimer's security clearance might be challenged. The committee was meeting at the Institute for Advanced Study, of which Dr. Oppenheimer was then head, and it was at an evening social gathering at Dr. Oppenheimer's residence that these disturbing rumors were discussed and realization dawned that he might be excluded from our ODM committee. I had seen enough of him during the meetings of this committee to be convinced of his integrity, responsibility, and loyalty despite his occasional naiveté.

These experiences in the Truman administration prepared me well for some later and more spectacular assignments by President Eisenhower.

PRESIDENTIAL SCIENCE ADVISER AND THE CREATION OF PSAC

I come now to a brief account of my pinnacle experience as an adviser to government, my full-time service as special assistant for science and technology to President Eisenhower. In this role

I served as science adviser to the president, the first to be assigned this responsibility.

My appointment to this post came as a result of the successful launching of Sputnik I by the Russians. This Soviet achievement created a climate of near hysteria in the United States with many people jumping to the conclusion that the Soviets had surpassed the United States in science and technology and in military power. This shocked reaction in both the United States and other parts of the free world required prompt action by the president to reassure the nation, to restore the United States's position as the leader of the free world, and to demonstrate his own leadership.

One of the ways Eisenhower sought to exercise his presidential leadership was to turn to experienced scientists for advice and assistance. He had consulted with President Detlev Bronk of the National Academy of Sciences, who had reminded him of the existence of the ODM science adviser and science advisory committee originally suggested to President Truman by William Golden. On October 15, 1957, he met with this ODM commitee, then chaired by Isidor Rabi. At this meeting Rabi made a specific proposal. There was no one around the president, he pointed out, who could help him be aware of any scientific component that might exist in the important policy matters coming before him. Other professions were well represented on his staff but not that of science or engineering. "He should have," said Rabi, "a full-time science adviser— a person he could live with easily." I then carried Rabi's proposal one step further and urged that there be in addition to a full-time science adviser a strong science advisory committee reporting directly to the president to widen the range of the advice that could be made by a single science adviser.

Because of the crisis of confidence brought about by Sputnik I, the announcement of my appointment as Special Assistant appeared in the nature of an emergency act and became a front-page news story throughout the nation. My appointment was thus given spectacular impact beyond its intrinsic importance and beyond my own assessment of its importance. I was not a little astonished to read headlines reporting "MIT Head Placed in Charge of All Defense Science" or Killian appointed "Missile Czar." It was not the intention of the president to assign me these unmanageable responsibilities, but the public seemed to expect this new officer to discharge them. Too little coverage was given to the president's announcement that he had also appointed an advisory group of outstanding experts—the President's Science Advisory Committee—to have the active responsibility of helping him and his special assistant follow through on a program for strengthening American science as well as space and defense technology. It was under these conditions that I obtained leave from the presidency of MIT and became a full-time member of President Eisenhower's staff for just under two years.

I was not unaware of the problems associated with introducing in such a spectacular way an addition to the White House staff, and I proceeded with the greatest tact to obtain the understanding and support of this staff. One presidential assistant, the late Gordon Gray, had been heard to remark wryly that it appeared that the president had brought in a "miracle worker," and I proceeded diligently to counter this notion.

I was greatly helped in achieving admission to the inner sanctum of the Eisenhower White House by several earlier appointments which I have described in this memoir. I had, for example served as chairman of a secret task force, the Technological Capabilities Panel, which in 1954–55 undertook a searching review of our military and intelligence technology, reporting directly to the National Security Council and to the president. The work of this panel did not receive the "pigeon-hole" treatment of so many presidential reports. Eisenhower followed through systematically in insisting on scheduled responses by government agencies to the recommendations of the report. It was this study, dealing primarily with ways to avoid surprise attack, that led to the acceleration of our ballistic missile development program, including Thor, Jupiter, and Polaris missiles. This panel also originated the concept of the U-2 system, which was to be of enormous value to the nation in bringing to the president hard intelligence about the Soviet missile program.

As Eisenhower's term approached conclusion, this hard U-2 intelligence gave him confidence that the "missile gap" alleged by Kennedy was not based on fact but was irresponsible campaign fiction. As general and then president, Eisenhower went to great lengths to secure reliable intelligence.

The Technological Capabilities Panel also alerted the president to the growing role of science and technology in the formulation of defense policy, and it created in his White House staff a better understanding of the contributions which scientists could make to the work of the president. It led to President Eisenhower's request in 1956 that I chair his board of consultants on foreign intelligence activities and thus served to bring science more effectively into use to gather hard intelligence.

As suggested by President Eisenhower, the Technological Capabilities Panel devoted studies in depth to the gathering of hard intelligence by the CIA and other intelligence agencies. These studies achieved results welcomed by the president and the National Security Council. It was undoubtedly my directorship of this TCP task force that led Allen Dulles and the president to turn to me to organize and chair a watchdog board to keep an eye on the intelligence organizations. Some members of Congress were making nervous noises about the CIA and urging more congressional oversight of its conduct and program. The thought of congressional penetration of his organization produced cold shivers in Allen Dulles, and there were senior members of Congress who felt firmly that they did not want to have the responsibility of knowing secrets of great sensitivity. Conclusions were drawn by some journalistic watchdogs that the appointment of the board was a move to quiet congressional unease. Actually the president had more convincing reasons for appointing a watchdog committee. Some years back the Hoover Commission had recommended such a board. More important, Eisenhower apparently concluded that the resources of science should be drawn on to achieve more and better hard intelligence.†

In *The Eisenhower Diaries*, published in 1981, appears Eisenhower's entry for January 24, 1956:

Today I had a conference with the members of the new president's board for intelligence activities. All were present except Bob Lovett, who is suffering from the flu. The other civilian members are Ben Fairless, Dr. Killian of MIT, and Edward L. Ryerson; on the service side are Admiral Conolly, General Hull, and Jimmie Doolittle. Each will be required to take an oath to reveal nothing to any nonauthorized person of any information he may gain while on his task. The charter of the board I intend to be very broad.[9]

Before the close of my chairmanship of the Eisenhower intelligence board, additional appointments were made, including Ambassadors David Bruce and Joseph P. Kennedy. The board decided that it should go into the field and make contact with various CIA staff in various parts of the world. Together with two members of my staff, I went to Paris, Berlin, Athens, and various other stations. Joseph Kennedy, who had a home on the Riviera, offered to visit Rome, which he did. While there and conducting an interview with the local head of the CIA staff, he espied a black box in the corner of the room. This led him quickly to jump to the conclusion that his interview was being bugged. A subsequent check proved that his interpretation of the black box was totally erroneous. It had no ears and no bugging purpose. From the very beginning of his membership on the Eisenhower board, Joe Kennedy found himself uncomfortable. He expressed from time to time a concern about the board, as organized and manned, being inadequate to meet the task imposed on it by the president. He seemed to fear that some great issue would arise which would result in the board's being charged with inadequacy or other dire faults and, as he frankly said, he didn't want to be a patsy, he being a Democrat and the board being appointed by a Republican president.

In fact when Mr. Kennedy finally decided to resign from the board, he gave me as his reason that he anticipated that his son might be seeking the vice presidency and under those circumstances he did not want to be associated with a Republican administration. I sought to dissuade him, but to no avail.

It must be said that a number of members of the Eisenhower board were nonplussed when they found out the vast array of activities and obligations that vested in the intelligence community, and in the early meetings I found it important to provide reassurance to these uneasy members that the basic job assigned to us by the president was doable.

I myself found membership on both the Eisenhower and Kennedy boards to be not wholly to my taste. I remember when a public announcement was made of the membership of one of the boards, one of my associates made the comment, "Well, Jim, I see you have become one of the 'spooks.' " If I found the assignment on the two boards difficult and occasionally disagreeable, it was because of the sense of pressure, secrecy, and controversy that inevitably impacted on the members of the board. It was not very comfortable, for example, for me to be told that my office at MIT must be regularly "swept" to make sure that it was not bugged, even though I never discussed any classified materials in that office.

On the plus side was the pleasure of being associated with the collection of experienced and distinguished men that made up the membership of the two boards. I gained much in outlook and understanding, particularly with respect to the role of government in foreign affairs, through my associations on these boards. I recall with especial respect and affection Ambassador Bruce, Robert D. Murphy, who later held many other important foreign service offices, and historian William L. Langer. Bruce had filled several ambassadorships, including ambassador to the Court of St. James; Murphy had been President Roosevelt's personal representative in North Africa as military operations were getting under way there; and William L. Langer, Harvard historian, had played a major role in the formation of the CIA. It was he who organized and made extraordinarily effective CIA's Office of National Estimates, and he brought scholarship and confidence to this key intelligence organization. Murphy proved to be one of the most fascinating raconteurs I ever encountered, a talent that had been enormously multiplied by his experience in so many hot spots around the world during the time that he served the State Department. I could go on naming other members of the two boards who were people I found memorable and with whom I was proud to be associated.

On a trip to European centers I was welcomed in Bonn by James Conant, who talked about the great CIA feat of building in the mid-1950s a tunnel under the border dividing the Soviet-controlled east sector of Berlin and the west sector, one of the CIA's greatest achievements because it permitted listening in for an extended period on the communications between the East German sector and Moscow, until it was discovered and sealed off in 1956. Conant spoke wryly about this accomplishment because the tunnel had been built and brought into operation without informing our American representative in Berlin.

Later one of the subjects on the agenda of the board of advisers was whether the CIA should undertake ventures in a given country without notifying our ambassador in residence there.

While I was in Germany, Ambassador Conant offered the use of his train to facilitate my travels about Germany, a train no doubt that he had inherited from the days when our American representative in West Berlin was high commissioner. Among the cities in Germany I visited was Munich, and while there I was lodged in one of the great residences once belonging to a prominent Nazi and then used as a guest house for visiting VIPs. I recall with some pleasure that in one of these elegant places I found myself assigned to a bedroom on the wall of which was a plaque "General Dwight D. Eisenhower slept in this room."

In 1957 my acceptance and effectiveness as special assistant were greatly facilitated by a remarkable letter written by President Eisenhower to Cabinet officers, White House staff, and all members of the National Security Council, which stated his wish that I and PSAC have access to all documents and other material, however sensitive, that we might need for our work and which indicated further that the science adviser and PSAC would be available to be of help to these other officers at the top level of government. I was invited to be present at National Security Council and Cabinet meetings and sessions of lesser policymaking bodies.

Under the favorable conditions that I describe and under the direction of President Eisenhower, the special assistant and PSAC were able to move expeditiously to accomplish a number of objectives important to the president and to give support to his policies. We moved immediately to formulate a space policy for the nation and to design an organization to administer non-defense space activities. PSAC and the president together came to the conclusion that our space program should be under civilian and not military control except for highly specialized defense space programs. This agreement on civilian control led rapidly to a coordinated effort by PSAC members and representatives of the Bureau of the Budget to develop plans for reconstituting the National Advisory Committee for Aeronautics into the National Aeronautics and Space Administration. A bill for this new organization was quickly formulated and presented by the president to Congress, and although there were many debates and numerous changes in detail, the essential elements of the PSAC proposals found expression in the bill finally passed.

When I assumed my responsibilities as special assistant to the president and as chairman of PSAC, I quickly realized that we would need a range of talents that was much beyond the membership of PSAC if we were to cope with the many problems that came our way. Together with PSAC I established a system of panels, some standing and some ad hoc, so that we could bring in specialists and outstanding scientists and engineers to help in meeting problems before the president. At one time the total number of scientists and engineers mobilized by this panel system approached two hundred.

The invention of the panel system gave exceptional strength and reach to Eisenhower's science advisory arrangement.

In his introduction to the Kistiakowsky diary, *A Scientist at the White House*, historian Charles S. Maier made observations about the different ways in which the first three science advisers handled their presidential assignments: "As coordinators of this advisory effort Killian, Kistiakowsky, and Wiesner (under Kennedy) brought different talents to bear and played different roles. In retrospect there is general agreement that Killian probably performed the function of organizing the PSAC effort with more tact and conciliatory capacity than Kistiakowsky would have brought to bear. Not a scientist himself, as president of MIT Killian had the knack of eliciting high confidence from the specialists with whom he worked. Killian himself probably recognized that once PSAC was organized and the American space effort under way, the special assistant should himself be a scientist. As might be expected in such a situation, Killian sought primarily to get consensus and unified recommendations from his major scientific advisers, whereas Kistiakowsky strove more to master the technical side of an issue."

A 1958 study by one of these panels, which I had asked Emanuel Piore to chair, resulted in a report, "Strengthening American Science." This report recommended the establishment of the Federal Council for Science and Technology, but it also presented recommendations responsive to President Eisenhower's desire to further a many-pronged effort to underwrite the strengthening of American science and technology as one of our essential resources for our national security and welfare. Among these recommendations was the following outline for federal policy in its encouragement and support of basic research:

This year's Federal money will pay for about one half of all the scientific research, engineering, and development carried out in the U.S. The other half will be paid for by industry, by universities, and by private research foundations. Less than half of the Federal research and development budget is spent in laboratories owned and operated by industry, universities, and other private groups. . . . It is apparent from the size of this effort that the Government exerts a powerful shaping influence on all U.S. science and technology. Not only the nation's security but its long-term health and economic welfare, the excellence of its scientific life, and the quality of American higher education are now fatefully bound up with the care and thoughtfulness with which the Government supports research. If this support is halting and erratic, if it emphasizes mechanism and "hardware" to the neglect of fundamental understanding, if it lavishes money on a few popular fields and starves others of importance, if it fails to encourage exceptional men and exceptional programs, the net result could be an impoverished science and a second-rate technology.

One of the clearest lessons to emerge from the history of science is that various scientific disciplines—seemingly unrelated—have a way of stimulating and fructifying each other in an unexpected manner. This complex back-and-forth interplay is the life and soul of science and technology—there can never be too much of it. The most impractical thing that can be done in designing and directing programs of scientific research is to worry overmuch about how "practical" they are. The secrets and treasures of Nature are hidden in the most obscure and unexpected places. It is clear, therefore, that the strongest scientific program is the program with the greatest breadth and scope. It is impossible to predict from which quarter the next scientific advance will come; but we can try to make sure that the Nation has able people at work across the whole scientific frontier.

Considering the speed and recency with which the U.S. has been thrust into the new age of science, the Nation must be more determined than ever before to shape its policies and methods to achieve new levels of excellence. In the past major advances in the Government's management of science have come about under the pressure of emergencies. Ways now must be found for recognizing the importance of stability and other long-term goals, while preserving the flexibility to respond to emergencies.

This PSAC panel report, in my judgment, takes its place as one of the three great state papers formulating national policy for the advancement of science, the other two being, of course, "Science: the Endless Frontier," prepared by Vannevar Bush, and the PSAC report prepared under the chairmanship of Glenn T. Seaborg entitled "Scientific Progress, the Universities, and the Federal Government." These three reports together contributed to the federal policymaking that made a vital contribution to the growing brilliance of the constellation of American-style research universities.

Dr. Piore presented his report to a full-dress meeting of the Cabinet. His presentation was enthusiastically applauded and his recommendations were accepted by all, with one exception. Lewis Strauss had from the beginning taken a dim view of almost everything proposed by me and by PSAC. Prior to the president's establishment of this new group of advisers, Strauss had by default served as a purveyor of science advice to the president, and he was unhappy that this role was preempted. He also organized opposition to thwart Eisenhower's ambition to negotiate a nuclear test ban with the Soviets.

When President Eisenhower initiated a reorganization study of the Department of Defense, he asked PSAC to make recommendations for the management of the huge defense research program. A PSAC panel recommended the provisions later embodied in the Defense Reorganization Act of 1958 and in effect created the office of director of Defense Research and Engineering, to which Herbert York, with my strong support, was the first appointee. This was an example of the role that the special assistant and PSAC played in strengthening the organization in government for administration of science programs. As a result of our campaign a number of departments appointed assistant secretaries for research and development.

Another important initiative taken by Eisenhower's science advisers was to propose to the president and to the secretary of state an office for arms limitation and control. Although the specific recommendations made by PSAC did not gain acceptance before the close of the Eisenhower term, they did lead later to the creation of the U.S. Arms Control and Disarmament Agency.

As I write, Washington still buzzes with controversy over the MX missile. I wish it were practical for the Reagan administration, as it copes with controversial scientific issues, to duplicate the panel system which was used by the Eisenhower Science Advisory Committee. Panels of experts were called together to study a specific defense problem and, in doing so, to review both sides of the principal issues. The conclusions reached by the panel after it had had this kind of competitive review in depth were brought to PSAC for its discussion, approval, or rejection.

I think if some similar process were available to the present administration, both the president and the secretary of defense, they would be better served than by the advisory process and the arrangements now used.

The PSAC group kept the president informed about the progress of our missile and space programs, it gained the president's support in opposing Air Force plans to develop a nuclear-propelled aircraft, and in a nontechnical domain it prepared, and President Eisenhower released, a report on "Education for the Age of Science."

Eisenhower was harassed and at times deeply troubled by the criticism of his defense policy by elements of the military-industrial complex. We who sought to advise him obviously were able to help him in rejecting many extreme proposals and in achieving a more balanced plan for the development of our advanced military technology. It was this experience in being under constant attack for his military policies that was a factor leading to Eisenhower's famous statement, in his farewell speech, on the military-industrial complex.

This is a quick, freehand sketch of the achievements of PSAC under my chairmanship. Many others came later when Professor George Kistiakowsky had succeeded me as science adviser. Fortunately President Kennedy continued the arrangements that had been set in place by President Eisenhower and, with Dr. Jerome Wiesner as his science adviser, continued to bring science into the service of the president and his national policy-making.

As Donald Hornig, who was to become science adviser to President Johnson, was to write in a special issue of *Technology in Society*, "Thus began a unique experiment in modern government." Eisenhower had recognized science and technology as instruments of national policy, and as events turned out, he had added an important mechanism of control for dealing with runaway military technology, most of which, as Herbert York once wrote, was "loaded more with engineering virtuosity than with good sense." What the science advisers brought to the White House was common sense—scientific common sense.†

I hope that there will yet be adequate studies of Eisenhower's achievement in bringing science for the first time into effective use in policymaking during peacetime. When this aspect of the Eisenhower administration, together with his ready acceptance of innovative scientific proposals, comes to be better understood, it will contribute to a still further upgrading of Eisenhower's reputation as an able president.

IN THE SERVICE OF PRESIDENT KENNEDY

Early in his administration President Kennedy concluded that he should do as Eisenhower had done and appoint a president's foreign intelligence advisory board. At his behest, his assistant for National Security Affairs, McGeorge Bundy, called me and asked me if I would again chair such a committee. He expressed the president's desire to have available scientific talent, as did Eisenhower, to strengthen the gathering of hard intelligence and to have a board of civilians to serve as his watchdog on the foreign intelligence activities of the government. I accepted this assignment and chaired the Kennedy advisory committee for two years.

I recall receiving a telephone call from the White House while on a visit to New York just after the failure of the Bay of Pigs venture had become public. President Kennedy urgently wanted advice. "What shall we do about the CIA?" he asked. "Should we change its name?" "What should we do about Dulles and Bissell?" He made it clear how strongly he felt that there should be in his administration no repetition of this kind of disastrous effort. Although recognizing that Allen Dulles and Richard Bissell should be replaced, the board advised no precipitant action, feeling as it did that failure of the plan was not wholly the fault of these two officers. President Kennedy courageously acknowledged his own responsibility but later asked the board to present suggestions for a sucessor to Allen Dulles. While still searching for candidates, the board was disturbed to learn by grapevine that Kennedy had already asked John McCone to take the post. This proved to be a fortunate selection, for McCone did an excellent job. But at the time of his selection there were strong feelings, particularly in the scientific community, that McCone, while chairman of the Atomic Energy Commission, had not been wholly loyal to President Eisenhower during the debate on the limitation of nuclear tests. I remember calling Robert Kennedy, who was on a hunting expedition in the Rocky Mountains, telling him of this concern. Later, while the board was meeting with the president, he apologized for his failure to inform it in advance of his selection of McCone. He remarked that any concern that we might have about McCone should be a challenge to the board carefully to appraise McCone's performance. It accepted this challenge, and its appraisal led to its conclusion that the president had been wise in his choice of McCone.

In 1962 I found it difficult to say no to President Kennedy when he asked if he might nominate me for the directorship of the National Science Foundation. I reached the reluctant conclusion to decline because of my obligations to MIT, and I wrote to the President: "I am mindful of the growing importance of the National Science Foundation and of the increasingly important role it can play both in terms of advising on policy with respect to the Federal Government's research and development program and of strengthening our civilian science. I find it all the more difficult to decline because you were generous enough to consider me an appropriate candidate for the post."

I count it my good fortune that my modest public services at the apex of our government fell within the administrations of three exceptionally great presidents: Truman, Eisenhower, and Kennedy. To be associated with the White House during their presidencies was a great adventure. Standards were high, and the moral clarity with which they endowed the White House made one feel very proud to be there and to be an American.

SCIENCE ADVICE FOR PRESIDENTS

In 1970 the House Committee on Science and Astronautics held many hearings on a bill to provide legislative underpinning for a scientific presence in the White House. On November 8 of that year, I expressed to the committee my hope that it would also initiate the preparation of a science policy statement updating the influential manifesto that Bush wrote in 1945 under the title "Science: The Endless Frontier." Several members of the committee, notably Charles A. Mosher, seemed to take note of my brash proposal and my pleas for a coherent science policy formulated by Congress. With this incident in mind I found satisfaction that the bill did more than provide for a presidential advisory system. It expressed a strategic philosophy bearing on science policy for the nation.

In *Sputnik, Scientists, and Eisenhower* (1977), I describe the reaction, in fact the dismay, that greeted President Nixon's decision in 1973 to eliminate the entire White House science and technology structure.[10] This decision by President Nixon prompted me to turn activist by joining the many members of the scientific community who felt strongly that a scientific presence should be restored in the White House.

Immediately after the Nixon decision I talked with George Schultz, who then was secretary of the treasury and assistant to the president, to express concern over the Nixon action. He made it clear that the action was final but that he would welcome any suggestions about the relationship of the scientific community and the president, a relationship that had seriously deteriorated partly because a member of the President's Science Advisory Committee had taken a public position opposing a policy of the president. Following this conversation, I wrote to Schultz expressing my hope that some arrangement could be preserved whereby the president would have the benefit of objective scientific advice that in no way would be colored by departmental- or agency-vested interests. I also emphasized the importance of improving relationships between the executive branch and the scientific community and of achieving, I said, "a healing of differences between the scientific community and the administration for the good of the country." Secretary Schultz acknowledged my letter and reported that its substance "has been relayed."

Before the end of 1973 the council of the National Academy of Sciences voted to establish an ad hoc blue ribbon committee to "look into the questions of scientific and technical advice to the government, including the advisory and coordinating functions previously carried out by the White House science advisory complex." I agreed to chair this committee, and it promptly went to work. Its studies resulted in a report, "Science and Technology in Presidential Policymaking, A Proposal."

This NAS report played a catalytic role in the congressional debates about the establishment, through legislation, of a science advisory arrangement in the White House and in the considerations by the executive branch itself. It prompted President Ford to ask Vice President Nelson Rockefeller, together with a panel of scientists, to advise him on legislation to restore an Office of Science and Technology Policy in the White House. With their assistance the president reached an agreement with the House Committee on Science and Technology and indicated that he would look with favor on a bill then in process, H.R. 10230: "To establish a science and technology policy for the United States, to provide for scientific and technological advice and assistance to the President, to provide a comprehensive survey of ways and means for improving the Federal effort in scientific research and information handling, and in the use thereof, to amend the National Science Foundation Act of 1950, and for other purposes." This bill was passed by Congress, and I had the pleasure of being present in the Rose Garden when it was signed by President Ford on May 11, 1976. In the explanation that accompanied the bill that was signed by President Ford, a statement was made that "undoubtedly one of the suggestions which has had the biggest impact is that of the National Academy of Sciences' Killian committee."

When Mr. Carter became president, he promptly selected Frank Press of MIT to be his personal science adviser and director of the restored Office of Science and Technology Policy in the White House.

After President Reagan's election, many months elapsed before a decision was reached to include a science adviser as a member of the White House staff. Before this action was taken, there had been a chorus of scientists and congressmen urging him to appoint a science adviser. I joined this chorus by writing for the Op Ed page of the March 10, 1981, *New York Times* a statement, excerpted as follows:

My experience in bringing science advice to the apex of Government in past years leads me to hope that President Reagan will find it appropriate to appoint a science adviser at an early date. . . .

President Reagan is confronted, as was Mr. Eisenhower, with critical policy decisions requiring sound technical judgment. . . . He will find it useful to have on call unbiased and competent technical advice from advisers totally loyal to him and skilled in working closely with the Office of Management and Budget and other White House staff members. . . .

The President's science adviser should be a member of the White House staff with direct access to him and other key members of his staff. He should be the President's man and a person with whom the President would feel comfortable. He should also have the stature to command the confidence of the scientific community so that he could mobilize for the President the nation's best scientific advice when needed, but he should never consider himself a parochial protagonist of the scientific community.

When President Richard M. Nixon abolished the advisory mechanism in the White House for providing scientific advice, he substituted for it an arrangement calling for the director of the National Science Foundation to serve as science adviser. Despite the talents of H. Guyford Stever, the able scientist-engineer who served in this double-harness arrangement, the dual responsibility proved inadequate. There should be no divided responsibility and no allegiance to any department or agency except the White House. Inevitably, there will be competitive views expressed by Cabinet officers and agency heads, and the President must mediate these contending positions.

During Gerald R. Ford's presidency and in response to his leadership, Congress passed The National Science and Technology Policy Organization and Priorities Act of 1976, a carefully crafted act that represented an impressive joint effort by the President and Congress. It is still in full force and provides a permanent legislative base for a science adviser. . . .*

Later in 1981 President Reagan appointed Dr. George Keyworth as science adviser and director of the continuing Office of Science and Technology Policy. My letter in the *New York Times* certainly was not the decisive argument that led President Reagan to appoint a science adviser, and I cite it mainly as an example of my activist participation in the campaign for a continuation of a science presence in the White House.

One of the most persuasive and urgent voices supporting a science adviser in the White House was that of William T. Golden, who had drawn a plan in 1951 that led to the appointment by President Truman of a science advisory committee. Golden in 1980 had made an important contribution to a better understanding of the origin, organization, and procedures for advising presidents on science and technology when he edited a special issue of the journal *Technology in Society*. This brought together "an unprecedented collection of original articles written by former members of the President's Science Advisory Committee, with other perspectives provided by a highly knowledgeable group of distinguished scholars and industrialists."

It is hard to believe that President Reagan had the benefit of adequate scientific advice when he made his 1983 proposal for a *Star Wars* antimissile defense system. His proposal has been widely challenged in the scientific community as technically unachievable, and many thoughtful arms control analysts have pointed out that a major program to develop such a system could undercut important arms control agreements such as the Anti-Ballistic Missile Treaty and the Limited Test Ban. Even were it technically feasible, such a system might well impose a dangerously large levy on the nation's resources.

PUBLIC BROADCASTING: TOWARD
A CIVILIZED VOICE

I come now to an engagement in the public domain which I undertook with enthusiasm. I speak of my chairmanship of the Carnegie Commission on Educational Television, which in its 1967 report drew a blueprint for a national system of public broadcasting.

The stimulus for the formation of the commission was provided in December 1964 at a conference convened by the National Association of Educational Broadcasters in cooperation with the U.S. Office of Education. At that conference Mr. Ralph Lowell of Boston—after discussion with his associates at the Lowell Institute Cooperative Broadcasting Council and Station WGBH, which it sponsored—proposed the establishment of a commission to study the financial needs of educational television and the manner in which they might be met; a formal proposal for the establishment of such a commission was then drawn up by Mr. Lowell and Mr. C. Scott Fletcher of the National Association of Educational Broadcasters. The interest of John W. Gardner, then president of the Carnegie Corporation, prompted by his Carnegie associate, Arthur Singer, was immediately engaged, and his efforts, together with those of Alan Pifer, vice president of the Carnegie Corporation, led to the creation of the commission. It is important to note that MIT was from the beginning a constituent member of the Lowell Institute Cooperative Broadcasting Council. This council was the brainchild of President Conant of Harvard, who had been under pressure to support radio programs generated and sponsored by Harvard University. It occurred to him that the Lowell Institute would find it an appropriate extension of its work in supporting public lectures if it were to fund radio broadcasts sponsored by the major cultural institutions in the Boston area. I had been asked to represent MIT at a meeting President Conant called at his home in Cambridge to consider such a council with

Ralph Lowell, the sole trustee of the Lowell Institute, sponsor of the Lowell Lectures in Boston. At that meeting I indicated MIT's strong support of the formation of the council, and later MIT rented facilities to the council for its early use. The council's initial venture into broadcasting was of course a somewhat elementary undertaking. The quarters it rented from MIT were across the street from an entrance to the Institute, and when WGBH entered the educational television field, my secretary recalls a representative of its television staff coming to our office to make use of our large-type (loudmouthed) typewriter for preparing captions for some of the station's early TV programs.

In forming the commission, John Gardner and Alan Pifer came to me with the request that I chair what was to be called the Carnegie Commission on Educational Television, and this request was strongly supported by Ralph Lowell.

From the beginning the plan for a commission had the endorsement of Lyndon Johnson. It was first thought that the commission might be presidentially sponsored, but on reflection Johnson concluded that because of his own family's involvement in commercial television in Texas, it would be better if the commission were privately appointed and financed. It was also felt that a private commission would provide better insurance for the protection of artistic independence and freedom of speech. These considerations led the Carnegie Corporation to sponsor and finance the commission.

Once I had agreed to be chairman, Alan Pifer solicited my recommendations for members of the commission, and we brought together a list of distinguished participants.[11]

President Johnson's interest in the commission and the moral support that he provided were doubtless stimulated and guided by the advice he received from his able staff associate, Douglass Cater.

The members of the Carnegie Commission brought imagination and sound judgment to the work of the commission, and they were also a delightful group with whom to work. I recall an evening at MIT's Endicott House when one of our members, Rudolph Serkin, agreed to play a brief piano concert for the pleasure of the commission. It was a lovely June evening, with the Endicott gardens in full array. The occasion lives in the memories of all of us.

In the beginning few of the members knew much of the art and technology of television, but under the tutelage of Stephen White, Hy Goldin, and other staff members, we learned rapidly. The commission also insisted on looking ahead and not backward and on moving boldly to conceive of a national, publicly funded, prime-time medium of entertainment and information in contrast to the underfinanced, disorganized, local stations we found struggling to maintain a system of severely limited television.

We coined the term "public television" to capture the broader goals we sought to further, and we drew clear distinctions among the several forms of television programming. We said:

All television, commercial television included, provides news, entertainment, and instruction; all television teaches about places, people, animals, politics, crime, science. Yet the differences are clear. *Commercial television* seeks to capture the large audience; it relies mainly upon the desire to relax and to be entertained. *Instructional television* lies at the opposite end of the scale; it calls upon the instinct to work, build, learn and improve, and asks the viewer to take on responsibilities in return for a later reward. *Public Television,* to which the Commission has devoted its major attention, includes all that is of human interest and importance which is not at the moment appropriate or available for support by advertising, and which is not arranged for formal instruction.

With these distinctions clearly in mind we moved adventuresomely to conceive of a new kind of indigenous noncommercial institution arranged to serve American society in all its diversity.

In a classic expression of our goals, E. B. White, in a letter to Stephen White, reproduced in our report, stated our purpose with precision and eloquence:

Noncommercial television should address itself to the ideal of excellence, not the idea of acceptability—which is what keeps commercial television from climbing the staircase. I think television should be the visual counterpart of the literary essay, should arouse our dreams, satisfy our hunger for beauty, take us on journeys, enable us to participate in events, present great drama and music, explore the sea and the sky and the woods and the hills. It should be our Lyceum, our Chautauqua, our Minsky's, and our Camelot. It should restate and clarify the social dilemma and the political pickle. Once in a while it does, and you get a quick glimpse of its potential.

Then we added in our report:

We have become aware of television as a technology of immense power, growing steadily more powerful. What confronts our society is the obligation to bring that technology into the full service of man, so that its power to move image and sound is consistently coupled with a power to move mind and spirit. Television should enable us not only to see and hear more vividly, but to understand more deeply.

We have come to see that since the technology of television lends itself readily to uses that increase the pressure toward uniformity, there must be created means of resisting that pressure, and of enlisting television in the service of diversity. We recognize that commercial television is obliged for the most part to search for the uniformities within the general public, and to apply its skills to satisfy the uniformities it has found. Somehow we must seek out the diversities as well, and meet them, too, with the full body of skills necessary for their satisfaction. . . .

To all audiences should be brought the best energies, the best resources, the best talents—to the audience of fifty million, the audience of ten million, the audience of a few hundred thousand. Until excellence and diversity have been joined, we do not make the best use of our miraculous instrument.[12]

These words caught the spirit of the commission's vision. We proposed a system that we hoped would gain the support of the public, the government, and the faltering educational television system. Our original terms of reference, concerned with relieving the poverty of educational television, never envisaged any such upspringing, far-reaching concept as public television as the commission came to conceive it. Happily we were inspired to conceive of something bolder and more imaginative than a financing plan. With the skilled writing and editing of commission members and of Stephen White and Edward Weeks, we also achieved a lucid, eloquent report that stands as one of the great documents or institutional charters of my generation. I hasten to emphasize, however, that public television was created not just by our report but by the spontaneous support that the concepts in the report generated. We had mined ideas whose time had come.

The Carnegie Commission had finished its work and reported in January 1967. With remarkable expedition the commission's report had resulted in the introduction into Congress of the Public Television Act of 1967, and by April 12, 1967, Senator John Pastore had scheduled a formal hearing on this bill for the purpose of hearing directly from the members of the Carnegie Commission. The recommendations of their report had largely provided the substance of the bill introduced into Congress with the support of the White House.

I had come to realize that important studies which are expected to achieve action by the governmnent require not simply the preparation of a thorough report but a systematic effort to present and explain this report to members of the administration and of the Congress. There have been many studies that have contained solid substance but have had little impact. They were pigeonholed because there was no systematic effort by their authors to explain their recommendations and argue for their support. The Carnegie Commission had made a public presentation of its recommendations at a press conference on January 12, and we were gratified that President Johnson promptly adopted a number of the commission's basic proposals and supported their incorporation in the Public Broadcasting Act of 1967. The bill was introduced by Senator Warren Magnuson, who was the prime sponsor of the original Educational Television Facilities Act, and it was highly fitting that the first hearings on the Public Broadcasting Act were conducted by the subcommittee which Senator Pastore chaired. This subcommittee of the Senate Committee on Commerce also had provided constructive leadership in the complex field of national communications policy. We of the commission had the good fortune to have both the executive and the legislative branches consider our recommendations with a sense of urgency. Members of the commission, particularly Drs. DuBridge, Land, Patterson, and I, participated in presenting our report in detail to the White House and to other officers of federal administration and then to congressional committees. The result was that Senator Pastore invited the commission to present its recommendations to the Pastore Subcommittee on Communications at a well-publicized televised hearing. Later of course we made a similar presentation to the cognizant House committee. Senator Edward Kennedy had taken a special interest in our proposals, and he assembled for a memorable luncheon more than twenty senators to hear Franklin Patterson and me express our hopes and aspirations. We also visited with Wilbur Mills, chairman of the House Ways and Means Committee, then in his heyday and long before his downfall, and found him responsive. We covered numerous other bases both in Congress and in the executive branch. The result of the hearings on the part of the Senate committee and of the cognizant committee in the House was that Congress accepted—and passed by overwhelmingly large votes—the substance of our recommendations and embodied them in the carefully crafted Public Broadcasting Act of 1967. In later years there were to be numerous other congressional hearings on public broadcasting, with particular attention given to the problem of long-range financing, which, regretfully, the first bill passed by the Congress had neglected. The presentation to the Pastore committee in behalf of the commission was made by L. A. DuBridge, Edwin Land, and Leonard Woodcock. During the hearings many questions were asked of members of the commission, a particularly large number about the presidential appointment of the board of the proposed Corporation for Public Broadcasting.

During the hearing Mr. Woodcock asked permission, readily granted, to file with the committee a statement from Mr. Walter Reuther in behalf of the international union, United Automobile Workers, and later in the day the committee heard from Fred Friendly and McGeorge Bundy of the Ford Foundation, all of whom in substance strongly urged a major effort to achieve a strong system of public television.

The rapid action of the Congress in passing, within nine months of receiving the commission's report, the Public Broadcasting Act, which provided for both public television and public radio, was heady progress; the exigencies of reducing this act to an operating system were not so heady. In passing the Public Broadcasting Act, the Congress provided only a minimal amount of financing and left to later presidential recommendation and action the question of how adequate federal funds would be made available. The Corporation for Public Broadcasting, as provided for by Congress, was brought into being, and under the leadership of John Macy, Jr., as president, and Frank Pace as chairman of the board, moved to create the Public Broadcasting Service as an operating body for the interconnection and to take the other measures necessary to implement a national system built on localism that the Carnegie Commission had, in its fervor, outlined. It was not easy, and a solution to the problem of federal financing lagged, to the desperation of staff and stations. In general, Congress was very supportive although at one time members of the House criticized the modest salary paid to President Macy, and he generously, but I think wrongly, offered to reduce this salary. The board declined to accept his offer.

As matters developed, however, it was the Nixon White House and not the Congress that proved to be an enemy of public broadcasting and its independence. At one point Clay T. Whitehead of the Office of Telecommunications Policy, which derived from the recommendation I have already reported of the Stewart Committee during the Truman administration, made a dismaying speech in Florida in which public television was attacked, particularly for not being adequately under local control. This expression of White House attitude was so meanly critical that both Macy and Pace were profoundly discouraged. When President Nixon vetoed a reasonably generous bill which Congress had passed and which would have ushered in an impressive period of development for public broadcasting, both officers concluded that fighting the president was a losing game, and they resigned.

In its attack the White House had made clear its objection to public television's engaging in public affairs broadcasting and its specific objection to some of the public affairs broadcasters who had been engaged by local stations and whom the Nixon administration considered to be unfriendly. Along with these troublesome and disconcerting actions by the White House, the selection of presidential appointees to the board of the Corporation for Public Broadcasting appeared at times to represent an effort by the White House to control the corporation. Later the White House occasionally viewed with malign neglect its responsibility as outlined in the legislation to fill vacancies with "eminent" citizens.

Actually all Nixon appointees to CPB in action came to defend the corporation's independence. Another Nixon selection, Henry Loomis, was elected president of CPB, but he too quickly demonstrated his strength of character by fully supporting the board's independence.

It was at this point that I felt moved to accept an invitation by the board to come in for a spell as chairman publicly to reassert the independence of the board, to work out acceptable agreements with PBS, then under the strong leadership of Ralph Rogers, and to reaffirm the right and necessity of public broadcasting's engaging in programs on public affairs, programs opposed by the White House. My first act as chairman was to obtain a unanimous vote from the board, including the Nixon appointees, to support each of these policies. I thus found myself in direct conflict with the Nixon administration and relished the fight, finding deep satisfaction in a determination to reassert the independence and freedom of this new system against the machinations of the Nixon White House and at least three members of its staff who were concerned with telecommunications.

The story from this point on was one of a sustained effort to achieve a reasonable degree of harmony with PBS. It also became clear in those early days that the public broadcasting community was highly volatile and easily tempted to fuss about all and sundry matters. This also made it difficult for its leaders to achieve coordination and harmony. As chairman of CPB for a brief period under these conditions, I felt not unlike Br'er Rabbit in the briar patch.

Even though most of the recommendations of the first Carnegie Commission had been accepted by the Congress and embodied in the Public Broadcasting Act, there were a few which were not, and these changes were to prove troublesome. The commission had recommended a twelve-member board, six of whom were to be appointed by the president and the remaining six selected by the board. The act enlarged the board to fifteen, all appointed by the president and subject to Senate confirmation. This arrangement for presidential appointments to the board has not worked well. The White House appointive process has not always produced members with appropriate qualifications and eminence. Several presidents have repeatedly neglected to fill vacancies, leaving a substantial portion of the board as lame duck. In fact a total of 107 months of director vacancies over a period of 12 years, as reported by CPB, were occupied by these lame-duck members. It also appeared that the selection by the president of new members was at times influenced by political considerations, and certainly during the Nixon administration by an effort to infiltrate the board with members in support of the president to influence board decisions. The Carter administration also proved to be unexpectedly insensitive to the need for strong appointments to the board and for protecting its independence.

When I knew it, the board at times demonstrated difficulties in exercising its trusteeship responsibilities. A number of the members of the board seemed to find it difficult to exercise the arts of compromise and leadership, with the result that the board was beset by disagreements and lack of cohesion.

Another omission from the Public Broadcasting Act was its failure to provide any method of long-range federal financing, although the approval of "advanced funding" during the Ford administration was a great help.

Despite these problems public broadcasting has made steady progress. The number of television stations rapidly increased, total income grew, programming improved, and satellite broadcasting arranged. The Public Broadcasting Service was established by CPB to operate the interconnection, and in exercising this responsibility, PBS sought and achieved a major influence in the total system. Under the aggressive leadership of its chairman, Ralph Rogers, greater local participation of community leaders was enlisted, and PBS became a strong membership organization. In fact it became the stations' organization. CPB brought into existence, as required by the Public Broadcasting Act, National Public Radio, which has given new scope and vigor to radio broadcasting. At one stage, however, PBS sought unacceptably to obtain for itself the funds CPB felt necessary to allot to public radio as it was struggling to get started. In 1983, when it faced a financial crisis, friends and stations, under a plan devised by CPB, rallied to rescue it because it also had demonstrated power to move mind and spirit and to serve, as no other radio network, practical needs for information, discussion, and entertainment.

Since the inception of noncommercial television, the Ford Foundation was one of its prime supporters. Not only did it contribute generously and imaginatively life-giving funds but it also generated important new ideas and goals. When the ultimate history of public broadcasting is written, the Ford Foundation will be seen to have had a decisive impact.

As I reflected, ten years after the original Carnegie report, on the agonies of the evolving system and the many difficulties that were plaguing it, I concluded that a new and objective appraisal should be made of the organization and conduct of public broadcasting. This led me to propose to the Carnegie Corporation, as did CPB, that it appoint another commission to review the system's growth and development over the decade that had elapsed since the original Carnegie Commission report. After a careful survey conducted by its own staff, the Carnegie Corporation agreed to sponsor Carnegie II and appointed a commission under the chairmanship of William McGill, president of Columbia University, with a strong group of members. This commission brought in a good report, under the rubric *A Public*

Trust, and made many constructive recommendations. In its findings and recommendations, Carnegie II emphasized:

Public broadcasting is now firmly embedded in the national consciousness, financed by the people who use it, as well as by an array of organized elements within society, including businesses, state, and local governments, universities and school boards, foundations, and, of course, the federal government. It was the Congress and President who, in 1967, set up the organizational framework and turned on the flow of much-needed federal dollars [including advanced funding] supporting the operations and programs of public radio and television as we know them today.

There is a necessarily ambivalent relationship between public broadcasting—a highly visible creative and journalistic enterprise—and the government. The dynamics of a free press and a democratic government are unpredictable enough without adding the additional complication of federal financial support.

Herein lies the fundamental dilemma that has revealed itself over and over again in public broadcasting's brief history and led to the empanelment of this Commission: how can public broadcasting be organized so that sensitive judgments can be freely made and creative activity freely carried out without destructive quarreling over whether the system is subservient to a variety of powerful forces including the government?[13]

In its numerous recommendations, Carnegie II, in a spirit of positive support, noted: "In less than a dozen years, among the most turbulent and pivotal in our history, public broadcasting has managed to establish itself as a national treasure. From the backwaters of an industry long dominated by commercial advertising, the public system has come into its own. Millions now watch and hear, applaud, and criticize a unique public institution which daily enters their homes with programs that inform, engage, enlighten, and delight. In that sense the ideal has been realized: public broadcasting has made a difference."

While the recommendations of Carnegie II have not been extensively translated into changes in the Public Broadcasting Act and too little effort has gone into securing legislative underpinning for the changes proposed, I am still hopeful that some of them will be, particularly its proposal of a better method of making presidential appointments to the board of the Corporation for Public Broadcasting.

Let me conclude this truncated account of the tribulations and achievements of public broadcasting by emphasizing the delight I have experienced in watching the rich and varied programs that have come into my home by way of the "public treasure" of public broadcasting. We the people should not be denied in the future programs of the quality of Clark's *Civilization* and Hughes' *The Shock of the New; Julia Child, the French Chef;* Arthur Fiedler's magnificent Boston Pops program on July 4, 1976, celebrating 1776; science programs such as *The Ascent of Man* and *Nova; The Adams Chronicles;* and *Vietnam.* I am also proud that public television has made available *Sesame Street* as well as the hour-long *The MacNeil-Lehrer Report*, which uniquely contributes to public affairs broadcasting depth and balance. The audience has steadily grown as citizens have come to welcome the opportunity to hear and see opera, music, plays, fiction, political events, ballet, movies, news, and vigorous independent public affairs broadcasting, all free of meretricious commercials.

Having extolled public television for its delights, I must acknowledge its fragile economic structure. An expansion of pay cable television and video cassettes is apparently imminent, and the television audience that wants broadcasts devoted to arts, culture, and entertainment may find paying for them as acceptable as making donations in response to the over-the-air begging of public television stations.

Carnegie II was explicit in its discussion of the challenges of the new telecommunications environment which is coming to surround public broadcasting. It recommended that public broadcasting move rapidly to develop a stronger, ongoing, and more fully integrated research and development capability to assist the system in adopting new technology. It further concluded that public broadcasting must broaden and become more flexible in its approach to the delivery of programs and services to the public. The achievement of satellite interconnection represents a major extension of the physical system. The commission cited two striking examples of what can be accomplished in public communications development—the South Carolina Educational Television Network and the consortium of community-licensed public television in educational institutions represented by the West Central Illinois Educational Telecommunications Corporation. In its regional approach this Convocom system is arranging a multifaceted production and distribution system employing television, radio, cable television, common carrier microwave, and video cassette.

I find much encouragement in the accomplishment of these highly motivated systems, and I am unwilling to jump to any conclusion that the new technologies may create conditions beyond the capacity of public broadcasting to embrace them for its benefit and that of our society. I find great encouragement, too, in the creative station leadership that came to the fore as the system developed. At the risk of being invidious, I cite Jay Iselin of WNET, David Ives of WGBH, and James Loper of KCET, Los Angeles.

The Corporation for Public Broadcasting is now administering a fund contributed by Walter Annenberg in the amount of $10 million a year for fifteen years to enable it to create in effect a "university of the air." Apparently he agreed to make this great gift after beng assured by the Reagan administration that no effort would be made to abolish the corporation. He also observed that college-level courses should be made available by television in view of the fact that the universities, through their high tuitions, may be pricing themselves out of the market. (There is yet no evidence to support this lugubrious view.) The Annenberg-CPB project provides further justification for the continuation of the Corporation for Public Broadcasting despite past efforts to abolish it. Among educational goals supported by the Annenberg-CPB project is the use of computers in the teaching of languages at MIT.

EXPERIENCES WITH CONGRESSIONAL COMMITTEES
In addition to my work with congressional committees in behalf of legislative underpinning for science advice in the White

House and the legislation for creating public broadcasting, I recall another memorable experience, this one at the peak of the ABM controversy during the Nixon administration.

In March 1969 the Subcommittee on International Disarmament Affairs of the Senate Committee on Foreign Relations sponsored a series of seminars on the ABM weapons system. For one of these it turned to George Kistiakowsky, Herbert York, and myself for a nationally televised seminar to dramatize its own skepticism about the Sentinel version of the ABM, then advocated by President Nixon and Henry Kissinger.

The committee was aware that the three of us had, in 1967, participated in a meeting with President Johnson to give our views on the ABM. At that time Secretary Robert McNamara was in opposition, and he hit upon the interesting plan of bringing all available past science advisers together in the Cabinet Room to make comments for the benefit of President Johnson. All these advisers were critical of the ABM at its then stage of development. Secretary McNamara sought in this manner to buttress his own negative view, but some months later he called each of us who had appeared in the Cabinet Room and had said our piece to President Johnson to tell us, to our surprise, that he was going to defend the ABM in a forthcoming speech. Apparently he had caved in to pressure.

At the Senate hearing both Kistiakowsky and York attacked the ABM on technical grounds, and I, mainly on strategic considerations.

At the 1967 meeting called by Mr. McNamara, I had expressed grave reservations about the desirability of deploying an ABM system under conditions operating at that time. I felt that deployment should be deferred in the hope that some progress could be made in restraining escalation in the arms race but that research, development, and testing of the system should continue.

The senators had numerous questions and comments. They asked, for example, whether President Nixon had sought our comment, and we said of course that he had not. Would we be willing, they asked, if they arranged an appointment for us, to go to see the president and present our views. We of course replied that we would be.

The committee then invited us to join it for lunch, and while we were together in the Senate restaurant, they reported that they had made contact with the White House and that we had an appointment that afternoon. We were not a little astonished by all of this, but of course we appeared at the White House under the arrangements which the committee had made. We were ushered into the office of Henry Kissinger, then special assistant to President Nixon for National Security Affairs. We found, hardly to our surprise, that Mr. Kissinger took a dim view of our seeing the president and made clear his conviction that the president already had availed himself of adequate comment and advice. Kissinger did take occasion to argue in behalf of the ABM, particularly for its value in negotiating with the Soviets on arms limitation. He also made clear that in his view, his own staff had provided wholly competent and objective advice, and so we found that not even an august Senate committee could achieve a breakthrough in the barriers arranged around President Nixon.

On another occasion Nixon had been outraged by criticism voiced by scientists who questioned the reliability of the ABM system then advocated. His angry reaction led the president to issue a choleric directive to cut back on MIT's federal research grants in view of Jerome Wiesner's "antidefense bias." MIT as an institution had taken no position, but Wiesner, an MIT administrator, had vigorously and publicly opposed the ABM system then advocated by the White House. It is reported that a year later Nixon formally inquired whether MIT had been punished as he had requested. This smacked of Hitler's famous inquiry "Is Paris burning?" Apparently wiseheads among his staff associates had sidetracked Nixon's retaliatory orders, and there was no cutback in MIT federal grants. (As this memoir is readied for printing I fortunately find an extended description of this episode by Deborah Shapley in *Science* 181, July 20, 1983, pp. 244–246.)

In looking back on my score of appearances before congressional committees, I would be ungrateful if I did not express my admiration for the services to science, education, and public broadcasting of the group of able chairmen who presided over the hearings at which I appeared. The nation has been fortunate in the quality of the congressmen who took leading roles in the several committees that dealt with science, technology, communications, and astronautics. I found guidance and stimulation in my association with these thoughtful members of Congress. I record too my indebtedness to Nicholas Zapple of the staff of the Pastore committee, and to Philip B. Yeager of the staff of the Committee on Science and Astronautics. I salute these senators and representatives and supporting staff, each of whom in my experience contributed importantly either to the space program, the advancement of American science, the restoration by legislative action of a science advisory presence in the White House, or the achievement of public broadcasting.

SERVICE ON NATIONAL COMMISSIONS

In addition to my work on the Carnegie Commission on Educational Television, I participated over the years in a variety of other studies that sought to clarify the national purpose and to define major goals for the oncoming decades. In 1956 the Rockefeller Brothers concluded that it was appropriate to plan a major, large-scale study whose objective would be addressed to the broad topic "Prospect for America." Six groups were organized for this study, involving more than one hundred American citizens, and each group issued its own report. At the conclusion these separate reports were brought together in a comprehensive volume published in 1961. Perhaps the most notable achievement of this study was a widely published statement on education prepared by John Gardner entitled "The Pursuit of Excellence." Not only were there famous people in the study group; there were also staff members who were later to become national figures, including Nancy Hanks and Henry Kissinger.

As his presidency drew to a close, Eisenhower encouraged the American Assembly to appoint a Commission on National Goals with the purpose of projecting programs for action in the sixties. This report, in addition to a statement drawn by the commission as a whole, contained sixteen essays written by men and women of acknowledged competence, the most notable of which were probably Warren Weaver's eloquent statement, "A Great Age for Science," and Henry Wriston's humane essay on the individual and our paramount goal in America to guard the rights, ensure the equality, and enlarge the opportunities of all citizens regardless of sex and race.

The two reports, *Prospect for America* and *Goals for Americans*, were given wide distribution and became the subject of discussion groups about the country. There was no effort in the reports to engage in "futurology," but it is interesting to look back and see how many spectacular developments in the decades immediately following the reports found no place in their vision. I note particularly that there is no anticipation of student unrest and no mention of the technologies of space weapons or of the computer revolution.

The *Goals for Americans* report prompted the well-conceived Cubberly Conference that was sponsored by Stanford University in 1961. Out of this conference came a first-rate book, *Education: An Instrument of National Goals*, to which I contributed a chapter under the rubric "New Goals for Science and Engineering Education." But for me the most meaningful statement presented to the conference was the paper by Senator Fulbright, in which he said: "The task of shaping national consensus, I have suggested, is pre-eminently one of Presidential leadership. The task of cultivating the qualities in which consensus must be rooted—qualities of wisdom, imagination, and maturity of judgment—is the task of our society as a whole but especially our schools and universities." This statement voices the conclusions that have come to me out of experiences both in academe and in Washington.

My concern about government intrusion led me to accept membership on the Sloan Commission on Government and Higher Education in 1977, chaired by Louis Cabot. It titled its report *A Program for Renewed Partnership* (1980). I quote the following observations or proposals in the overview of the Sloan report because they so adequately give expression to my views:

We urge our colleges and universities to take a new hard look at themselves. Academics have been pioneers in calling for change in other social institutions but have not always been ahead of society in changing their own. Many of the current demands resented by academic spokesmen are neither extraordinary nor illegitimate. The academy claims special status as the disinterested custodian of truth. But some of the advertising by "academic" institutions is as extravagant as any in the commercial sector.

Both sides must work to restore the goodwill and feeling of partnership they enjoyed for so long. The prevailing adversarial mood is dangerous, particularly in the coming period when the dependence on the government as a patron will be so great. Those in higher education must anticipate problems, must educate the regulators, and above all, must themselves make the changes that are needed. They are in the best position to decide how to change and keep their capacity to do what society needs them to do. . . .

There are now seventeen federal laws and executive orders relating to equal opportunity to be enforced. There are eight different agencies, with many regional offices, responsible for enforcement. The federal courts, of course, have ultimate jurisdiction. This diffusion of responsibility is one major source of confusion. Another is that Congressional legislation never spelled out clear standards or powers for any of these agencies. Compliance standards and enforcement procedures vary among them, and even within them, as officials are replaced or succeeded. Also, there is considerable duplication of effort on all sides, making the process expensive for both government and higher education. . . .[14]

My participation in these studies clearly widened my acquaintanceship with a great array of lively minds. It broadened my horizons and added to my vision of what our nation may become if it ardently pursues the great goals stressed in these reports.

CARNEGIE-MELLON UNIVERSITY: THE STORY OF A MERGER

After I had announced my resignation in 1959 as special assistant to President Eisenhower, I was approached by Paul Mellon and William Baker, who inquired whether I would consider a post of leadership at the Mellon Institute in Pittsburgh. I explained to them that my commitment to MIT precluded my considering such a post, but in 1960 I did accept Mellon's invitation to join the board of trustees of the Mellon Institute. This membership was to lead to one of the most interesting and satisfying episodes in my career.

The idea of an institution of applied research mainly to serve industry had been proposed in 1906 to members of the Mellon family by the late Robert Kennedy Duncan. The plan appealed to A. W. Mellon and R. B. Mellon, who invited Duncan to establish the Mellon Institute of Industrial Research. These Mellon founders provided a substantial endowment, and in 1937 Andrew Mellon dedicated a palatial, neoclassic building to house the Institute.

In its early days, under the leadership of E. R. Weidlein, the Mellon Institute became widely known for its services to industry and as a center of applied research, but when Paul Mellon discussed the institute with me in 1960, it was clear that its status and future required fresh study if its full potential was to be achieved. More and more, industries were developing their own research programs, and even the addition of a large grant from the Mellon family for basic research did not achieve a full realization of the institute as a major center for research. At the time I accepted membership, the board of trustees included Baker, Lee DuBridge of the California Institute of Technology, and Warren C. Johnson of the University of Chicago. Paul Mellon's desire to develop the best possible plans for the institution led him to turn to these trustees to advise on the administration, the role, and the future of the institution. Along with these trustees I became quickly convinced that the contributions of the institute would be enhanced were it to have an affiliation with an educational institution, especially one with a strong graduate school and engaged extensively in pure and applied research. As we pondered this question, we concluded that if the institute were to be merged with an educational institution, the most likely prospect would be its neighbor, the Carnegie Institute of

Technology. At the request of Mellon, I proceeded to an off-the-record meeting with the president of the Carnegie Institute and the chairman of its board, a meeting that was held in 1960 in Cleveland to avoid any possibility of setting off rumors in Pittsburgh.

These representatives of Carnegie Tech indicated positively that in their view their institution would be interested in a merger. This initial exploratory effort, however, came to naught because a member of the Mellon family had a close relationship with the University of Pittsburgh and was hesitant about any move that might be interpreted as a rejection of the university. The idea of an affiliation with Carnegie Tech was then put on the shelf.

It was not until 1965 that possibilities of a merger again came under intensive discussion. Paul Mellon visited me at MIT and indicated anew his conviction that the best interests of the Mellon Institute would be served by relating it to a university. He further indicated that he believed the way was now clear to consider some affiliation with the Carnegie Institute of Technology, and he asked me to chair an informal committee of the Mellon Institute trustees once again to explore this possibility. In the same year, and quite independently of these discussions, Guyford Stever, head of the Departments of Mechanical Engineering and Naval Architecture and Marine Engineering at MIT, was elected president of Carnegie Tech, and when he learned of the possibilities of a merger, he gave clear indication that he would welcome joint discussions.

This led to the preparation of a carefully detailed plan which was developed in consultation with the faculties and trustees of both institutions with full consideration given to their interests. A plan based on these discussions led to an agreement to go public with an indication that both institutions were prepared for a merger. The discussions that followed resulted in the creation of a new university bearing the name Carnegie University. Following this announcement I received a letter from Mellon reporting that there had been nothing but favorable reactions from all concerned in Pittsburgh, and then he generously added: "I am sure that with the good groundwork that has been accomplished, thanks to you, the merger will eventually go through with a minimum of trouble. And that is something which I know we will all be grateful for."

During the year following the announcement all of the legal steps were completed for the establishment of Carnegie University in 1967 with the Mellon Institute of Science as one of its six colleges. Later the trustees of the university reached the appropriate conclusion that it should not be called simply Carnegie University but be named Carnegie-Mellon University. Thus the name of the new institution pays tribute to the founder of Carnegie Tech, Andrew Carnegie, and to the Mellon family.

One of the major dividends of this experience was my pleasure in coming to know Paul Mellon and to realize his devotion to art and to the great institution in Washington founded by his father—the National Gallery.

AN INTERNATIONAL INSTITUTE OF
SCIENCE AND TECHNOLOGY?

In December 1957 President Eisenhower invited me to accompany him to Paris to be available for any scientific matters that might come up at the NATO heads of nations meeting scheduled for that month. The agenda for that meeting included a proposal for the establishment of a science advisory committee for NATO and for the appointment of a science adviser to the secretary general of NATO. With strong support on the part of the United States, these proposals were approved by the NATO Council, and Professor Normal Ramsey of Harvard was appointed the first science adviser. There was a strong feeling that NATO could appropriately undertake to stimulate the further development of science and engineering in the Atlantic Community.

In 1959 this NATO science committee, in cooperation with the Ford Foundation and the Foundation Universitaire of Brussels, appointed a study group chaired by M. Louis Armand, which came forward with a recommendation that the North Atlantic Council authorize the secretary general to appoint a "small . . .

high-level Working Group . . . to study the question of the establishment of an international institute of science and technology," and to formulate for the council "recommendations on specific possibilities and their feasibility."

In late 1960 I was visited at MIT by the secretary general, Paul-Henri Spaak of Belgium, who invited me in behalf of the council to chair a Working Group to study the feasibility of such an institution.

I was encouraged to accept this responsibility by President Kennedy and the secretary of state, Dean Rusk, each of whom wrote a letter expressing his great interest in the concept. In his letter President Kennedy wrote:

The proposed Institute, the plans for which it is your task to formulate, could prove to be a most significant addition to the strength and unity of the North Atlantic Community. It would augment our graduate education facilities for science and strengthen our basic and applied research in new as well as traditional fields. It would serve as a means of bringing together the scientific and technological resources of the Community in a manner which will be of the greatest benefit to the future welfare of the Community. Moreover, such an Institute would be a unique public demonstration of the breadth of common purpose of the North Atlantic Nations.

The members of the Working Group were duly appointed, and the deliberations of this group were lively and enriched by consultants throughout the Atlantic nations.[15] The group had plenary meetings in Cambridge, Paris, and Bellagio, Italy. In October 1961, I, as chairman, presented to the members of the North Atlantic Council in Paris a formal report stating the unanimous conclusion of the Working Group:

. . . it is both feasible and desirable to establish in Europe an International Institute of Science and Technology devoted to graduate and postdoctoral studies and operating at the pinnacle of the university system; and that the benefits which such an institution could bring to science, engineering and education, and thus to the welfare and security of the Western countries, make its establishment urgently important.

The Working Group concludes, further, that today the widely recognized advantages of international efforts in science, together with the growing facility and effectiveness with which Western countries undertake group efforts for the common good, provide an unprecedentedly favourable climate for the establishment of an international educational institution devoted to science and technology. The increasing interdependence of nations—in part the result of science and technology—and the importance to scientific progress of free and cultivated international exchange set the stage for new joint efforts among nations.

The North Atlantic Council authorized the report to be referred to the member nations for their consideration.

As the consultative process proceeded, the British government suggested that it would be helpful if there could be a bilateral meeting in London so that the Americans and the British could compare their views. The American government was enthusiastic about the proposed international institute, and it had even moved to the point where it was agreed that American funds could be made available to help get it started. The British had questions. The proposed meeting was to take place at the time that the discussions were under way as to whether Britian would join the Common Market, and it was perhaps this factor that led the British to suggest that the conference be turned into a trilateral meeting with the French participating also. There was general agreement in this July 1982 meeting that the creation of such an institution was desirable, but there was also concern that it might compete with existing institutions for staff. There was also concern that NATO was not the best sponsor of such an institution because of its military responsibilities, but it was felt alternatively that a group of representatives from selected European countries might well constitute a governing group for the institution.

The Americans who were selected by the State Department to be present at this meeting included scientists I. I. Rabi, Frederick Seitz, and William Nierenberg; a State Department representative, Irwin Tobin; and myself. In addition to a representative of the British Foreign Office, the British delegation was headed by Alexander Todd, then chairman of the United Kingdom Advisory Council on Scientific Policy. That council, with responsibilities similar to the President's Science Advisory Committee in the United States, had reached a prior conclusion that an alternate scheme should be devised under which internationally assisted centers for advanced research and postgraduate teaching would be located at existing universities. Among the French representatives was Pierre Aigrain, a scientist who has served tours of duty in the French Cabinet and in other high government posts and who had had associations with American institutions including MIT. While the meeting was in session, an emissary arrived from France who conveyed to the French group instructions to favor a governing body limited to Europe and excluding the United States. This message reflected at that time the prevailing views of President Charles de Gaulle. It should be noted that the proposal of my Working Group had not been initiated by the U.S. government and that the report had been prepared by a group that consisted mainly of European scientists with me serving as chairman. Of course the French veto of American representation on the governing board would have killed U.S. interest in making U.S. funds available to help launch the institute as it had been prepared to do.

There had been an earlier (March 1962) discussion between the then secretary general of NATO, Dirk Stikker, and Lord Hailsham of England, who served for a period as science adviser to the British government. At first Hailsham was also vehemently unfriendly to American participation, expressing the astonishing view that the establishment of the proposed institution might lead to American domination of European education, but eventually he expressed support if the institute's programs could be dispersed among several institutions.

Outside of these reservations on the part of Britain and France, the report of the Working Group had the strong support of most of the NATO countries, and indeed some of them were campaigning to have the institution located in their territory. Secretary Stikker, I must acknowledge, always felt that the British took the back-of-the-stairs lead in killing the plan.

This outcome was of course regrettable. I think all of the members of the Working Group favored the proposed institution. I for one had written in a NATO letter in April 1962:

I find the prospect of the creation of the International Institute of Science and Technology a moving and exciting testament to the inventiveness of Western society.

I believe the achievement of such a university, located in Europe, but serving and being supported by the entire Atlantic Community, could be another one of those "transforming" institutions contributing uniquely to the cultural, economic and political resources of the region. These institutions may well provide an unmatched example to all the world of the strength and appeal which derives from the free exchange of ideas, the promotion of comity among nations of like interests and objectives, and the steady striving of international forces to release the full intellectual and imaginative energies of free peoples.

During the summer of 1971 I spent a month or so at the Villa Serbelloni, the Rockefeller Conference Center on Lake Como, working on a book and while there learned that Dirk Stikker was at his villa on the other side of the lake. I invited him over, and we spent several hours in exchanging gleaming anecdotes about NATO and gossiping about the international community. It was then that he told me this story about my admired friend, Robert Lovett.

When Lovett was under secretary of state, an ambassador to the United States sent word that he wanted to come and present a strong protest to some undertaking of the United States. Lovett promptly said he would see him and listened impassively to the vehement protest presented with unalloyed French ill grace and then said: "Mr. Ambassador, your facts are wrong, your statement is offensive, and in addition, your fly is open." The ambassador quickly moved to zip up, caught his tie in the zipper, and left the office unable to straighten up.†

At the meeting in London when the French emissaries knocked the props from under the International Institute of Science and Technology, I rather wish the session might have ended as did the one Stikker described in Lovett's office.

In 1965 Shepard Stone, director of the International Affairs Program of the Ford Foundation, asked if I would undertake under the foundation's sponsorship a series of visits to England to engage in discussions with Lord Vivian Bowden, who had been appointed minister of state, Department of Education and Science, in the new Labour government. In addition, he asked that I visit two institutions in Berlin, the Technical University of Berlin and the Free University, both of which were recipients of foundation aid. In fact the Ford Foundation had played a major role in the establishment of the Free University in Berlin, and it had arranged for MIT to provide faculty assistance to the Technical University. He wished to have my reactions to the programs of these two institutions.

The visits to England were the foundation's response to a request from Lord Bowden that he have the benefit of discussions with American educators as he undertook his duties as head of the Department of Education and Science in the Wilson government. Stone said that the foundation was prepared to finance up to eight trips to the continent and to England and that Mrs. Killian could accompany me.

We elected to go first to Berlin, stopping by Paris so that I could visit Pierre Aigrain, who was then director of French Higher Education, and the great Jean Monnet, who was providing intellectual leadership for new cooperative relationships among the Common Market countries.

I was greatly encouraged by the progress being made by TUB (Technical University of Berlin) and the value of MIT's contributions to its progress. I was puzzled by the status of the Free University. Its creation had been a major achievement, but I was disappointed to find that it had adopted the traditional German university organization. While in West Berlin, Mrs. Killian and I had an opportunity to observe the notorious Wall and to make a journey into East Berlin, escorted by an American foreign service officer. This was a depressing visit, but it did afford an opportunity to pass by the locus of what had once been the University of Berlin.

In England, in the course of the three visits that I made, I had an opportunity to visit the Universities of Warwick, Essex, and Sussex, new institutions all of which were developing innovative programs that departed from Oxbridge traditions. I was invited to make my base at Churchill College, Cambridge Uni-

versity, through arrangements the Ford Foundation had made
with Sir John Cockcroft, master of Churchill. Cockcroft recommended my appointment as an overseas fellow of the college,
and I met with Alexander Todd, Eric Ashby, and others. The
high point of one of the trips was the opportunity to visit the
prime minister at Chequers. In addition to the visits I made to
the new "plate-glass" universities, I visited a technical college, a
college of advanced technology, and a comprehensive high
school. I also had a memorable evening with Lord Oliver
Franks, who gave me a summary of the work of his commission
that was undertaking a study of Oxford. Altogether these visits
provided fascinating experiences and contributed notably to my
own education. Lord Bowden arranged for me to visit the House
of Lords and to have lunch in the Lords' dining room with C. P.
Snow.

Lord Bowden I found an extraordinary character. He spent an
extended visit at MIT and at government agencies in Washington concerned with science and technology and returned to England "to bang Britain's universities into the twentieth
century," as the journal *The Observer* reported. At the time he was
appointed by Prime Minister Wilson as a minister of state, he
was principal of the College of Science and Technology in Manchester and dean of the Faculty of Technology at Manchester
University, posts to which he returned after his brief excursion
into government service. His ecstatic speeches about MIT and
American education verged on the embarrassing. He stood
apart from the Oxbridge elite, and *The Observer* quoted a critic as
describing him as "a philistine product of the Manchester school
turning out an endless woof of khaki-coloured ideas." Perhaps
this lack of sympathy with his ideas may relate to some of the
problems now besetting England.

Although I have not had an opportunity to visit it, I have
watched with great interest the creation and progress of a new
university in England, The University College at Buckingham.
Its founder, Max Beloff, I had met at a time when he and I were
guests at the Villa Serbelloni in Bellagio. He was a distinguished
historian at All Souls College, Oxford, and became convinced

that England should have a university wholly independent of government funds and completely master of its own destiny. Max Beloff has visited his friend Harold Hanham, MIT's former dean of the School of Humanities and Social Science, several times, and I have had a chance to hear reports of the almost miraculous achievement he brought about in the establishment of this new institution.

THE BIRLA INSTITUTE OF TECHNOLOGY
In addition to my association with the aborted NATO effort to sponsor an international institute of technology in Europe, I had a sense of genuine accomplishment in being of some assistance to a distinguished Indian industrialist, the late G. D. Birla, who had embarked on a program to create in Pilani, India, under the Birla Education Trust, the Birla Institute, a privately supported technological institute to be modeled on MIT. The Birla family had already established and long supported a Birla Institute in Pilani, but its original objectives and curriculum were more pre-college than college.

Mr. Birla's new goal was an impressive one: to transform the institute into a degree-granting institution that would be to India what MIT is to the United States. I recall that he once said: "Most of the current products of Indian schools are at best copyists and not even good copyists." Mr. Birla envisioned an institution that would not produce "copyists" of textbook knowledge but who would be able to approach engineering and scientific problems with professional competence, originality, and imagination and would provide a unique resource and opportunity for Indian industry, Mr. Birla himself being a leading Indian industrialist.

Because I was impressed with Mr. Birla's enthusiasm and bold educational ideas for India, I agreed to help him find an American engineering educator who could help formulate the plans and assist in the launching of the new Birla Institute. After consulting faculty members at MIT, I arranged a meeting for him with Dr. Thomas B. Drew, professor of chemical engineering at Columbia University. Mr. Birla requested that Professor

Drew make a trip to India to talk over the plan and to visit the Institute at Pilani which Mr. Birla wanted to upgrade.

In 1962 Professor Drew accepted Mr. Birla's invitation to be his academic consultant and to help shape the new institution. He went to India, where he visited a number of Indian engineering schools, and met with industrialists who expressed interest in the project and in the training of Indian engineers who could build and put into operation plants suited to the Indian scene, eliminating the need to import engineers from abroad for these jobs.

After this initial visit Professor Drew returned to India in 1963 with Professor Howard R. Bartlett from the Department of Humanities at MIT "to evolve an actual plan for reorganizing those Birla colleges at Pilani into the desired new institution." I am pleased to have been associated with the early implementation of this important educational venture. Mr. Birla also obtained the support of the Ford Foundation, who aided both MIT and the Birla Institute in working together in creating a full-fledged institute of technology. The year 1963 also saw the drawing up of a roster by Mr. Birla and Mr. D. Ensminger, Ford Foundation representative in India, of Indian industrialists who were to be invited to form a corporation of the institute. These prominent industrialists and professional men would manage a corporate board, suggested by Dr. Drew, analogous to the boards of trustees of American institutions.

Thus it was that the framework for the Birla Institute of Technology and Science was begun, with the proposed corporation formed during the winter of 1963–64, and the institution evolving, not without growing pains, in Pilani. It was unusual among Indian education institutions because it was privately supported and it received a charter giving it the authority to award degrees and thus allowing it to have relative independence from the Indian university system, and it used the American pattern of instruction as a guide. Activities over the next two years culminated in a proposal in 1966 for "A Joint Program in Education and Research, Massachusetts Institute of Technology, Birla Institute of Technology and Science, and the Ford Foundation."

The joint MIT-BITS-Ford Foundation program was reviewed in July 1966, when Mr. Birla came and met with the MIT faculty advisers and Ford Foundation representatives. MIT Professors Nathan Cook, David White, Paul Gray, Gordon Brown, and others became associated with the new institution and contributed importantly to its development. An MIT alumnus, Dr. Chitta R. Mitra, is now director of the Birla Institute.

At one of the anniversaries of the new Birla Institute, I was invited over to give the convocation address. My wife accompanied me and we were guests of the Birla family at their Pilani home, Chandra Bhawan. It was a memorable experience and left us with admiration and affection for the Birlas. They were a deeply religious family of high ideals, and as hosts, they were thoughtfully sensitive and wonderfully gracious. The meals served in their home were entirely vegetarian. Even so they were Lucullan in their attractiveness and variety. My wife and I had never realized that vegetables could be served with such imagination. I must confess that occasionally a member of the Birla staff surreptitiously provided us some carefully camouflaged bacon at breakfast.

Clearly Mr. Birla commanded the love and respect, not only of his family, but of the people of Pilani. I went with him to the place where he was born and to other locations important in his life, arriving at one of these astride a camel, and in each place there was pageantry and ceremony, all bespeaking devotion to Mr. Birla and hospitality to his guest. After I made some ceremonial remarks, many in the audience came forward with gifts of fruits and vegetables. My wife and I also visited the beautiful marble Saraswati Temple he built in Pilani. We had of course left our shoes outside, and our feet were somewhere near frigid by the end of the visit.

My first experience with Mr. Birla preceded those related to the Birla Institute of Technology. He visited me in Cambridge to pave the way for the admission to MIT of one of his grandsons. I am indebted to former Ambassador John Kenneth Galbraith for the interesting information that all sons of the Birla family are expected to go into the Birla firm, but not sons-in-law: "Business acumen is thus assumed, in effect, to be inherited, and there is considerable practical evidence to support the view." Given this family policy, I better understand Mr. Birla's visit to me in behalf of his grandson's gaining admission to MIT. It turned out that his grandson was admitted on his own record, thus avoiding any possible embarrassment on the part of Mr. Birla or me.

After the convocation at his institute, Mr. Birla had arranged for his plane to take Professor and Mrs. White, Dr. and Mrs. Mitra, and the Killians to several places of great tourist interest. This sight-seeing trip included Jaipur and then Udaipur, where he had arranged for us to spend the night at the Lake Palace Hotel located on an island in Pichola Lake, which Galbraith has described as the "nearest thing to a child's fairy castle anywhere in the world." We found it so, but as usual in many old buildings in India, however magnificent, the great marble bathroom was embellished with a display of tiny lizards, all harmless but disconcerting. Even so, we enjoyed the stay even more than the night we had spent some years before in the striking hotel Le Corbusier designed in Chandigarh.

In my discussions with Mr. Birla I described how American colleges and universities sought to accumulate endowments of which they used only the income. I expressed the hope that he would ensure the future of the Birla Institute by endowing it. Apparently he had already established the Birla Education Trust, but I am not sure he approved of my suggestions that he endow some named professorships at the Institute. There were no precedents for such funds.

While at the Lake Palace Hotel, arrangements had been made for us to go to a nearby Wild Game Sanctuary where, if our luck held out, we might shoot a panther during an all-night hunt. We tactfully but firmly begged off, not one of us summoning the courage to face a panther. Instead, we flew on to Delhi, where several days and dinners had been arranged for me to meet prominent Indian government officials and educational leaders who were far more cordial than panthers.

This memorable trip was concluded by a visit to Kanpur, where a new Indian institute of technology had been built under the direction of a consortium of American universities, of which MIT was one. Before returning to the States, our trip was delightfully capped off by dinner at the home of Dr. and Mrs. Norman C. Dahl, an MIT professor then with the Indian office of the Ford Foundation who had earlier served as program leader during the creation of the Indian Institute of Technology.

We count it a privilege to have had these experiences in India thanks to Mr. Birla. I shall always think of him as one of the most remarkable and gifted men I have encountered in my visits about the world.

TECHNOLOGY SQUARE AND URBAN RENEWAL
In the foreword to this book I speak of fresh initiatives in education and research as providing an interconnecting theme for this memoir. A quite different example of innovation is to be found in the story of MIT's role in the building of Technology Square in Cambridge. To accomplish this urban renewal project, MIT entered into a collaboration with a redevelopment firm that was then unusual for an educational institution.

Shortly after I returned from Washington in 1959, I was visited by Edward Crane, then mayor of Cambridge, who spoke of the difficulties the city was encountering in redeveloping the Rogers Block, a noisome slum all too close to the MIT campus. The city, under a federal statute, had acquired the Rogers Block and removed the blighted buildings that occupied it, this being done with the intent of replacing them with appropriate modern buildings to produce jobs and taxes. Mayor Crane reported that so far, the city had been unable to find a developer and that he was discouraged by the outlook. At about that same time I had been approached by Mr. Gerald Blakeley, head of the real estate development firm of Cabot, Cabot & Forbes, with the thought that I might have suggestions as to how MIT could use its good offices to bring additional science-based industry into the metropolitan Boston area. MIT had already served to attract research firms to "Research Row" along Memorial Drive in Cambridge and to Route 128, a circumferential highway west and north of Boston. I told Mr. Blakeley I was primarily interested in Cambridge and would be glad to join in an effort to promote development in our home city. It then occurred to me that the languishing Rogers Block project offered an opportunity for such a joint development effort. Not only was this area available for development, but adjacent to it was an abandoned soap factory that was for sale and that could be combined with the Rogers Block to make an adequately large area for development.

The upshot was that MIT and Cabot, Cabot & Forbes agreed to join forces in the creation of a research center, with MIT providing out of its endowment necessary capital to acquire the soap factory and finance the development and Cabot, Cabot & Forbes providing its entrepreneurial resources to bring the project into being.

Plans were promptly developed for an industrial research center. To undertake the project, a corporate entity was formed by the participating institutions, and the program for the new center moved rapidly ahead with the enthusiastic support of the city and all others interested in urban renewal in the metropolitan area. The center was designed as a taxpaying development and thus offered the potential of contributing to the economy of the city and to employment opportunities.

As developed, Technology Square was to become the fourth largest source of property taxes in Cambridge and was to provide a far more benign environment for all adjacent properties than existed before the center was built. In 1971 MIT was able to withdraw its investment in the center, since it had used endowment funds which needed to be replaced. At the time the program for Technology Square was announced, Paul R. Corcoran, chairman of the Cambridge Redevelopment Authority, blessed the project by saying: "The Cambridge Community owes MIT a debt of gratitude. It is heartening to note that in this undertaking the new corporation will pay taxes and is joining its neighbors in the joys and sorrows of day-to-day living in its home city.

"This public demonstration of cooperation and competence together with the physical improvement and tax support which accompany the proposed development, is of the highest value, both now and for the future."

In addition the press and public officials hailed the new project as a novel and unprecedented undertaking that provided a demonstration of how educational institutions and business organizations can combine for the generation of new business and property resources in their communities and for attracting high-technology companies.

Originally three buildings were erected at Technology Square. Subsequently it proved feasible for the Draper Laboratory to build near the square a complex of buildings for its purposes, and this has contributed further to the beneficial effects of this concentration of research activities. A major science-based occupant of the center is the Polaroid Corporation.

Later on, MIT was to embark on a program of helping Cambridge enlarge and expand the amount of housing available in the city, particularly for the benefit of the elderly. The Institute also joined Harvard in creating the Cambridge Corporation, which served for a limited period to promote still additional housing. These undertakings came in response to organized efforts in the Cambridge community to offset any possible impact of the universities in preempting housing that was needed for the elderly and low-income families.

When the state appeared to be moving inevitably to the building of a bitterly opposed Inner Belt highway through Cambridge, MIT found itself in the difficult position of having to oppose a route that would have isolated its campus and have other baneful effects on its future development. To replace any housing that might be destroyed by the Inner Belt, the Institute acquired sites for substitute housing. Fortunately the Inner Belt has never been built.

At another time the National Aeronautics and Space Administration undertook to build an Electronics Center in Cambridge, motivated by a desire to be near the two major educational institutions. Early plans for this Electronics Center would have placed it so close to the MIT campus that it too might well have blocked future developments. This led the Institute, against opposition, to support the city in a redevelopment project that resulted in a better location for the Electronics Center. Because of a rapid cutback by Congress in federal funds for the space agency at about the time the Electronics Center was being completed, the agency was forced to announce that it would not use the facilities it had built and would put them up for sale for unspecified use. At that time I made a determined effort to persuade the government not to abandon this property, which had been arranged for with so much difficulty and grief by the city. This effort was successful in that what was to be a center for NASA was converted into a research center for the Department of Transportation.

My initial interest in urban redevelopment in Cambridge had resulted from my participation in the Citizens Advisory Committee which had been appointed in 1956 by the Cambridge City Council "to foster comprehensive city rebuilding and redevelopment by private enterprise." Both President Pusey of Harvard and I served on this committee along with a dedicated group of concerned citizens. It was an important educational experience for me.

The creation of Technology Square as a research park certainly played a role in influencing the current redevelopment now proceeding in Kendall Square. Four great buildings are already changing the skyline, and there are more to come. It is not boastful to say that the presence of MIT has been a major factor in bringing this highly underdeveloped area to a point where it will provide additional jobs, new high-technology enterprises, increased tax receipts, and much-welcomed amenities.

WALTER L. MILNE: AMBASSADOR TO CAMBRIDGE

In Great Britain his title would be private secretary to the prime minister; at MIT we call him assistant to the chairman and the president. Given the range of his duties external to the Institute, he might be dubbed foreign minister since he has been the principal officer at MIT who represents it in its relations with the city of Cambridge.

After having served as assistant to Jim Rowlands, director of the News Office, and then to Francis Wylie, director of public relations, he joined the presidential staff in 1958, during the period I was in Washington, and there provided my successor, President Stratton, with valuable continuity. Later during my chairmanship, when I began to give special attention to MIT's Cambridge relationships, he carried on the work that had been assigned to James Kelso and Frank Colcord. Although he concentrated mainly on maintaining MIT's good relations with Cambridge, he also shared many of my burdens as chairman.

It was soon recognized within and without the Institute that he had special gifts for the cultivation of amiable town-and-gown relationships. When the officials of the Cambridge city government wished to pursue a matter at MIT, they usually turned to Walter to be the liaison officer. So skillful were his relations and negotiations with the civic leaders and politicians of our city that on one happy occasion he was dubbed by Cambridge officials MIT's ambassador to the city. His diplomacy in handling affairs led me to conclude that MIT had the best civic relations of any institution in the city.

Beyond these more formal responsibilities he had qualities that led officers of the Institute to turn to him for counsel and advice on many matters, as, for example, in the preparation of state papers, and for assisting Vincent Fulmer in supporting the Corporation members in their duties and in their goings and comings.

Although he began his career at the Institute as a journalist, he has come to serve five different presidents, each of whom turned to him for advice and to benefit from him in the role he developed as trusted counselor as they dealt with the weals and woes of the presidency.

VENTURE CAPITAL FOR SCIENCE-BASED COMPANIES ON ROUTE 128

The same innovative risk-taking spirit that animated teaching and research at MIT in the postwar period also found expression in a burst of entrepreneurship on the part of scientists and engineers studying or working at MIT, some still in their larval stage as graduate students. A canard widely expressed in the decade of the thirties claimed that young Americans had lost their zeal for taking risks, especially for engaging in economic ventures. Possibly the Depression had imposed a deadening play-it-safe attitude or a loss of entrepreneurial bravery that once was the hallmark of many young.

As the postwar generation of academic scientists and engineers began to see the economic potential of ideas that were then being generated in research laboratories, they sought to form companies to exploit these ideas but were frequently discouraged by the difficulty of finding venture capital to finance new enterprises.

For some time Karl Compton had been preaching "Put Science to Work" from his bully MIT pulpit, pointing out the potential contributions it could make to invigorate our sluggish society as we were emerging from the Great Depression. He and others such as Merrill Griswold, chairman of Massachusetts Investors Trust, recognized the need not only to put science and technology to work but to stimulate the financial community to provide the venture capital that would be needed to finance new science-based companies. They recognized that nearly half of the wealth of New England was frozen in fiduciary institutions including insurance companies, trust companies, and universities. Some of this capital might be put to venture use. Fortunately another prescient New Englander, Ralph Flanders, was reaching similar conclusions. His experience as an engineer, the builder of high-technology industry in Vermont, senator, and MIT Corporation member incited him to encourage new science-based enterprises, and he and Compton joined forces with imaginative business leaders and two other technologists from MIT in encouraging the formation of a venture capital firm that was to be called American Research & Development Corporation. Senator Flanders was the first president, but he soon found a permanent leader to head this new firm, Professor Georges Doriot of the Harvard Business School. This group, together with a handful of enlightened Boston business men, inspired a cohort of bankers to see the opportunities in high technology for the creation of new industries.

The result was an industrial boost for Massachusetts, largely based on electronics and a new concept of companies performing research and development as the main purpose of their business. It was to be dramatized by the shorthand "Route 128 Effect" as new enterprises built laboratories and factories on the new circumferential highway, Route 128, around Boston (and later, Route 495). These encouraging developments incited other scientists and engineers in MIT and Harvard laboratories to put their inventions and ideas to work by creating high-technology companies. Especially did the great research laboratories sponsored by the federal government at MIT become seedbeds of new science-based industry. Gordon Brown's Servomechanisms Laboratory, Stark Draper's Instrumentation Laboratory, the Research Laboratory of Electronics, and then the newly established Lincoln Laboratory all became sources of new products and processes and new entrepreneurs to commercialize them. Vannevar Bush already had provided examples of entrepreneurship through his role in launching the Spencer Thermostat Company and his participation in the formation of Raytheon. One observer has estimated that MIT personnel and research have engendered more than 400 companies.

This surge of efforts to found new companies inevitably resulted in some failures. But in new assets created, the successes exceeded the failures, and there occurred a benign epidemic of new corporate formations. Perhaps the most spectacular example of a new enterprise launched by an MIT engineer from an MIT laboratory is the Digital Equipment Corporation. In 1957 Kenneth H. Olsen, a graduate engineer in MIT's Lincoln Laboratory, saw the possibility of developing transistorized computers that would be smaller and more flexible than the then-existing large computers. With the help of $70,000 in seed money obtained from American Research & Development, Olsen launched a company located in an old mill in Maynard, Massachusetts. He and his young associates "confounded the conventional wisdom of Wall Street and the management experts and made a phenomenal success of being a maverick," and Digital grew to be second in size only to IBM. In an address before a meeting of the Newcomen Society, Olsen explained that he brought to his new company some organizational ideas from MIT: "There was an attitude and environment at MIT that we wanted to duplicate. It's hard to describe but MIT was and, I think to a large degree is, a very generous, a very trusting, and a very challenging environment. That environment was one of the things we wanted to capture and bring to our own company. We had so much confidence in MIT that we even followed the MIT operations manual. We took the same hours, we took the same vacations, we paid the same holidays. The state came by and said you can't pay on those days, it's illegal. We said MIT does; the state said we can't control MIT, but we can control you."

Other entrepreneurs building new companies have noted the special ways MIT has aided them. "We chose to be near MIT," said one, "because it helped us. It is not a matter of proximity. It is a matter of never having left." Others have mentioned the access MIT provides to special equipment and research, others the close relationship between faculty members and students.[16] These mutually beneficial relationships help to explain studies by Professor Edward Roberts which show that of 215 high-tech companies he studied in the Boston area, 156 were created in MIT departments and laboratories.

There is reason to believe that the experience that young engineers and scientists had in the military services or that the education they received in postwar laboratories encouraged them to abjure academic constraints and become technically bold or, to use Kenneth Olsen's word, "brave" in developing and commercializing high technology.

With the spectacular growth of Kenneth Olsen's Digital Equipment Corporation, American Research & Development became the most conspicuously successful of the venture capital organizations that appeared in this period. It became quite fashionable to promote institutions for providing funds to back new products, particularly new products emerging from university laboratories. It also became necessary for university administrators to give tough-minded thought to patent policies and the professional standards of staffs and institutions. Several of us at

MIT were associated with the formation of the Baystate Science Foundation. Still other funds or venture capital organizations were formed as, for example, the New England Enterprise Capital Corporation, and earlier, William Coolidge had established his Enterprise Associates. Still earlier and outside the boundaries of New England, Laurance Rockefeller, J. H. Whitney and Company, and the Phipps family fund were among the venturesome pioneers in finding productive uses of venture capital. A spirit of adventure was abroad both in the technical community and the financial community, with MIT personnel moved by the stimulating entrepreneurial climate that marked the decades following the war. To recognize the failures with the successes, I must add that the financial communities both in Boston and New York are still very inadequate providers of venture capital. They seriously lack staff broad-gauged enough to understand the uses of technology. With brilliant exceptions they timidly ignore good opportunities for venture capital investments as well as their social responsibility to "put science to work" for the economic benefit of their communities and the nation.

In the second lustrum of the 1970s and on into the 80s, a new surge of entrepreneurial energy appeared both on the part of high technologists and venture capitalists. Biotechnology, microelectronics, and robotics were domains of daring, and research universities, particularly those strong in molecular biology and electronics, were finding themselves confronted with novel new issues of policy as they struggled to conform academic integrity with the exploration of the exciting entrepreneurial research ventures that offered opportunities for new Route 128's.

14
EXCERPTS FROM A PERSONAL JOURNAL

EPISODES 1, 2, AND 3—NOTES ON AN ILLNESS
I have spoken of the essential responsibilities carried by the wife of a college president. From the very beginning of my term I was deeply dependent on my wife, Liz, as was the Institute community, and she in turn had easily carried her partnership duties, as both wife and mother, with joy, grace, and complete commitment.

Liz had always seemed exceptionally strong physically. We had hiked together in the mountains and gone to remote fishing camps for vacations. One mountain climbing expedition was an overnight trip in August to the top of Maine's Mt. Katahdin, which we found embroidered with feather ice. Before starting up, I sought out the ranger to get information about the trail. I asked him if in his judgment my wife could climb with a small pack to a lean-to half way up the mountain, where we wished to spend the night. He looked Liz up and down and gave his answer: "She could carry fifty pounds!" In all the chapters of our life she has never hesitated to carry fifty pounds, however demanding the trail.

So it was with staggering impact on us all when she was felled in 1955, at the early age of forty-eight, by a sequence of three strokes, the first and third massive in their hurt. The first stroke came on February 24. I was out of town, as I so frequently had to be, this time in Toledo for an Engineers Week dinner of the Toledo Technical Council and to visit potential contributors. She was taken to the hospital by James Howard Means, MIT medical director, and by her friend Carol Brooks (wife of E. P. Brooks, dean of the Sloan School), who had called in the early morning for a visit.

By the end of two weeks, happily, she was back in the President's House to convalesce and to start the long recovery.

In the spring there came a second episode, this time when I was reading to her one evening from one of Henry Mencken's *Prejudices* his vivid salute to Beethoven. Fortunately this stroke was mild, but the doctors decreed that she should go back to the hospital for the ligation of veins in her legs to prevent the escape of blood clots. There had been other disconcerting symptoms.

We ventured an evening at the theater for a benefit performance of *Most Happy Fella*, and Liz saw not one performance but two, as double vision was imposed on her sight. We were seated at this event alongside Dr. George Berry, dean of the Harvard Medical School, and his concern was obvious as he became aware of her plight. From this cerebral accident she seemed rapidly to recover.

But the worst was yet to come. In October of that year 1955, another stroke occurred, a massive one. After leaving her at the hospital this time, I was almost bereft of hope and despairingly wandered the streets of Boston for half a day. Her throat, right side, arm, hand, and leg were paralyzed. For a period all too long, it was touch and go. The anticoagulant Dicumerol, only then being introduced, was used, and Liz was one of the first patients to be placed on it. The determination of the proper dosage was tricky; in fact hemorrhaging sent Liz into shock, there was a frightening crisis, and the children were called, our son from his Army assignment at Ft. Devens.

Good medical care by Raymond Adams, famous neurologist of the MGH, Liz's vitality, and her determination, however, brought her out of the crises. I shall never forget, while in some of her lowest moments, hearing her quote from Robert Frost:

The woods are lovely, dark and deep.
But I have promises to keep,
And miles to go before I sleep,
And miles to go before I sleep.[1]

The first solid food she managed to swallow was a bit of banana, and when he heard of this, our friend Hartley Rowe of the United Fruit Company offered to send her whole bunches of bananas. Later he and his wife accompanied us on a United Fruit banana boat to Honduras, a health-restoring trip for a convalescent.

One of the memorable celebrations in our family was the Thanksgiving following this third episode, when Liz was allowed to come home from the hospital for Thanksgiving dinner with the family. She was on crutches as she was to be for many months, and required other assistance, but she was gay and shared our joy.

Her recovery over the years could only be partial, although it was steady and reassuring, and she candidly coped with residual effects and resumed many of her activities. Superficially her recovery seemed miraculous, but she and I have been acutely aware that massive strokes always leave their signature.

When I was called to Washington in 1957 to be special assistant to the president for science and technology, Liz, as advised by her physicians, decided to keep her home base in Cambridge. It was lonely for me and her thus to live apart, but we sought to ease the separation, she traveling occasionally to Washington and I to Cambridge. When she traveled to Washington, it was usually for the purpose of attending state dinners at the White House or other special events, and I came to Cambridge for MIT events.

Back in Cambridge in 1959 the lives of both of us underwent drastic change, with the most difficult adjustments falling on her. She never flinched and found greater strength and spirit, in our new context, to share with others, of which I am ever-gratefully one.

This account permits me to reiterate the extraordinary support that she—and I—received from the MIT community during her illness. Sustained expressions of thoughtfulness had left us with a deepened understanding of its humanitarian and wondrously kind support. A group of alumni offered to install an elevator in the President's House, and at Christmas time, 1955, the MIT Choral Society assembled at the President's House to sing carols and madrigals to cheer her along her way.

In 1983 the MIT Women's League arranged for a portrait to be added to the array of past and future portraits of presidential wives, and our daughter, Carolyn Staley, blessed our fifty-fourth wedding anniversary (August 21, 1983) by writing, "Fifty-four years is a beautiful achievement of stability, commitment, and love." While addressed to both of us, this note might have justly been addressed to Liz alone.

A VERY SPECIAL PROFESSORSHIP

In 1966 an endowed chair in the humanities was underwritten by my classmates with the request that it be called in perpetuity the Elizabeth and James Killian 1926 Professorship. Liz and I felt deeply grateful for this act of generosity and friendship, the more so since we knew how much the Institute needed endowed chairs, especially in the humanities.

In addition two wonderful men associated with the establishment of the chair gave it very special meaning for us. One of these was my colorful classmate, I. Austin Kelly, who led the campaign to fund the chair; the other, Professor Elting Morison, the first full-time Killian Professor, whose achievements as historian, biographer, and humanist endowed the chair with humane and scholarly distinction.

In 1983 the MIT Libraries invited Austin, its honorary curator of rare books, to present a lecture on his experiences and goals as a collector and to exhibit some of his rarities. Inspired by the lecture, Professor Richard Douglas later remarked that Austin was a passionate man—passionate, I added, in his good works, in his good taste, and in his devotion to institutions he had attended for his education. Especially had he become an ardent advocate of the humanities at his alma mater, where he majored in general engineering.

Elting Morison joined MIT in 1946, having already made his mark as a biographer and historian with his book *Admiral Sims and the Modern American Navy*. After joining the MIT faculty, he published *Turmoil and Tradition: A Study of the Life and Times of Henry L. Stimson* and edited *The Letters of Theodore Roosevelt* (in eight volumes). After these major contributions to history, his scholarly interests began to take a new direction, influenced, no doubt, by his immersion in the excitements of MIT. "Virtually all the work done in its buildings," he noted, "is directly related to the extended applications of old forms of power and the development of the means to produce new forms of power. Simply to live and work as an historian in such a place was a liberal education. . . ."

The new directions his interests were taking found first expression in a book he published in 1966, *Men, Machines, and Modern Times* (The MIT Press). He directed his attention more and more to the development of American technology and ways to bring this technology humanely into the service of man. And his most recent book, *From Know-How to Nowhere: The Development of American Technology,* contains essays on episodes in the history of American technology and, more important, his philosophical considerations of how the great impact of ever-widening technological achievement could be adapted to humane use in our society. "If we are to build a new firmament fit for us to live in out of the materials and forces now available," he concluded, "our first order of business is to develop a knowledge of ourselves, and a respect for ourselves, certain enough to enable us to build a technological firmament that will really fit us."

With the encouragement of President Wiesner, Elting designed a new highway to this firmament—a new program of teaching and research at MIT, the Program in Science, Technology, and Society—and once expressed the hope that it might be called New College within the MIT complex. I supported him in the development of this program.

Jerry Wiesner has spoken of the profound influence that Elting Morison came to have on his life, beginning with their meetings as members of the subcommitee on environment of the Lewis Committee.

I also had the opportunity, as a trustee of Educational Services Incorporated, of encouraging the development of a program in social studies for lower schools. Two of the people associated with Elting in this project were Professors Franklin Patterson and Jerome Bruner. Bruner was to present in his own autobiography, *In Search of Mind,* a play-by-play account of the triumphs and political controversies engendered by this interesting educational effort along with a splendid tribute to the insights, the influence, and the intellectual powers of Elting.

In his writing and in his speaking, Elting achieved a luminous, often metaphorical style. His gift for writing with irony, wit, and allusion has lent admired liveness to his scholarship.

During his active career at MIT, he was the center of gravity, the convenor, of a fellowship representing both Harvard and MIT, and in this capacity he contributed importantly to the collegiality of what we can appropriately call the University of Cambridge. His wide reach as a humanist together with his scholarship and his attracting visions made his appointment to the Killian chair an occasion for celebration by Liz and me—and by Austin Kelly, representing the class of 1926.

THE ROSE OF SHARON

In the tiny village of Sharon, New Hampshire (population 188), my wife and I recharged our batteries in a country retreat, now regretfully sold, a two-hundred-year-old farmhouse perched on a windy flank of Temple Mountain at an elevation of 1,300 feet. From this point of vantage we had a sweeping view of the Contoocook Valley and of Mount Monadnock.

We struggled to maintain on this site a hostel for family gatherings, a modest, shaggy cottage garden, a small arboretum consisting in part of trees and shrubs, some exotic to the region, and a marble statue in the outmoded neoclassic Canova style and bearing the signature S. Albano F. Firenze 1882.

The provenance of this sculpture in this woodland setting makes a story for telling. The piece had been commissioned for his music room by Gordon McKay, donor to Harvard of a large fund in support there of engineering education. When Harvard and MIT agreed on a plan for all instruction in engineering to be given at MIT for both institutions, Harvard also agreed that the McKay endowment income would be used in support of the joint program. This use of the McKay fund was challenged, and in November 1917 the Supreme Judicial Court of Massachusetts declared the plan invalid, much to the distress of Presidents Lowell of Harvard and Maclaurin of MIT, who shared enthusiasm for the arrangement.

McKay also provided by bequest for this music room statue, but it ended in the estate of Mrs. Stanley McCormick, MIT's great alumna and donor. After having kept it stored in a warehouse in her lifetime, she in turn bequeathed it to Radcliffe

College, which declined to accept it, probably because of the
problem posed by displaying an explicit nude figure, however
delicate, on a college campus. Under the terms of the McCormick will, any rejected bequest provided for in her will became a
part of her major bequest to MIT. The Institute also backed away
from displaying the statute and was tempted to consider its sale,
perhaps to a stone cutter or tombstone maker who might value
it only for its beautiful marble. Because of my association with
Mrs. McCormick over the years, as well as the historical background of the statue, I had indicated that in the event that the
statue would be disposed of, I would like to have a chance to
purchase it. As a result I received a letter from Vincent Fulmer,
then chairman of the Board of Governors of MIT's Endicott
House, indicating that it would like to acquire the piece from
MIT and offer it as a gift to me. But what could I do with it? After
deliberation and guided by sentiments of appreciation and respect for Mrs. McCormick, I replied that I had spotted at my
place in New Hampshire a retreat for the Sleeping Girl, "a
woodland bower where it will be surrounded by 'sounds and
sweet airs that give delight and hurt not' and where appreciative
dryads will give it loving care." And so the Sleeping Girl twice
rejected came to rest in Sharon in front of arranged hemlocks at
the distant end of an upsloping allée lined on both sides by
Rhamnus frangula columnaris.

In this discrete setting, as a piece of garden sculpture, the
Sleeping Girl served the vagaries of my gardening in the wild.
Inevitably members of my family came resignedly to speak of it
as the Rose of Sharon.

Shortly after acquiring our Sharon home, "Big Maple," I had
become a devoted participant in the affairs of the nearby Sharon
Arts Center. (I was acting out Walter Lander's epigram, "Nature
I loved, and, next to Nature, Art.") I admired the community
energies that had been brought to bear to create and maintain
this interesting woodland institution and even now that I am
sixty miles away, I maintain my association with the enterprise.
When we sold our house, I decided to give the statue of the
Sleeping Girl to the Sharon Arts Center, which it accepted with

enthusiasm. With a generosity and friendship that I shall always cherish, the government of the Sharon Arts Center voted that its gallery should bear the Killian name, and on the occasion when this was announced, there was a community gathering that will remain in my memory because of the warm friendships that it represented. I found special satisfaction in concurrently being a trustee of Boston's great Museum of Fine Arts and of Sharon's unique Arts Center.

Soon after we purchased Big Maple in 1967, we planted a pagoda tree (*Sophora japonica*) not then aware that pagoda trees sometimes delay blooming for a score or more years after they are planted. Our tree, it seemed, was programmed this way, but no: shortly before we gave up our retreat, the tree burst into bloom for the first time. It seemed that our "Chinese scholar tree," by being "hung with bloom," was staging for us a gracious good-by.

My sister, Ruth, and her lawyer husband, Richard Nichols, have long had a place in Sharon as well as their home in Wellesley, Massachusetts, and it was they who first made clear to us the seductions of Sharon. Ruth is learned in the identification of wild flowers and brings a kind of witchcraft to bear in the cultivation of gardens whether in Wellesley or Sharon. Dick finds pleasure in the druidic mysteries of forests and in their care. He is also handy with ax and chain saw.

Both Nicholses have contributed in humane and loving ways to the life of the Killians far beyond Sharon.

ANECDOTES AND TRIVIA

"Anecdotes," said Churchill, "are the gleaming toys of history." I have collected over the years for my journal a handful of episodes that can be described as such gleaming toys.

● A wartime visitor, famed but abdicated, was brought to the Institute under bizarre circumstances. At that time our MIT Information Office was presided over by a rotund figure of modest status and quite routine responsibility by the name of Willie Jackson. He had read in the press that Wallis Warfield, Duchess of Windsor, was to bring her Aunt Bessie to Boston for medical reasons and that she would be accompanied by her husband, the Duke of Windsor. In an outbreak of hospitality Willie sat himself down and addressed a letter to the Windsors inviting them to come to MIT during their stay in Boston, but he forgot to tell the front office that he had done so. I received one day a phone call from the British Consul in Boston asking me what our plans were for receiving the Duke of Windsor, who had accepted, he said, MIT's invitation to visit us, and I had to explain with embarrassment that I had no knowledge of his visit but that we would welcome such a distinguished guest. My associates and I promptly went into action, and through the good offices of Dr. DuBridge, director of the Radiation Laboratory, we arranged to get the duke enough clearance to show him some of the parts of this American radar project, which owed so much to British science. And so with great fanfare the duke appeared, and we had a very good time with him and with the British Consul, who took the matter in stride. After the duke's departure I firmly instructed Willie Jackson to notify the front office before he issued any more formal invitations to distinguished personages even though we could welcome them with the same enthusiasm that marked our reception of the duke.

As we escorted the duke through the labyrinth of laboratories, the wave of surprise and excitement was clearly visible in these carefully guarded precincts. At one spot I heard a voice cry out: "For God's sake look who's broken through the guards."

● Jan Christiaan Smuts, the great prime minister of South Africa and natural philosopher, came secretly to the Institute during the war to visit MIT's large Metallurgical Project and Professor of Metallurgy Antoine Gaudin.† The atomic bomb research in the Manhattan Project had launched an intensive search for uranium, and deposits had been discovered in the Belgian Congo and South Africa. But the uranium in Africa required unusual extractive processes for which the talents and technology of Professor Gaudin were needed. Gaudin informed me of General Smuts's incognito visit, and after the technical discussions, the three of us forgathered for a secret luncheon. I was aware that Smuts had been a student at Cambridge during the period that Richard Maclaurin (later to be the sixth president of the Institute) was there and that they had become close friends. After the luncheon I took Prime Minister Smuts to see a portrait of Maclaurin that then hung in the president's office, and he recalled that at one time he had sought to attract Maclaurin, some sixteen years or more after their Cambridge days, to head an educational program for the new Dominion of South Africa. A guerrilla fighter against the British during the Boer War, Smuts was later to become a British subject.

● In 1949 Jawaharal Nehru, first prime minister of independent India, made a state visit to the United States, and Harvard University and MIT were on his itinerary. The Killians were just moving into the President's House, but at the request of the State Department we undertook a reception there for the prime minister. Again at the request of State, we invited Indian students studying in the metropolitan Boston area but also students from recently created Pakistan, a total of several hundred. My wife recalls that as Nehru and his party arrived at the front door, the workmen who had been reconditioning the President's House were just leaving by the back door. He was accompanied by his distinguished sister, Madam Pandit, and other foreign officers of the Indian government.

Nehru had indicated that he did not wish to speak. His sister was ready, even anxious, to speak and did so in the garden, but Nehru sat brooding in the living room, with the students too awed to talk to him. I finally decided to bring the meeting alive by saying some words of welcome, which of course the occasion demanded. To my surprise and everyone's delight, Nehru arose and spoke graciously and at length to the assembled group. Part of his remarks were in Hindi and part in English. His presence and his informal remarks made it a great occasion for the Indian and Pakistani students who were present. It is not likely that in their home countries they could ever have had the opportunity to be so close in an informal setting to the distinguished prime minister.

We at the Institute were on pins and needles because of the mixture of Indian and Pakistani students, Pakistan having been created as a separate nation a short time before by the British when they agreed to an independent India. Happily the occasion went off without incident, a memorable event for those of us at MIT.

Later, in the early 1960s, when I was in Delhi, the Ford Foundation arranged for me to call on the prime minister at his modest office. Again his brooding presence made it difficult to engage in conversation, but when he did talk, he dwelt at some length on student unrest in universities especially in Indian universities, and inquired whether such unrest was occurring in America. His inquiry and comments were prophetic because they came only a few years before the disruptive events began in American universities in 1964.

When I was in India in January 1970 to speak on the occasion of the tenth anniversary of the Birla Institute's transformation to a full-fledged institute of technology, I remembered my conversation a decade before with Prime Minister Nehru about student dissent and unrest. A cable had been sent to me by MIT officers in Cambridge reporting that students had broken into and occupied the office of MIT's President Howard Johnson and then moved on to occupy mine, which was in the same suite. As the cable trailed me about Delhi, its sensational message was quoted place after place as the cable office sought to catch up with me. It confirmed the prime minister's earlier concern and almost made me a celebrity.

• 1965 brought to Cambridge a visitor of quite a different kind, Mrs. Harold Wilson, wife of the recently elected prime minister of Great Britain.

Earlier that year, during a Ford Foundation-sponsored trip to England, I was invited to visit Chequers to lunch with Prime Minister Harold Wilson and his family. This visit had been arranged by Lord Bowden; the purpose of the visit to Chequers was to discuss British education. This luncheon occurred not long after Wilson had become prime minister, and after lunch he asked Lord Bowden and myself if we would like to explore Chequers guided by its "curator," who had served in that role under a succession of prime ministers. He noted that he and

Mrs. Wilson had only recently begun to use the great house and they would welcome this first opportunity to explore it and learn more about its colorful history.

At this luncheon I of course met Mrs. Wilson. Later, on a trip to Washington, the prime minister brought his wife, and she slipped away from official affairs there to visit her son who temporarily was at MIT. She was alone on this trip, unaccompanied by any retinue such as our Secret Service, and she had quietly secured a room at a modest inn in Cambridge. We discovered her presence and invited her to join us in going to one of the Coolidge luncheons which I described earlier in this memoir. It is hard to imagine, I later reflected, the wife of an American president traveling alone in a foreign country or even in America.

• Back in the days when American cities were calling attention to themselves by staging salutes to great foreign cities, Boston followed suit in 1955 by arranging a fanfare for Rome, Italy. One of the events associated with this Salute to Rome was a visit to Boston by the Mayor of Rome, Professor Salvatore Rebecchini, who came under the sponsorship of the State Department and the U.S. Information Agency.

MIT was delighted to receive the mayor-professor not only because an academician had achieved this post but because MIT had a number of distinguished Italians on its faculty. On being asked to receive the mayor, we arranged a morning reception and invited to it all the professors of Italian background who were on the faculty of the Institute. These MIT professors included Dean Pietro Belluschi of the School of Architecture and Planning, Professor of Humanities Giorgio de Santillana, Professor of Electrical Engineering Robert Fano, and Professor of Physics Bruno Rossi. Our welcome to the mayor was the greater because it turned out that he was professor of applied physics in the University of Rome's Faculty of Architecture. He in turn enthusiastically stopped by MIT because he wanted to visit with our dean of architecture, Pietro Belluschi, a native-born Italian and an alumnus of the University of Rome.

Among those in Mayor Rebecchini's retinue was John A.

Volpe, then commissioner of public works of the Commonwealth of Massachusetts and later to become, during the sixties and seventies, respectively, governor of Massachusetts, U.S. secretary of transportation, and finally U.S. ambassador to Italy.

The mayor was obviously pleased with the distinguished array of personages who gathered to greet him, but a latecomer was to add another kind of glamour to our receiving line— pugilist Rocky Marciano, at that time world heavyweight boxing champion. In an exhibit of his acute political sensitivities Mr. Volpe had thought to add Rocky to the list, and indeed he proved to be the hit of the day. He confronted the array of academicians with the same poise and confidence with which he faced opponents in the ring.

Rocky was one of Boston's greats, and his early death was a grievous blow. His graceful venture into the academic world left a spoor that I at least continue to identify with pleasure.

● The 1903 report of the Committee on the Charles River Dam chaired by President Henry Pritchett based on engineering plans executed by MIT alumnus John R. Freeman resulted in the creation of the Charles River Basin in 1908. The necessary legal actions taken by the state and surrounding municipalities did not provide for securing forever the protection of all the land under the water of the basin. Many years later, realtors, discovering the fact that some of the land now under water might be purchased and developed, began a campaign to find ways to build buildings in the basin. This came to the attention of a bold and adventurous realtor in New York, who called me as President of MIT to ask if he could come up to see me with his architectural adviser to discuss plans developed in his office for the use of available land in the Charles River Basin. With this advance information I panted to see him, and he arrived with a roll of plans and a young architect, a graduate of MIT, subsequently a "hero" of the architectural profession. These plans were in effect proposals for the erection of buildings offshore. They were dramatic and in many ways beautiful, but I was startled by the thought that there should be any significant action to desecrate the great lake so important and useful to metropolitan Boston. This realtor was Zeckendorf; the young man accompanying him, his architectural consultant. They rolled out their plans on the floor of my office and in the process of examining them, Zeckendorf came forward with the question of the day. "Would MIT have any objection to the developments in the basin conceived by him and his office?" My response was immediate and unmistakably final. "MIT," I said, "would use every resource at its disposal to prevent any kind of development that would disturb the basin and desecrate its loveliness."

Mr. Zeckendorf was a perceptive man when dealing with problems of this kind, and his immediate response was, "President Killian, that's all we need to know. I'll forget about the whole concept." And he rolled up his plans and departed from an encounter that was startling but amiable in understanding by both parties.

And the young architect who came with Zeckendorf? I. M. Pei, no less. Since then he has designed a number of MIT's finest buildings, has been a member of the MIT Corporation, and is one of America's most honored architects.

● Numerous episodes involving students occurred while we were living in the President's House. One year during Freshman Orientation Week two freshmen rang the bell of the big front door and when they were admitted, they said they were in an argument, one being from Texas, the other from California, and each was sure that the longest straight line from border to border could be drawn in his home state. They wanted a map or a globe to settle their argument; could we provide one? We did, and California proved to be the right answer. But the moral of the episode was that the freshmen from different parts of the country were rapidly coming to know each other.

On another occasion the doorbell rang around midnight. My wife and I reluctantly came downstairs to see who the caller was. It turned out that he was a student who had just discovered that the next day was a holiday and that he could combine this with the weekend to go skiing. His trouble was that he didn't have any cash, and would we please lend him some money so that he could get away early the next morning to go for a long skiing weekend. It happened that we kept a cache of money for just these kinds of emergencies or even more serious ones when a student needed money to go home as a result of illness.

When I told this story, at a senior dinner, about the student borrowing money to go skiing and remarked that the check he had given me had not bounced, I noticed in the audience a number of students pointing to one of their comrades and thus indicating that the event was recalled four years later.

Another night at the President's House I was working into the small hours of the morning in my study, which was located on that side of the house nearest to the adjacent dormitories. The telephone rang and I grumpily went to answer it and it turned out to be a student calling from the adjacent dormitory who said they noticed that my light was on and wondered if I might come over and join a bull session. I had the gumption to accept the invitation and as a result, spent a highly informative as well as pleasant hour discussing what was wrong with the Institute.

• Professor Frederick G. Fassett and his wife, Julie, were beloved figures at the Institute in my day. He had taught in the Department of English and History and then succeeded me as editor of the *Technology Review*, and from that position he went on to become dean of residence. On one occasion something that the police would probably have called a panty raid aimed at Radcliffe seemed to be gathering force on the campus, and in moving in to quell the disturbance, they arrested several whom they thought to be participants. One of these was Dean Fassett himself, and it was not long before I received a plaintive call from the police station that Fassett was there. I moved rapidly to free him from the clutches of the police and to make clear that this gentle man had nothing riotous in his makeup and that clearly there had been a mistake in identity.

• In its green days the magazine *Esquire* occasionally published for its center spreads photographs of nubile ladies. In April 1975, in an act of surprising editorial anomaly, it published for this center spread a photograph of thirteen elderly Bostonians, certainly not nubile, then ranging in age from seventy to eighty-eight. The former editor of the *Atlantic*, Edward Weeks, had selected the group and brought them together in his living room. The implication of the photograph was that Boston is a good place in which to grow old, and indeed the beaming faces in the photograph, of which I was one, seem to express this theme.

Included in the picture were former Speaker of the House the late John W. McCormack, Harvard classics professor John H. Finley, Jr., the late Arthur Fiedler, conductor of the Boston Pops Orchestra, the late historian Samuel Eliot Morison, the late U.S. Senator Leverett Saltonstall, poet David McCord, and other worthies. A number of these I had come to know well through memberships in conversation or dining clubs such as the famous Saturday Club, the Examiner, the Library Society, the Thursday Evening Club, and other venerable groups which flourish in the benign Boston cultural environment. I should say in Cambridge too, where I live and work, but let's simply say that Boston is a part of metropolitan Cambridge.

The Library Society, the most intimate of these clubs, derives its name from its role in founding the Athenaeum, Boston's famous private library. The club meets mostly in members' homes, and black tie is in order. Van Bush had been a member before he died, and Din Land almost always shows up for the meeting.

These clubs provide rich opportunities for comradeship and conversation, and I have found in them fellowship and intellectual stimulation which have taken me out of the cloistered academic life, an important dimension for one who has spent most of his days in an educational institution.

15
THE EMERGENCE OF A UNIVERSITY POLARIZED AROUND SCIENCE

ON THE "REAL BUSINESS" OF THE UNIVERSITY

In various parts of this book I have sought to identify those forces and influences that have brought MIT to a place among the institutions in the forefront of the world's leading universities. I was therefore encouraged to receive, in August 1982, from Elting Morison a letter reporting that he and Walter Rosenblith were planning an oral history project "to retrieve some of the parts of MIT's past . . . that can't be obtained from the paper record. . . ." "We thought," he wrote, "we would begin with the years 1945–1960, when the Institute began the transition from, essentially, a school of engineering toward a university polarized around science."

Later, as the oral history was delayed and in response to my eager importuning, Morison composed for me a statement in which he presented, with the perception of an historian, some of the reasons leading him to conclude that from 1945–1960, "MIT was moving very rapidly into the real business of a modern university." In his statement, Morison quotes as his text an astonishingly prescient observation made many decades ago by the British natural philosopher, Samuel Alexander (1859–1938).[1] "If I were asked to point to the most distinctive feature of university work," declared Alexander, "I would say it was the inclusion of technology and that that inclusion is the best key to the understanding of the real business of a university."

Recognizing the enormous impact of World War II on the Institute, Morison notes that from MIT's founding "the central mission had been to work with things and ideas that were immediately useful and in the public interest. This commitment was reinforced by the fact that many faculty members had had during the war direct and personal experience in public service." Elting concluded:

Compton and Bush had started things off during the 30's . . . and the creation of the Radiation Lab during the war had provided invaluable experience in systematic research and development. During the years 1945–1960 the Institute built steadily upon these foundations.

There was another way in which the rapidly expanding knowledge exerted its influence. New findings in many of the fields that dominate traditional universities—history, literature, for example—can ordinarily be easily assimilated in the existing body of knowledge and contained within the familiar departmental structure. In the dominant fields at MIT new findings can not only change profoundly the understanding of what has been known but they continually seek connections with learning in other departmental categories. So the Institute was being constantly shaken up not only intellectually but also structurally. This may have made it more confusing but also more responsive than more settled institutions to change and more readily subject to resourceful direction as, for instance, in the development of Centers.

Morison went on to discuss some of the subtle aspects of the attitudes toward learning at the Institute:

Historically the object of a lot of scholarship in traditional universities has been to obtain a more accurate description and fuller understanding of the given conditions—of the nature of things and of human experience. At MIT the aim, for much of its history, has been to learn what you needed to know to improve the machinery and so, presumably, to make things work better. As a result the Institute tended to become more directly engaged in the world around it than its older counterparts did. And then, as in the period in question (1945–1960) when the expanding machinery increasingly altered the given conditions of this world and brought pressure to bear on the conduct of its affairs, it was natural for those in the Institute both by the work they did and their cast of thought, to take a larger part in what was happening. Since what was happening was, in general, an effort by society to find appropriate accommodation to all the new instrumentation that MIT had helped to make available, it seemed also natural for the Institute to extend its range of learning to meet the current needs.

Here Morison was referring to new fields embraced by the Institute such as political science, psychology, the Sloan School, and "the search for the appropriate contribution of the humanities."

Morison went on to emphasize the influence of many distinguished scientists who came to MIT from Europe. "These people [and I would add several brilliant scholars from Asia] had a more cosmopolitan view than that contained in our historical psyche, wider cultural perspectives, and since they were also very good in their fields they were, I think, a very significant leaven in the existing substance." It is a startling fact that of the total present-day MIT community—students, faculty, and staff—twenty percent originally came from foreign countries. Currently we view this concentration of international scholarship as an enrichment of our intellectual resources and as a contribution to world amity, but the day may come when the urgent manpower needs of the U. S. together with aggressive foreign competition in technology may make it desirable to lean toward an increased percentage of American students.

As I summarize my explanation of the emergence of the Institute as a university, I give central importance to the role of its cosmopolitan faculty. In the postwar period it was inspired to build a complex of intellectual highways and organizations for increasing the mobility of ideas throughout the Institute. The great success of the wartime laboratories demonstrated that when the specialist is placed in such an environment, a communication network facilitating contact with other specialists, unexpected kinships, and interactions—and feedback—occur and reach out to stir new intellectual impulses in unexpected places. Such subtle changes have influenced dramatically the teaching and research society of the Institute.

In an address in 1980 Lewis Thomas used his talent for talismanic words to capture the effects I have in mind. "When human intellects," he said, "are brought close together under amiable circumstances and when the air is right, the minds keep touching each other and rebounding into other orbits, recycling and starting up new forms of energy in a mechanism rather like a Bach fugue, and there is no entropy."[2]

These arrangements, both structural and intellectual, to help minds touch each other and to rebound into other orbits dramatically speeded up the transformation of the Institute into a university. A single, unfragmented faculty in consort with one central administration, the close articulation of research and teaching, of basic science and applied science, the continuous spectrum of undergraduate and graduate studies, the mobility of ideas resulting from the high permeability of the boundaries of both departments and centers, and even the extensive interconnection of its buildings—together these all have encouraged the intellectual free enterprise, cohesion, and creative integration that turned MIT not only into a university but into a new species of university.

Next, the structural changes at MIT in the postwar period contributed profoundly to its success in carrying forward the revolutionary changes started by Compton in 1930. In a postscript to his classic lectures, *The Uses of the University*, Clark Kerr makes the flat statement that "the big research university is particularly impervious to structural changes." This has not been true of MIT. In his statement Morison speaks knowingly of MIT's being constantly shaken up not only intellectually but also structurally. His statement is supported by the successful introduction of centers such as the Research Laboratory of Electronics, the creation of the Lincoln Laboratory as an off-campus research center, and the Sloan School of Management. Several spinoffs such as Educational Services Incorporated, the Mitre Corporation, and ultimately, the Draper Laboratory also were structural changes. More recent years have brought about the establishment of Whitaker College of Health Sciences, Technology, and Management and related programs in the neurosciences and the brain sciences, the Harvard-MIT Division of Health Sciences and Technology, the Center for Cancer Research, the introduction of the Program in Science, Technology, and Society, the Arts and Media Technology Program, and the unconventional Whitehead Institute for Biomedical Research (structurally independent but intellectually conjoined). In my years at MIT I have witnessed this succession of structural changes, Clark Kerr regardless.

Kerr makes another, even blunter, observation at the end of his second postscript to *The Uses of the University*: "The research university in America still has a long way to go." Here he is on target, both about the research universities as a group and about

MIT in particular. In his statement Morison quotes from Eric Ashby, who said, "science, sociology, technology, and a liberal education are indivisible." Said Morison:

I think he means—if it's not too flowery a simile—that if one is to understand the modern world it is necessary to look upon all the different kinds of knowledge as in a single solution in which the various contributing elements, if not of equal valence, must at least be taken into equal account and accorded equal significance in their interaction.

If Sir Eric is right, and if a university is what that word itself means, then MIT is not yet a modern university (nor is any other place). During the last decades we have added new fields and beefed up some old ones, which has altered the character and enlarged the vision of the place. But in spite of some determined efforts to do so, we have not succeeded in demonstrating how these fields necessarily interact with each other or how this diverse learning is comprehended in indivisibility.

CONCLUDING REFLECTIONS ON THE RESEARCH UNIVERSITY

The indivisibility envisioned by Ashby is a goal to inspire us. But no university, MIT included, yet has the resources to launch such a daunting reform with "majesty instancy" or even "deliberate speed." We have not come far enough in demonstrating how diverse learning is comprehended in indivisibility, and such an effort, given current rigidities, could be implosive if pursued with impetuous zeal. Yet the modern research university is unique in the opportunities it offers to achieve new integrations among the liberal arts, the social sciences, and the sciences, and MIT already has demonstrated progress in accomplishing this. The Research Laboratory of Electronics in its heyday achieved an extraordinary interdisciplinary congeniality that attracted philosophers, linguists, artists, and other intellectual explorers. The Schools of Engineering and Management have on their own arranged a long-needed federation. Whitaker College achieves a confederacy of biology and the neurosciences, including the brain sciences, and finds artificial intelligence an eager ally. Marvin Minsky has defined artificial intelligence as "the science of making machines do things that would require intelligence if done by men." Despite an inadequate send-off at its launch, the Program in Science, Tecnology, and Society seeks to construct an institutional focus—"a place where men and women from different fields, at various stages of their intellectual training, from MIT and elsewhere, can be brought together to search for fuller understanding of the way scientific ideas, technical systems, and human energies and intentions interact to give shape to society." Morison, in emphasizing the need for the program as he originally conceived it, quoted a faculty member as saying, "There is no adequate focus in the Institute for what everybody talks about all the time."

In addition to formal programs, one finds throughout the Institute efforts to bring science and technology more sensitively and effectively into the creation of a humane technological society. The artist and scientist are increasingly recognizing their common origins and their current kinship. As Professor Thomas Kuhn has said, we have only begun to discover the benefit of seeing science and art as one. The ideal, William James said long ago, "is the union of the mathematician with the poet, fervor with measure, passion with correctness." Spontaneously formed academic partnerships are one of the surest routes to an ultimate comprehensive indivisibility.

The 1970 report of Kenneth Hoffman's Commission on MIT Education expressed views less sanguine than mine about the progress being made by MIT to achieve a closer relationship between science and the humanities. Stressing the need in university education of a tie between knowledge and values, the report concluded that MIT must face the question of why, after much effort, "we have still not overcome the separation of the humanities and the sciences in the intellectual life of the Institute." The report candidly concluded: "Within the university, the separation of scientific activity from broader cultural and intellectual concerns has all but destroyed the capacity of academics to think of themselves as members of one common profession with shared intellectual and moral concerns."[3]

There are academic Jeremiahs today who express despondent

views about the future quality of our universities. The impact of disarray in precollege schools, of government regulation and intrusion, of demographic trends, and of decreased funds for research taken together have created anomie and loss of self-confidence in some institutions. A disturbing loss in public confidence has also occurred. In an essay, "Higher Education in the Nation's Consciousness," Alan Pifer has bluntly written that "during its great period of expansion, the academic community did acquire some unattractive faults. For all its great achievements it became somewhat arrogant and pretentious, lax in its intellectual and moral standards, and insensitive to the needs of the individual student. . . . Many voices can now be heard attacking it and discounting its value; others are badly needed to defend it now, before the present wave of disenchantment goes so far that irreparable damage is done."

Among my contemporaries are many who have performed brilliantly as engineers and then caught a vision of how engineering and the social sciences together establish a new frontier. In a provocative statement in the 100th anniversary issue of *Technique*, MIT's student-edited yearbook, Professor Jay Forrester (of Whirlwind fame) observed: "For more than a hundred years MIT has pressed forward into technology and its scientific foundations. But how long can a frontier last? At today's pace, probably not much more than the past hundred years. Technology is no longer the great frontier. . . . Can MIT continue as a pioneering institution unless it finds a new frontier?" And then he concludes: "It is now timely to use the technology to solve the problems of social systems. Therein lies the frontier for the next hundred years."

Although I welcome his always provocative views and support his search for a new frontier, I am not yet persuaded that technology is becoming a diminishing, worked-out frontier. I see all about us new intellectual fields on the frontiers of technology already challenging great talents—voraciously demanding great funds. The exciting fields of the brain or cognitive sciences along with artificial intelligence and its fifth generation computers are clearly enlivening and extending technological frontiers. On the occasion of the 100th anniversary of the Department of Electrical Engineering, a committee of its professors presented a report, entitled "Lifelong Cooperative Education." The report expressed their conviction that "the future vitality and competitiveness of U.S. high-technology industry depend on widespread acceptance of lifelong formal educational activities as integral components of productive engineering work." Clearly they envisaged the indefinite continuation of our present technological frontier, as do I.

As we seek today to stem a decline in American scientific and technological leadership and to introduce new stability and competitive strength into the American economy, let us not forget what has happened in other nations. The Industrial Revolution started in England with an extraordinary outburst of energy and intellectual vigor. British science policymaking, however, faltered, and the British fell behind while Germany forged ahead. Later the United States achieved leadership over the war-weakened Germans, and today Japan aggressively seeks to surpass us. It may well do so if we, like Britain, fail to sustain policies that can ensure our future technological strength.

In contemplating this and other challenges that face our private research universities, let me reinforce some of my earlier comments on key factors in maintaining the financial stability and integrity of these institutions. In compensating for government-sponsored research, the government has almost never recognized that our universities must have adequate capital if they are to continue to be successful in undertaking research needed by government. Their present capital has come almost completely from nongovernment sources. It includes, as Walter Rosenblith has said, both "grey capital"—the human talent they have recruited—and "green capital." It has been the grey capital over the years that has given to universities the intellectual, spiritual, and moral capital, that special endowment that makes them unique among the major institutions of our society.

The need for green capital grows steadily greater if the grey capital is to be adequately supported.

In recent years it would appear that higher priority has been given to the raising of funds for buildings and projects, with the result that new funds to sustain and strengthen the heart of the institution have lesser priority. Buildings and projects of course can be of crucial importance, but the core strength of the institution is still more important. Raising endowment funds for salaries, student aid, and innovation requires a new degree of imaginative effort.

A higher priority, I repeat, needs to be given to raising funds that keep endowments in proper balance with increasing levels of operating and program costs. This is especially true for those institutions that depend on soft money. When portions of tenured faculty salaries are charged to government funds or to other kinds of soft funds or when an institution must take risks or borrow, it needs adequate endowment to protect its independence. In my judgment many of our research universities are so inadequately endowed that they are forced to take excessive risks and find themselves timid in the degree of boldness they can bring to bear in undertaking new ventures that are clearly important to their future effectiveness. And always they have high-priority need for funds that are unrestricted and that can be applied flexibly in behalf of the core strength of the institution.

In the immediate years ahead the scramble for funds by private institutions from private sources will be desperately competitive. Success in these ravenous efforts will depend not alone on the quality and prestige and honorable ingenuity of the institutions but on their clearly demonstrated commitment to the public welfare. It will also depend on innovative fund raising that brings donors and recipients into an intellectual partnership that serves the legitimate interests of both. Mere begging will not be enough.

And of course every prudent institution must avoid obesity and middle-age spread. It must limit its scope and not try to cover the whole waterfront even though emerging new fields appear intellectually seductive. It must not sacrifice mobility of ideas and intellectual coherence by creeping toward a "megaversity." Undue growth can spawn costly bureaucracies as well as disaggregated academic programs.

In contemplating the present and new frontiers and new fields that are beckoning, I hasten to inject, as a digression, my conviction that MIT's effectiveness in the future will rest on its disciplined control of growth, lest it may lose the advantages of a quality shop to become a supermarket, to use a Compton metaphor.

In this period of depression in the national academic community, I have not become a Jeremiah obsessed with concern about the future of our universities; in fact I find much encouragement in the quality of university leadership that I have watched emerging in the past lustrum and in the fighting determination on the part of both university leaders and scholars to achieve needed reforms in our higher education and bold opposition to actions by government and the military hardliners who seek to impose restraints on the essential freedoms of our universities. These inept and dangerous proposals, I note with great encouragement, have resulted in an annealing effect on the present cohort of university leaders. I have watched with confidence their hard resistance to the imposition of restraints on free publication of scholarly research.† The battle may not yet be won to prevent such encroachment, but a mobilized effort is in place to prevent damage to the delicate fabric of university education. The failure of the federal government to recognize the central role of the universities in maintaining our national security and the continued deterioration in our lower schools can put the nation at risk.

I also find encouragement in the efforts of the National Academy of Sciences to establish a "round table" that brings together representatives of government and the universities to exchange views and to renew the kind of partnership between government and higher education that was so effective in the fifties and sixties. This effort to bring about better communication and discussion is vitally needed because there is presently no central organization in government that brings it into constructive relationship with universities or affords an opportunity for the universities to have a person, a bureau, or an office to which they can go to air their needs and present their proposals.

Public criticism of our universities since the sixties has resulted in part from the abuses that have grown up in the televising of "big-time" college basketball and football. The exploitation of student athletes and the system of high finance associated with these big-time arrangements have added to the public disesteem for all of higher education.

Recently, growing conflicts between public and private institutions could further diminish public confidence in higher education. In 1800 President Eliot of Harvard and President McCosh of Princeton set a bad example when they joined in opposing the extension of public higher education as represented in the Land Grant College system. In his *History of the American College and University*, Frederick Rudolf commented that "McCosh and Eliot indulged in one of the shabbiest episodes in American academic history. . . ." Fortunately their views gained little support, and the nation proceeded, greatly to its advantage, with the parallel development of a dual system of public and private institutions. At times the two systems have feuded, but until recently the rivalry has been conducted under reasonable, cordial Queensberry rules.

Today there is growing tension between the two systems as they engage in hard competition both for students and dollars. Unless conducted with educational statesmanship, this competition can grow bitter and destructive and contribute further to public criticism. At least one public university unusually gifted with funds has publicly and egregiously announced its intention to strengthen its faculty in science and technology by paying whatever salaries are required to attract outstanding professors away from other institutions. This kind of raiding can only be hurtful to the national university community.

I observe with hope current efforts to achieve a benign university-industrial connection. It seems inevitable that the research universities will be increasingly dependent on industrial support of research and that industry itself increasingly will recognize its obligation and in fact its need to ensure the ongoing strength of the research universities. What is needed is to achieve, in spirit at least, the kind of partnership that prevailed between the universities and the government in the postwar period and to find ways acceptable both to the universities and industry to avoid arrangements in which intellectual property and university values become mortgaged by proprietary goals and narrowly conceived commercial benefits.

We in the universities cannot wholly disclaim responsibility for an unmistakable decline in the quality of everyday life as so frequently reflected in American craftsmanship, in the unreliability of too much of our technology, and in the low quality of many consumer products and their service. I cannot forget a cartoon that appeared several years ago that highlighted this shoddiness. "This toy," said the caption under the cartoon, "is designed to prepare the child for the modern world. No matter how you put it together, it won't work."

The central challenge facing American universities is the imperative to be relentlessly first rate, to maintain such high credibility, creativity, and luminous excellence that they enlarge the national vision and enhance the national confidence. By their demonstration of a contagious excellence and high moral purpose, they may help our society avoid a slough of Despond.

It may be within the power and vision of American universities to help rebuild consensus in American society. The achievement of a working consensus has become increasingly difficult as "single-issue minorities" uncompromisingly and belligerently assert their special interests without regard for the larger welfare of society. James Madison, in the tenth essay of the Federalist Papers, expressed his fear that consensus might break down and factions occur. "By a faction," he wrote, "I understand a number of citizens, whether amounting to a majority or minority of the whole, who are united and actuated by some common impulse of passion, or of interest, adverse to the rights of other citizens, or to the permanent and aggregate interests of the community." Increasingly many citizens refuse to give a little when by their modest sacrifices we might all gain a lot. When differences occur, too often the current style is to litigate or regulate rather than arbitrate. We in the universities are in an advantageous position to demonstrate the values of reconciliation and cultivate the arts of persuasion and civility more, coercion and litigation less.

A philosopher and humanist I admired, the late Charles Frankel, spoke eloquently of the need to work steadily at clearing a path "toward an image of a better society, and a strategy for attaining it, which will recommend itself to the imagination of liberal men."[4] To this challenge, those in our universities will surely continue to respond. As Sir James George Frazer wrote in the last chapter of *The Golden Bough*, "The advance of knowledge is an infinite progression toward a goal that for ever recedes." The business of the university and its survival power lie in its total commitment to this advancement of knowledge.

When the inauguration of Paul Gray began in Killian Court, the sky was overcast and rain threatened, but as I ended my apostrophe to our new president, the sun dramatically broke through the overcast and in a moment of inspiration I turned to Paul and exclaimed: "Sir, the sun shines upon you." This statement and this sentiment can appropriately be applied not only to the fourteenth president of the Institute but to the institution itself and comprehensively to the research university as a central institution in our society.

Above: The cover of *Newsweek* for November 18, 1957. *Top Right*: Being sworn in as special assistant to the president for science and technology in the presence of the President, Sherman Adams, and the author's daughter, Mrs. Paul R. Staley. *Bottom right*: Officers and trustees of Atoms for Peace Awards, established to honor Henry and Edsel Ford. Pictured, from left: M. Bryce Leggett, executive secretary; Harvey H. Bundy, secretary; Mildred McAfee Horton, trustee; James R. Killian, Jr., chairman of the board of trustees; Joseph J. Snyder, treasurer; Mervin J. Kelly, Detlev W. Bronk, and Alan T. Waterman, all trustees. Absent: Ralph J. Bunche and Arthur H. Compton.

Jerrold Zacharias, pioneer of science curriculum reform in the secondary schools, demonstrates apparatus for physics teaching in high schools, showing the "pressure of light," a pressure that provides an essential structural element of the stars. *Right*: "Tubby" Rogers never appeared in this guise in his classes teaching English literature.

Katharine McCormick (nee Dexter), one of MIT's great benefactors,
conducting experiment as a student of biology at MIT in the Class of
1904.

Above: The Carnegie Commission on Educational Television whose report led to the passage by Congress of the Public Broadcasting Act of 1967. Seated, from left: James B. Conant, Oveta Culp Hobby, Killian (chairman), Lee A. DuBridge; standing, from left: Franklin Patterson, Terry Sanford, Robert Saudek, Leonard Woodcock, Joseph H. McConnell, Edwin H. Land, David D. Henry, J. C. Kellam, and Ralph Ellison. Commission members Rudolph Serkin and John S. Hayes were absent. *Top right*: President Lyndon Johnson presents to Killian the pen with which he signed the Public Broadcasting Act of 1967, which created the Corporation for Public Broadcasting. *Bottom right*: Members of WGBH's *Zoom* public television program cast traveled to Washington to perform at a dinner for the author upon completion of his term as a director of the Corporation for Public Broadcasting.

Members of the General Advisory Committee on Arms Control and
Disarmament meet with President Nixon, March 21, 1972.

Meeting with Vice President Gerald Ford to discuss the recommendations of the National Academy of Sciences Blue Ribbon Committee report, "Science and Technology in Presidential Policymaking, A Proposal," which contributed to the legislation reestablishing a science advisory organization in the White House in 1976.

Six former special assistants to the president for science and technology assembled at MIT in October 1973. From left: the author, Kistiakowsky, Wiesner, Hornig, DuBridge, and David.

President Jerome Wiesner presides at the dedication of Killian Court at MIT in 1974.

The wives of five presidents of the Massachusetts Institute of Technology. From left: Mrs. Jerome B. Wiesner, Mrs. Howard W. Johnson, Mrs. Julius A. Stratton, Mrs. James R. Killian, Jr., and the late Mrs. Karl T. Compton.

In an issue devoted to growing old and how to do right, *Esquire* magazine pictured this group of Bostonians over seventy. Standing, from left: former Speaker of the House John W. McCormack; Harvard classics professor (now emeritus) John H. Finley, Jr.; author and former editor of *Atlantic*, Edward Weeks; Killian; journalist and commentator Erwin D. Canham; advertising executive Francis W. Hatch.

Seated, clockwise from left: Pops conductor Arthur Fiedler; Mrs. George C. Shattuck of Brookline; historian Samuel Eliot Morison; bookseller George Goodspeed; former Republican Party officer Mrs. Charles P. Howard; poet David McCord, and former U.S. Senator Leverett Saltonstall.

Left: Vice President Nelson Rockefeller presents the first Guglielmo Marconi International Fellowship to the author at the annual dinner of the National Academy of Engineering in Washington on April 23, 1975. *Above*: As recipient of the 1978 Sylvanus Thayer Award, Killian receives an engraved saber from Cadet First Captain John Cook at West Point. Observing the presentation is Lt. Gen. Andrew Goodpaster, superintendent of the U.S. Military Academy.

Killian receives the first Vannevar Bush Award from Norman Hackerman, chairman of the National Science Board, at a National Science Foundation dinner held in Washington in May 1980. The citation reads: "For his outstanding contributions to science and technology through public service to the Nation as one of the leading spokesmen for educational innovation and curriculum reform, for strengthening and broadening engineering education, for support of basic research, and for his distinguished record of service from World War II to the present time."

The author, who served MIT both as president and chairman of the Corporation, is flanked by the current holders of those offices, Paul E. Gray and David S. Saxon, as he receives a resolution in recognition of his eightieth birthday on July 24, 1984. MIT photo by Calvin Campbell

Stark Draper (founder of the Draper Laboratory); David Shepard, class president; and the author exchange anecdotes at the 1926 fiftieth reunion.

After the convocation of the Birla Institute of Technology, the author rides a camel to a celebration at one of the scenes of Mr. Birla's childhood. Mr. G. D. Birla, founder of the institute and friend of Gandhi, is standing at the far right. Mr. Birla sought assistance from the author and other MIT personnel in raising the institution to full college status.

Killian and Harold Edgerton, who coauthored *Moments of Vision: The Stroboscopic Revolution in Photography* (MIT Press, 1979), with photography by Edgerton and text by Killian. *Right*: One of Edgerton's most famous strobe photographs. MIT photo of author and Edgerton by Calvin Campbell

MIT in the author's green days—1938.

Recent view of the MIT campus showing dinghies on the Charles and developments (in lower right corner) on the West Campus, including examples of how new forms of architecture were embraced by MIT in the 1950s: Aalto's Baker House, Kresge Auditorium, the Chapel, Stratton Student Center, and McCormick Hall.

"Big Maple," formerly the Killian's second home, Sharon, N.H., 1982. At right: the "Rose of Sharon" statue now at the Sharon Art Center.

The author at the Henry Moore *Three Piece Reclining Figure, Draped* (1976) in Killian Court, 1983. Photo by Jamie Cope

16
AN END AND A NEW BEGINNING

. . . Or say that the end precedes the beginning.
And the end and the beginning were always there
Before the beginning and after the end.
——T. S. Eliot, "Burnt Norton" *Four Quartets*

Alia Initia e Fine
The above epigraph selected by President Maclaurin is carved
on the marble fireplace in the president's office at MIT. Freely
translated it says: "From an ending, other beginnings."

This theme of new beginnings aptly describes my transition to
"years of grace as a pensioner entirely free of any executive
responsibilities but with a ringside seat."

I undertook the writing of this memoir, knowing full well that
it would be interrupted by periods of benign neglect. The teem-
ing, dynamic life of the Institute provided constant diversions. I
had all the opportunities but none of the obligations of a visiting
professor to take full advantage of the incandescent life of the
institute including a formidable menu of lectures, seminars,
ceremonials, concerts, alumni and Arts Council meetings, and
other hard-to-miss events. I kept up to date with current news
about headlined achievements of the Institute and its people.
For example, in 1984, MIT had once again dominated the National Science Foundation graduate fellowship program. Recipients of these NSF fellowships can choose the institution they
prefer to attend, and of the 540 persons nationwide who won
these fellowships, eighty-three chose MIT, more than the number electing Stanford, Berkeley, Princeton, Harvard, Cornell,
Cal Tech, and Chicago. It was with special satisfaction that I
noted that of the sixty who won minority fellowships, MIT again
attracted the most.

Among the usually pleasant interruptions were inquiries and
visits from graduate students and scholars from a variety of
institutions who were seeking information about periods and
events in Washington in which I played a modest part. During
the past few years a number of historians have been preoc-
cupied with the Eisenhower administration, stimulated by the

recent release of many of his papers long classified. These scholars were studying episodes in which I was once involved: nuclear test ban negotiations, the origins of the U. S. space program, the formation of NASA, the Polaris submarine program, and the U-2. They want to know why the Gaither report was leaked to the press and the more important Technological Capabilities Panel report was not. The progress of public broadcasting, along with its tribulations, prompted inquiries and correspondence. I now know that conspicuous participants in topside policymaking in Washington never escape this kind of ardent pursuit by historians. My trouble is that I relish responding to these incessant inquiries.

I have found stimulating the visits from Larry Owens, a talented Princeton graduate student pursuing the history of science. He has done a brilliant dissertation on Bush's development of the differential analyzer, and in the course of his research he has turned up much fresh information about Bush and his computing machines. Owens is now inspired to undertake a full-scale biography of Bush and an illumination of the engineering culture that shaped his career and his machines.

From these many contacts with succeeding generations, I began to realize that I was engaged in a boot-camp experiment to demonstrate "lifelong cooperative education."

As I approached retirement in 1971, the Alumni Association proposed that Liz and I make a swing around the country to pay farewell visits to selected alumni groups. All together, we met with alumni in eight different gatherings ranging from Mexico City to Dallas to San Francisco and including Chicago, Philadelpha, and New York, the latter being a concert in Philharmonic Hall by the MIT Symphony Orchestra. The number of alumni we met with on these farewell occasions totaled nearly 5,000 of the 78,000 living alumni. It was a wonderful opportunity to get a grassroots feeling for the greatness of this institution by observing close up what its alumni have accomplished, what they contribute to the welfare of this country, and the variety of ways they have enriched the quality of American life.

My association with Institute alumni for nearly six decades has afforded me an almost unique opportunity to know a vast number of graduates, and after years of observing, I realize that a brusque reticence characterizes the majority of our alumni fellowship and that this tends to leave unspoken but not unfelt a deep loyalty and pride on the part of the sons and daughters of MIT. This has led me to conclude that the ethos of student life at MIT, with its professional orientation, its intense work ethic, and its unrelenting stress on excellence does not lead to a superficial rah-rah spirit in the MIT constituency. It does, however, bring about a singularly loyal fellowship that I have come greatly to admire as the hallmark of our corporate body.

I was the first MIT alumnus to become president of the Institute and won among its alumni the accolade "Mr. MIT," thus providing another example of the generous amiability of our alumni.

I see more clearly now than I did at the start of this book how World War II profoundly shaped MIT's future. The Rosenblith-Morison oral history project concluded at its very beginning that the war was a cultural divide for the Institute. Some institutions, they noted, simply struggled to establish what they had been before the war. In contrast, MIT saw what it might become after the war and set out in hot pursuit of a broader intellectual franchise and of government grants to fund it. I find continued evidence that this turn to the future rather than return to the past was a major factor in transforming a small but distinguished institution into the university polarized around science we know today.

Another of the rewarding freedoms of my retirement arrangement, this time of new beginnings, has been the freedom to explore and identify in this memoir the inner qualities of MIT and the machinery below decks that reliably propel it forward. What is its inner logic? What qualities of style shape its institutional personality? What is its special cache of excellence? What have been the visions and virtues that have made this both a happy institution and an unyieldingly challenging one? To add to what I have included in the preceding parts of the book, I continued to persist in this effort more completely to identify, in the poetic words of Gerald Manley Hopkins, "all things counter, original, spare, strange" which mark our "inscape" and to give primary attention to these internal singularities rather than to tables of statistics, however impressive they may be.

I finish this memoir in my eighty-first year, still in pursuit of new beginnings. The traumas, distempers, and decrepitudes encountered during my trudge to this venerable age might have forced me into limbo; but no, the hot pursuit of times past, the raptures of the *backward* view, and the manic excitements of university life have so enlivened my days, and freed me from boredom, that I still "hang in."

As sung in *Gaudeamus igitur*, "let us therefore be joyful."

I have also been well served by clinging to a melioristic view that our future is best served by an acceptance of what Sir Peter Medawar has aptly termed "the *hope* of progress." "To deride the hope of progress," he has said, "is the ultimate fatuity, the last word in poverty of spirit and meanness of mind."[1] This view is tempered only by fear of nuclear war and of an intemperate, militaristic spirit eroding the most precious values of our society. American society, I deeply believe, can still be shaped by an "attracting vision" and still has firmly in place—but badly in need of repair—a majestic infrastructure for the achievement of equality and the pursuit of excellence.

My hope of progress comes naturally from my having lived so long in the regenerative sanctuary of a research university deeply committed to the pursuit of the first-rate. Along with this circumstance has come the sustained invigoration provided postmeridian by association with a singular fellowship of young men and women working in a contagious atmosphere of excellence, discovery, and high spirits. "What is more agreeable than an old age surrounded by the enthusiasm of youth?" exclaimed Cicero in his essay, *De Senectute*.

Since, at eighty, time is running out for me, I cannot contemplate including in this casual memoir more about these students of the Institute, their work and their achievements, and my experiences in living a collegial life in their company. The MIT student body taken altogether is nonpareil, cosmopolitan, brilliantly versatile, and life giving, and I would have found it joyful to write about my experiences in serving them. Now that I have been around long enough to observe the computer culture now engulfing us and to learn from Sherry Turkle's book, *The Second Self: Computers and the Human Spirit*, I might even have gotten into challenging discussions of hackers and the student philosophers of artificial intelligence who dwell in the brave new world she has penetrated. Perhaps I might yet have words to say about these exciting, provocative matters but not in this book.

The Turkle book is an impressive example of one of the contributions our Program in Science, Technology, and Society can make in leading an institute of technology polarized around science and technology into the "wondrous strange" new age she describes.

In the concluding chapter of his book, *As I Remember Him*, the late physician and bacteriologist (*Rats, Lice, and Men*), Hans Zinsser, spoke of compensatory adjustments that took place in his mind in his concluding days. "It seemed," he said, "from that moment, as though all that his heart felt and his senses perceived were taking on a deep autumnal tone and an increased vividness . . . his sensitiveness to the simplest experiences, even for things that in other years he might hardly have noticed, was infinitely enhanced." I have experienced similar compensations as the years have crept along. My devotion to members of my family and my dependence on their love has grown strikingly greater and so has my affectionate veneration for cherished friends and colleagues. With a surprising increase in perception I find beauties all about me unnoticed before. Aldous Huxley once said that of all the glories of this world, none exceeds the sky. I see the glories too as I watch from our apartment scores of sunflecked dinghies sailing on the Charles or visit the MIT Chapel with Bertoia's soaring screen or sunlight dancing on its inner walls.

John Henry Newman spoke of the snapdragon growing outside his window at Oxford's Trinity College. I vividly recall the crab apple and rhododendron blossoms viewed from the windows of the MIT president's office. As Newman did in leaving Oxford, I have taken these blossoms as "the emblem of my own perpetual residence . . . in my university."[2]

In "Sailing to Byzantium," William Butler Yeats expressed a poetic theme appropriate for me at this stage of my life:

An aged man is but a paltry thing,
A tattered coat upon a stick, unless
Soul clap its hands and sing, and loudly sing . . .

As I sail on to Byzantium, I still clap my hands and loudly sing.[3]

EPILOGUE

FOR RIDERS ON THE EARTH

Nowhere in this memoir have I mentioned my preoccupation with arms control, but I now recognize, given my background, that it would be irresponsible for me not to end with a few convictions about the fateful debate on issues relating to nuclear weapons.

• I find it difficult to believe that any "Star Wars" defense system to make nuclear weapons "impotent and obsolete" is technologically achievable.

• I feel strongly that all our efforts to proceed with a "Star Wars" program would be destructive of past and current efforts of the superpowers to moderate the arms race. I feel instead that attempts to develop an impenetrable shield will surely and understandably encourage the Soviet Union to achieve comparable improvements in its offensive and defensive capabilities.

• The baroque adventurism in space-warfare technology can only have the effect of abrogating the Anti-Ballistic Missile Treaty.

• During the past four years I have favored significant increases in defense expenditures but hardly at the profligate rate we are now witnessing. I agree with Professor William Kaufmann that no organization, however skillful, can spend money so fast and succeed in maintaining the quality control needed in our defense system. The current almost unlimited defense budget has inevitably resulted in extravagant purchases, hasty planning, and unreliable equipment.

• If pursued with obstinate fantasy, efforts to achieve a "Star Wars" antiballistic missile system could be dangerously costly to the nation.

• My concerns about current and projected defense policies are further amplified by searching studies that indicate "bureaucratic infighting, ideological conflict, and personal antagonisms" which are now making it virtually impossible to achieve and sustain a rational foreign policy.

• I am encouraged by the steady growth in an insistent public examination of nuclear issues and the way they are being handled by our government. One does not have to agree in detail with all the studies, reports, and statements by clergymen, physicians, scientists, strategic experts, and plain citizens to recognize that they have made enormously helpful contributions to the public understanding of the nuclear threat.

I am further encouraged by the response of qualified scholars in our research universities who have been speaking with knowledge, integrity, and responsibility about nuclear issues and helping others to understand the complexities of arms control and the hazards of nuclear weapons. In my time there have been no issues so fateful to mankind where we need scholars courageously speaking out of intensive study and profound wisdom.

• It appears that the military-industrial complex, as described by President Eisenhower and so worrisome to him, is still having a profoundly dangerous impact on our government.

• I find it impossible to accept the view of a persistent few that we can fight a nuclear war and survive.

My views and alarms have deep roots in my experience while mobilizing science advice for President Eisenhower in the decade of the 1950s, when the agenda for his advisers included space, intelligence, weapons technology, and the achievement and verification of nuclear test bans. These heady assignments gave me a view of Eisenhower's sustained efforts to moderate the arms race, to minimize defense expenditures, to initiate negotiations to achieve a limited ban on nuclear tests, to keep space a sanctuary unmolested by war-fighting technology, defensive or offensive, and to keep the image of America before the world as a nation secure in its might but deeply committed to peace and peacekeeping, a nation that refrains from unrestrained rhetorical imprecations that result in a dangerous escalation in belligerency and hardening of views.

The need for public understanding and aroused action has never been so urgent. Our goal, the goal of all the nuclear powers, is that we avoid a war that will make our planet uninhabitable, that we make sure that all that mankind has accomplished over the centuries will not be continued at risk, that the majestic achievements of human civilization, the great art and architecture, the great discoveries of science, the temples and universities, the spiritual and intellectual achievements, and the human species itself will not be destroyed.

Shortly before he died of cancer, George Kistiakowsky, talented scientist who succeeded me as science adviser to President Eisenhower, sent to the *Bulletin of the Atomic Scientists* a statement moving by its despair and challenging by what it said to all who wish to preserve the life of this planet:

The political leaders of powerful nations continue uttering pious words about their love of peace, but the arsenals keep growing, the stability of nuclear peace is being undermined, and the proposals for arms controls negotiations on both sides are so unbalanced as to be obviously non-negotiable.

As one who has tried to change these trends, working both through official channels and, for the last dozen years, from outside, I tell you as my parting words: Forget the channels. There simply is not enough time left before the world explodes. Concentrate instead on organizing, with so many others who are of like mind, a mass movement for peace such as there has not been before. But the threat of annihilation is also unprecedented. Then lead the movement so that, instead of the few now in Washington, many will be elected to Congress who have a true and unbreakable commitment to search for peace.[1]

When the Apollo Mission in 1968 returned from space, it brought back spectacularly beautiful photographs which showed our earth as seen in all its beauty from out beyond the moon. The late Archibald MacLeish turned his poetic skill to speak the sentiments so many felt on viewing their planetary home. In concluding a piece he wrote for the *New York Times,* he said: "To see the earth as we now see it, small and blue and beautiful in that eternal silence where it floats, is to see ourselves as riders on the earth together, brothers on that bright loveliness in the unending night—brothers who *see* now they are truly brothers."

Cannot we as "riders on the earth" summon our skills and our determination to reduce the ever-growing nuclear threat to our planetary home lest it become a bourn of malignancy and megadeath?

COMPTON ACCEPTS THE MIT PRESIDENCY

Karl Compton's inauguration as president of MIT on June 6, 1930, initiated the transformation of the Institute from an outstanding engineering school to a leading research university. In 1945 he took time out to write "for the files" a private memorandum, until now unpublished, a play-by-play account of how the invitation to accept the presidency of the Institute came to him and how he was persuaded to accept.

I reproduce Compton's memorandum describing events leading him to accept the presidency of the Institute because much of my memoir deals with the realization of the vision that Dr. Compton revealed in his private memorandum "for the files."

One day early in 1930 in Princeton I received a letter from Mr. Gerard Swope, President of the General Electric Company, asking if I would drop in to see him on my next trip to New York. I had for a number of years been a consultant for the General Electric Company in connection with its Vapor Lamp Division in Hoboken and its work in the general field of discharge of electricity in gases at Schenectady. I assumed that Mr. Swope wished to ask me some question in regard to the research program of the General Electric Company.

This expectation was correct. Mr. Swope talked to me about some of the problems of organization, personnel and program of the Research Laboratory and asked me if I would think over these problems and let him have the result of any ideas which I might wish to suggest to him.

I felt decidedly complimented by this inquiry and felt that if as busy a man as Mr. Swope took the time to ask for my ideas, it was certainly up to me to reply as fully, frankly and helpfully as I could. I consequently wrote him a rather long letter on the subject of the Research Laboratory and included certain ideas with reference to broadening the base of selection for new employees in this laboratory.

Mr. Swope then asked me to come up to discuss the matter further with him. When I arrived at his office in New York he expressed interest in my report and said that he had referred it to Dr. Whitney for consideration and comments. He then said that what he had really had in mind in his first interview with me was to get acquainted with me as a possible candidate for the presidency of the Massachusettes Institute of Technology. He then went on to tell me something about the problems, the business operations, and the future opportunities of the Institute, and told me of the plan to promote Dr. Stratton to be Chairman of the Corporation, and asked me whether I would be interested in the presidency of the institution.

This was a total and complete surprise to me. I had never given any thought whatsoever to an administrative post and had never had any desire or ambition for one. I was wholly happy and enthusiastic about my position and opportunities as head of the Department of Physics of Princeton University. While I knew something about the difference between an electron and a proton, I knew very much less about the difference between a stock and a bond, and had never had much interest in any theories of education except the belief that a good educational job can be performed by an inspiring teacher who lets his student cooperate in some way with him in his investigations.

Without, I fear, very much enthusiasm for the prospect but with respect and admiration for the way in which Mr. Swope had broached the subject, I told him that I would like to think the matter over a bit and would particularly like to discuss it with Dr. Frank B. Jewett, then President of the Bell Telephone Laboratories, whom I knew very well and who was a member of the MIT Corporation.

Shortly thereafter I made arrangements to meet Frank Jewett en route from the South to New York. I met him on the train at Trenton and rode with him to New York and then went to his office to continue the discussion. I had promised Mr. Swope to give him my answer on that day, and when I had left my home in Princeton, I had pretty well decided that I had better stay at Princeton on a job about which I was enthusiastic and which I felt that I could handle.

Dr. Jewett made no personal argument or effort to urge me in the decision. However, he painted a picture of the opportunities at MIT in such a way as to convince me that there was a real obligation for someone with a good scientific background to tackle the job which he described in the following way.

During the period of the 1800s and the first decade or two of the 1900's, Jewett said, the industries of the country were technologically in their beginnings so far as any real applications of science were concerned. Consequently the industries had to look to the engineering or technical school to secure men who had the technical training in the various arts or manipulations necessary for the industry. As a result these schools took on a strong slant of immediate practicality, training their students in the particular techniques, shop practices, etc., which industry might require of them.

Along in the early 1900's, however, the more important industries had developed to the point where they possessed strong scientific and technical staffs of their own, and they had developed their own practical arts and techniques. They no longer needed or even wanted such training from the engineering schools. They much preferred to give it to their new recruits in their own way.

Along with this development, however, came a rapidly increasing industrial need for men with a good sound foundation in fundamental science and mathematics, and the basic principles of engineering. This was primarily to enable industry to grasp and quickly develop new technological opportunities opened up by the rapid advances in science. Such men industry could not train for itself. It was increasingly true that industry needed men who had the type of fundamental training given in physics, chemistry and mathematics, as distinct from the more practical training which had been traditional in engineering.

On this basis Dr. Jewett maintained that the leading institution of technology had a great obligation and a great opportunity to break away from the traditional program of engineering education and introduce a much more powerful element of fundamental science. He felt that this should be done not only by strengthening the scientific departments and emphasizing their role in the institution, but also by bringing into the staffs of the engineering departments an increasing number of men of research type, whether trained initially as engineers or as scientists. In this way he felt that MIT could perform its best function, not only in its own educational program, but in its example to other engineering schools. Jewett said that it had been this thought in the minds of the committee on selection, headed by Mr. Swope, which had inclined them to the selection of a research physicist for the presidency of the Institute.

On the basis of this discussion it appeared to me that here was a real challenge, that the job at the Massachusetts Institute of Technology would not be an abandonment of my professional career, but would be an opportunity to draw on this background of experience and my scientific contacts in order to enlarge the scope of their value and influence in the educational and research fields generally.

Following my interview with Dr. Jewett I called up my wife in Princeton and told her that I had decided to accept the offer. Her exclamation at this news may have been caused by astonishment or by a sudden realization of what she was in for. However this may be, she was then, as always, a good sport.

Following this telephone conversation, I called on Mr. Swope and told him that I had decided to accept the offer. I think it was at this time that he brought in Mr. Owen D. Young, and it was also at this time that he invited me to come with him at an early date to Boston to meet other members of the Executive Committee.

Shortly thereafter my wife and I came to Boston and went to the Dartmouth Street home of Mr. Edwin S. Webster for breakfast and to meet members of the Executive Committee. It was a most gracious occasion, and I recall that Mr. Webster asked my wife to select for herself one of his orchids. When she pointed out her choice he gallantly plucked it and pinned it on her dress, and then told her that this was a new variety which had only one bloom and would not have another for seven years.

I subsequently made another visit to the Institute, where Dr. Stratton introduced me to the faculty at a special meeting. I do not know whether or not this was the first word which had reached the faculty regarding the new change in the administration of the Institute.

In connection with the discussions relative to my acceptance of the new position there are two or three incidents which stand out clearly in my mind and to which my thoughts have subsequently frequently returned. One of these was my comment to Mr. Swope to the effect that I had no gift nor desire for money raising, and also that I had no ability as a public speaker and, except for talks on scientific subjects, any prospect of a public address ruined my peace of mind for weeks in advance. To these objections Mr. Swope made the following reply. He said that money raising was the business of the Corporation and that my attention could be devoted to administration of the operating affairs and to the policies of the Institute. As regards speech making, he said there were only two speeches per year which were necessary: one was to welcome the incoming freshman class, and the other was to bid them Godspeed at the graduation exercises. Everything else he said was entirely within my own control. Maybe so, but if so, my control has been weak. A little later, in reading the biography of the late President Maclaurin, I was interested to note that he raised the same two questions about money raising and speech making when he was approached with reference to the presidency of the Institute. I take it that we may serve as examples to all future presidential prospects.

A second incident occurred on a New Haven train when my wife and I were en route to the inauguration exercises in June 1930. We were invited to share a compartment with Gerard Swope and Owen Young. During the conversation Mr. Young discussed his ideas on the responsibilities of an administrative officer. He emphasized his belief that the first responsibility of any administrative or executive officer was to insure the immediate availability of his successor, and most especially of someone who could carry on the work of the organization with good effectiveness in case the officer himself should suddenly be removed by death or accident. This is a program which I have always tried to follow in connection with the selection of our Deans and Vice-Presidents.

A third incident was a letter received from my friend, the late Henry Gale, who was Dean of the Graduate School of Science and head of the Physics Department of the University of Chicago. Gale cautioned me against making any high pronouncements on educational policy for a long time to come. Based on his observations he said that the typical performance of a new college president was to accept an invitation to make a speech before he had anything to say. To meet the emergency, however, he cudgeled his brains to think up something which would get by. After his speech well-wishers and flatterers told him how good it was, and he was prone to believe it. In this way he soon became persuaded that the half-baked ideas which he had pulled out of thin air were a great educational doctrine, and from that time on his career as a really great educator was ruined.

I should not conclude these comments without expressing my firm conviction that the plan of selecting the president while his predecessor is still of an age and vigor to contribute to the institution from his background of acquaintance and experience is very sound policy. My first year at MIT would have been very much more difficult and less effective had it not been for the unfailing backing and helpfulness of Dr. Stratton and for his excellent judgment in not usurping or undercutting the responsibilities of the new president. With goodwill and good sense on both sides, I believe there should never be difficulty in finding the proper line of demarcation between the two offices and in securing a good degree of mutual assistance across this boundary line.

I believe that this concludes my recital of recollections prior to my inauguration as President of the Institute. Unfortunately I kept no records of correspondence, diary or newspaper clippings in connection with these events.

LETTER TO A DRAFT BOARD

Over the years I have debated with myself from time to time as to whether I should have accepted the invitation in 1939 to be Dr. Compton's executive assistant, given all that this appointment was to lead to for the Institute and for me. Recently, in 1980, a letter written by Dr. Compton to my draft board in 1942 was found in the MIT archives. Now that I have seen it for the first time, it adds a mite of assurance that it was appropriate for me to stay at MIT instead of leaving for some war job or enlisting. Herewith the letter:

June 8, 1942

Local Board #106
Needham, Massachusetts
Ref. Order No. 11260

Gentlemen:

Permit me to amplify the statements made in the enclosed affidavit in support of the request of *Mr. James R. Killian, Jr.* for 3-b classification.

As my Executive Assistant, Mr. Killian is the key executive officer of our institution. He has been in this position for a sufficient number of years to be thoroughly acquainted with our administrative problems, with the personnel, with the details of our budget, and with our problems of public relations and contacts with governmental and business concerns. There is no other member of our staff who has the background to perform these duties.

Since the active program of national preparedness began

about two years ago, I have been devoting at least three-fourths of my time to government business in connection with the work of the Office for Scientific Research and Development. This has thrown on Mr. Killian a much greater share of the executive responsibilities of this institution. Were he to be called to military duty, I and various of my other administrative colleagues, such as deans and heads of departments, who are also devoting substantial time to war projects, would have to reduce their contributions to the war effort to help carry the administrative responsibilities now handled by Mr. Killian. It is proper to point out, that among Mr. Killian's administrative duties at MIT a considerable amount of his attention is even now being devoted to the war in connection with the administration of war contracts for research, or for the training of personnel. The aggregate of these contracts exceeds by several fold our ordinary annual MIT budget. From this it is evident that a substantial portion of Mr. Killian's time is already being devoted to the war program.

Because of these facts, it seems clear that Mr. Killian's best contribution to our national war effort will be secured by permitting him to continue his present activities which are essential and for which he is practically irreplaceable under existing conditions. I hope therefore that your Board may feel justified in classifying Mr. Killian under 3-b for occupational deferment.

Very sincerely yours,
Karl T. Compton
President

MEMORANDUM LEADING TO THE APPOINTMENT OF THE LEWIS COMMITTEE

August 5, 1946

Memorandum to Dr. Compton
Subject: Proposal for the Appointment of a Faculty Committee to Study Our Undergraduate Educational Program

During the summer, there have been a number of discussions of the need to promote here at the Institute more interest in the study of educational objectives and procedures. At a recent meeting of the Administrative Council, there was a consensus that a strong faculty committee ought to be set up to make a long-range study of our undergraduate program. Members of the Council indicated not only that they feel our program needs such a study but that the by-products of the study would be important—as, for example, bringing to the attention of the Faculty current and advanced thinking on educational methods; helping to revitalize the Faculty as an operating body (it lost ground, of course, during the war as a deliberative body); and giving a clear indication outside of the Institute of our steady and constructive work in the field of educational policy and method. The great increase in our research program and the fact that research is more news-worthy than education indicates that we need to make special efforts to call attention to our vigorous educational activity.

I would suggest that a committee be appointed made up wholly of members of the Faculty and excluding administrative officers other than Department Heads. The academic deans can be available to the committee for any assistance or counsel, but I think they might best remain in the background.

The committee might well be given ample scope and urged to look at our undergraduate program as comprehensively as possible, reexamining its objectives, its organization, and its operation. It might well ask itself some very fundamental questions (the wording of these questions does not presuppose any answers): Do our admission requirements need revision? Are we too specialized in our undergraduate program in the upper two years, and is our course system the most effective organization? Have we swung too far in the direction of theory as distinct from practice, or have we not gone far enough? Have we yet allotted enough time for humanistic studies? Do we require too much routine and scheduled work of our students, leaving too little time for self-development? Do we have a sufficiently strong corps of instructors available for undergraduate instruction? Are we exercising the educational leadership in our undergraduate program which should properly come from the Institute?

The Millard Committee made its study during the war, and we are now operating under the plan they developed. Has the simplification of curriculum carried out under this plan worked well? How much of the plan should we retain permanently in our program? Are the changes made in the

freshman year by way of lightening the freshman load
to be continued? . . .

I think that Lewis is the logical person to be chairman because of his great prestige and his strong interest in teaching.
He has talked with me several times about his feeling that
we were not making use of all the educational advances now
available, and he has also a strong feeling that the Institute's
Faculty has tended to abdicate its position as a body determining educational policy. He strongly favors more widespread and active discussion of educational matters. I know
that he will hesitate to take the chairmanship because of his
present heavy responsibilities, but I am certain that he is the
ideal man for the post and that he will command unques-
tioned respect throughout the Institute. . . .

If you believe that this committee can make an important
contribution and that we should proceed with this study, I
would suggest that we set the committee up and announce it
at the first Faculty meeting in the fall. . . .

Yours sincerely,
J. R. Killian, Jr.

FACULTY ACHIEVEMENT AWARDS

In 1971 a committee of the faculty, generously wishing to establish an annual tribute to the tenth president of the Institute and
retiring chairman of the Corporation, ingeniously designed the
James R. Killian, Jr., Faculty Achievement Award to recognize
extraordinary professional accomplishments by full-time members of the faculty, to provide an honorarium, and in addition to
provide a means for the communication of these accomplishments to the faculty, students, and other members of the MIT
community and to the general public. Thus the Faculty Achievement Award honors and rewards a member of the faculty while
paying tribute to a retired president and chairman.

I find pleasure in listing below the faculty members who have
received this award through the year 1984:

Nevin S. Scrimshaw, Victor F. Weisskopf, Morris Cohen,
Frank Press, Hans-Lukas Teuber, Robert M. Solow, Morris
Halle, David J. Rose, Alexander Rich, Chia-Chiao Lin, Herman
A. Haus, Robert W. Mann, and Philip Morrison.

THE NAMING OF KILLIAN COURT: REMARKS BY PRESIDENT JEROME WIESNER

On June 3, 1974, during the Alumni Days program, a ceremony was staged "on one of spring's brightest days" on the steps of the Richard Cockburn Maclaurin Building to change the name of the Great Court to Killian Court. This was in response to a resolution of the Corporation and president voted at its meeting preceding commencement on the previous Friday.

Below is presented the address of President Wiesner on that memorable and beautiful occasion.

Said I in response to President Wiesner and the Corporation resolution read by Chairman Howard W. Johnson: "No accolade which has come to me in my lifetime has moved me so deeply as this action of the MIT Corporation. I simply do not know how to respond to a resolution so magnanimous, so felicitously phrased and so heartwarming in spirit."

Mrs. Killian gave her own "heartfelt thanks" and added, "Always may Killian Court be a lilting legacy to us all."

President Wiesner's address:

We have asked you to join us here today in a tribute to Mr. MIT, Jim Killian. The MIT Corporation at its meeting on Friday voted to name this Great Court "Killian Court" in recognition of Dr. Killian's singular contributions to MIT and all of humanity.

Throughout all of its history, MIT's sons and daughters have made unique contributions to the development and welfare of our beloved country—inspired alumni have contributed to the greatness of MIT through their teaching, their leadership, their financial support and through the inspirational examples of productive, creative, happy lives. The parade of MIT alumni stretches forward in time from the Civil War across two centuries and spans more than 100 nations; it numbers more than 80,000 persons. Its members have had a mighty role in the building of America, its industries, its educational institutions, and its government. In this parade a few stand tall, visible to all—respected for their outstanding accomplishments and revered for their human qualities. Such a man lives among us—he has for half a century—and his contributions to the greatness of MIT and the nation are indeed awe inspiring. It is safe to say that no one has served MIT more devotedly or with greater effectiveness or for longer than the man we honor today. He guided the Institute through the dislocations of World War II, helped steer the wartime Radiation Laboratory, provided the inspiration and leadership for the postwar development of MIT— revitalizing and strengthening traditional disciplines and extending the reach of academic programs in the social sciences, humanities and management. He played a major part in the development of MIT's world renowned faculty, in the building of its superb physical plant, and the endowment that supports both. Across the length and breadth of this land there are many who speak affectionately of Jim Killian as their most expensive friend. His enthusiasm for MIT is highly infectious.

Dr. Killian's public structures match his local monuments. The Public Broadcasting System, now grown to maturity, was fathered by Jim Killian and only recently was given a much needed parental assist by him.

Dr. Killian's many accomplishments as President Eisenhower's Special Assistant for Science and Technology would require a symposium to do them justice, but a few stand out in my memory—the successful reorganization of the space program, enhanced basic research and higher education programs for the United States, the rationalization of the Defense Department research and development effort, and effective technical support for the President's efforts to halt the arms race and stop nuclear testing. Dozens of other public-service accomplishments are equally part of Jim's stamp on America.

Dr. Killian has served with wisdom as a director of several great corporations and foundations where his unique mixture of courage, readiness to learn, wisdom and humility have made him an exceptional contributor.

I have had the rare good fortune to be associated with Dr. Killian most of my professional life here at MIT and in governmental activities, and I must confess that my admiration and affection for him and awe of him still continue to mount. He approaches each day and each problem that he confronts with enthusiasm, care, grace and total commitment. He enriches his life and ours with involvements in art and literature and through his own artful prose.

In reflecting on Jim's powers, wonderful human qualities, and magnificent accomplishments, one's thoughts inevitably turn with affection and admiration to the person who shared it all with Jim—a great woman—Elizabeth Killian, our beloved Liz. In thinking ahead to this occasion Liz remembered an earlier day here about which she sent me a note.

"In the balmy Spring of '56, three people took a walk from the MIT President's House to the Great Court—grandfather, grandmother, and grandson. They wanted to partake of the regreening of the world. Grandfather was the sturdiest of the walkers and was very protective. Grandson had the excessive energy and uncontrollability of an 18-monther, and grandmother lacked balance after paralytic strokes. (A footnotish aside, grandson is now in college and grandmother is much stronger.)

"Upon reaching the Great Court, grandmother very readily sat down on one of the benches there and let grandfather watch over grandson's response to the extensive space. In looking at grandfather against the MIT dome, grandmother remembered his reference to the dome in his inaugural address as MIT's 'marble index'—like Wordsworth referring to the statue of Newton in his college days in Cambridge as the

Marble index of a mind for ever
Voyaging through strange seas of Thought.

Grandfather's great loves were well represented then and there grandmother thought—his family, nature and MIT. The picture in the mind is one grandmother will never forget."

Signed, Grandmother Killian

This Great Court has existed for slightly more than the 50 years of Jim Killian's association with MIT, waiting, it seems to me, for a felicitous name. Jim Killian and the Great Court appropriately honor each other. This is a memorable moment in the history of the Institute. To mark it, Chairman of the MIT Corporation Howard Johnson will read the resolution the Corporation passed by acclamation at its meeting last Friday.

CHRONOLOGY

1926–1927	Assistant managing editor, *Technology Review*, MIT
1927–1930	Managing editor, *Technology Review*, MIT
1928–1929	Secretary, MIT Alumni Association
1930–1939	Editor, *Technology Review*, MIT
1939–1943	Executive assistant to President Compton, MIT
1943–1945	Executive vice president, MIT
1945–1948	Vice president, MIT
1948–1949	President-designate, MIT
1949–1959	President, MIT
1957–1959	(On leave as president, MIT) Special assistant to president of the United States for science and technology
1959–1971	Chairman of the Corporation, MIT
1971–	Council for the Arts at MIT, member
1971–1979	Honorary Chairman of the Corporation, MIT

1949–1952	Air University, U.S. Air Force, member, board of visitors (chairman, 1951–1952)
1950–1952	President's Advisory Committee on Management Improvement, member
1950–1951	President's Communications Policy Board, member
1951–1956	Army Scientific Advisory Panel, chairman
1951–1957	Science Advisory Committee, Office of Defense Mobilization, member
1953–1955	U.S. Naval Academy, member, board of visitors
1954–1956	Committee for the White House Conference on Education, member
1954–1955	Technological Capabilities Panel, Science Advisory Committee, Office of Defense Mobilization, chairman

1956–1957	President's Board of Consultants on Foreign Intelligence Activities, chairman
1957–1961	President's Science Advisory Committee, member (chairman, 1957–1959; consultant, 1961–1972)
1960–1961	President's Commission on National Goals, member
1961–1963	President's Foreign Intelligence Advisory Board, chairman
1962–1965	National Academy of Sciences Committee on Utilization of Scientific and Engineering Manpower, chairman
1963–1964	President's Committee on Public Higher Education in the District of Columbia, member
1967–1968	Latin America Planning Group, Organization of American States, member
1969–1973	U.S. Arms Control and Disarmament Agency General Advisory Committee, member
1973–1974	National Academy of Sciences Ad Hoc Committee on Science and Technology, chairman
1982	National Academy of Sciences, National Academy of Engineering, Institute of Medicine Panel on Scientific Communication and National Security
1982–1984	Truman Centennial Committee, member
1984–	Advisory committee in support of the continuation of the ABM Treaty, member
1984–	Advisory committee for the development of the Charles H. Townes Center, South Carolina State Museum, member

1954–1970	The Nutrition Foundation, trustee (chairman, 1956–1957; 1959–1965)
1954–1977	Alfred P. Sloan Foundation, trustee
1977–1980	Alfred P. Sloan Foundation, member, Commission on Government and Higher Education

1955–1958 1959–1979	Atoms for Peace Awards, Inc., president and trustee
1956–1957 1959–1969	Institute for Defense Analyses, trustee (chairman, 1956–1957; 1959–1961)
1956–1957 1959–1961	Rockefeller Brothers Fund Special Studies Project, member
1960–1963	National Merit Scholarship Corporation, director
1960–1967	Mellon Institute, trustee
1960–1969	Tulane University, member, board of visitors
1960–1982	Mitre Corporation, trustee (chairman, 1967–1969)
1960–	Winston Churchill Foundation of the United States, Ltd., trustee
1961	North Atlantic Treaty Organization Scientific Affairs Division, Working Group to study feasibility of establishing an international institute of science and technology, chairman
1962–1972	Mount Holyoke College, trustee
1964–1965	Ford Foundation International Affairs Program, consultant
1965–1967	Carnegie Commission on Educational Television, chairman
1965–1966	Churchill College, Cambridge University, overseas fellow
1966–1970	Washington University, trustee
1967–1973	National Academy of Engineering Committee on Public Engineering Policy, member
1968–1975	Corporation for Public Broadcasting, director (chairman, 1973–1974)

1946–1957	Boston Lying-in Hospital, trustee (president, 1947–1949)
1949–1952	Massachusetts General Hospital Scientific Advisory Board, member
1954–1957	Federal Reserve Bank of Boston, director
1956–1957	Cambridge Citizens Advisory Committee to

1959–1966	the City Council, member (chairman, 1963–1965)
1959–	Boston Museum of Science, trustee
1959–1967	Educational Services, Inc., trustee and chairman
1962–1965	Massachusetts Board of Education, member
1966–1979	Boston Museum of Fine Arts, trustee
1967–1969	Education Development Center, trustee (honorary chairman, 1967)
1967–1974	Committee of the Permanent Charity Fund, member
1983–	Council of Friends of the History of Science Society, member
1975–	Sharon, N.H., Arts Center, director (chairman, 1977–1978)

1957	Research Corporation, director
1959–1962	International Business Machines Corporation, director
1959–1975	General Motors Corporation, director
1959–	Polaroid Corporation, director
1963–1975	Cabot Corporation, director
1963–1977	American Telephone & Telegraph Company, director
1971–1976	Ingersoll-Rand Company, director

AWARDS

1944	Fellow, American Academy of Arts and Sciences
1948	President's Certificate of Merit
1953	Certificate of Appreciation, Department of the Army
1957	Decoration for Exceptional Civilian Service, Department of the Army

1957	Public Welfare Medal, National Academy of Sciences
1957	Officer, French Legion of Honor
1958	Gold Medal of the National Institute of Social Sciences
1958	World Brotherhood Award of the National Conference of Christians and Jews
1958	Award of Merit, American Institute of Consulting Engineers
1959	Washington Award, Western Society of Engineers
1959	Distinguished Achievement Award, Holland Society of New York
1960	Gold Medal of the International Benjamin Franklin Society
1960	Good Government Award, Crosscup-Pishon Post, American Legion
1963	Honorary Member, American Society for Engineering Education
1963	Hoover Medal, American Society of Mechanical Engineers
1967	Member, National Academy of Engineering
1968	George Foster Peabody Broadcasting Special Education Award
1969	New England Council "Man of the Year" Award
1969	Golden Omega Award of the Electrical Insulation Conference
1970	Prometheus Award, National Electrical Manufacturers Association
1975	Recipient of the first Marconi International Fellowship
1976	George Foster Peabody Award (for work in public broadcasting)
1978	Sylvanus Thayer Award, U.S. Military Academy, West Point

1980	Vannevar Bush Award, National Science Board, National Science Foundation
1945–1972	Recipient of honorary degrees (LL.D., Sc.D., D.Eng., D.Appl.Sci., Ed.D., HH.D., D.P.S.) from thirty-nine colleges or universities

I thus experienced an outburst of unearned academic kudos. This leads me to recall that Winston Churchill once said that he was surprised "that in my later life I should have become so experienced in taking degrees when as a schoolboy I was so bad at passing examinations."

NOTES

The following notes are included here to present supplementary information appropriate for the chapters indicated. In addition to the sources noted, I have drawn on numerous MIT documents that are now part of the MIT Library-Institute Archives.

INTRODUCTION

1. Johann Wolfgang von Goethe, as reported by *The Practical Cogitator*, selected and edited by Charles P. Curtis, Jr., and Ferris Greenslet (Boston: Houghton Mifflin Company, 1962), p. 3.

CHAPTER 1

1. Eric Hodgins, *Trolley to the Moon* (New York: Simon and Schuster, 1973), p. 147.

2. Frank Aydelotte, ed., *English and Engineering*, A Volume of Essays for English Classes in Engineering Schools (New York: McGraw-Hill Book Company, Inc., 1923), pp. xv–xvi.

3. I have derived ideas, stimulation, and inspiration, as frequently expressed in this memoir, from my reading of the English poet and novelist George Meredith (1828–1909). Meredith was an advocate of women's rights, long before women's liberation, and both his novels and poems were marked by psychological insights and content that is perhaps closer to the literature of the 1980s than it was to the periods in which he wrote.

I turn again and again to the famous essay which he first presented as a lecture and then published in 1877 under the title "An Essay on Comedy and the Uses of the Comic Spirit."

4. James Russell Lowell, "Agassiz," *The Poetical Works of James Russell Lowell* (Boston: Houghton Mifflin Company, 1904), p. 129. These lines appear in a long poem paying tribute to Agassiz, one of Lowell's admired friends.

5. W. H. Auden, "September 1, 1939," was published in *Collected Poems*, copyright 1941 by W. H. Auden (reprinted in *The Oxford Book of American Verse* with permission of Random House, Inc. and Faber and Faber Limited, London).

6. Winston Churchill, *Their Finest Hour: The Second World War*, Vol. 2 (Boston: Houghton Mifflin Company, 1949).

CHAPTER 2

1. Vannevar Bush Oral History Collection, IASC-MIT, Vol. 7, p. 374.

2. Henry E. Guerlac, August 17, 1945, letter to James R. Killian, Jr., vice president, MIT, Library-Institute Archives AC 4. My version of the decision to locate the Radiation Laboratory at MIT is based on contacts, as executive assistant to the president, with the principals, Drs. Compton, Bush, and others, and by the carefully prepared statement of Guerlac. This Guerlac statement differs in some respects from an interview with Edward Bowles.

3. James Phinney Baxter III, *Scientists Against Time* (Cambridge: The MIT Press, 1968). Reprint of 1946 edition. John E. Burchard, *Q.E.D., MIT in World War II* (New York: The Technology Press, John Wiley & Sons, Inc., 1948).

4. Louis D. Smullin. Professor Smullin was interviewed by an MIT student, Roslyn R. Romanowski, for her thesis, "Peacetime to Wartime: Transitions in Defense Research Policy at MIT." I pay tribute to Miss Romanowski for the opportunity to quote from her able thesis.

5. Consultation with Professors Reintjes and Gordon Brown provided insights and greater authenticity to this account of the Servomechanisms Laboratory.

6. Julius A. Stratton, *Science and the Educated Man* (Cambridge: The MIT Press, 1966), p. 175.

7. Ibid. p., 174.

8. Kent C. Redmond and Thomas M. Smith, "Project Whirlwind: A Case History in Contemporary Technology" (Bedford, Mass.: The Mitre Corporation, 1975), manuscript, p. 2.26.

9. In the same letter in which he made the comment, Brown added a further bit of MIT computer history that deserves preserving: "I recollect clearly, during the period that led to the building of the present Information Processing Center, that I was motivated to recommend that at MIT we drop the use of the term 'Computer Center' and use the term 'Information Processing Center' as a way of inducing all the potential users of the facility who were not principally mathematicians . . . to join the act. I was influenced by my observation of the Forrester-Everett-ONR difficulties. I think now that the Information Processing Center at MIT has done a lot to promote multidisciplinary work and to establish cross linkages between totally different disciplines."

10. Larry Owens, "Vannevar Bush and the Differential Analyzer: Authorship and Context in the History of an Early Computer," an essay in

preparation for publication, Program in the History of Science, Princeton University.

11. Ibid.

12. Norbert Wiener, *Cybernetics, or Control and Communication in the Animal and the Machine* (New York: The Technology Press, John Wiley & Sons, Inc., 1961).

13. Jerome Bruner, *In Search of Mind, Essays in Autobiography* (New York: Harper & Row, Publishers, 1983), p. 121.

14. The pioneering form of government support under an ingenious tripartite contract with the three military services was largely invented by the representatives of MIT working with civilians in the military organization, notably Harold Zahl of the Army, John Marchetti of the Air Corps, and Emmanuel Piore of the Navy.

15. MIT's experience in handling research contracts with the government during the war and in the 1950s led to its development of an accounting system that is singularly adapted to the handling of government and industry contracts of the 1980s. The recent death of retired Vice President Paul Cusick recalls the major contributions he made to the management of government contracts and to his achievement of national recognition for his skill in bringing government and the universities together in devising contractual procedures.

16. Vannevar Bush Oral History Collection, IASC-MIT, Vol. 9, p. 505.

CHAPTER 3

1. Among the recruits from the Radiation Laboratory who were to occupy important posts at MIT were Malcolm Hubbard, Lan J. Chu, Ivan Getting, H. Guyford Stever, Malcolm W. Strandberg, George E. Valley, Jr., and Jerrold Zacharias. From the Los Alamos Laboratory came Victor Weisskopf, Bruno B. Rossi, Bernard T. Feld, David Frisch, and Martin Deutsch. All told, a stellar group!

2. Jerome Bruner, *In Search of Mind: Essays in Autobiography* (New York: Harper & Row, Publishers, 1983), p. 210.

3. Robert Nisbet, *The Degradation of the Academic Dogma: The University in America, 1945–1970* (New York: Basic Books, Inc., 1971), p. 81.

CHAPTER 4

1. In a paper presented at an MIT symposium in 1980, the novelist John Hersey noted how the Lewis Committee confronted the challenge of the "two cultures" a decade before C. P. Snow delivered his famous

Rede Lecture. He went on, however, to detail the many barriers inherent both in science and the humanities to closing the gap. I take a more hopeful view. Science can embrace the humane, and a science-based university can be a home for the liberal arts.

CHAPTER 5

1. I was interested to find that the Institute catalog for 1867–68 listed four vice presidents under Rogers. In 1984 there were five.

2. Richard G. Hewlett and Oscar E. Anderson, Jr., *The New World, 1939–1946: A History of the United States Atomic Energy Commission* Vol. 1 (University Park, Pa.: The Pennyslvania State University Press, 1962), p. 650.

3. As I sought to reconstruct and understand the events associated with the decisions to develop and test an H-bomb, I was greatly aided by McGeorge Bundy, who directed me to the documents I needed.

4. *In the Matter of J. Robert Oppenheimer*, Transcript of Hearing before Personnel Security Board, Washington, D.C., April 12, 1954 through May 6, 1954 (Washington: U.S. Government Printing Office, 1954), p. 562.

5. Bush's Washington battles and frustrations after World War II are discussed in *The Physicists* by Daniel J. Kevles (New York: Alfred A. Knopf, Inc., 1978), pp. 361–366.

CHAPTER 6

1. John E. Burchard, *Mid-Century: The Social Implications of Scientific Progress* (Cambridge: The Technology Press, John Wiley & Sons, Inc., New York, 1950).

2. MIT Library-Institute Archives, Compton-Killian File, AC 4.

3. *William Barton Rogers, Life and Letters*, Vol. 1 (Cambridge, Mass.: The Riverside Press, 1896), p. 405. Report from the Committee of Schools and Colleges [of the Legislature of Virginia], Doc. No. 41. Prepared by W. B. Rogers, chairman of the faculty, 1845:

. . . While referring to those features in the organization of the University which distinguish it from most of the leading institutions in this country, and which are regarded by its friends as among its highest merits, it is appropriate to state that by an express law its authorities are forbidden to grant honourary degrees, and that accordingly no diploma of compliment has ever yet received its imprimatur. In most other colleges and universities, as is well known, such honours are extended not only to those who have earned some reputation in divinity, medicine or law, or even in the uncongenial pursuits of party politics, but are accorded, as of course, in the case of Master of Arts, after the interval of a few years, to all who have taken their first academical degree. Rejecting a system so little friendly to true literary advancement, the legislators of the University have, we think, wisely made their highest academic honour, that of Master of Arts of the University of Virginia, the genuine test of diligent and successful literary training, and, disdaining such literary almsgiving, have firmly barred the door against the demands of spurious merit and noisy popularity. . . .

Rogers' opposition was doubtless influenced by the firm decision of Thomas Jefferson that the university he founded should not bestow honorary degrees. In this report of Rogers may be found an explanation of why MIT has resolutely refused to grant honorary degrees. When Mr. Churchill participated in the 1949 convocation, he would have been the ideal recipient of an honorary degree, but the Corporation's Executive Committee adhered to this policy that goes back to MIT's founder.

4. Sir John Colville, *Footprints in Time* (London: William Collins Sons and Co., Ltd., 1976), pp. 256, 258.

5. Sir John Colville, *Winston Churchill and His Inner Circle* (London: Wyndham Publications Ltd., 1981), pp. 158–159.

CHAPTER 7

1. In Scottish universities their *Senatus academicus* performed a different role; see Eric Ashby, *Technology and the Academics* (London: Macmillan & Co. Ltd., 1959), p. 71.

2. John Burchard and Albert Bush-Brown, *The Architecture of America: A Social and Cultural History* (Boston: Little, Brown and Company, 1961), pp. 493–494.

3. It is worthy of note that Secretary of State George P. Shultz, while a member of the MIT faculty, was secretary of the staff section of the Staff-Administration Committee at the time these recommendations were made in 1952.

4. In the Julius Stratton administration, faculty committees, including one chaired by Elting Morison, continued consideration of the topics dealt with in the Soderberg committee report.

5. When first organized, the University of Virginia had a single faculty with a single curriculum. Later Jefferson introduced the first separate faculties.

6. Edward Shils, "The Hole in the Centre: University Government in the United States," *Minerva* 7 (January 1970), p. 6.

7. Karl Jaspers, *The Idea of the University*, ed. by Karl W. Deutsch (Boston: Beacon Press, 1959), p. 84.

8. Talcott Parsons and Gerald M. Platt, *The American University* (Cambridge: Harvard University Press, 1973).

9. George F. Kennan et al; *Democracy and the Student Left* (Boston: Atlantic Monthly Press, Little Brown and Company, 1968), pp. 3–4.

10. Vannevar Bush, *Science Is Not Enough* (New York: William Morrow & Company, Inc.).

CHAPTER 11

1. Reductionism and modernization of the laboratories of the Mechanical Engineering Department similarly occurred. As I see in my mind's eye the elegant Corliss Triple Expansion Engine and similar Victorian machines in the Steam Laboratory, I think of Rupert Brooke's line "the keen unpassioned beauty of a great machine." Before this laboratory was modernized, it displayed some beauts that could have inspired Brooke's rhapsodic line, but these beauts had become technological dinosaurs.

2. Sir Eric Ashby: *Technology and the Academics* (London: Macmillan & Co. Ltd., 1959), p. 58.

3. Paul A. Samuelson, *Economics*, 8th edition (New York: McGraw-Hill Book Company, Inc., 1970), pp. 1, 5.

4. Samuel C. Prescott, *When MIT Was "Boston Tech"* (Cambridge: The Technology Press, 1954) p. 115.

5. Bernard Newton, *The Economics of Francis Amasa Walker: American Economics in Transition* (New York: Augustus M. Kelley Publishers, 1968), p. ix.

During his presidency, Walker was doubtless furthering the valiant struggle of the faculty to accomplish the "General Cultivation" desired by founder Rogers which inevitably resulted in a pluralism if not a hodgepodge of titles for units of instruction in the broad area of the humanities and social studies. Economics at times was called "Political Economy" or "Economics and Statistics," and General Studies at various times were dubbed "General Science and Literature," "Science and Literature," "Elective Course," "General Course," "General Science," and "General Engineering." Ultimately these nonprofessional subjects came to be grouped in an established program called Course IX.

This Course IX of the early days was later to be designated General Science or General Engineering and is now a graduate program in

Psychology and Brain Science. The general subjects once grouped in this natal Course IX are now replaced by a required program of at least eight electives in the humanities, arts, and social sciences.

6. In preparing my record of the early days of biology at the Institute, I am indebted to Professor Bernard Gould, the "Clio" of the Biology Department, who read my manuscript and suggested important emendations and additions.

7. Kenzo Tange and Noboru Kawazoe, *Ise: Prototype of Japanese Architecture* (Cambridge: The MIT Press, 1965).

8. W. H. Auden, "In Memory of Sigmund Freud" [1940] (as published in *Bartlett's*).

9. The funds granted for the PSSC physics program alone exceeded $6 million, and the PSSC textbook has had worldwide sales totaling over a million copies.

10. Isaiah Berlin's essay on what he called the divorce of the sciences and humanities appeared in a collection of his essays entitled *Against the Current, Essays in the History of Ideas* (New York: Viking Press, 1978), p. 80.

11. In recalling Adam Smith's *History of Astronomy*, I draw on an article by Herbert F. Thomson in *Quarterly Journal of Economics* 79 (1965): 212 ff.

12. Pp. 137 ff.

13. George Sarton, *Six Wings: Men of Science in the Renaissance* (Indiana University Press, 1957), pp. 130–131.

14. Frederick Mosteller and David L. Wallace, *Inference and Disputed Authorship: The Federalist* (Reading, Mass.: Addison-Wesley Publishing Company, Inc., 1964).

15. Susan Hockey, *A Guide to Computer Applications in the Humanities* (Baltimore: The Johns Hopkins University Press, 1980), pp. 133–134.

16. Timothy Friberg and Barbara Friberg, "A Computer-Assisted Analysis of the Greek New Testament Text," in *Computing in the Humanities,* Peter C. Patton, Renee A. Holoien, eds. (Lexington, Mass.: Lexington Books, 1981), pp. 15–51.

17. Paul A. Samuelson, *Economics*, 8th edition (New York: McGraw-Hill Book Company, Inc., 1970), p. 4.

18. Richard P. Feynman, Robert B. Leighton, and Matthew Sands, *The Feynman Lectures on Physics* (Reading, Mass., Addison-Wesley Publishing Company, Inc., 1963–1965).

19. Norbert Wiener, "Mathematics and Art," *Technology Review*, 32 (January 1929), pp. 129 ff.

20. Gyorgy Kepes, *The New Landscape in Art and Science* (Chicago: P. Theobold, 1956).

21. *Gyorgy Kepes, The MIT Years: 1945–1977* (Cambridge: The MIT Press Visual Arts Series, 1978), pp. 3–4.

CHAPTER 12

1. Roger M. Williams, "The Quality of Commitment," *The Lamp* 64 (Spring–Summer, 1982), p. 92.

2. Joseph A. Schumpeter, "The Creative Response in Economic History," *Journal of Economic History* 7 (May 1947), p. 151.

3. The decades before and after World War I were other periods, among several, when MIT educated men who were to become illustrious leaders of American industry. Of this constellation of talent let me offer this partial list: James M. Barker, '07 (Sears Roebuck); Rexford A. Bristol, '26 (Foxboro Company); Charles A. Cary, '12 (du Pont); Bradley Dewey, '09 (Dewey & Almy); James H. Doolittle, '24 (Shell Oil); Donald W. Douglas, '14 (Douglas Aircraft); Lewis W. Douglas, '17 (Southern Arizona Bank & Trust and former U.S. Ambassador to Great Britain); Luis A. Ferré, '26 (Ferré Industries); Guy S. Frisbie, '26 (Hobart Mfg.); Eugenio Garza-Sada, '14 (Mexican industrialist); Cecil H. Green, '23 (Geophysical Service and Texas Instruments); Crawford H. Greenewalt, '22 (du Pont); Edward J. Hanley, '24 (Allegheny Ludlum); Robert T. Haslam, '11 (Standard Oil of New Jersey); Lester C. Hopton, '26, and Robert H. Johnson, '26 (Ingersoll-Rand); John R. Kimberly, '26 (Kimberly-Clark); Fred C. Koch, '22 (Koch Industries); Frank S. Mac-Gregor, '07 (du Pont); Theodore A. Mangelsdorf, '26 (Texaco); H. W. McCurdy, '22 (Puget Sound Bridge & Dredging Co.); James S. McDonnell, Jr., '25 (McDonnell Aircraft); E. V. Murphree, '23 (Standard Oil of New Jersey); Edward L. Ryerson, '09 (Inland Steel); David A. Shepard, '26 (Standard Oil of New Jersey); U. A. Whitaker, '23 (AMP); I. W. Wilson, '11 (Aluminum Company of America); Robert E. Wilson, '16 (Standard Oil of Indiana).

4. Daniel J. Boorstin, *The Americans: The Democratic Experience* (New York: Random House, 1973), p. 542.

5. Ibid., p. 540.

CHAPTER 13

1. In 1983, the Alumni Association elected her its first alumna president.

2. The origin of this visiting committee plan is given from the following abstract from records of the Corporation meeting of November 10, 1875: "Visits to the School: On motion of Mr. Atkinson, it was voted that the Secretary notify members of the Corporation of a vote by which they are requested to visit certain specific departments of the school with which they are familiar and in which they take specific interest. He thought that the management of the school would be greatly facilitated by such visits."

In the next meeting of the Corporation on December 8, 1875, appears the entry: "Committees of Visitation: Mr. Atkinson presented a scheme for the apportionment of the members of the Corporation as Visiting Committees of the school which, after some explanation and a few modifications, was finally adopted. . . ." From "Report of the President, MIT, 1936–1937," Vol. 75, No. 1, pp. 22–23.

3. Harold Macmillan, *Riding the Storm, 1956–1959* (London: Macmillan Publishers Ltd., 1971), p. 567.

4. My association with the Lying-in Hospital prompts me to recall a jesting remark at the Faculty Club dining table that "a breach has occurred in the MIT administration. Karl Compton is an evangelical supporter of the Planned Parenthood Association, and Jim Killian has currently agreed to serve as the president of the Boston Lying-in Hospital." My trustee service to this hospital was a most agreeable and educational experience.

5. Frederika Louise Thyra Victoria Margarita Sophia Olga Cecilia Isabella Christa, Princess of Hanover, Princess of Great Britain and Ireland, Duchess of Braunschweig-Lüneburg.

6. In 1939 the book value of the Institute's endowment funds totaled $36,230,000. In 1971, when I retired, the treasurer reported a total of $216,364,000.

7. Herbert F. York, *The Advisors: Oppenheimer, Teller, and the Superbomb* (San Francisco: W. H. Freeman and Company, 1976), pp. 105–106.

8. Ibid., p. ix.

9. Robert H. Ferrell, ed., *The Eisenhower Diaries* (New York: W. W. Norton & Company, 1981), p. 312. Names of all members of the PBCFIA from *The Eisenhower Diaries* (p. 422n.1) for January 24, 1956: "Robert A. Lovett, former secretary of defense; Benjamin Fairless, president of the United States Steel Corporation; James R. Killian, president of Massachusetts Institute of Technology; Edward L. Ryerson, iron and steel manufacturer; Rear Admiral Richard L. Conolly, Lieutenant General John E. Hull, Lieutenant General James H. Doolittle."

10. James R. Killian, Jr., *Sputnik, Scientists, and Eisenhower: A Memoir of the First Special Assistant to the President for Science and Technology* (Cambridge: The MIT Press, 1977).

11. Listed were James B. Conant, former president, Harvard University; Lee A. DuBridge, president, California Institute of Technology; Ralph Ellison, author; John S. Hayes, United States ambassador to Switzerland; David D. Henry, president, University of Illinois; Oveta Culp Hobby, chairman of the board, Houston Post Company; J. C. Kellam, president, Texas Broadcasting Corporation; Edwin H. Land, president, Polaroid Corporation; Joseph H. McConnell, president, Reynolds Metals Company; Franklin Patterson, president, Hampshire College; Terry Sanford, former governor of North Carolina; Robert Saudek, Robert Saudek Associates, Inc.; Rudolf Serkin, concert pianist; Leonard Woodcock, vice president, United Automobile Workers of America; James R. Killian, Jr., chairman of the Corporation, Massachusetts Institute of Technology, chairman.

12. *Public Television, A Program for Action: The Report and Recommendations of the Carnegie Commission on Educational Television* (New York: Harper & Row, Publishers, 1967).

13. *A Public Trust: The Report of the Carnegie Commission on the Future of Public Broadcasting* (New York: Bantam Books, published by arrangement with the Carnegie Corporation of New York, 1979), pp. 9–10.

14. *A Program for Renewed Partnership: The Report of the Sloan Commission on Government and Higher Education* (Cambridge: Ballinger Publishing Company, a subsidiary of Harper & Row, 1980), pp. 5–6, 10.

15. (Proposal for) *An International Institute of Science and Technology,* Report of the Working Group appointed by the Secretary General of the North Atlantic Treaty Organization, May 1962, pp. 7, 11–12. Members were Professor P. Caldirola, director, Institute of Physics "Aldo Pontremoli," University of Milan, Italy; Professor H. B. G. Casimir, director of Research Laboratories, N. V. Philips Gloeilampenfabrieken, Eindhoven, Netherlands; Sir John Cockcroft, master, Churchill College, Cambridge, England; Dr. P. G. A. Piganiol, Délégué Général à la Recherche Scientifique et Technique, Paris, France; Professor A. Rucker, Technische Hochschule, Munich, Germany; Professor W. A. Nierenberg, assistant secretary general for scientific affairs, NATO, Paris, France; Dr. James R. Killian, Jr., chairman of the Corporation, Massachusetts Institute of Technology, Cambridge, Massachusetts, U.S.A. (chairman). Assisting me was Eugene Skolnikoff of the Office of Science and Technology in the White House and now director of MIT's Center for International Studies.

16. For the sources of these and other comments on the "128 effect" see *Technology Review* (May–June 1984), pp. 6, 8, 9.

CHAPTER 14

1. Robert Frost, "Stopping by Woods on a Snowy Evening" (1923), st. 4.

CHAPTER 15

1. This statement was called to Morison's attention in a conversation with Lord Ashby.

2. Lewis Thomas, *Bulletin: Inside Brigham and Women's Hospital* (January–February 1981), p. 18.

3. This excellent report never commanded the attention it deserved. As its title, *Creative Renewal in a Time of Crisis,* indicates, the study, suggested by Howard Johnson, was prepared in the heated wake of student unrest in the sixties. Hoffman, sometime head of the Department of Mathematics, is admired both as humanist and mathematician.

4. Charles Frankel, *The Case for Modern Man* (New York: Harper & Brothers, 1955), p. 2

CHAPTER 16

1. P. B. Medawar, *The Hope of Progress* (London: Methuen & Company Ltd., 1972), p. 127.

2. John Henry Newman, "Leaving Oxford," *Apologia pro Vita Sua,* Part VI.

3. Another ending was the retirement of Elizabeth Pigott at the close of 1984. She had served MIT with acclaimed skill and grace for thirty-four years, and for thirty-two of these she indefatigably assisted me every step of my way as I undertook the new beginnings reported in this memoir. Beyond this she assisted me in the final editing of this book for publication. Without her cheerful patience this ending would have been beyond me.

EPILOGUE

1. George Kistiakowsky, *Bulletin of the Atomic Scientists* (December 1982), editorial.

POSTSCRIPTS

PAGE 38

Norbert Wiener also became involved in the evolution of computers. In his autobiography, *I Am a Mathematician* (p. 112), he recalls that he was closely associated with Vannevar Bush during the early days when Bush was developing some of the various forms of computing machines that were later to make him famous. Wiener wrote:

> From time to time he would call on me for advice, and I tried to do what I could in designing computational apparatus on my own account. . . .
>
> One time when I was visiting the show at the old Copley Theatre, an idea came into my mind which simply distracted all my attention from the performance. It was the notion of an optical computing machine for harmonic analysis. I had already learned not to disregard these stray ideas, no matter when they came to my attention, and I promptly left the theater to work out some of the details of my new plan. The next day I consulted Bush.
>
> The idea was valid, and we made a couple of attempts to put it into working form. In these, my contribution was wholly intellectual, for I am among the clumsiest of men and it is utterly beyond me even to put two wires together so they will make a satisfactory contact. Bush is, among other things, one of the greatest apparatus men that America has ever seen, and he thinks with his hands as well as with his brain. Thus, our attempts in a new sort of harmonic analyzer were quite reasonably successful, and since then they have led to work even more successful.

PAGE 38

In *Moments of Vision: The Stroboscopic Revolution in Photography*, which Professor Harold Edgerton and I published in 1979, I wrote an essay of tribute to Edgerton which included a nontechnical description of how he conceived of the modern stroboscope. The way that students were to use Bush's mechanical differential analyzer to support the further development of Edgerton's studies provides one of those anecdotes which Churchill described as the gleaming toys of history. It was also a striking example of the memorably close companionship among students and faculty in those freewheeling days in the Department of Electrical Engineering.

Knowing that my memoir was approaching completion, Edgerton brought me a description he had just written on how these pioneering engineering developments enabled him, as he said, to be "on the cutting edge of both." While a graduate student, Edgerton was participating in a study of what electrical engineers call power system stability, the ability of synchronous generators and motors to stay in step after disturbances such as a sudden load of lightning striking transmission lines. Edgerton was seeking to determine the transient changes in the angular displacement of the speeding rotor of the synchronous electric motor he had rigged up in the laboratory so that he could induce angular displacements too fast to be seen by the unaided eye. While using mercury arc rectifiers, Edgerton suddenly observed that he could see the rotating poles of the machine oscillate about a midposition after a simulated system disturbance. The mercury arc rectifiers happened to be placed close enough to the generator for their flashes to illuminate its rotor stroboscopically. Edgerton's prepared mind immediately recognized the opportunity to develop stroboscopes for the purpose of stopping motion.

Edgerton and his associates then undertook a study of how a displaced synchronous motor might be brought back into step, and this required the solution of a nonlinear differential equation. Edgerton had happened to read an article in a British engineering journal that commented on the "nonsolvability" of nonlinear differential equations. He knew better since he was fully aware of the latest of the differential analyzers Bush had developed which had the capability to handle equations of this type. Edgerton's knowledge of the Bush machine led him to inspire graduate student Frederick Zak and two MIT seniors, Kenneth Germeshausen and Gordon Brown, to undertake the integraph solution of the problems of the synchronous motor.

PAGE 61

In November 1981 Bruce S. Old and his associates delivered to the Office of Naval Research a study of three research programs to which ONR had made substantial grants: Project Whirlwind, the Laboratory for Nuclear Science and Engineering, and the work of Professor Morris Cohen and students. Bruce Old was one of a group of young Naval research officers who played a major role in conceptualizing and bringing into being the Office of Naval Research.

This report is an important contribution to the history of Project Whirlwind. It concludes that "the return to the Federal Government in taxes for its estimated $17.4 million investment in basic engineering research would certainly reach many billions of dollars." Old's report shows that von Neumann visited Whirlwind in February 1948 and was ecstatic over technical progress. Old claims that von Neumann, on seeing the Whirlwind multiplier complete five billion multiplications without error, became so excited he kissed one of the Whirlwind staff members on both cheeks.

PAGE 76
In the postwar period we have witnessed a trend toward the establishment of specialized research centers independent of the universities. Some of these are important and necessary, but I find reason to be troubled by the recent multiplication of research institutions separate from universities. Too great a separation of research from the teaching function can only diminish the "thin, clear stream of excellence" that results from the marriage of teaching and research in a university environment. In his essay, "A Great Age for Science" (1960) in *Goals for Americans*, the report of the President's Commission on National Goals, Warren Weaver gave eloquent expression to the importance of preserving this marriage.

"For centuries," he wrote, "intellectual and cultural leadership has resided in universities. The great traditional role of universities has involved the preservation of knowledge, the advance of knowledge, and—as the central educational function—the passing of knowledge and of the zest for new knowledge to the oncoming generation. A half century ago there were in the universities many, many instances of the great scholar-teacher. These individuals were dedicated to scholarship and research, but they also considered it a high privilege and a clear duty to teach younger students [including undergraduates as well as graduate students]."

PAGE 162

The incident described to me by Mrs. Compton did occur but not exactly in the way she remembered it. The circumstances that prompted Compton to urge Bush to call more physicists into action and to press ahead are described in Hewlett and Anderson's authoritative history, *The New World, 1939/1946* (pp. 35 and 36). They report that on March 17, 1941, Ernest Lawrence and Alfred Loomis met with Compton in his MIT office to discuss plans for radar research. This led to a discussion of the status of the uranium program and prompted Compton both to telephone and write Bush. Bush no doubt was irritated. "His responsibility," wrote Hewlett and Anderson, "covered the whole range of contributions science might make to national defense. He was anxious to support the uranium program . . . but he did not want to have to cope with pressure tactics that might dangerously warp the scientific effort." It turned out that both Compton and Bush were acting with wisdom, and all irritation and worry on the part of each soon happily evaporated.

PAGE 174

When I tried to reach Land to ask him to head the intelligence panel of the Eisenhower surprise attack study, I was told that he was in Hollywood discussing the technology of 3D motion pictures, which was commanding his attention at that time. I later learned that he had been observing Alfred Hitchcock filming his movie *Rear Window* with Grace Kelly and James Stewart. When Land impatiently inquired of him why he found it necessary to repeat over and over the filming of certain scenes involving Grace Kelly, Hitchcock told him that he simply was enjoying the experience of watching a beautiful woman! Upon receiving word while on the movie set of my invitation to take part in the Eisenhower study, Land—bless him—put aside for the nonce 3D movies and undertook the assignment to head the TCP intelligence panel.

PAGE 185

In reporting the several events that led to a renaissance in engineering education in the postwar period, I should note one serious neglect: the lack of effective academic preparation available to educate a cohort of engineers competent to contribute to the efficiency and productivity of the manufacturing process in industry.

So much attention was devoted to the necessary introduction of more science into engineering education that both faculty and students gave low priority to the technology of manufacturing. Fortunately but belatedly, teaching and research in this field are now commanding enough attention to ensure the education of a cadre of engineers who are interested and competent in advanced manufacturing technology. In the years when we were neglecting this aspect of engineering education, the Japanese were energetically educating engineers who proudly devoted their creative talents to productivity and sophisticated manufacturing technology. This has unquestionably been one of the factors in the achievement by the Japanese of a competitive advantage in numerous fields of manufacturing.

PAGE 244

In an article in *Time* magazine for November 19, 1984, Kurt Andersen described a current exhibit at the Museum of Modern Art of Aalto's furniture, saying that it was "still fresh after 50 years." He also noted Aalto's buildings "are modern all right, sleek and sensible and just a bit Martian, but Aalto never took the final vows of modernism. Strict symmetry and monoliths left him cold. Rather, an Aalto building is apt to swell or zigzag confoundingly, to have lines and textures that seem more botanical and geological than geometrical. Ahead of his time, he declined to enforce the brittlest dogmas of the new. Thirty years before the phrase was coined, Aalto was a postmodernist, the first."

PAGE 313

When I think of Viki, I am prompted to mention again Adam Smith's *History of Astronomy* in which he gave priority not to utility but to the intellectual or aesthetic sentiments of wonder, surprise, and admiration.

PAGE 328

In 1950 William Webster, who succeeded Karl T. Compton as chairman of the Research and Development Board of the Department of Defense, appointed a committee under my chairmanship to review the RDB organization and its work. My associates on this committee were Detlev W. Bronk, Lee A. DuBridge, Frederick L. Hovde, Mervin J. Kelly, Merle A. Tuve, and Robert E. Wilson.

This committee concluded that the Research and Development Board also should support the development of new scientific techniques for securing hard intelligence.

We were not convinced that the board would ever be successful. It was not until the DOD had a director of research and engineering, as suggested by PSAC, that it had adequate direction of R & D.

PAGE 337

I have devoted much discussion in this memoir to MIT's success in developing creative integrations and interdisciplinary congeniality among a variety of research fields. There is an analogy here with what took place in the Eisenhower staff when those individuals who served on the Technological Capabilities Panel, on the President's Board of Consultants on Foreign Intelligence Activities, and on PSAC provided this creative integration of which I speak. For example, the fact that William Baker, Edwin Land, and I were engaged concurrently in several of these groups made it possible to achieve an extraordinary synthesis of minds and ideas to aid the president in achieving his goals in shaping our defense and intelligence programs and policies. The fact that a number of us, including Baker, Land, Zacharias, Wiesner, Beckler, Kistiakowsky, and many others, worked together with interdisciplinary congeniality made possible the success of such achievements as the Polaris, the acceleration of our intercontinental ballistic missile program, the U-2, new techniques of undersea warfare, and spectacular advancement in our reconnaissance capabilities. Coupled with this concert of minds was the fact that the results generated could be brought directly to the president for his consideration. My ready access to President Eisenhower made it possible for me promptly to bring to him, and to open opportunities for others to bring to him, new and important technologies, concepts, and analyses that added to the strength of our nation.

I will always remember the times when George Kistiakowsky and I were presenting to the president U-2 photographs that gave him direct evidence of the status of the Soviet missile program and proved there was no missile gap.

PAGE 367

My association with Robert Lovett during the period he was Secretary of Defense left me with the abiding impression that he was one of the best defense secretaries of all those I came to know during my Washington days. My admiration for his exceptional qualities of wit, wisdom, and administrative judgment led me to recommend him to the MIT Corporation's nominating committee, which readily proposed him to the Corporation.

One of the most unusual experiences I had during my days of service in Washington was to be asked by Secretary Lovett to join a quartet of civilians not connected with government to help him resolve a budgetary conflict among the heads of the three services. He asked if we would do this off the record and provided us with a suite of offices in the Pentagon to do our work unobtrusively. The Air Force, it seemed, had pressed for a larger piece of the budget pie than the other services deemed fair. Lovett authorized us to interview, *in camera*, each of the secretaries and each of the chiefs of staff and such aides as we wished. In these interviews our little committee, not one of whom was an officer of government, was startled by the willing but savage candor of the Army and Navy officials. In our first session with Generals Vandenberg and LeMay of the Air Force, they refused to respond in providing the information we requested, and we had no choice but to return to Secretary Lovett and report that we could not reach a useful conclusion without the information requested of top Air Force officers. Secretary Lovett promptly asked that we meet again with Generals Vandenberg and LeMay after he had requested their cooperation, and so we did. In this second round they responded fully to our questions but not without a touch of abashed dignity.

It was a novel exercise, but we were able to reach conclusions and make comments to Secretary Lovett which we hoped he would find useful in resolving the interservice conflict before him. The procedure he used was unique in another way: not one word ever leaked about this unusual meeting, which was perhaps the most miraculous aspect of the episode.

PAGE 391

In commenting on Professor Gaudin's contributions, Lt. General Groves wrote in 1955: ". . . Professor Gaudin not only performed the difficult management duties inherent in the guiding of a large group of scientists working in a new field, he also played the dominant scientific role in the developments. Without him, we certainly would not have started them with the confidence which is always so important to prompt successful achievement."

Professor Gaudin's Metallurgical Project was one of the largest wartime programs at the Institute.

PAGE 408

In introducing Paul Gray at his inauguration, I spoke of my confidence that a new cohort of university presidents would demonstrate the will and the strength to oppose government regulations harmful to the universities. In confirmation of this judgment I have read with encouragement an article by Colin Norman in *Science* for October 26, 1984, and let me quote:

The long battle between the universities and the Department of Defense (DOD) over restrictions on the publication of academic research appears to have been resolved in the universities' favor—at least for the time being.

A memorandum written by Under Secretary of Defense Richard DeLauer, dated 1 October, specifies that no restrictions should be placed on the publication of unclassified fundamental research sponsored by DOD. The memo, which was sent to research chiefs in the Pentagon and establishes DOD policy on the matter, defines fundamental research to include virtually all DOD-supported research performed on university campuses.

DeLauer's memo clarifies and puts into effect a policy announced last May (*Science*, 8 June, p. 108) that relies on classification as the primary means of controlling fundamental research publications. Announcement of the new policy effectively signaled an end to DOD's efforts to restrict dissemination of the results of unclassified but militarily sensitive research, but left open the question of how fundamental research would be defined. DeLauer's memo clarifies this.

The determined and skillful efforts of university presidents had much to do with bringing about this wise decision on the part of the DOD. I speak specifically of Kennedy (Stanford), Goldberger (CalTech), Bok (Harvard), and Gray (MIT). I must add, however, a cautionary note that their achievement could be thwarted by continuing policy debates within the government.

INDEX